STUDIES IN THE HISTORY OF LATIN AMERICAN ECONOMIC THOUGHT

We do not know any work that has tackled the study of Hispanic American economic ideas over such a long period. Its originality, the rigour of the analysis, the value of its conclusions and its pioneering character assure this work a good reception from all those interested in the evolution of economic thought.

(José M. Mariluz Urquijo, National Council of Scientific and Technological Research of Argentina – from a review of the Spanish edition)

This is the first study of the development of economic thought in Latin America. It traces the development of economic ideas during five centuries and across the whole continent. It addresses a wide range of approaches to economic issues including:

- the scholastic tradition in Latin American economics;
- the quantity theory of money;
- cameralism;
- human capital theory;
- economic development.

Oreste Popescu was born in Romania. He has held a number of academic posts, including technical consultancies on various UN/UNDP programmes, and has published more than 100 papers in addition to several books. He currently teaches at the Argentine Catholic University of Buenos Aires and directs the Institute of History of Latin American Economic Thought. He has been distinguished with honorary academic titles from the University of San Marcos, Lima, the University Simón Bolívar, Colombia, and recently the University of Bucharest in his native Romania.

ROUTLEDGE HISTORY OF ECONOMIC THOUGHT SERIES

A HISTORY OF JAPANESE ECONOMIC THOUGHT
Tessa Morris-Suzuki

THE HISTORY OF SWEDISH ECONOMIC THOUGHT
Edited by Bo Sandelin

A HISTORY OF AUSTRALIAN ECONOMIC THOUGHT
Peter Groenewegen and Bruce McFarlane

A HISTORY OF CANADIAN ECONOMIC THOUGHT
Robin Neill

A HISTORY OF INDIAN ECONOMIC THOUGHT
Ajit Dasgupta

STUDIES IN THE HISTORY OF LATIN AMERICAN ECONOMIC THOUGHT

Oreste Popescu

London and New York

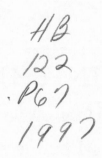

First published as *Estudios en la Historia del Pensamiento Económico Latin americano*
in 1986 by Plaza & Janés Editores - Colombia Ltda, Bogotá

First published in English 1997
by Routledge
11 New Fetter Lane, London EC4P 4EE

Simultaneously published in the USA and Canada
by Routledge
29 West 35th Street, New York, NY 10001

Typeset in Garamond by Routledge
**Printed and bound in Great Britain by
T. J. International Ltd.**

British Library Cataloguing in Publication Data
A catalogue record for this book is available from the British Library

Library of Congress Cataloging in Publication Data
A catalogue record for this book is available from the Library of
Congress

ISBN 0–415–14901–0

To my brothers
Valerian and Vespasian
and my sister
Virginia
in memoriam

CONTENTS

ACKNOWLEDGEMENTS

In the first place, I wish to thank the editors who have previously published certain articles of mine who have granted me permission for their reproduction in this book. Thus I thank the Kiel Institute of World Economics for 'Lehrgeschichtliche Anfaenge der Sozialoekonomischen Entwicklungsbestrebungen Lateinamerikas', *Weltwirtschafliches Archiv*, Kiel, Sondernummern für Latein-Amerika: 64–96 (1966); Professor Barrie P. Pettman Chairman MCB University Press for the article 'Price Theory in the Hispanic American Scholastics', *International Journal of Social Economics* 14: 132–9 (1987); Professor Lazaros Houmanidis from the International Society for Intercommunication of New Ideas, for permission to publish the paper 'Latin American Economics during the Hispanic Domination', *Economic History and Economic Theory* (Festschrift in Honour of Lazaros Th. Houmanidis), University of Piraeus: 288–309 (1991); and Professor Jürgen Schneider from the Otto-Friedrich-Universität for 'Latin American Contributions to the Development of the Quantity Theory of Money', in J. Casas Pardo (ed.) *Economic Effects of the European Expansion, 1492–824*, Stuttgart: Steiner Verlag: 99–172 (1992).

In the second place, I wish to thank Mark Timothy Waldorf (MA), University of Kentucky, and my disciples Juan Manuel Castro, Guillermo Gómez, Noelia C. Lucini and María Cecilia Minguillón – all fellows of the Institute of Latin American Economic History and currently assistant professors in the chair of History of Economics at the Catholic Argentine University of Buenos Aires – for their assistance in preparing the English version of my *Estudios en la Historia del Pensamiento Económico Latinoamericano*. Special thanks to Lic. Maria Angelica Tietjen and Carlos Romano – my assistants during more than ten years on my research programme – for their cooperation in the documentary area and responsibility in supervising the manuscript.

1

INTRODUCTION

A historiography of Hispanic American economic thought

A project on the History of Latin American Economic Thought may seem daring but it is in reality imperative. Efforts towards integration and economic and social development, in accordance with each region, and the establishment of an economic order formed and moulded in the authentic national Latin American culture, compel us to give a high priority to the study of the history of Latin American economics. Now, from the simplest analysis of the few works on the history of culture in Hispanic American culture, it is evident that while contributions coming from the fields of philosophy, politics, law, and sociology, together with literature, archeology, the arts, music and folklore, occupy a central place in the development of this discipline, contributions from the field of economic thought, if not utterly absent, get just a brief mention.

Taking this into consideration, and, facing the fact that the majority of our future programmers of development and integration in Latin America are students of economic sciences who number over 100,000 in more than 130 colleges of higher education, in which – except in a few cases – in the subject of the History of Economic Thought no mention is made of Latin American Economics. This leads us to realize the serious responsibility that falls on the professors and researchers in this field.

The past binds us. However, this is not so in the field of Latin American economic thought. It has been more than a century and a half since the subject of political economy was established in our universities and more than half a century since the foundation of the faculties of economic sciences, some of which demand more than 500 professors per academic year. Still, researchers would hardly find a work on the economic doctrines of the twentieth century that gave them access to the thinking of three or four of the greatest recent thinkers in almost any country in the region. If this accounts for the national level of the Latin American region in the twentieth century, the situation worsens when considering the nineteenth century, and it is utterly depressing if we look at the period of Spanish domination in America.

About thirty-two years ago, a journal (and later a magazine) published a

1

brief retrospective exposition on Latin American economic thought, which I had presented in a radio conference sponsored by the United Nations. An economics scholar in his final year of studies published in 'El Correo del Domingo' of the journal *El Espectador*, a series of encouraging reflexions, but there was also a shadow which I regard it as my duty to reproduce: 'To me [said Julián Jaramillo], it has been more than astonishing to learn that in my country there have been people worthy of mention in the history of economic thought' (Jaramillo 1965: 2f).

This spontaneous reaction does not represent an isolated case. Jesús Silva Herzog, one of the great names in the history of Mexican economic thought, reports that a friend of his, back in his country after studying in one of the most prestigious European universities, claimed that in Latin America as in Spain, there had never been any notable economist or economic concerns (Silva Herzog 1947: 7). I have met this same disease repeatedly during more than forty-eight years of teaching and researching in almost all the Latin American countries. These circumstances would be enough to justify my boldness in compiling my *Studies in the History of Economic Thought* in a volume. But, on top of them, we should add other reasons of a more profound nature. In the region, works on the doctrines of national economic thought are beginning to be published. To add to the timid works of Guillermo Subercaseaux (1924) in Chile and Gastón Lestard (1937) in Argentina, substantial studies started appearing, such as those of L. Nogueira de Paula (1942) in Brazil, César Augusto Reinaga (1969) in Perú, Jesús Silva Herzog (1947) in Mexico, and José Consuegra Higgins (1984) in Colombia. Almost simultaneously, there appeared viewpoints at the regional level, such as those of I. F. Normano (1945), Felipe S. Vázquez (1961), and Isidro Parra Peña (1984) and also Salvador O. Brand's, in the form of a dictionary (1984). In 1966, the magazine founded by José Consuegra, *Desarrollo Indoamericano*, embraced studies on the history of economic thought, greatly encouraging specialists in this subject. Moreover, in 1980, Consuegra widened his scientific dedication by starting the collection called *Antología del Pensamiento Económico y Social de America Latina* (APESAL) (Anthology of the Social and Economic Thought of Latin America). Consuegra also insists that on the subject of economic doctrines in Latin America there exists a vacuum. Thus the idea of compiling the most important studies on the history of Latin American economic thought came about. In other words, it is a step taken from the isolated studies in our subject to a systematic work spanning five centuries of our cultural past. I hope that this global view will be welcomed by my readers, and will help fill the vacuum mentioned above.

Regarding my readers, may I take this opportunity to speak with absolute clarity. Strictly, the 'step' mentioned in the previous paragraph is not actually a 'step further': I must emphasize that it is a 'first step in a new stage of development' of my research activities. This step could have been delayed, as

I have delayed it for the last forty-eight years. But I am now convinced that we will draw greater advantage by taking it now rather than by postponing it. Besides, sometimes, as Hesiod in his profound wisdom warned about 3,000 years ago, the half is worth more than the whole.

2

INDIAN ECONOMICS

INDIAN ECONOMICS AND THE CLASSICAL SCHOOL

The history of Latin American economic thought during the Spanish and Portuguese domination covers over three centuries. Such a long period has still not been thoroughly researched. Ricardo Levene (1885–1959) who devoted his career closely to this matter, coined the phrase 'Indian economics' (Levene 1952: 33). This chapter closely follows the work of Levene, except that it will trace the works only of those thinkers who were born in what we shall refer to as the New World (Spanish America), or who were there long enough to know and understand the Indian cultural and economic systems. This group would include scholars as Alonso de Zuazó, Bartolomé de las Casas, Tomás de Mercado, José de Acosta, Miguel Agía, Juan de Solórzano y Pereira; and those excluded from this group would be Spaniards such as Uztáriz, Ulloa, and Campomanes, etc., who had never set foot on American soil.

The task to be undertaken in this chapter is a difficult one and one assuming great responsibility, but its treatment cannot be postponed any longer.

The structure of Indian economics can be seen as a three-storey building. At the base, there is an imposingly solid building block, representing the foundations of scholastic philosophy, which covers a period of a little more than three centuries of Spanish and Portuguese domination in the Americas. Upon this base, there is a second, equally thick building block, meant to represent the typical patterns of the mercantilist lineage, which covers at least an identical period of time, if not lasting up until today. Finally, on the top of the building, there is an attractive and graceful turret representing the classical school. This turret is placed on the right-hand side of the building, to indicate that the time period in question is only the last decades of the era of Spanish domination in America.

When seen from a distance, only the turret appears clearly, and this is precisely the impression received when reading the writings on the history of economic thought during the period of Spanish domination. But, upon closely examining the building, one gradually discovers the influence of the vast output of the mercantilist school (as a school of economic development) as well as the deeply rooted writings of the scholastic school.

Thus, Indian economics looks like a structure of three superimposed schools of thought, or the superimposition of all three schools (the scholastic, the mercantilist and the classical schools) in the last phase of colonial times. If one is able to accept this vision of the development of Indian economics as being built by superimposed layers, the first point to consider is the topic of the different periods. According to the traditional scheme, valid in Western Europe, the scholastic period ends some time in the middle of the fifteenth century, when mercantilism takes a steady foothold, only to be itself displaced by the classical school towards the middle of the eighteenth century.

For the entire Mediterranean area, especially Italy and the Iberian peninsula, the scholastic period is extended, due to the discovery of late scholastic economics, or as it is also called, the 'school of Spanish scholastics'. This prolongation now covers the period from the sixteenth to the middle of the seventeenth centuries. This extension, with the consequent superimposition of the scholastic and mercantile periods, will present Spanish scholars with the difficult problem of periodization, that is, of being able to state clearly the time periods of the different schools.

The problem is even worse for Latin American scholars. I do not consider this the best place to develop it. It is enough to insist that a great effort must be made, and that it should be carried out at the subcontinental Latin American level, so as to obtain through the Weberian method of the ideal types, a more or less manageable scheme, which should promise better results in the future.

The vast Latin American bibliography dealing with the classical period is very well known, and has been intensively studied in all the thirty-three Latin American universities since 1780, as Robert Sidney Smith's study shows (Smith 1957). Nevertheless, it will be convenient to note that even the majority of the writings where the names of the great men of Europe (Genovesi, Galiani, Quesnay, and above all Adam Smith) are invoked on every page, make up writings of a mercantilist tendency.

The number of Latin American scholars dedicated to the studies of classical economic theory is indeed small. It is true that there are illustrious men, who, captivated by the novelty of the language of 'political economy', translated into Spanish the prodigious texts of Quesnay (Manuel Belgrano (1770–1820) (1794) in Madrid and Joaquín Camacho (1766–1816) (1810) in Bogotá); and Adam Smith (the abstract offered by Francisco García Peláez (1785–1816) (1814) at the University of San Carlos in Guatemala). In addition, Professor José Agustín Govantes (1796–1844) (1821) in La Habana translated Thomas Malthus, while Jean Baptiste Say was honoured by a translation of the first edition of his 'Treatise' done by the capable hands of José María Benavente (1785–1833) (1814–15) in Mexico, only to be followed by a translation of the second edition of the same work by Don Justo Vélez, professor of Political Economy at San Carlos de La Habana (1818–24). While in universities in Bogotá, Caracas, Cartagena, Quito and Sucre, Jean Baptiste Say's work was used as a textbook, in Buenos Aires, due to a decree of 28 November 1823, James Mill's *Elements of Political Economy*, published in London in 1821, with a Spanish version published in Buenos Aires in 1823 as well in the *Imprenta de la Independencia*, was chosen as a university textbook. This book has had great success in the Spanish speaking world.[1] It is also said that there was a translation of Mill's book into Portuguese dating from 1832, done by Professor Pedro Autran de Mata e Albuquerque, but I still have not found it myself. Finally, sometimes works were even translated without giving credit to any translator, as was the case of Jean Jacques Rousseau's 'Économie Politique', from the French *Encyclopaedia*. Only after much time had passed was Diego Padilla (1751–1829) given credit for performing this monumental task in 1810.[2] Although the undertaking of all these translations was a difficult job to perform, the handling of the theoretical tools of the classical school by these scholars was in general very poor.

One of the best qualified for this job in all of colonial America was the Brazilian José da Silva Lisboa, Visconde de Cairú (1756–1831). He enjoyed the first professorship of Economic Science in all the Americas, which was created at his insistence in 1808. He began writing on economic theory in 1798, and continued without interruption until the end of his life. But the most important of all his writings is *Estudos do Bem Comun e Economia Politica*, written and published in two volumes in Rio de Janeiro in 1819. The title itself proudly displays his deeply philosophical scholastic roots. The work is indeed a true version of the new language that Adam Smith introduced to economic science. To avoid the pitfalls of repetition, the author wisely precedes the volume of economic theory with another volume dedicated solely to the history of economic thought, choosing the contributions on a country by country basis as a method of analysis: England, Italy, France, Germany, Portugal, Spain, Switzerland, etc. It is one of the greatest legacies received from this period.

As a complement to Cairú's work, although at a different level, are the writings of the Honduran scholar, José Cecilio del Valle (1770–1834). These writings contain a three-fold meaning in the history of culture: for his integrationist vision of 'the most meritorious research of an American is America'; for his fervent economic liberalism, defined as 'Free trade has always been a principle for me: it stems from property, and property is sacred' (Valle 1958: 112); and for his increasing fondness of the usage of mathematics in economic science, such as had been carried out by the Frenchman N. F. Canard, whose work, which del Valle knew and admired (Valle 1958: 39,105), and which had already been used successfully in the development of some aspects of spatial theories in economics, thus anticipating the work of A. Lösch. Canard's influence in the Río de la Plata countries can be proved by a publication in the *Telégrafo Mercantil del Río de la Plata*, 2 May 1802, IV, 5, folio 65, where an extensive and enthusiastic book review, in which formulations of 'equations that represent the state of economic equilibrium in the competitive market' and of 'flows of monetary circuits and its branches . . . just as those of the aorta' are mentioned for the first time, can be found. In a last commentary, the critic formulates his opinion about Canard's work and says that 'not approving all the principles that the author feels nor all the consequences he deduces from such principles, we can say that his work takes the science of Political Economy to a point never reached before'. The econometrists of today, knowing that the quotation refers to the work of N. F. Canard, will surely applaud this conclusion.

As is known, José de Lavardén (1754–1808) and Pedro Antonio Cerviño (1757–1816), carried out similar works along the Río de la Plata basin. Cerviño dedicated himself with much interest to the same matter in a work entitled *Nuevo Aspecto del Comercio del Río de la Plata*, thus anticipating the ideas of Von Thünen. A separate mention should be made of the work 'Economía Política', penned by 'Almada' and published in the *Correo del Comercio* in 1810, but which seems to have been selected six years previously by Manuel Belgrano, due to the abridged and concise development of the theory of the just price in the later version.

Was there no 'preclassical' period in Indian economics? This question was raised on various occasions and it has received some very elaborate answers from men such as the Peruvian Pedro José Bravo de Lagunas y Castilla (1704–62), Antonio de Narváez y la Torre (1753–1812) and Pedro Fermín de Vargas (1770?–1808?) in New Granada. The two latter authors are, to me, mercantilists of a Christian hue, beyond any doubt. If they seem to favour agriculture in certain parts of their writings, it is evident that they are just trying to conceal their enthusiasm for industrialism, perhaps in order not to harm the standard of their works. The Peruvian Bravo de Lagunas y Castilla is most difficult to place in a specific school of thought, since he shows an indisputable preference for farming activities, yet at the same time has deep scholastic, Aristotelian, Thomistic roots.

INDIAN ECONOMICS AND MERCANTILISM

A profile of Indian mercantilism will now be undertaken. Between the beginning and the ending of the colonial era, there was a huge amount of writing of a mercantilist hue. Mercantilism begins with Christopher Columbus' (1451–1506) *Diario de a Bordo* and ends with an immense number of memorials, records, and essays read in the presence of the consular personnel, or sent to the viceroys and governors or to the Council of the West Indies, right up to the last moment of Hispanic domination in

America. Most of the works are empirical studies which deal with local economic problems carried out as part of a given economic development policy, said policy being general, sectional, or regional.

Christopher Columbus did not hide his bullionism. He wrote that gold was excellent: from gold, treasure was made, and he who possessed it could do what he wished in the world; nor did he hide his Christian motives for bullionism, for the hope of respect and increasing the Christian religion in the Province of the Indies and, of course, to finance the crusade to liberate the Holy Land, then in the possession of pagans.

Though there was a strong inclination towards bullionism in Spanish America, this was not all of it. Bartolomé de las Casas (1474–1566) walked the straight and narrow path of using the central ideas of Indian mercantilism as a doctrine of economic development, and he himself elaborated highly ambitious projects and plans for the colonization of the lands by farmers, and for evangelization in the New World. This was the path trodden for the next three centuries, until the last of the writings of the colonial era.

The avalanche of memoranda read by consulate secretaries, magistrates and trustees in all the remote parts of the Americas during the last decades of the colonial era is also important: Francisco de Arango y Parreño (1765–1837) in Cuba; Pedro Fermín de Vargas (1760–1807) from Zipaquirá; José Baquijano y Carrillo (1751–1817) from Lima; Victorián de Villava (d.1802) from Chuquisaca; Manuel de Salas (1755–1841) from Santiago de Chile; and Manuel Belgrano in Buenos Aires. This is by no means an exhaustive listing, it merely reflects the names of those most prolific in the production of writings about economic development at the end of the eighteenth and the beginning of the nineteenth century.

In addition to the Christian nuance, Latin American mercantilism also has a profound liberal hue. The authors know that the 'Indias' are a province of Spain and/or Portugal, which means the fine points of any policy of economic development should agree with those set forth by the mother countries. Nevertheless, those mercantilists of a liberal persuasion persisted in their demands for liberalization of trade with the mother countries by any means. At the outset, they did so timidly and as an exception, as it was done in 1629 by the trustee of the Cabildo (city hall) of Buenos Aires, Antonio de León Pinelo (c.1590–1660), who presented a memento of protest to the Council of the West Indies. But, as time passed, the mercantilists began to ask for free trade as a scientific demand of the progress attained by the classical school: laissez-faire, laissez-passer.

Of course, projects smacking of utopian socialism are not absent, such as that begun by Vasco de Quiroga (1470?–1565) in Michoacán between 1530 and 1562. This project was to build towns in each region in which the natives, under the guardianship of the friars, were to become farmers in an agrarian community where working and tilling the soil, they may, by their work, support themselves and live orderly and under the control of the authorities and with saintly, good and Catholic ordinances; in this way, with GOD's aid it would be possible to establish a well organized Christian community like the primitive Church.

(Zavala 1937: 45)

The foundation of the doctrine was taken by Quiroga, as he states specifically, from Thomas More's 'Utopia' (1516). Due to this, Quiroga implemented the following measures in his hospital-towns: the corporate organization of families; the importance of agriculture in combination with crafts; the institution of common ownership of the means of production; the elimination of the usage of money in national transactions; the fair distribution of the national income; a six-hour working day; and an ardent and growing spiritual activity, particularly religious activity.

Projects with an anarchist influence are not missing either, such as Lope de Aguirre's (1518–61), known through letters to and records of the civil and religious authorities of the Province of Venezuela, and letters to King Philip II (1561), sent during his stay on Margarita Island, and in the towns of Burburata and Nueva Valencia. Lope de Aguirre's idea is but a projection of Max Stirner's (1806–56) in 'Der Einzige und sein Eigenthum', especially as regards his support for the thesis that the Indian authorities should be eliminated. Like Stirner, Aguirre fought for this, as is shown in his statement that 'all the presidents, magistrates, bishops and archbishops and governors, lawyers and solicitors were to be slain' (Macía 1972: 455). However, there was an exception which distinguishes him from Stirner: his statement of expressed obedience to the church and his fondness for the religious order of La Merced. This was shown by his statement that these people did not themselves take a special interest in the business of Spanish America. This Christian forerunner of Stirner had, nevertheless, something in common with the other two great men of anarchism, Michael Bakunin (1814–76) and Prince Peter Alexeyevich Kropotkin (1842–1921): he was 'hijodalgo' (a nobleman) as they were; and at the same time, he was a revolutionary and the author of histories and essays, just as they were, with courage that almost reached the brink of insanity.

The Jesuits established an economic system in the Indian culture that lasted for more than 150 years, reaching from the Paraguayan missions to those in California, following a line from the inner side of the Andes mountain range, which is commonly known today as the Carretera de la Selva. This system has had its supporters and its enemies, which still exist today and though it is not convenient for this discussion to be dealt with here, we cannot overlook one piece of writing of the colonial era by an authentic missionary of San Ignacio de Miní and professor at the University of Córdoba, in which an attempt at defining the essence of the Jesuit economic

9

system is made by means of the comparative method. The author is José Manuel Peramás (1732–93), and his posthumously published work was rendered into Spanish as *La República de Platón y las Reducciones Jesuíticas del Paraguay*. One may disagree with the author in many aspects of the work, especially as he confronts an economic system with an economic doctrine. Still, one cannot help emphasizing at the same time the double importance of this work by a Jesuit from the Río de la Plata mission, who was also a university lecturer in moral theology (1755–67). On the one hand, the importance of this work in the history of economic doctrines, is due to the author's capacity for pointing out the specific economic features of Plato's *Laws* and his *Republic* as no one in America had done before; and on the other hand, the importance of Peramás' valuable contribution in explaining the characteristics of the missionary economic system. Thus, from the point of view of development policy, he declares himself an opponent of the bullionist doctrine and prefers a model based on land productivity for the development of the farming and industrial sectors, and favours technological progress and human capital accumulation. As far as ideology is concerned, Peramás is as much an opponent of the individualism of the liberal philosophers, as of the individualistic egalitarianism that was determined to open the way for collectivism. Peramás is a true defender of the doctrine of organic solidarism.

In Indian mercantilism, just as in the Old World, a number of schools also began to appear in connection with originally established doctrines of economic development. Such was the case with writings devoted primarily to the development of sea trade, similar to those of Dutch and British authors. In the inventory of the specialized works dealing with commercial mercantilism, the 'Representación' of Miguel de Uriarte y Herrera in Quito in 1757, must not be excluded. In addition, there was the 'Memorial del Consulado de la Ciudad de los Reyes sobre el Estado de la Real Hacienda y el Comercio en las Indias'. This was written in Lima in 1726 by one of the great eighteenth-century figures, Dionisio de Alcedo y Herrera (1690–1776). Alcedo y Herrera was only surpassed in the economic field by the wise Peruvian Pedro José Bravo de Lagunas y Castilla, who, with his 'Voto Consultivo' of 1755 (reprinted in 1761) should rightfully be regarded as the founder of the Indian system of economic nationalism, as the Peruvian Emilio Romero (1945: 275) suggested. But another Peruvian, César Augusto Reinaga (1969: 20–7) sees Bravo as the forerunner or even founder of Quesnay's Physiocracy.

There also existed an Indian school of cameralism. It began timidly with a 'Parecer' by Fernando de Santillán (d.1576), magistrate of the 'audiencia' of Lima, and later of Quito. He was a mercantilist, with strong traces of what is referred today as the social economics of the market. He formulated, anticipating by centuries, the root of the adage of laissez-faire, laissez-passer, often ascribed to Boisguilbert, or to Gourney, or even to Quesnay. As a matter of fact, it occurred when, rejecting the system of forced labour used in the mines of Potosí, Santillán stated that

> it was better to leave them in freedom so that those who want to go to the mines can do so of their own will, and the best guidance for them [was] to let the Indians themselves take part in their contracts and melting activities in agreement with their customs.
>
> (Santillán 1950: 112)

The work of Santillán is an excellent brief treatise in which the author very carefully examines the tax system applied to the Peruvian Indians during the Hispanic regime, and compares this to that applied during Inca rule, with the conclusion that the Incas' system was superior. With this conclusion, he establishes a link with his forerunner Juan Polo de Ondegardo (1532–96), a distinguished jurist to the court of viceroy Francisco de Toledo, whose 'Relación' was written in 1571 and who, with his successor, Francisco Falcón, was present at the Lima Council of 1582. Falcón's 'Representación' offered the opinion that the Spaniards had no right whatsoever to impose taxes on the Indians; even more daringly he stated that in order to stimulate economic development in the New World, it was imperative that the revenues of the Peruvian kingdom were to be consumed in that same kingdom for the creation of new jobs and for encouraging new economic activities. Of course, Falcón's 'Representación' was harshly criticized by his contemporaries, who were mostly of the mercantilist spirit.

The most important works in Indian cameralism flourished, however, in the first half of the seventeenth century, as can be established firmly, though provisionally, since only a fragment of the enormous output of Indian economics is known.

The author of the first work is Francisco de Alfaro, who was a university professor and later a district attorney in the magistrate's office of Panamá in 1594, of Charcas in 1597, and finally a magistrate of the latter location in 1607. In 1610 he was appointed 'visitador' for the Tucumán, Paraguay, and Río de la Plata provinces. On this occasion, he travelled extensively throughout what is currently Argentina. As a result of these positions, which lasted until the beginning of 1612, he drafted the famous 'Ordenanzas' from 1611–12, known in the history of Argentina as Alfaro's Statutes, by virtue of which the system of *encomiendas* was suppressed. The author's son, Father Diego de Alfaro, SJ, born in Panama, is also remembered in our cultural history. He worked in the Jesuit missions in Paraná and Uruguay, and later while serving as Superior of the Missions he had to confront the invasion of the Paulists and died fighting against the *bandeirantes*, shedding his blood upon missionary soil. Alfaro's cameralism has been presented in a work written in Latin, in accordance with the Western tradition of the universities and countries which prided themselves on their culture. *Tractatus de Officio Fiscalis deque Fiscalibus Privilegiis* was

11

published in Valladolid in 1606; it spread all over the West and enjoyed great recognition, as is confirmed by the fact that it went into three editions.

But in Latin America, where the study of Latin has been eliminated from the mandatory subjects for the formation of our university students, because it is regarded as a foreign language, Alfaro's 'Tractatus' just like many other works from the colonial era – and even from our own era up to 1850, when the norm that established that doctoral theses should be presented in Latin was valid – remained inaccessible to American scholars of the last two centuries. It was due to the acute need to incorporate this work into the publishing funds of the Library of Latin American Economic Thought during the Hispanic Period that I requested and received, in 1974, the generous support from Conicet, and from the Universidad Católica Argentina, to start a post-degree seminar, which continues to this day, as well as a Doctoral programme at the same school, also started in 1974. The seminar is based on a general and methodological investigation, century by century, nation by nation, and author by author of the writings which were to become the building blocks of Indian economics. But, as I have already stated, we are still in the infancy of such work.

The approach of Alfaro's work is highly cameralistic. The main purpose is the study of the public sector, as it was for the German and Austrian cameralistic authors of that time, from the viewpoint of the sciences of the state, legislation, public administration and economic science, as they are currently treated, based on documentation of a highly scientific level.

As a result of this multi-disciplinary vision, a large number of Alfaro's reflections of an economic nature turn out to be important to the history of economic thought. Among those which deserve special attention are the rules of taxation, the wage policy, the just price, the elements of spatial analysis, and many ideas on political economy for the Indias as a peripheric area of Spain and Portugal.

Alfaro's 'Tractatus' allows Gaspar de Escalona y Agüero (1592–1650) to reach the highest position in Indian cameralism and to succeed in producing the first treatise on Indian public finance, with the highest scientific responsibility. Nearly 350 years ago, this volume appeared in Madrid, with a title page that is a real work of art, written half in Latin and half in Spanish and titled *Arcae Limensis Gazophilatium Regium Perubicum*.

As we can determine from the title page of the book, Escalona y Agüero declares himself to be an 'Argentinian Peruvian', a native of Chuquisaca. There are three editions, all printed in Madrid, in the years of 1647, 1675, and 1775. There is also a 'modern' abridged edition, according to Ots Capdequí, published in La Paz in 1941, limited to a selection of chapters from the section written in Spanish, moreover omitting all marginal notes in Latin (which, despite its limitations, is better than nothing).

The *Gazofilacio Real del Perú* is the product of the knowledge and long experience of Escalona y Agüero, who was famous as a consultant to courts, a politician, and an administrator of public finance, as much in his professional life as he was in his scientific writings. As soon as he had finished his university studies in Chuquisaca and Lima, he held various official positions one after the other: he was a magistrate in Tarija, governor of Castro Virreina, a solicitor in Cuzco, and collector of royal revenues. His performance in this last position induced him to prepare his aforementioned great work.

The section in Latin is devoted to public policy and to fiscal administration in general, as a direct duty of the American viceroys. The section in Spanish is devoted to administration, legislation, and tributary accounts, as a duty of the royal officials 'in the Ministry of Royal Finances' and of the 'auditors of the Exchequers', on the one hand, and to the thorough study of each and every one of the different classes of Indian taxes on the other hand. The author critically analyses each topic inspired by the doctrine – widely and totally ignored by the modern researcher – of the authors ranging from Greco-Roman antiquity up to his own day, without omitting his own criticism, even in cases where caution should impose silence on his part. The criticism was exceedingly favourable to Escalona's work. Solórzano, who shortly thereafter published the last volume of his *Política Indiana*, on Indian public finances, besides being constantly guided by our Argentinian Peruvian, spares no praise or admiration for the learned and wise cameralist of Chuquisaca.

INDIAN AND SCHOLASTIC ECONOMICS

The Indian scholastic school covers the same time period as Indian mercantilism: from the beginning to the end of the colonial period. Its true representatives are the doctors, generally theologians, whose work places are the universities or the convents of the religious orders. As a transplant of the Spanish scholastics, the Spanish-American scholastics have equally deep Aristotelian roots, and as such, the business world has its place, according to Hugo de San Victor (1096–1141), within moral philosophy and its three disciplines: ethics, politics and economics. But it has also, according to doctors in law, with their seats in the universities, and in the sites of the royal audiences, an origin in the world of contracts of bargains and sales, commonly called 'agreements and contracts' (*tratos y contratos*). The treatises on moral philosophy, on justice and law, and on agreements and contracts, are the three basic sources in the business world for the scholastic economics in the New World.

The identification of the works of interest for the business world is more difficult in the case of the scholastic works, as they were usually not published in Spanish. The perceptive reflections of Professor Guillermo Furlong (1889–1974) on the occasion of the publication of his *History of the Philosophy in the Río de la Plata during the Colonial Era*, should be borne in mind.

It is obvious to say that almost all the documentation of which we have made use is written in Latin. The non-familiarity of those who have wanted to write on the philosophical doctrines of the [colonial] past, has prevented them from resorting to the sources. That accounts for so many and so regrettable extravagances, even in writings that carry at the foot of the page the names of scholarly and well intentioned men.

(Furlong 1952: 29)

In order to explore the process of the spread of the late scholastics in Latin America we have made a sampling of the principal written works, with the aim of guaranteeing, on the one hand, its temporal distribution during the three centuries of the colonial period, and on the other, its regional expansion in the whole of Spanish America. As a result of this procedure, we have come to prove the significance of these authors for the period starting in 1550 and ending in c.1700, but with a dispersion circle from the beginning of the sixteenth century until the end of the eighteenth century, as is shown in the writings of the Dominican friars for the first half of the sixteenth century, and those of the Jesuits for the end of the eighteenth century.

Its regional distribution revolves around two centres, Mexico in the north, and Chuquisaca and Córdoba in the south, from which arise the names of the two economic schools, the School of Mexico and the School of Chuquisaca and Córdoba. In the following chapters, we shall examine the life and work of some scholastic authors.

3

JUAN DE MATIENZO[1] AND TOMÁS DE MERCADO[2]

More than 400 years ago, in the last months of 1580, a work in Latin enti-
tled *Commentaria Ioannis Matienzo Regii Senatoris in Cancellaria Argentina
Regni Peru in Librum Quintum Recollectionis Legum Hispaniae*[3] left the printing
presses of Francisco Sánchez in Madrid. This work was written by Juan de
Matienzo (born on 22 February 1520 in Valladolid, Spain), magistrate to the
Court of Charcas, in the city of La Plata or Chuquisaca (today Sucre) of the
Viceroyalty of Peru, from 7 September 1561 until his death on 15 August
1579.[4]

It is a voluminous work, impregnated with wisdom, with an eminently
jurisprudential focus, in which our Royal Magistrate (Regii Senatoris), using
resources from his personal library and surely reinforced by the La Plata
Tribunal (Cancellaria Argentina), enlarges upon the *Comentarios al Libro
Quinto de la Recopilación de las Leyes de España* (Commentaries on the Fifth
Book of the Digest of the Laws of Spain) established by King Philip II and
published in Madrid in 1567.[5]

In order to carry out such a commitment, the work must have been
arduous and one assumes that it would have required intense dedication,
through many years of effort; much reading and deep meditation, stimulated
by the pleasant and sunny environs of an eternal spring, on the slopes of the
Churuquella and Sicasica peaks; and also a lot of permanent documentation,
which was limited by this same environment so far removed from the world
of books.

But Matienzo had accumulated a great reserve of experience in scientific
research carried out the decade before. Actually, it was during this time that
he finished three works, of which one was published, when he was still in
Spain, in the Chancellery of Valladolid (Matienzo 1623); while the other two
had been finished in 1567 in the La Plata Tribunal of the province of Charcas.[6]

Matienzo took the opportunity, when remitting these two final works to
the mother country, to send a letter dated 28 November 1567, in which he
refers to the putting in motion of a new set of investigations which he had
already begun, and anxiously desired 'to bring them out into the light in
order to be used' by those who of his 'sweat and labour wanted to get help'

15

(Levillier 1918, I: 238). It is evidently a reference to the *Commentaria*, the great work which we already know about, and which he completed later upon sending it to the Council of the Indies of the 'Gobierno del Perú'[7] and the 'Estilo de Chancillería' (Style of the Chancellery).[8]

The second and final time that we discover a reference by Matienzo to the progress of his scientific research, and that is to his *Commentaria*, is a letter sent to the king from La Plata on 14 October 1576. After pointing out that the manuscripts of his two earlier works remained in the long queue at the Royal Council of the Indies from eight or more years ago, he lets it be known, with no great introduction, that he had already sent one book in Latin and one book in Spanish, not forgetting to add that this activity required all the leisure time he had when not working at his official charge (Levillier 1918, I: 402).

Of the book written in Spanish, nothing is known of its existence today. But it is believed, and with good reason, that the book in Latin was the *Commentaria*, since the author adds in the final text of this work that he had finished writing it in the beginning of 1576 (Matienzo 1623: Title 25, Law 3, Gl.1).

With what does the *Commentaria* deal? It is difficult to give a correct answer to this question. In the first place, this is due to the work lacking a general index which would have allowed scholars to know at first glance all the contents and the organic structure of the book, as often happens when the author dies during the printing process. Second, the work, like many others of its time, had an alphabetical index on the basis of the special indices of each title and subtitle of the work, prepared by Matienzo himself. As the book is built upon a structure of twenty-five titles, Matienzo took special care in heading each of them with a very neat index on the contents of the title, which at times occupied several pages. In this way, an unprepared scholar may take the special index on the contents of the first chapter to be the general index to the whole work, especially since it is written in a dead language, Latin.

It should then come as no surprise that some people have thought that the *Commentaria* deals with jurisprudential aspects related to the family in its multiple facets: constitution; integration; specific aspects of each group which integrates the family; aspects of disintegration; of inheritance; etc. Actually, the first third of the twenty-five chapters of this work are dedicated to these matters. Nevertheless, the remaining two thirds touch upon subjects which, though rigorously respecting the jurisprudential focus, involve the world of business, from the empirical point of view. In the foreground, Matienzo deals emphatically with what today is called economic law and this takes up the second part of the book. But the last third touches upon problems more directly related to the economic science of his time, as for example: Title 11 deals with problems of sales and purchases; Title 12 upon the sale of cloth; Title 13 is dedicated to weights and measures; Title

14 is on hucksters; Title 18 is on money exchangers and bank account-ability; Title 19 deals with public robbers and bankruptcy; Titles 20–24, on mints, the monetary system and the types of money; and Title 25 looks at the already famous 'bread tax'.[9]

In addition to this subject classification of business from an empirical standpoint, it is possible to contemplate the topics from the point of view of the type of knowledge we wish to reach, which at times is a function of the way in which we pose our questions: be it on the normative front; on the administrative or instrumental front – or, as we would say today, in the implementation of adequate measures to reach a determined objective; or finally, on the eminently analytical front (Popescu 1985: 40ff).

Matienzo is outstanding in all three of these areas. Just like the Roman jurists and the scholastic theologians, Matienzo took as the central point for his economic theorizing in the *Commentaria* the Doctrine of the Just Price, and managed to achieve this from a triple focus: the doctrine of the just price as an economic philosophy; the doctrine of the just price as an instrument of order in the market; and the doctrine of the just price as the analytical foundation of the theory of value, of the theory of prices, and of the value of money.

Matienzo is among the first Hispanic American thinkers who developed the doctrine of the just price in a profound and systematic manner. It is true that before him in the New World, a religious man from a preaching order, Tomás de Mercado (1525–75), studied the subject in 1569.[10] However, it is disputable whether Mercado's ideas reached the depth and breadth of Matienzo's. This by itself makes Matienzo's *Commentaria*, the only work in which he discusses the theory of the just price, an extremely valuable work in the history of economic thought in general and specifically in that of Latin America.

As a consummate jurist, Matienzo establishes the connection between the doctrine of the just price and the 'Institutions' and 'Digest' of the Justinian code (533–64), this relation enjoying a highly valued position in the economic doctrines of today (Dempsey 1935: 471–86; Kaulla 1940: 10–20; Spengler and Allen 1971: 60–74). One of the basic sources of the doctrine of the just price of classical scholasticism is contained in the commentary of the jurist Paulus (170–230), in a law named Falcidiana, which was incorporated in the 'Digest'. Dempsey reproduces this entire law, because, as he emphasizes: 'it is difficult to deny the commentary of Paulus on the Falcidiana law a place among the influences formed by the medieval theories on value and price' (Dempsey 1935: 63). Paulus's main idea is: prices of things should not be established according to the fondness or the utility of individuals, but according to the common valuation.

Matienzo begins the exposition of the doctrine of the just price with exactly the thesis of Paulus and makes direct mention of the law of Falcidiana. This is an important and correct methodological move. And it is necessary to emphasize this fact, even more so because, unfortunately, we economists over the following centuries have distanced ourselves from the doctrines of the Roman jurists, to the point where they are now largely ignored. Matienzo subscribes without hesitation to the commentary of Paulus and re-transmits it almost textually. 'The just price of everything is not determined by taste or expense, it is determined by the common estimation' (Matienzo 1580: Title 11, Law 1, Gl.2, No. 1). After more than 1,300 years of the law of Falcidiana, it was impossible to distinguish a Hispanic tinge[11] in the formulation of the thesis of Paulus. But what is important is the emphasis that Matienzo and a handful of predecessors placed upon the social or common estimation as the basis for and measurement of the just price.

Another Roman maxim, one quite celebrated among the jurists, that an object was worth whatever it could be sold for, was known to Matienzo. What Matienzo did with it was to bend it to fit not only Paulus's theory, but also to blend in nicely with all prior scholastic thinking on the moral philosophy of the just price.[12] Matienzo faithfully followed the views of Thomas Aquinas and Domingo de Soto, and reformulated this second great maxim of the jurists to state: 'an object is worth as much, without fraud or injustice, as it can be sold [for] in agreement with the common valuation, to those who know its conditions' (Matienzo 1580: Title 11, Law 1, Gl.2, No. 1).

To these selected normative reflections, it is necessary to add others, related to the possibility and the feasibility of using the doctrine of the just price as an instrument for putting the market in order. To this end, Matienzo makes a distinction between two types of just price, which goes back to the idea of Thomas Aquinas and Aristotle: 'one legal and the other natural' (Matienzo 1580: Title 11, Law 1, Gl.2, No. 9). Matienzo states that 'the legal just price is that which is determined by a law from the sovereign or from the civil society itself' (Matienzo 1580: Title 11, Law 1, Gl.2, No. 9). He later parts from the premise that the social authority by its very nature is capable of touching on and capturing the idea of the just or unjust social price, and especially on the idea of social or common valuation.

The natural price is the 'spontaneous or free just price, provided that no law restrains it' (Matienzo 1580: Title 11, Law 1, Gl.2, No. 9). And taking up a suggestion of Saint Thomas, later expressed concretely by Saint Antonino of Florence (1389–1459), Matienzo calls attention to the fact that while the legal just price is just one unalterable price, or as he says, 'it consists of that which is indivisible' (Matienzo 1580: Title 11, Law 1, Gl.2, No. 9), the natural price enjoys a certain latitude, oscillating between 'in one extreme, rigid; in the other, merciful; but in the middle, it is moderate' (Matienzo 1580: Title 11, Law 1, Gl.2, No. 9).

Once the conceptual instruments are inventoried for the objectives of ordering the market, the question arises of the choice of path to reach the supreme goal of a society ruled by just prices. To tell the truth, Matienzo confesses that due to his manner of conceiving things, stimulated by an identical attitude displayed by his teachers Diego de Covarrubias y Leyva and Domingo de Soto, his sympathy is decidedly on the side of those who opt for the doctrine of the legal just price. So here is proof of Matienzo's sympathy for direction in economic matters. To the question as to who will be concerned with the responsibility of establishing this price and value for merchandise, Matienzo answers: 'Certainly the governors of the provinces and the administrators of the republic' (Matienzo 1580: Title 11, Law 1, Gl.2, No. 9). Of course, he accepts that this policy would not always be very feasible although it would be wiser if all were appraised in this manner: 'but if not everything could be appraised, at least appraise that which one could do easily, as Domingo de Soto suggests' (Matienzo 1580: Title 11, Law 1, Gl.2, No. 9).

If one accepts Schumpeter's thesis that the sources of liberalism, of eighteenth-century laissez-faire, go back to the Hispanic scholasticism (Schumpeter 1971: 138), the doctrine on the officially set prices supported by Matienzo could be described as retrograde or reactionary in the elegant terminology of our century. But if a more detailed examination is made of Hispanic scholastic thought as regards the ordering of the market, Matienzo's situation does not seem unique. At a first glance in this area it seems that this ideological current of economic control and the official fixing of prices were not insignificant and that, consequently, Matienzo would find himself in good company (Weber 1959: 124–35).

If other references were taken into account, as for example some of the fundamental ideas inserted in the encyclical 'Quadragesimo Anno' (Valsecchi 1941: 563–84), or in the *Código Social de Malinas* (Unión Internacional de Estudios Sociales 1953: 59ff), his doctrine would be labelled quite frankly as progressive, and perhaps even good.

If the jurist from Valladolid was inclined to directivism and a systematic fixing of prices, the magistrate in Chuquisaca did not share the same opinion. It is not that Matienzo's opinion changed over time. Matienzo continued to be faithful to his point of view, but what changed were the circumstances. In his reflections on Spanish America Matienzo started out from a situation of economic spaces which lacked foodstuffs and other goods which had to be imported from the exterior. He warned that a policy of price fixing by the public sector, no matter how fair it might be, could provoke a sharp decline in imports, which could result in a reduction in people's welfare and perhaps even a disaster for the whole economic system.

It is what truly concerns the administration of our kingdom of Perú, that merchandise is carried here from Spain whose duties could turn out to be harmful, especially for the imperial city of Potosí, so sterile, that nothing is produced there but silver, in which most of the inhabitants work.

(Matienzo 1580: Title 25, Law 1, Gl.17, No. 2)

19

And he went on to state: 'if merchandise and foodstuffs are not introduced there, coming from the exterior, the great and famous commerce of that city would be paralyzed, damaging all Christendom, as it is well known' (Matienzo 1580: Title 25, Law 1, Gl.17, No. 2).

Confronted with such a possibility, the magistrate of Charcas does not hesitate to take the most liberal measures for the ordering of the markets of Potosí: 'reason for which we have never permitted the officials of that Royal Chancellery to impose there any duties on the merchandise and the foodstuffs' (Matienzo 1580: Title 25, Law 1, Gl.17, No. 2).

These few brush strokes are enough to give an idea of the normative and administrative fundamentals of the doctrine of the just price in the works of Juan de Matienzo. Nevertheless, hardly are the basic questions in each of these areas of knowledge posed than further questions arise from the answers. What are the forces that generate the social or common valuation of things? By what criterion are the legal prices of objects established? Is there any difference between the forces which act upon the determination of the natural price and those which act upon the legal price? How are the prices of things formed? What is the price? What is value? Which are the causes of value? What are the determinant elements in the formation and variation of prices? These and many other questions of this type, which are today called analytical, rushed through Matienzo's mind, and in as far as his reading and attentive observation permitted, he attempted to present the respective answers. In order to come as close as possible to his analytical thinking on the doctrine of the just price, we have grouped his reflections around three sets of strictly interconnected problems: the theory of value; the theory of prices and the theory of the value of money.

Matienzo's attitude when confronted by what is today called the theory of value based on the costs of production or its variant, the labour theory of value, was not very favourable. It could best be interpreted as an open and decided rejection. However, it is true that he ignored the role which the costs of production played in the economic process, or that he stubbornly opposed the idea of relating the price of goods with their labour input and the expenses thereof.

A man of his training, with so penetrating a spirit of observation in the labyrinth of commerce of the old and new worlds was not, and could not have been, an amateur in economic phenomenology. Consequently, Matienzo could not refuse to accept that all products, precisely by being such, were made by means of human efforts and instrumental and raw material costs: the 'labor et expensae' of the Romans jurists and the scholastic doctors. And Matienzo had no objection to stating (in the middle of the battle against the labour theory of value which was at that time so attractive to the emerging capitalists and bourgeoisie) that 'in the sale of merchandise, the expenses of the sellers must be considered' (Matienzo 1580: Title 11, Law 1, Gl.2, No. 3). This point of view is in line with the moderation and prudence of

Aristotle (384–22 BC) and Thomas Aquinas, when they remembered that the expenses formed the basis of the sustenance of labourers, artisans and businessmen, and that one moment's carelessness in the cost of production policy could well be the cause of a long-run collapse of an industrial activity (Aquinas 1946: 124).

But in his theory of value and cost of production Matienzo was not ready to support the position of John Duns Scotus, one of the greatest men of classical scholasticism. This much respected thinker, one of the most influential after Thomas Aquinas, who felt great sympathy and understanding for the role undertaken by merchants, ended up creating a 'rule' in virtue of which, in all cases, a reasonable benefit for the sellers should be added to the costs of production before determining a just price.[13] And Matienzo was right, because to accept such an idea would mean accepting that the costs of production were the most logical source or cause of value, a thesis which he was not ready to embrace because for him, the level of the costs of production 'had nothing to do with the true and proper value of things' (Matienzo 1580: Title 11, Law 1, Gl.2, No. 4).

Encouraged by the writings of the great Hispanic scholastics of his time, such as Francisco de Vitoria, Juan de Medina, Diego de Covarrubias, Martín de Azpilcueta and especially Domingo de Soto,[14] Matienzo set himself on the path towards the *Treaties and Contracts* of Conrado Summenhart de Calw (1450?–1502), the first of the high-level opponents of the Scotus doctrine,[15] and one who did much to demolish it. Matienzo then allows his point of view to mature into a tight synthesis. Alluding in a direct form, without naming the author, he makes his feelings known in the following manner:

> That rule according to which one must always sell the object at the price that was paid to buy it or the price of the labour and risks taken in acquiring it and moreover the merchant's profits, is a great fallacy. Actually, if one merchant, ignorant of his profession and the art of business in which he is occupied, buys it for more than the just price, or if luck is quite the adverse, if an unexpected surplus of merchandise comes to pass, he could not be fairly compensated for the expenses he had. And, vice versa, if another more capable or more fortunate man, who bought for less and upon whom luck smiled and a shortage of foodstuffs came to pass, for example, he could undoubtedly sell the same merchandise at a higher price the same day and even in the same place, even though the merchandise had not improved in the slightest way. It is that the art of business is at the mercy of fortuitous events, the reason for which businessmen must assume the risk of fatality and take advantage of good luck.
>
> (Matienzo 1580: Title 11, Law 1, Gl.2, No. 10)

For Matienzo, as for Conrad, de Soto, Covarrubias and a legion of Hispanic scholastics who reached the same conclusions as would be drawn by Molina and Lugo, the thesis of the cost of production theory of value or the labour theory of value is condemned as a great fallacy, and the arguments for this are the same as those given above (Höffner 1941: 110).[16] The fact that the radiating power of the economic doctrine of the Hispanic scholastics was strong not only in the universities of Spain and Portugal but also in Italy, France, Belgium, Germany and Austria, has been known for a long time. However, it never occurred to us that it could have reached our university centres, in the far regions of the New World, as has in fact happened.[17]

Juan de Matienzo was the great disseminator of these lessons in La Plata de los Charcas. Tomás de Mercado, under the same influences, transplanted the new seed to the other part of the Kingdom, New Mexico, and maintained the same negative thesis as Matienzo as regards the objective theory of value, even though neither of the two knew anything of the existence, the writings or the accomplishments of the other.[18]

Matienzo crosses the threshold of the subjective theory of value in the company of Aristotle and Saint Augustine (354–430), two of the main sources in this area,[19] having Diego de Covarrubias and Domingo de Soto as contemporary witnesses of 'authority', who in their turn, Matienzo considered, completed a whole tradition of knowledge accumulation from the sources of jurists and glossarists of Roman law and scholastic theologians of the Late Middle Ages, respectively, as well as Conrado de Summenhart, to whom Matienzo expressly refers. The security and confidence with which Matienzo manages this set of sources is impressive, and contrasts with the lack of interest and surprise of many scholars of the twentieth century who are accustomed to thinking that the first principles of the subjective value theory could be traced only as far back as the eighteenth century. The fact that a minority of the historians of economic thought had turned back to look at the Aristotelian and Augustinian legacy on the subject of the theory of value, and are now exercising strong pressure upon the orthodox majority that believes the study of our science begins with Quesnay and Smith, is evident proof that Matienzo's position, even if regarded as 'humble' in the Hispanic scholastic current, should be placed next to that of the group of forerunners in the debate about the origins of the subjective theory of value.

Once the elements from Aristotle and Saint Augustine are gathered and synchronized, Matienzo proceeds to the elaboration of an essay on the theory of value as he understands it and which can be summarized in the following manner. First, he distinguishes between two different manners of appraising goods: one is by the nature of the good or its intrinsic quality; and the other by the importance it is given 'from outside', by its appearance. Consequently, we discover an attempt at classification which emphasizes, on the one hand, an objective concept, considering value as an individual property of goods, independent of the value schemes of men; and on the other hand, a subjective concept, considering value not as an inherent property of goods, but imbued by the importance given to them by men. From whence came this theory, which would be studied by scholars for centuries to come? The original source is none other than Saint Augustine, whose text would be one of the most quoted works in the history of economic thought until the advent of the classical school,[20] even though one may suspect that historians of economic science have not shown it the interest it deserves.

To understand Matienzo's theory of value, knowledge of the work of Saint Augustine is essential. Saint Augustine incorporates it in his work *La Ciudad de Dios* (The City of God), making it the object of his consideration in a separate chapter which carries a suggestive title: 'Of the degrees and differences among the creatures, as are in one manner estimated by their usage and utility, and in the other as regards the order of reason' (Saint Augustine 1948: Book 11, Chapter 16). Upon reading the paragraph reproduced by Matienzo, a total coincidence in the substantial distinction between the two focuses of valuation is observed, but at the same time, one sees a slight adaptation of Saint Augustine's quote used in the technique of presenting the illustrative examples of said distinction.

Keeping in mind the alternative presented by Saint Augustine, Matienzo thinks that a valuation conforming to the nature of things, far from serving in the business world, is but a source of confusion, which it is necessary to avoid. The correct criterion is the second one: 'In the contracts of purchase and sale and the like, things are not valued according to their nature, but by the common valuation of men, no matter how vain and incorrect this valuation can be' (Matienzo 1580: Title 11, Law 1, Gl.2, No. 2). In the following lines, Matienzo provides the justification for this idea:

> Since if one would have to look according to the nature of things, he would have to value a horse more than a precious stone, by the utility of the horse and because all living things are, by their nature, more precious than any inanimate object.
>
> (Matienzo 1580: Title 11, Law 1, Gl.2, No. 2)

Wherein, then, lies the fruit of Matienzo's adaptation of the passage by Saint Augustine? First, we observe that the concept of 'things by their nature' receives new support, since to the ontological argument of Saint Augustine of 'living things versus inanimate objects' is now added a technical economic argument based on the antinomy of 'useful things versus useless things'; the horse is superior to the precious stone for two reasons: because it is a living thing and for being an intrinsically valuable object. Second, one observes that the same comparative example of 'horse versus precious stone', which even if it is an adaptation from the work of Saint Augustine, is quite ingenious in the manner in which it allows us better to explore the double meaning of the 'nature of things'. Third, the utility of the horse is identified with the objective concept of value, as if by the term utility itself one would intend to mean the intrinsic quality of objects; and the reference to Conradus, as an authority who supports such an interpretation,[21] could actually be traced further back in time to Saint Bernardino of Sienna (1380–1444) and Saint Antonino of Florence, who already had given the term utility (*virtuositas rei*) the meaning of the intrinsic quality of goods. Consequently, and together with the concept of scarcity (*raritas*), this definition could be used as a foundation for the objective theory of value. And finally, the new twist given to Saint Augustine's theory of value clearly shows the danger of the confusion, and consequently gives birth to the paradox of the theory of value. Matienzo's horse and precious stone will be replaced some 200 years later by water and diamonds in Adam Smith's famous paradox. Like Smith, Matienzo puts forth his paradox but, unlike Smith, Matienzo solves it: the cause of value does not lie in utility, but in the appraisal or importance we give to goods due to the '*indigentia*' or necessity we have for them. They make us need them, as Saint Augustine said – that is, we lack them and feel their absence. We want them to fulfil some need (*necessitas*) or to satisfy a whim (*voluptas*), which in Saint Antonino's and Saint Bernardino's language would be *complacibilitas*.[22]

Matienzo opts for the expression *indigentia* to designate the second type of value, subjective value, profiled in Saint Augustine's *La Ciudad de Dios* (The City of God). Matienzo had rejected the nature of an object as a cause for its value in the business world,

> And the reason which de Soto gives in his 'Of Justice and Law', is that the cause and measurement of the human permutations lies in the *indigentia*, just as Aristotle had pointed out in the fifth volume of his *Ethics*. . . . Then, if no one had lacked the object or the work of another, all permutation of things by humans would cease. Consequently, it is due to *indigentia* that we must calculate the value of things.
>
> (Matienzo 1580: Title 11, Law 11, Gl.2, No. 2)

Matienzo does not feel attracted to the progressive focus of Saint Bernardino of Siena and Saint Antonino of Florence either in the substantive or the lexicographical aspect. He resolves, as a consequence of his usual conservative attitude, to put himself on the ancient path, part of which is the doctrine of *indigentia*, inaugurated by Albertus Magnus (1193–1280) (Willeke 1961: 5) and Thomas Aquinas (Aquinas 1946: 149–53), and adjusted and reinforced by the strong subjectivist essence of Jean Buridan (1300–58), rector of the University of Paris (Brants 1895: 72), and Henry de Langenstein (1325–97), professor at the University of Vienna (Brants 1895: 71), and carefully preserved by Domingo de Soto.[23] Henry de Langenstein stated that the '*indigentia* should be estimated in terms of the abundance and the scarcity of things' (Brants 1895: 72).

With this we are in the presence of a definite advance in the determination of the phenomenon of scarcity, until now only considered to be autonomous and objective. The necessity is a concept which reduces the neo-classical utility and scarcity notions to just one subjective phenomenon. And when Victor Brants became aware of the emergence of the neo-classical school and its new focus, characterized precisely by the reduction of utility and scarcity to just one phenomenon and its concomitant subjectivism, he exclaimed spontaneously: 'This is what the authors of the Middle Ages understood by *"indigentia humana"*, presenting it as a criterion of value' (Brants 1895: 171).

One can concede that with the expression *indigentia* the scholastics had in mind a much wider concept, which could have included not only need and/or utility but also a level of intensity conditioned upon greater or lesser abundance or scarcity. It could also be in accordance with this concept that the term was maintained by the scholastics throughout the period in which Latin was used as an ordinary working language. But when we also state that for Aristotle *indigentia* was the cause and measurement of exchange, it is necessary to remember that he wrote in Greek and employed the word *'chreía'*, which in Spanish has usually been translated as necessity. Thus, for example, we read in the Spanish version of the *Nicomachean Ethics* prepared by Francisco de Samaranch that 'this measure is the necessity we have for one and another, which sustains social life, since without needs and without similar needs, there would be no exchanges or the exchanges would be different' (Samaranch 1967: 1231).

But without much delay scholars of economics became aware of this deficient interpretation. The first reaction is due to the translator of the Fermín Didot (Paris) edition, who translated from Greek to Latin Aristotle's *Opera Omnia* between 1848 and 1850, in which *chreía* is translated into Latin as *usus seu indigentia* (Langholm 1979, 1983; Chafuén 1986; Lowry 1987; Cravero 1993). Glauco raised the point that the original word in Greek can be translated into Italian not only as necessity, but also as utility, or even common usage; and that the meaning of utility seems to have been the original intent. And Tozzi warns that only by giving the word *chreía* this latter meaning can a coherent idea be attributed to Aristotle, in the sense 'that the different values of objects depend upon their diverse degrees of utility, or . . . of the intensity with which we perceive their necessity' (Tozzi 1968: 137).

As regards the Spanish language, the contribution of the Argentinian economist Julio Meinvielle deserves mention. According to Meinvielle, the Greek word *chreía* can be translated into Spanish as use, utility, and also as necessity, adding that 'as that which is useful and necessary, man claims it, asks for it, demands it, also it can be translated as demand, which Ross has done on many occasions' (Meinvielle 1973:142).

This series of interpretations of the meaning of the Greek word *chreía* allows the re-establishment of the congruency between the concept and the *indigentia* used in the Latin texts of the scholastic authors, and to emphasize in this manner the common denominator of both doctrinal sources as regards the respective attitude to the subjective theory of value.[24] Now one can better understand the procedure used by Matienzo to base his subjective theory of value on the scholastic doctrine's authority, and at the same time the sources of Saint Augustine on the one hand, and Aristotle on the other. Correct or not, Matienzo's procedure is still an antecedent of, or an advance on, the contemporary preoccupations of historians of the subjective theory of value.

Matienzo deserves a special mention for his contribution to what today we call the law of supply and demand. Such mention is mandatory if one remembers that in truth there already existed forerunners in this area. In the *Encyclopedia Internacional de Ciencias Sociales* (International Encyclopaedia of Social Sciences), Raymond de Roover credits Luis de Molina (1554–1623) with having formulated the law of supply and demand. Luis de Molina published his work *On Justice and Law* in 1593, and it is to this work that Roover refers when mentioning Molina's formulation that 'a concourse of buyers, more considerable in one moment than another, and its greater disposition toward purchasing, would drive prices up, whereas the paucity of purchasers will bring them down' (Roover 1968: 435).

As a consequence, this deals with two important contributions, one of terminology related to the introduction of the term *concurrentium* in the economic lexicon, and the other of the law of supply and demand. The fact that these contributions have been granted to a Spanish scholastic is of major importance. But, more importantly for the scholars of economic history, is that besides Molina and even before him, there were other Spaniards and even some Spanish Americans, who made contributions which led to the solution of the two presented problems. In this group we find Juan de Matienzo, whose writings are clear testimonies of his active participation in the arguments related as much to the incorporation of the word and concept of *concurrentium* (concourse) in the technical language, as to the formulation of the law of supply and demand.

We shall begin with the contributions in the terminological area. The usage of the word 'concourse', discovered in Molina's work at the end of the sixteenth century, has produced a commotion among the twentieth-century critics. Joseph Höffner, cardinal and archbishop of Cologne, pointed out in 1941, 'As far as I know, here is used for the first time the word concourse' (Höffner 1941:177). For Raymond de Roover, in 1955, not only does it deal with the incorporation of a technical term, but also in this case with the introduction to our science of a new concept, that of competition in the market, with a clear meaning of rivalry among the members of the participating groups.[25] And the same would be maintained in 1961 by Franz-Ulrich Willeke.[26] How should these interpretations be evaluated? The best path towards an answer to this question is to begin by stating what Molina did not say on this subject. It can be confirmed that Molina never thought of a confluence of buyers and even less of a concurrence or rivalry among buyers. Molina's interest was not centred around peace or war among buyers. From his own conclusions, it is clear that Molina was interested in the situation of a greater or lesser quantity of buyers and its effects on the price level. Therefore, his concourse of buyers dealt with the state of having more or less buyers in the market, and nothing else.

This demonstrates that the influence of Domingo de Soto upon Molina was great, as it was upon Matienzo, Mercado and others. De Soto used the precise expression 'frequency of buyers' – emptorum frequentia – in the market as a possible factor in the variation of prices (Soto 1556: Book 6, Q.2, Art. 3). As if he had been able to foresee the headache that could be produced by the introduction of such progressive expressions, Juan de Matienzo opted for reproducing almost textually de Soto's conclusions, and consequently stated that among the many factors which influence the formation and/or variation of prices, one must also mention the 'frequency in the market of buyers and sellers' (Matienzo 1580: Title 11, Law 1, Gl.2, No. 7). Of course, the same could have been expressed using the term 'concourse' rather than 'frequency' in the market of buyers and sellers, but Matienzo stuck to the traditional path.

The same could not be said of Luis de Molina, who probably tired of the repeated reproduction of de Soto's text, and thought it convenient to change the terminology. He opted for concurrentium, a term which was misinterpreted well into the twentieth century, just as was Saint Antonino's use of the term 'industry', until Edgar Salin managed to halt the enthusiasm of those who wanted to apply to it the modern meaning of the word.

But Matienzo was familiar with the concept of industry in Saint Antonino's sense, and the concurrentium in the sense given thirteen years later by Luis de Molina. Actually, Matienzo uses the word 'industry' as did Saint Antonino to mean eagerness, application and creative activity, even going as far as to coin the phrase: 'The industry of the merchant' (Matienzo 1580: Title 1, Gl.2, No. 7). And the same could be said of the term concurrentium, but first we should look in depth at Matienzo's ideas.

Matienzo appears to be the forerunner in the long process of incorporating the concept of concourse or competition in the lexicon of economics, although by two very distinct paths. The first, as is well known, was to anticipate the use of the word 'frequency' to refer to the quantity of buyers in the market, which would be later changed to 'concourse', But the second was done in a more direct way, as Matienzo frequently used the verb 'to concur' and the noun 'concourse' in direct relation to economic facts. The first case is found in the title of one of his commentaries on the regulation of the advanced buying of bread, and in this case it is clear that the family of words derived from the verb 'concur' could not have escaped the notice of any Spanish jurist after the year 1528.[27]

The other case appears in a work by Matienzo in 1567, that is, twenty-five years before Molina's Justice and Law. Referring to the Royal Roads of the Inca Empire, Matienzo points out that some of these were still used in his time and it is precisely 'due to the great concourse of people who come . . . for the negotiating and contracting in Potosí (Matienzo 1967: Part I, Chapter X). It is no secret that such expressions were common property of the ancient thinkers, as is proved by the doctrine of the Jurist Julius Paulo, whose text on the origin and function of currency (where the verb *concurrebat* was used in economic phenomenology) was well known by all the Hispanic scholastics.[28] This does not overshadow Matienzo's participation, as the latter's contributions do not discredit Luis de Molina's works either, in the history of economic thought. It allows us to view the matter as one of the Spanish scholastic school. The best proof is given in the famous sentence: 'C'est la concurrence qui met un juste prix aux marchandises' ('It is concourse that sets a fair price for goods'), a sentence hidden amidst Montesquieu's 'De l'Ésprit de Lois' in Book XX, Chapter 9. This idea is also found in Castillo de Bovadilla (b.1547), who states that the need for a proper organization of the Spanish merchants would lead to the 'lowering of prices' as a consequence of the abundance, emulation and concourse of the sellers – which is an idea suggested by Matienzo himself. And this was stated in the *Política para Corregidores* (Castillo de Bovadilla 1775), first published in 1585. Could it be that this work, in which Matienzo's influence is evident due to the great amount of quotations from the *Commentaria*, is the first one where the term 'concourse' refers to the rivalry among sellers, as Roover intended, that leads to the lowering of prices of the goods sold?

Now, an examination of Matienzo's contribution to the substantive area is in order. Matienzo observed that the formation and the variation of prices depends among other factors on the level of abundance in the market of 'buyers and sellers' (Matienzo 1580: Title 11, Law 1, Gl.2, No. 7). It is worthwhile analysing this in relation to Luis de Molina's law of supply and demand.

It is noteworthy that both authors have in mind the same concern, that is, an interest in scrutinizing the formation of prices in a free market, and also both have the same vision about such mechanism of formation and variation of prices. But they also have certain slight peculiar differences. Molina's judgement that 'a concourse of buyers much greater in one moment than another, and their greater disposition toward buying, will raise the prices, whereas the scarcity of purchasers will bring them down' appears susceptible to objection. Actually, by looking at this statement in greater detail, one sees that Molina is talking about the law of demand, more than about the law of supply and demand. In this 'model', as we would call it today, only buyers appear. Sellers are not ignored, as they are necessary for Molina's formulation of prices, they just are not on the scene at this point; they lurk hidden in the wings, or as we say today, the supply is given.

On the other hand, Matienzo embraces from the beginning the processes of formulation and variation of prices by means of the interaction between buyers and sellers. This is an aspect that deserves emphasis, but one should also be aware of the high cost of the imprecise nature of his vision. If Matienzo did clearly present a certain relationship between the variation of prices and the gravitation of buyers and sellers, one could correctly object that between his formulation and that related to the mechanism of prices, there is a great distance.

But as if he were aware of this, Matienzo poses the matter again, this time focusing on it more closely and yielding to the reader a better perspective of the mechanism of price variation. In a style which is almost identical to that of Molina, Matienzo expresses his thoughts in the following terms: 'The price increases or decreases due to the scarcity of buyers and the multitude of merchandise and sellers' (Matienzo 1580: Title 11, Book 1, Gl.2, No. 6). This formulation is appealing – even more so than that offered by Molina.

However, there are problems with Matienzo's model. First, he only further probes the phenomenon for the lowering of prices. The scarcity of buyers and the surplus of both merchandise and sellers will always drive down prices, and with this effect the second weakness of the model appears, for it is evident that there is no logic between the increase and decrease of prices and the causes of such movements, causes which appear in one direction only.

Matienzo took these ideas from the work of Diego de Covarrubias (Covarrubias y Leyva [1552] 1957: Book 2, Chapter 3, No. 5), who at the time, while serving as president of the Council of Castilla, was the second most important figure in all of the Spanish kingdom (Fraga Iribarne 1957: ix–viii). Actually, Matienzo based his ideas on Covarrubias' doctrine, but also pointed out certain doubts as regards its methodological bases. These reflections can be found in Matienzo's *Commentaria* and form new sources for this complex question.

The first doubt refers to the adequate formulation of the principle of scarcity in the process of price formation. Matienzo clearly perceives by intuition that it is the scarcity or abundance of merchandise which plays the most important role in the process, and not so much the scarcity or abundance of buyers and sellers. He must have read in de Soto's writings that the abundance or scarcity of buyers was inversely related to the abundance or scarcity of merchandise; and all of this held true for the simple reason that 'actually, when merchandise is in abundance, the number of sellers is greater, and less is the number of buyers' (Soto 1556: Book 6, Q.2, Art. 3, fourth conclusion). Whatever the reason, what is certain is that Matienzo left evidence of the important role of abundance or scarcity of merchandise in determining prices. Matienzo published in two of his works that the lowering and rise of prices was due to abundance or scarcity.

As an example, Matienzo writes about the high price of bread in Perú, in which case he correctly diagnosed that of the two causes behind the high price, one was 'the greater scarcity of bread in the West Indies than in Spain'

(Matienzo 1580: Title 11, Law 1, Gl.2, No. 2). Matienzo only missed one more step to perfect Covarrubias' formulation according to the ruling principle of abundance and scarcity and its effects on buyers and sellers. The Matienzo-Covarrubias sentence should read 'price goes up or down due to the scarcity (abundance) of buyers and the multitude (scarcity of sellers). The improvement lies in the text added in parenthesis and consists of two elements: the scarcity of goods and the multitude of sellers, the first one is in Matienzo while the second one is a logical offspring of the first.

Matienzo takes a first step towards widening the thesis taken from his admired Covarrubias,[29] but he resists the temptation of completing the above-named linkage. That is, Matienzo admits that in terms of merchandise, one must contemplate as much its scarcity as its abundance as factors in price variations, but as regards the situation of the number of purchasers, he only looks at it in terms of scarcity. So, Matienzo's conclusion to all this, as stated in his General Alphabetical Index, is: 'The price increases or decreases due to the scarcity of purchasers and the abundance of merchandise' (Matienzo 1580: Title 11, Law 1, Gl.2, No. 2).

The reason that led Matienzo to persist in a such an incomplete formulation can be explained partly by the fact that the scholastic doctrine of the just price denied that the special utility of the buyer (coined by Thomas Aquinas in his 'Secunda secundae') could be a cause for price increases, but here we are dealing with an analytical problem concerning the variation and formation of all kinds of prices. Regarding this aspect, beside problems arising from logical inconsistencies of his argument, Matienzo could have resorted to the bright concept, formulated in 1553, of Domingo de Soto,[30] whose influence on the majority of the thinkers of this time was noteworthy – especially his influence on Tomás de Mercado,[31] the compatriot of the magistrate of Charcas. De Soto also widely develops the doctrine of the 'special utility of the buyer' formulated by Thomas Aquinas, when he contemplates the normative aspects of price policy; but this does not stop him from looking into the analytical aspects of the subject.

It is precisely in this moment that Matienzo nears de Soto's *On Justice and Law*, so that, supported by the latter's authority, he can make a review and put in order all the factors which make up the analytical fundamentals of price formation. Matienzo presents two sets of factors, scarcity (abundance) of merchandise and the number of buyers (sellers) in the market, in the hopes of avoiding the methodological bottleneck presented by following Covarrubias' method. In addition, Matienzo presents other possible factors related to 'the necessity felt for the thing, the labour of the merchant and his underlings, his industry and its risks, and if the merchandise was improved or suffered deterioration' (Matienzo 1580: Title 11, Book 1, Gl.2, No. 7).

An interesting point is that Matienzo assigns to de Soto one more theory, which never appeared in de Soto's text. This is the abundance or scarcity of money which Matienzo adds not by mistake, but in an intentional form, and not to adulterate the doctrine of his respected teacher, but to give more support in his own theory to an idea based on what he had been living through in Spanish America for quite some time, just like Tomás de Mercado. That is to say, it was easier for Matienzo to use the name of a respected scholastic scholar than to state that a theory was based on personal observation, which would make it an authentically personal doctrine.[32] To this bit of mischief of Matienzo's we will return later.

In addition to the factors already mentioned which would help determine the variation in prices, Matienzo quotes Pliny the Elder[33] for using temporal and spatial factors and the influence of factors related to the people in the market,[34] the spatial position of real estate for sale that will lead to imperfections in the market,[35] the preponderance of monopolistic structures,[36] the more or less explicit expectations as to the future behaviour of certain variables and its effect on the actual level of prices, etc. Included in this list is the unusual distinction between the market for buyers and the market for sellers, which Matienzo diligently collects and critically examines: 'If it is the seller who searches out the buyer the price shall have to drop, since all that is offered loses value, which is the reason why at the auctions usually things are bought at lower prices' (Matienzo 1580: Title 11, Gl.2, No. 6).[37]

In order to evaluate correctly Matienzo's contribution in this specific area, it is also necessary to take into account that in this case what is at hand is an accumulative knowledge that goes beyond his direct sources, de Soto and Covarrubias. We know that the work *Sobre los Contratos* (On Agreements) by Conrado de Summenhart was a pioneer approach, a detailed analysis of sixteen factors which determined the price level, which the classical scholastics used to their benefit, particularly Thomas Aquinas, who in turn read the most representative writings of the Greco-Roman style, which never could be surpassed by later attempts to define a law of supply and demand, the first attempts being found in the earlier writings of Pliny the Elder and in the 'Poroi' of Xenophon (Tozzi 1968: 37ff, 308ff).

Of course, what is open to discussion is whether Matienzo actually determined a law of supply and demand. In my opinion, such an ambitious and coherent idea was expressed neither by Matienzo and his scholastic contemporaries nor by the Ancient Roman and Greek scholars. But we can say that thanks to these two groups of writers, we do have all the tools necessary to analyse the behaviour of markets. These were the pioneers of what at one time was called the law of supply and demand, and which today we find separated into three or four interdependent theories. Only in this way can we specify that Matienzo participated in the development of a law of supply and demand: of course, it was a preparation at a world scientific level, which is no small achievement for the history of our science and even greater for the history of Latin American economic thought.

4

SCHOLASTIC ECONOMICS

After repeated attempts that date from over a hundred years ago, Spanish scholasticism has finally managed to find a place in the history of economic thought. The cumulative efforts by Dempsey (1936), Höffner (1941), Larraz ([1943] 1963), and later by Grice Hutchinson (1952), Roover (1953) and Iparraguirre (1954), culminated in its incorporation in Schumpeter's posthumous work, *History of Economic Analysis* ([1954] 1971). Considering the exceptional prestige of this author and the outstanding quality of this work, which I dared to define more than three decades ago as 'the standard work of reference for several generations' (Popescu 1964c), Schumpeter's judgement on the achievements of the Spanish scholastics, or as he called them the 'late scholastics', strikes not only Spanish students, but all those who read it:

> In the systems of moral theology of those late scholastics, economics acquired definitively if not its autonomous existence, at least, a well determined one; these are the authors of whom it can be least incongruently said that they have been the 'founders' of scientific economics.
>
> Moreover: the basis they laid for a useful and well integrated body of analytical tools and propositions were sounder than much of the subsequent work, in the sense that a considerable part of economics of the later nineteenth century might have been developed from those bases more quickly and with less effort than it actually cost to develop it, and that some of the work between those two periods has had something of a labour and time consuming detour.
>
> (Schumpeter [1954] 1971 : 97)

This feeling of pride and contentment is fully shared by the Spanish economic scholars, and there are good reasons for this. The Americas were conquered and integrated with Spain during the zenith of late scholastic activity. It has been said that the 'New World' became part of the Spanish empire by means of the cross and the sword. The sword represents those who, thirsty for gold and silver, sowed the seeds of mercantilism. The cross is the symbol of the men of many religious orders, but especially the

Dominicans and Jesuits, who were both vigorous pioneers in the evangelization of the Indians and staunch defenders (Popescu 1966) and preachers of the doctrines their masters taught them in the School of Salamanca. But a common denominator for all conquerors, inhabitants, magistrates, and religious men, was the yearning for spiritual contact with the far-off mother country. From the first decades of the discovery of the Americas, this thirst for knowledge was quenched by the supply of books brought from Spain in ever increasing numbers; in 1785, one single consignment of books received in El Callao, the port of Lima, totalled 37,612 volumes (Henriquez Ureña 1947: 45). Certainly, the books sent from Europe included the most varied topics and, with the passing of time, they acquired a heterogeneous character. Nevertheless, the interest of the cultured classes, particularly those of religious men and magistrates, centred on scholastic writings and on their Aristotelian-Thomistic foundations. The works of Aristotle, whose *Ethics*, *Politics*, and *Economics* were already in the New World by 1536, Thomas Aquinas, Vitoria, Medina, de Soto, Covarrubias y Leyva, Azpilcueta Navarro (whose *Confesionario* enjoyed wide circulation due to its being written in Spanish), Molina and Lugo, to mention only the most renowned scholastics of the School of Salamanca, could be found in most of the private and public libraries until well into the period of independence of the Latin American republics.

The spiritual contact with the mother country became even stronger by means of the Hispanic-American universities. From 1538 to 1824, the last year of Spanish domination in America, the number of universities totalled thirty-three, not including the colleges and institutes of higher studies which easily would bring the total number of independent learning centres to well over fifty, for a population of not more than 15 million (Furlong 1969: 277). It should be noted that the first twenty-one universities were founded in the sixteenth and seventeenth centuries. This shows that most Hispanic-American universities were founded and intellectually nourished in the scholastic tradition and that most members of the faculties were disciples of the great Spanish scholastics from Francisco de Vitoria (1468–1524) up to Juan de Lugo (1613–38). These disciples, once established in the New World, became the teachers of native teachers and of fruitful writers of theological and philosophical treatises and of civil and canonic law. Guillermo Furlong says, 'Philosophy during the long, active and substantive period of Spanish domination was similar to analogous activities in the cultured Europe' (Furlong 1952: 51).

We should add that a new offshoot grew from the transplanting of Spanish scholastic economics to the New World: Hispanic-American scholastic economics. I must admit that it took me a long time to get accustomed to this new vision of the development of scholastic economics, but once I became conscious of it, I began to ponder a number of questions. How was this transplant made? Was there any Hispanic-American philosopher, theologian, or jurist who examined this process? Did some school or at least some trend of thought which would be worthy of mention in the economic thought of the Hispanic-American scholastics develop from this process? In what sense could the problems of the New World have widened the traditional horizon of the scholastics in Europe? And, faced with the maturity of the School of Salamanca between the years 1550 and 1650, would it not be possible to detect some participation of the philosophers, theologians, and jurists of Hispanic America at the end of the fifteenth and the first half of the sixteenth centuries in the foundation of this same School of Salamanca? These are some of the many questions that would hardly interest the European researcher, but that become sweet temptations for the scholar in Indian economic thought.

This chapter is not quite the place to answer so many questions. The only possible task which I dare undertake is to attempt to sketch, in a very provisional way, the outlines of some of these questions. In this manner, I would like to stimulate my colleagues in Latin America to carry on this research and wait for the definite answers. This is the spirit which has guided me throughout this chapter.

Schumpeter chooses for the 'late scholastics' a few representative names: Tomás de Mercado (1525–75), Leonardo Lessius (1551–1623), Luis de Molina (1535–1601), and Juan de Lugo (1583–1660), appointing Molina as the 'chief guide' (Schumpeter 1971: 133). I shall follow the same methodology, and shall consider a small group of Hispanic Americans who are very representative: Tomás de Mercado; Bartolomé de Albornoz (1520–75);[1] Juan de Matienzo (1520–79); Luis López (1530–95);[2] Pedro de Oñate (1568–1646);[3] and Domingo Muriel (1718–95).[4]

The fact that Bartolomé de las Casas is excluded from our listing is evident and annoying. As can be seen in his *Treatises*, the Apostle of America was at the same time one of the most learned Indian scholastics. But we must admit that the field of economic analysis was not his strong point, although he was interested in programmes of social development, and he will be mentioned in the discussion regarding the quantitative theory of money. In fact, his speciality was the field of social philosophy, which he used as a weapon to obtain his goal of the liberation of the aboriginal people, even if it were only by one more inch. From this section we might expect to obtain some of his recollections of the history of Indian economic thought. As an example, we notice the accurate use of the phrase *'ceteris paribus'*, which he mentions, or the repeated use of the expression 'natural liberty', so dear to the author of *The Wealth of Nations*.

The inclusion of Mercado simultaneously among the Europeans and the Americans may surprise the unwary reader, but it should be taken into account that present day Spain is not the Spain of the sixteenth century, in whose immense territories, extending beyond the Americas as far as the Philippines, the sun never set. Legally, Spanish America was a Spanish province, 'the Province of the Indies'. Besides the doubts over Mercado's place of birth which we have already pointed out, the most important fact in our research is his American experience. Speaking of Mexico, Mercado wrote in his *Summa*: 'I deal [in my book] with places, though very remote, because we are not only men of understanding, but even more of one Spanish country and one Spanish nation', pointing out further on, 'because that Empire [Mexico] is of Spaniards and Indians; both races and bloodlines are mixed and live under one governor, one jurisdiction and are all subjects of one King' (Mercado [1571] 1977). And what I have said of Mercado can be said in practically identical terms of most Hispanic-American scholastics. Undoubtedly, they were born in Spain, but because of their years of residence in the New World, and especially because of their work and of their complete identification with the problems of Hispanic America, they belong to it more than to Europe or to Spain. As Ortega y Gasset says,

> It is the work of men whose new life has made new men of them. Some of their pages have revealed the New World to the European imagination, which adopted from them a few exciting topics. But, in the incredible amount of papers they wrote was . . . the real discovery of America for European eyes. Only in America could this direct view be fully understood, because for them it was but an intellectual and imaginative perception.
>
> (Henriquez Ureña 1949: 55)

And to this opinion, voiced by one of the most respected historians of Hispanic-American culture, we must add that of another historian no less respected in Hispanic America, in the United States, and in Europe: Silvio Zavala: 'Partly, the political philosophy of the conquest should be attributed to thinkers who never went to see the "Indias". There were others with experiences of life overseas, that is "indianos". The difference, very understandable, between both is perceptible' (Zavala 1947: 21). And it is with this criteria that we have compiled our list of 'Indian' scholastics, i.e. Hispanic-American authors.

'Indian' scholastics, like European scholastics, takes as a starting point the theory of the just price. Father Tomás de Mercado dedicates 100 folios, almost 200 pages, to the subject. The treatment is substantial, serious, and well balanced. His sources of inspiration are his experiences in Spanish America and in Seville, and a profound knowledge of classic and late scholastics. In the latter case, Mercado reaches as far as the *De Justitia et Jure* of Domingo de Soto. To this he adds an impressive knowledge of the works of the Greeks, from Hesiod to Plato and Aristotle. Reference to the writings of Saint Thomas Aquinas is very frequent. The script is written in Spanish, but even today it is very easily read. To this book, the second volume of the *Summa*, a third one of about fifteen folios and with thirty pages, could be added. In it, Mercado studies the just price theory in relation to a single commodity: wheat. In modern economic language, we would say it is the first writing on scholastic microeconomic theory, and probably one of the best introductions to this subject for students desiring to understand the development of economic theory in Hispanic America.

The writings of Albornoz, López and Matienzo are completely different. In general, their treatment of the theory of just price is brief. In Albornoz, the sources for the theory of just price are the Holy Scriptures, mainly the Old Testament. The author, nevertheless, does not hide his debt to the *Summa* of the 'Reverend and learned Fray Tomás de Mercado', with whom he sometimes liked to hold polemical discussions. This is quite natural, as theirs was an old friendship from the times when Albornoz, as a professor of law at the University of Mexico, must have first met Mercado as a student and later in the cloisters and library as a member of the faculty and professor of Moral Theology. Sometimes, in his commentaries on the theory of just price, Albornoz places Mercado on the same level with Azpilcueta, calling them 'our Reverend and very learned teachers, Dr Azpilcueta and Master Mercado'. He also mentions Domingo de Soto and others, but the supreme distinction is for his beloved teacher of Osuna, to whom he dedicates his whole work, 'the most Illustrious and Reverend Don Diego Covarrubias y Leiva [sic]', one of the great Spanish scholastics, and at the time, president of the Royal Council of Spain. On the other hand, his dealings with the work of the Bishop of Chiapas, Fray Bartolomé de las Casas, are very cautious, mentioning that he had expressed his opinions regarding his doctrine in certain pages which were later lost at sea with his other writings. Undoubtedly, he refers to his *Tratado de la Conversión y Debelación de los Indios*, printed in Mexico and recovered, not by being washed up by the sea, but by the Inquisition. His contributions to the theory of just price, in spite of their brevity and juridical approach, are excellent and with many original ideas. Dr Demetrio Iparraguirre, a modern critic, points out that Albornoz' *Arte de los Contratos* is still unknown, because of its rarity: 'it is a rare book because it has been condemned by the Inquisition'. Oñate, nevertheless, mentions him, and so does Solórnoz (1648), who certifies that Albornoz 'resided many years in New Spain', and remembers that the author wrote his book about contracts 'with great distinction and clarity'. Albornoz has increasingly been mentioned since his biographical file was included in the *Ciencia Española* of Marcelino Menéndez y Pelayo, and the almost simultaneous reference by Rahola (1885). It is in the last decades, however, that the name of Albornoz has begun to be noticed and his works have been the object of research of various specialists in Spanish scholastics.

The name of Juan de Matienzo is better known in Hispanic-American literature, thanks to his work *El Gobierno del Perú* (1567), although the interest was centred around the political aspects of this writing. As we shall see, this manuscript contains some valuable economic considerations and also contributions to the theory of just price and monetary theory. But once again, thanks to the *Ciencia Española* of Marcelino Menéndez y Pelayo, we were able to discover the biographical file of his forgotten *Commentaria . . . in Librum Quintum Recollectionis Legum Hispaniae*, in which the magistrate of Charcas deals systematically and deeply with all the conceptual requirements of the theory of just price. Due to their juridical point of view, Matienzo's contributions are the best complement to those already made by Tomás de Mercado from the angle of Moral Theology. Armed with an extensive bibliography, Matienzo makes the understanding of the scholastic economic model easy.

The Dominican theologian López is a contemporary of Molina, and probably that is the reason why his writings, as well as his life, are hardly mentioned by Spanish speaking critics. Among the Hispanic-American scholastics, I noticed Oñate quotes him frequently. His theory of the just price, however, is quite well developed in Chapter 63 of his *Instructorium Conscientiae* (1585: Part II) and in Chapters 14 and 42 of his *Tractatus de Contractibus et Negotiationibus* (1589: Book I). His bibliographic references are extensive and quite up to date. The polemical content of his critical observations has been most fruitful for the continuous development in late scholastic economics, and the degree of influence, which he almost certainly exercised, in the writings of Molina and Lesio (Lessius), has not been sufficiently studied.

In Pedro de Oñate's *De Contractibus*, the first topic comprises a whole *Tractatus de emptione et venditione* (Treaty of bargain and sale), so typical of the methodology of the late scholastics, for the study of what we today call microeconomics, and which covers almost all the theory of just price, with a total of 200 pages in two columns. We must add to this the *Tractatus de cambiis* (Treaty of exchanges), with which the scholastics rounded off their theory of just price and which has about 80 pages of two columns each. This means that the theory of just price in Oñate covers a total of 280 pages of encyclopedic format. To these two parts, he finally adds a third under the title of *Tractatus de usura* (Treatise on usury), which covers eighty-five pages. We conclude that Oñate's economics almost reached the dimensions of Samuelson's famous 'Introduction'. Of course, we are talking of different languages and different points of view, but it cannot be denied that it is the most extensive and profound study in scholastic Hispanic-American economic thought. Oñate's work is impressively rich in bibliographic sources. A quick look at these sources shows us that, in addition to the inventory of Aristotelian and Thomistic bibliography and of all the great Spanish scholars of the early period (1150–1580), he focuses with preferential attention upon the scientific production of the period 1580–1620. As an example, I shall mention the works of: Domingo Bañez (1527–1604), *Decisiones de Jure et Justitia*, Salamanca, 1588 and Venice: 1595; Luis de Molina, *De Justitia et Jure*, Cuenca: 1593–1609; Juan de Salas (1553–1612), *Commentarii in Secunda Secundae*, Lyon: 1617; Leonardo Lessius, *De Justitia et*

Jure, Louvain: 1605; and of course, Francisco Suárez (1548–1617), *Tractatus de Legisbus ad Deo Legislatore*, Coimbra: 1612. At the same time, his colleague at Salamanca, Juan de Lugo, was carrying out the same task in Spain. While Lugo published his most important work, *De Justitia et Jure*, Pedro de Oñate was putting the finishing touches to his outstanding work, the first volume of which appeared four years later in Rome in 1646, the year of his death, while the third one related to our topic appeared posthumously in two volumes, in 1649–52. In both cases, we come face to face with magnificent works, one of Spanish scholasticism, the other of Hispanic-American scholasticism. Whereas in Spain, following the publication of *De Justitia et Jure*, we can speak of the beginning of the end of Spanish scholasticism, here in Hispanic America, the process of growth continued.

As for the theory of the just price, Domingo Muriel's starting point is the same as Mercado's: natural law. Muriel makes it clear in his writings that he knows perfectly well the work of Azpilcueta, Covarrubias, Francisco de Vitoria, Tomás de Mercado, Molina, Lugo, and their followers of the seventeenth and eighteenth centuries, but in his treatment of the theory of just price, he likes to quote sources from the Bible or from the ancient Greek and Roman writings, which he knows by heart. He also surprises us with his reference to Cicero's 'classic' case of the merchant of Alexandria who arrived at Rhodes with a cargo of wheat at a time when the Rhodians were suffering from hunger and scarcity, and also when prices were extremely high. This merchant also knew that behind him, a great number of traders had sailed from Alexandria, their ships loaded with wheat, bound for the island. We have here the empirical sources of the problem of the just price, which appears in the ancient days and which has been the origin of an enormous amount of literature, starting with Saint Thomas, followed by Conrado de Summenhart, Medina, Lesio, and, before Muriel, Hermann Busenbaum (1600–68), with his *Medulla Theologiae Moralis* of 1645.

The Hispanic-American scholastics look at the price doctrine from a three-pronged point of view: as an economic philosophy; as an instrument of order in the market; and as an analytical basis for the theory of value, the theory of price, and monetary theory.

All Hispanic-American authors, either jurists or moralists, focus on the doctrine of just price as an economic philosophy, taking as a starting point the 'Institutiones' and the 'Digesta' of the Justinian code (533–64). They considered, on the one hand, the idea of 'plurisubjectivity' of the jurisconsultant Julius Paulus (c. 170–230), which established as a basis for the theory of value the idea of common estimation, the *communiter fungi* and, on the other hand, the idea of complete freedom in the functioning of the market, attributed to Salvius Julianis (first century AD), later transformed into an axiom of classic Roman law, in the sense that a 'thing is worth whatever price it can be sold for' (*restantum valet cuantum vendu potest*). The principle of *communiter fungi* was incorporated without exception by all authors, as the backbone of the theory of value. This was all the more so, as it had previously been supported by the patristic, and later by classic, scholasticism (Thomas Aquinas), and the continental late scholastics (Vitoria, Covarrubias, and Soto). The same, however, did not happen with Juliano's thesis. All authors accept it with some suspicion and some, like Pedro de Oñate, severely criticize it

> this rule, or better said, destruction and breaking of all rules, is not approved by the Doctors; moreover it should be rightly excluded and erased for containing errors and injustices, for containing unbearable moral errors, and for subverting the whole doctrine of the contract of bargain and sale.
>
> (Oñate 1646: Tract 21, Disp. 63, Sec. 2, Nos. 32, 34)

Due to the legalistic mentality of those times, it was decided to follow the path already trodden by Accurcius (1185–1263), adding the words *sed communiter* to Julianus' axiom, to make it congruent with Paulus' principle and later adjusting it to Christian moral philosophy, ignoring the situations of *fraude et iniuria*. For the finest finished formulation and the one most in agreement with the Spanish doctor's doctrine, we are obliged to Matienzo: '*tantum enim valet res, cuantum absque fraude & iniuria communiter vendi potest, homini scienti eius contitionen*'. Albornoz' doctrine has a somewhat Julianus-type hue. It is true that in the general explanation of the contract and sale, we find the aforementioned limitations as regards fraud, force, and deceit, and even more, the need for a third party, preferably selected from among good men for the determination of the just value of a thing. But when he deals with the subject within the framework of the just price, he plainly underlines his legalist spirit: 'a thing is worth as much as it can be sold for'. On the other hand, it is surprising that Muriel, who writes in a period dominated by classical economics, would follow the orthodox line developed by López, Matienzo and Oñate.

As for the doctrine of just price as an instrument for regulating the market, the arguments of the Hispanic-American scholars are related to the alternative between the legal price and the natural price. Tomás de Mercado leaves no doubt as to his preference

> The merchant's will is universal, though as Saint Augustine says, it is always vicious to want to buy cheap and sell dear. The desire and the intention of the Republic is, on the contrary, to sell as cheap as possible, because it belongs to it to promote all utility and benefit to its inhabitants. From here we infer that it has authority for three things. First, to expel all merchants, especially foreigners, and replace them by three or thirteen, giving them enough means to buy all that is necessary, and to put price to all the merchandise. Secondly, it has the authority, inasmuch as it admits merchants, to keep for itself the

faculty of transport, entry and sale of some merchandise for a number of reasons. Thirdly, it has the right to establish and dictate laws which should be kept in the contracts to regulate and establish prices, which all are obliged to observe, for clothing. Because it is their business to appraise and assess the value of all things which serve human life.

(Mercado 1977: Vol. II Chapter VI)

It is not without reason, even though in the end this might be an error, that many authors include Mercado among the mercantilists. Albornoz' criterion is the complete opposite to that of Mercado. Albornoz actually observes, synthesizing his philosophy of the bargain and sales contract, that

Everything that has been said about this Contract, in the Titles and Observations, is understood so that the operation is free for both parties, for the seller to sell his thing to whom he wants and how he wants, for the buyer to give for it whatever he pleases, so that between the parties there is perfect freedom, and if this is missing it should not be called a Contract but Force.

(Albornoz 1573: Book 2, Title 16, C. 76)

It is true that Albornoz, when examining the law which fixed a maximum price for the sale of wheat, '*la tasa del pan*' (the bread tariff), gives his complete approval for this policy, due to the monopolistic characteristics of the market. He finds no other remedy to the 'Force' of the monopolists (for Albornoz, monopoly means, as it does etymologically, only an agreement among sellers), than the imposition of maximum prices. Luis López takes an almost identical position, although his source of inspiration, as he himself declares, was the *Manual de Cônfesores*, by Dr Azpilcueta. His emphasis, however, has an eminently social character, aimed at solving the misery of the lower classes, in which case the authorities could be induced to control hoarders and regulate the price of goods of prime necessity. Matienzo completely upholds Diego de Covarrubias' and Domingo de Soto's theses that all goods' prices should be fixed, and if it is not possible to appraise everything, at least appraise what can be done easily. Nevertheless, warns Matienzo, there are situations precisely such as those found in the New World, where the scarcity of some consumer goods makes it necessary to import them. In this case, a policy of price controls would cause a fall in imports, with well known effects.

This is what truly concerns the Kingdom of Perú, where merchandise is brought from Spain, especially to the Imperial city of Potosí, which is absolutely sterile except in the production of silver. If the goods were highly taxed, this measure would paralyze the great and famous commercial activity of the city, harming the whole Christendom, as it is well known. This is the reason why I have never allowed the civil servants of the Royal Chancellery of Charcas to impose any duties on merchandise and food.

(Matienzo 1580: Title 25, Law I, Gl.17, No. 2)

Pedro de Oñate starts his voluminous treatise on the just price with great reverence for the legal price, that is the price fixed by law; 'because it is most difficult to equate price and value of things, so that there will be no fraudulent buying and selling'; and for Oñate, this legal price, predetermined and fixed, has to be judged as the most just of all prices. He is not, however, servile in his attitude nor inflexible in his judgement. As he develops other forms of just price, he underlines the virtues of the natural and conventional prices, which are typical of the free market. And when he finally decides to compare the three types of prices, he surprises us by his open sympathy with market prices. What is more, he is not afraid to affirm that the legal price may be unjust or even obsolete, abrogated in order to suit the needs of the ruler, and a law which has been repealed not only does not oblige but is no law. There can be no doubt that Oñate was greatly influenced by the writings of the Hispanic-American Luis López and by the Spaniard Luis de Molina, whom he quotes frequently along with most of the scholastics of his time.

Muriel, albeit briefly, also gives his opinion about the regulation of the price system. He accepts that in exceptional situations of what he names 'general need', Spain always practised what was called the '*Ley de Tasas*' (Law of Price Fixing), but he also reminds us that even at the beginning of the conquest and colonization of Hispanic America, the free market had its virtues. 'I will mention, to this effect, the answer of Charles V in favour of Hispanic America, when he ordered the merchants overseas to sell their goods as best as they could'. In the same manner, he insists that the contracts of bargain and sale can be considered null and void when it can be proved that they lack estimative equality, whatever their nature and whether referring to legal or natural prices. Those measures are coherent with the trend of thought which prevailed in Muriel's time, and which he extends to other spheres of the ethics of the 'polis', which he likes to call society. This is the principle of sociability, which he introduced to the lexicon of the Hispanic-American scholastics. Here we have a seed which will later grow into 'social liberalism', 'social market economy', and the 'social doctrine of the Church'. This springs from Muriel's work at a time dominated by the cry of laissez-faire from the disciples of Quesnay and Adam Smith, and which Muriel does not even mention.

Finally, we must mention the analytical foundations of the doctrine of just price in the New World. In so far as the theory of value is concerned, their observations are centred around two themes: the cost of production theory of value, and the subjective theory of value. We shall consider first their attitude towards a cost of production theory of value. One of the

biggest errors of the merchants, observed Mercado, stems from their obsti-
nacy in taking the cost of their wares as a basis in the valuation and pricing
of their goods, without really understanding that the 'just price is either the
one fixed by the republic, or the one quoted day by day on the market and
which is flexible: today it is of much value, tomorrow of very little'. The
only reasonable method is that

> the merchant should be prepared in his mind either to gain or to lose,
> now losing because his costs exceed the price, now winning because
> the price exceeds the cost. Consequently, the trader must not sell taking
> his costs as a basis, but by the value which his clothing fetches today and
> as is sold in the city; for the art of trading is subject to this risk.
>
> (Mercado 1569: Book 2, Chapter 11, 4–5)

Albornoz, though ignoring Mercado's observations, refers to the multitude
of cases of the same sort as those exposed by his predecessor, and later
expresses it in almost the same words: the just price of a good is different
from the real cost of the good, and from what is in the good, and the real
cost of the good is different from that which is in the good. Juan de
Matienzo takes as his starting point an Aristotelian-Thomistic foundation,
and knows very well that in the exchange value of the good (the price), the
labor et expensas of the Roman jurists must be considered, but he also makes
it very clear that he does not think, as John Duns Scotus (1265–1308) does,
that the cost of production is the source or the cause of value. Referring to
the 'Rule' stated by Scotus, Matienzo states firmly:

> The rule which establishes that a thing must be sold covering the price
> paid for buying it, or the price of labour and risks incurred to acquire
> it, plus the profit of the seller, is most fallacious. . . . Because the art of
> buying and selling is very much at the mercy of fortuitous events, and
> for that reason the trader must assume fatality as his own risk, and take
> advantage of good luck.
>
> (Matienzo 1580: Title 1, Law 1, Gl.2, No. 10)

For Matienzo, as for Covarrubias and all the Spanish scholastics who
followed them, to be joined later by Molina and Lugo, the cost of production
theory of value is always condemned with the same expression: 'most falla-
cious', and using the same arguments which we have just exposed. We
should not be surprised to find the same argument, inverted, in Luis López:

> *haec est alea sortis et fortunae mercatorum, quoad duritia negotiantur debent*
> *victrix; sorti sicut lucrandi, ita et perdendi se exponere, iuxta temporum, et*
> *circustatiarum predictarum varietatem. Unde fallacissima regula est si semper*
> *quanto emit pretio; et quantum periculu, et laboris subivit, tantum valit*
> *vendere.*
>
> (López 1585: Part 2, Chapter 63)

This is easily explained, since both authors use the same source, the *De Justitia et Jure* of Domingo de Soto; and, like Matienzo and Luis López, Pedro de Oñate also widely develops the thesis of Scotus, as well as those of Covarrubias and Soto, although stating expressly that he is in agreement with the latter ones, and all who followed them, and that they all reproach Scotus for this 'rule'.

To determine the cause of value, Hispanic-American scholastics reject its foundation in cost. Value, they say, is not founded on the intrinsic essence of things, as value theory has no objective base. Things in and of themselves have no objective value, that is 'in themselves they do not have it', observes Mercado, adding, 'Aristotle admirably states in the fifth book of the *Ethics*, that things are not valued according to their nature'. Mercado also resorts to the authority of Saint Augustine, who

> in his book, *Civitas Dei*, states directly and delicately that our whims and thoughts are different from nature, otherwise a mouse, for being a living animal, would be worth much more than wheat, but actually there is no one that does not prefer even some little wheat in his granary to a lot of mice.
>
> (Mercado [1571] 1977: Book 2, Chapter 6)

In human matters, 'it is not wise or just to consider that they are worth for what they themselves are, but rather for what utility they bring to man', or as Aristotle said and Saint Thomas so rightly underlines:

> what gives value and price to things is our need, because if we would not need them, we would not exchange or value them; this is the measure and the weight of their value; they are not appreciated by more of what they are useful; and those that are more valuable are more useful. And the fact that men do not use the same things everywhere causes that the same thing can have more value in one place and less in another.
>
> (Mercado [1571] 1977: Book 2, Chapter 6)

Mercado arrives at the conclusion that 'there is nowhere in any nation anything that has ever been valued for its natural value, but for our need and use' and he reinforces this with Saint Augustine's words, 'and so, we do not price the things according to the dignity of their nature, but rather according to the advantage and well-being which they provide us'. This impressive outline of the subjective theory of value is profusely illustrated step by step, with abundant examples from the New World, especially from Florida, and is summarized by Mercado in his sentence: 'Men do not value things according to their nature, but rather as the Philosopher said, by our will and need, which gives them esteem and value'. Mercado's work had great influence among his contemporaries Bartolomé de Albornoz and Luis López, who embraced his theory of value. Albornoz even uses the same example as Mercado, trying to illustrate the important role of subjective estimation with the remarkable story of the New Spanish fleet that got lost off the coast of Florida and had to abandon on the beach treasure valued at nearly a million marks in gold. After four months, the treasure was found by other galleons sent by the viceroy of Mexico. It was untouched by the Indians because the metal had no value for them; the Indians scoffed at the importance the Spaniards placed on the gold. But in other original examples Albornoz approaches a very fertile soil from a theoretical point of view, and fell just short of launching into marginal utility analysis. On the other hand, Albornoz' great merit is to have underlined on various occasions the role played by scarcity in the development of the subjective theory of value. For Luis López, scarcity is the most important factor in the subjective approach to value, because the existence of human life depends on it.

Juan de Matienzo, completely isolated in the Audiencia de Charcas, quotes neither Mercado nor Albornoz, and knowing his intellectual honesty, we can be sure that those writings were unknown to him. The subjective theory of value is, then, a product of his own intellectual vision, though naturally he uses the same source as Albornoz: the *De Justitia et Jure* of Domingo de Soto. Matienzo also approaches the theory of subjective value in the company of Aristotle and Saint Augustine. In the first place, he distinguishes between the two ways of appraising things, on the one hand, for their very nature and intrinsic qualities; on the other hand, for the importance we assign to them for their outlook. Intrinsic value is related to objective value, while the extrinsic value, which considers the importance men assign to goods based on their exterior appearance, is the subjective value. In the 'contracts of bargains and sale, things are not valued according to the dignity of their nature, but according to the estimation of men even if that estimation were foolish'. This explanation is already well known. Now comes the justification of this option:

> If we were to look at things according to their nature, we would have to put a higher value on a horse than on a precious stone, first for the utility of the horse and because any living thing is naturally more valuable than any inanimate object.
>
> (Matienzo 1580: Title 2, Law 1, Gl.2, No. 2)

It is worthwhile repeating this idea in the original text, written in Latin, by Matienzo: '*Nam si ex natura rei foret observanda, pluris esset aestimandus equus, quam gemma, ob utilitatum equi, et quia omne animarum ex natura sua pretiosius est quolibet inanimato.*'

With this, Matienzo continues along the same path as Mercado and others, towards accepting the ontological Augustinian argument that gives greater hierarchy to living creatures than to inanimate objects; but what is new in his doctrine is that, at the same time, he understands that some things are more useful to men than to others, thus surpassing the

44

Augustinian argument. The horse is more useful than a precious stone, but this is also because of its nature. Matienzo rebels against the idea of the objective nature of value, founded on the intrinsic quality of things. Now it is clear that the 'horse' of Matienzo plays the same role as Adam Smith's 'there is nothing more useful than water'; and in the same way, 'the uselessness of the precious stone' for Matienzo is identical with the 'diamond that hardly has any intrinsic value' of the father of our science. But, while Adam Smith puts forth the 'paradox' and then abandons it, Matienzo proposes the same 'paradox' and solves it: the essence of the value lies not in its intrinsic or objective character, but in the quality which is eminently subjective and extrinsic to the thing in question, in the estimation we give to things according to our *'indigentia'*. As Saint Agustine says, 'We need it because we feel the lack of it, we want to satisfy some need'. Matienzo's *indigentia* is the same as the *indigentia* of Domingo de Soto and Saint Thomas Aquinas, and is identical with the Aristotelian *'creia'*, and is precisely what we today call the subjective utility of a good.

With Oñate, the scholastic theory of value achieves an even greater refinement. He shows that in addition to being completely up to date with the bibliography of the Old World, he is fully acquainted with the contributions of his Hispanic-American predecessors, whom he quotes on many occasions. His starting point is again the distinction between objective and subjective values. He clearly distinguishes and studies both aspects of objective value pointed out by Matienzo (the things which are intrinsically more noble, like a mouse is more valuable than gold, as underlined by Saint Augustine; and the things which are more necessary, like a loaf of bread is more valuable than any gems), and he refutes them both as not true in business life. 'Value is not an intrinsic and real property of the goods.' Instead, he puts forward the subjective idea of value: the estimation of man. He defines this idea rigorously:

> The estimation and value which we study are not referred to the divine order nor to the objective reason of things which springs from their nature, but rather to human estimation and human judgment when appraising tradable goods, and this is variable. The fact that this estimation might not be true or that the opinion of men and masses is false is not important; because what is false also has the property of establishing a just and true price.
>
> (Oñate 1646–54: Tract 21, Disp. 63, No. 1, 6)

That is to say, Oñate starts from a subjective theory of value and leads into a price theory. It is surprising that no other scholastic academic could find a definition for price when the answer is so simple: the price is the just measure of the value of what can be sold expressed in money. It is as if we were listening to Alfred Marshall, who in 1890 ruled that 'price is the value of a thing expressed in money'.

Domingo Muriel, who wrote in an age when the objective theory of value was predominant in economics, did not even mention it. He defined the basis of value, in the same way as stated by orthodox scholastics: according to the common estimation of the good.

In price theory, the contributions of the Hispanic-American scholastics are less spectacular, but nevertheless significant. They had a clear concept of the determining elements in the formation and variation of prices. They clearly distinguished between the open market and the closed market. In the open markets, they worked under the hypothesis of the 'natural just price' (sometimes also referred to as current, vulgar, or accidental), while in the closed markets, they did so with the theory of the 'legal just price' (or 'la tasa'). On the other hand, they distinguished clearly between markets of free competition and monopolistic markets. Already, Tomás de Mercado had drawn attention to trader agreements (which we call monipodio), for both the buying and the selling side of the market. Albornoz suggests maintaining the name of monipodio only for the buyers, since the sellers go by the name of monopoly, which is more correct, and in this Oñate also agrees, for in Greek *monos* means one and *poleo* means sell. This anticipates by several centuries the anxieties of Joan Robinson. Tomás de Mercado, Matienzo, and López even identify the market in which a monopolistic seller comes face to face with a monopolistic buyer. While Mercado continues to condemn this type of market, López thinks that the buyers' monopoly may be an effective way of confronting the sellers' monopoly, and as such justifies its existence. Oñate, on the other hand, not only christens it pandopolium, but better justifies its advantages. Actually, observes Oñate, pandopolium is almost a normal market in Panama. If, in answer to the cunning of the Peruvian buyers, who agree not to buy if the price is not lower than the just price, the Spanish traders reply with identical agreement and cunning to sell only at prices above the natural price

> they would compensate reciprocally for the two identical transgressors and as one nail knocks another out, one monopoly would prevent another one, or better, from the mutual agreement, there would result a just price. . . . In this joint determination of the price, there is nothing unjust . . . one could consider it a very just and fair global agreement.
>
> (Oñate 1646–54: Tract 1, Disp. 67, No. 50)

It is evident from this that we are dealing with a double monopoly and in fact he labels it *monopolia bina*, which is nothing more than the 'bilateral monopoly' of Bowley, foreseen by Marshall, and others. Oñate also points out its nature detected with almost the same foresight as Galbraith expresses in his theory of countervailing power in 1952. What is more, Oñate, following closely the conclusions of López in the discussion of the well known case of the merchant of Venice, becomes sharply aware of the duopoly, which he condemns as severely as monopoly. This will later be thoroughly investigated in economics by Cournot (1838), Bertrand (1880), and Edgeworth (1897). On the other hand, Oñate, following up the words of Tomás de Mercado and the warnings of Albornoz, will find various elements for the identification of the partially oligopolistic market, whether it be of buyers or sellers, which Oñate condemns, saying that its members commit frauds and use unfair ways. In this he is in agreement with Mercado, who described them as destroyers of the republic. However, this subject will later be researched by Chamberlin (1929–33), Schneider (1930–2), Frisch (1933), Stackelberg (1933–4), and others. With regard to the public monopolies, the attitude of the Hispanic-American scholastics was benign. The justification was based not only on fiscal considerations but also on reasons relevant to social welfare, as Mercado understood the *estancos* (government monopolies), and Albornoz understood the *cotos* (price limitations), which were formed to import goods and to protect the produce of the farmers, which was hoarded by the oligopolists and put up for sale at moderate prices; or for the promotion of certain trades, such as editorial firms and restaurants, as suggested by López; or finally, for the promotion of silver mining, like the well known *estanque del azogue* (monopoly of the market) in Huancavélica, in Perú, which Oñate considered a 'just monopoly'.

The theory of a natural just price was rooted in the idea of competition, and the Hispanic-American scholastics made their contributions, keeping in sight the writings of their Spanish masters, as well as empirical knowledge acquired as observers, for their observations are important. Actually, in spite of the fact that in their value theory they insisted on the idea of subjective value, in their price theory they took into account, in a Marshallian manner, the subjective elements on the demand side, along with the objective aspects on the supply side. It is true that they did not use the terms supply and demand, except accidentally. An exception is the case of Mercado, who several times emphasized the role of *demanda* in and of itself, a fact which is very significant in the history of economic thought. Nor did they give the word *concurrentia* the meaning which it has in the French and German literature of today, and which goes back to the times of the jurisconsultant Paulus. Scholastics have been inclined to use the words competition, outbidding, auction, or even struggle, expressions which appear at every step in their writings in Spanish and in Latin as well from Mercado, Albornoz and Oñate, up to Muriel. It is also true that our scholastics have sensed something related to the mechanism of supply and demand, but have never said it in these terms, with the exception of Oñate, who came very near to the goal when referring to Saint Augustine. The focal point of their reasoning was always centred around the factors which led to the rise and fall of prices on the free market. Mercado gives a beautiful example:

We see at the market that if there is a lot of clothing, it is cheap; if there are few buyers, it is cheaper; if there is little money, it is not worth anything and it is burned. On the contrary, if there is little clothing, it is expensive, if there are a lot of buyers, the price increases, and more so if there is an abundance of money.

(Mercado [1571] 1977: Book 2, Chapter 7, 1)

Matienzo is even more illustrative, as from the start he calls attention to the fact that for the determination of the just price, one has to consider a multitude of factors. The two pairs of fundamental factors, common to all Hispanic-American scholastics, are the abundance or scarcity of goods and the quantity of buyers and sellers in the market. But to these are added considerations such as the need for a thing; the work of the merchant; the care of the merchant; his industry and his risks; if the goods have been transformed into something better, or have simply deteriorated; and the abundance or scarcity of money. And above all, Matienzo continues to add to the price theory his empirical observations taken from the Chuquisaca market. Prices may change due to spatial and temporal variations; personality traits of the participants in the market; the preponderance of monopolistic or competitive structures within the market; and explicit expectations about the future behaviour of economic variables and their effect upon the general level of prices.

After putting together this inventory of the most important factors which affect his price theory, Matienzo considers it necessary to add the fluctuations in the price levels caused by those same factors undergoing continuous changes. This is a process he himself has been able to verify, as it happened every day in the market of Chuquisaca. Even more impressive is the inventory of factors drawn up by Oñate, who adds for each situation hundreds of cases, collected mainly by personal observations, frequently in Paraguay. We can therefore state that the Hispanic-American scholastics, when making this detailed inventory of nearly all the factors which intercede and shape the analytical tools of those who take part in the bargaining in the market, have made a pioneering effort to build up a theory of prices, in an age when not even Europe was prepared to take full advantage of such an enormous flow of knowledge.

As for price policy, Oñate agrees with the opinions of his predecessors that both the legal price and the free market price are compatible with the natural price, but he warns that neither of them are always just and consequently they require constant adjustments to the natural price of the scholastic theory of just price. 'The natural price does not always agree with the current market price', Oñate warns severely. He goes on to explain:

Those two prices are very different, and in our opinion should be well differentiated. Actually, the current price, even for all the country, may be unjust sometimes due to frauds, monopolies, and the influence of the rich. On the other hand, the natural price, that which is dictated by reason after giving a lot of thought and consideration to each case, can never be unjust, but corrects and rectifies both the legal price and the current price when they become overflowing.

(Oñate 1646–54: Tract 21, Disp. 64, No. 36)

Let us now try to examine more closely some considerations about the area of monetary theory, and particularly the quantitivist theory of the value of money. The aspect which most draws our attention is the attempt at integrating monetary theory with the general theory of prices, an imperative issue which lasted until the present time. The linking bridge of both subjects was the idea of *'estimatio'*, 'esteem' – that is, the purchasing power of money, which depends in its turn on *'ceteris paribus'*, of its *'abundantia vel penuria'*, abundance or scarcity. From this fundamental vision, product of the Indian experience and of the study of their teachers of classical and late scholastics, came forth two other contributions of great importance for the development of economics: one related to the internal value of money, the quantitative theory of money; the other a logical consequence of the former, related to the external value of money, the theory of the purchasing power parity.

The most brilliant representative of the monetary theory and the most celebrated by specialized criticism is Tomás de Mercado (Sayous 1927, 1928; Weber 1962 – who, like Marjorie Grice Hutchinson, knows he is talking about a Mexican scholastic; and Larraz 1963). The most interesting fact is that in his statements, Mercado develops both theories simultaneously. This is the key text found in Book IV, Chapter 5, of his *Summa*:

It must be taken into account that the value and price of money and its esteem are not the same thing. A very clear example of this is that in the Indies the value of money is the same as it is here; one real, thirty four maravedis, one mine peso, thirteen reales, and the same is its value [price] in Spain. But, notwithstanding the value and price are the same, the esteem is very different in both places: that much less is it esteemed in Indies than in Spain. . . . After the Indies where it is less esteemed, is in Seville, as it is a city that receives all that is good that comes from the Indies, then the other parts of Spain follow. It is very much esteemed in Flanders, in Rome, in Germany, in England. Such esteem and appreciation is caused in the first place because there is a great abundance and scarcity of these metals and as in those parts of the Indies they are found and gathered, they are lowly considered. . . . A very clear example of this is that even within the boundaries of Spain [having the ducados and the maravedis the same value] we see that they have a much greater esteem for them in Castilla than in Andalucía. And even in the same city, because of the diversity of the times we find the same discrimination: that thirty years ago 200,000 maravedis was a handsome sum, at present they are estimated in nothing, yet being the maravedis of the same price of money. Because, the same estimation that the times have made in the same town on account of several events, cause the reasons I exposed at the same time in different reigns.

(Mercado [1571] 1977: 388–90)

Once the essence of the purchasing power of money which he calls 'esteem' (estimation) is made clear, we should try to find a trace of the concept of the velocity of circulation of money. I believe he was bordering on the subject, as it follows from this text:

Money is better present than absent, many learned teachers say. . . . Finally, as they say, it is better to have a bird in the hand than two in the bush . . . speaking plainly it is better to have money in cash than to wait for it. Though for many men it is better not to have it. For the merchants present money is not better than the absent one, on the contrary, the absent money has more value than the one in the hand.

(Mercado [1571] 1977: 384)

It remains to find the theory of the purchase power parity in Mercado. Now then, this different esteem of money confirmed from one country to another and from one time to another in the same country is the dynamic resource of international exchanges; their cause and at the same time their support: the abundance or scarcity of money makes the exchange rates go up or down. Referring to justice he states that 'the justice of the exchanges now in use, lies upon and is originated in the different esteem of money that occurs in different places, and this suffices to justify them'.

Referring to the cause, he states his reality in the following way:

Modern changes are based in the different esteem of money, of the totality of a republic or reign: as we see that, in all Flanders, in all Rome, money is more esteemed than it is in all Seville, and in Seville more than in the Indies, and in the Indies more in Santo Domingo than in Nueva España, and in Nueva España more than in Perú. . . . And the money changers and the exchange have an eye to appraise this different esteem.

(ibid.: 384)

Mercado formulates the principle of purchase power parity in the following paragraph, meaning that the different esteem of money in different places equals itself by means of the different quantity of exchanged money.

In this way it happens in money, that because they are more esteemed in some places than in others, they come to be equal, even if the quantity is diverse: ninety-three in Flanders against a hundred in Seville, not because the ducado is another legal standard or it has another value, but because that land itself pays more attention to money. . . .

Three things are of the essence of exchange, namely: if the esteem of money be unequal, the unequal quantity makes it equal, this necessarily demands a diversity of places, as a hundred ducados in Seville and ninety-five in Antwerp are equal in esteem because they are unequal in quantity. The unequal quantity equals the different reputation of money there is in these places.

(ibid.: 391–5)

Mercado's doctrine found a wide acceptance among the other Hispanic-American scholars, but with different nuances: in Albornoz (*Arte de los Contratos*, Book II, Tit. XVI: f 64 C and Book III, Tit. IV: f 131–2); in Matienzo, who did not know either the author or his work (*Commentaria*, Tit. 11, Act. 1, Gl.2 Nos. 2 and 7); in López (*Tract. de Contr.*, Book 11, Chapters 7 and 9; *Instr. Consc.*, Part II, Chapter 63), to reach, in Oñate, the dimension and grandeur of a complete treaty (*De Contractibus*, Trat. XXIV: 521–603).

The monetary problem has not, from the formal point of view, a separate treatment in Matienzo's *Commentaria*. This must undoubtedly be due to the fact that its systematic consideration, together with the theory of usury, would be incorporated in another work which was planned or was probably being prepared and whose destiny we ignore. Consequently, his theory is expressed in fragments that are dispersed in the corpus of his writings, making difficult the work of inventory and analysis of his considerations in this field.

In spite of this formal difficulty the effort of searching for and integrating materials in the economic area is compensated by his contributions being so substantial. Effectively as we have seen above, and it is worth repeating, the money variable is one of many that have to be taken into account in the formation of prices. Prices rise or fall, he said 'with the abundance or scarcity of money': '*Pecunia abundantia vel penuria*'. Putting it in other words, Matienzo's monetary theory is another chapter, and as such forms part of the general theory of prices. The desire of contemporary scholars to integrate the theory of money with the general economic theory is, for our author, a problem that has been solved. If we could ask Matienzo about the basic ingredients of the so called law of supply and demand, he would undoubtedly answer that at least in this area, we should incorporate the theory of demand, the theory of supply, the theory of prices and the theory of money.

The incorporation of the theory of money in the theory of prices should take place also on account of another reason. Actually Matienzo states that money, like any other merchandise, fluctuates in its value, price or esteem. Of course, it is necessary to distinguish between the intrinsic and the extrinsic variations of money. In the intrinsic variation money is modified in its weight and material, while in the extrinsic variation: 'with the same weight and the same material, it increases or decreases extrinsically in regard to price or esteem'. '*Vel quoties pecunia eodem pondere et materia manentibus, vel*

51

augetur, vel minuitur extrinsecus quoad eius pretium, vel aestimationem.' But Matienzo does not consider that this very important subject could be further analysed in the chapter about 'Weights and measures to buy and sell goods and maintenance and iron-works' which is the object of Chapter 13. And in Book 8 of the *Recopilación*, he interrupts the development of the subject, excusing himself thus: 'This due to lack of space here we shall expound in another place': *'cuius examinatio, quia non vacat modo alibi fiet'*. And yet, from the scanty considerations about the intrinsic and extrinsic factors of the variations of the value of money, we can extract the conclusion that effectively for Matienzo, in the consideration of the monetary problem also they should have resorted to the tools of supply and demand, of abundance and scarcity. This is a quite familiar idea among the Hispanic scholastics of the sixteenth century, as Wilhelm Weber demonstrates.

The other monetary aspect we can find in the *Commentaria* is related to the delicate question of money interest. The discussion of this issue is also delayed by Matienzo, as we have already mentioned in the comments about Book 8 of the *Recopilación*. But Matienzo's brief statement respecting the possibility of the loaning of money being licit, to the concept 'just interest' – *'interesse justum'* – and the compatibility of just interest with an annual rate of 10 per cent, is astonishing. Surprise is increased due to the spontaneous association of ideas produced in readers' minds when they remember that Matienzo knew and frequently quoted Carolo Molineus' treaty, nowadays well known by historians of economic thought. But if we bear in mind that formerly the Church, in the Fifth Letran Assembly of Bishops in 1515, and the Spanish monarch himself in 1534, had laid positive foundations for the doctrine sustained by Matienzo, the question changes its aspect. Actually, we know today that there were very few authors in the sixteenth century who followed the doctrine of 'just interest', and this sole fact is enough to emphasize Matienzo's presence among the very few inventoried up to now for that century.

The third monetary subject and one which undoubtedly will interest most contemporary learned men, is Matienzo's contribution in the field of the money value theory. The aforementioned thesis that prices rise or fall 'with the abundance or scarcity of money' is in itself a consideration which contains the germ of the quantitative theory of money. We should avoid, of course, the dangerous statement (Matienzo [1567] 1967: 99, 260) that this was being propounded for the first time, as the critics implied when they dealt with the treaty *Sobre la Justicia y el Derecho* (On Justice and Law) by Luis de Molina. Today we know that at least four non-American authors whose works were written before Matienzo's, sustained an idea that was identical or fairly similar. Around 1557 the Spanish chronicler, Francisco López de Gómara (1511–c.1565) wrote in the *Anales del Emperador Carlos V* that the level of prices had risen 'because the great quantity of silver and gold that has arrived here from the Indies'. In December 1556 and January

1557 Dr Martin de Azpilcueta Navarro (1492–1586) published in Salamanca the first edition of his work *Comentario Resolutorio de Cambios*, which the criticism of our time considers as a pioneer work in Spain in the development of the quantitivist theory of money value. About thirty years before, Nicholas Copernicus (1473–1543) had stated in his work *Monetae Cudendae Ratio*, written in 1526 at the suggestion of King Segismund of Poland, that 'money is normally despised when it becomes too abundant'. However, these works were surpassed by Columbus' reflections which sprang out of the American reality. Besides, almost a century before Copernicus, Saint Antonino of Florence (1389–1459) affirmed still more vigorously, that 'one of the causes of things being more or less valuable is the scarcity or abundance of money among the citizens'. Of the four works only the *Summa Theologica* of Saint Antonino of Florence was known by Matienzo, and two of the other three remained unpublished, Gómara's until 1912 and Copernicus' until 1861. It is incredible that Matienzo ignored this particular writing of Dr Azpilcueta, whose other works he knew since he was at the University of Valladolid, and who he quotes quite frequently; but it is so. Neither does Tomás de Mercado quote him (Azpilcueta) in his *Summa* – also incredible but true. And also respecting the *Summa* of Saint Antonino it must be made clear that though he was acquainted with the work of Saint Antonino, Matienzo seemed completely unaware of the thesis related to the influence of money on the general level of prices, because if he had known it he would gladly have resorted to the authority of the Archbishop of Florence whom he quotes on several occasions, and not to the authority of Domingo de Soto.

There is a second text in the *Commentaria* of great interest for the history of the quantitivist money theory. In it Matienzo ratifies and enlarges the thesis formulated in the former paragraph. The approach is genuinely inductive and it contemplates, together with the quantitative theory, aspects related to the purchase power parity. The starting point of his consideration is the problem of the price of bread:

> Bread [Matienzo states] is of the same nature in Spain and in the Indies. But here, it is sold dearer than in Spain, because this product is scarcer, but also because there is an abundance of gold and silver, which are the causes of the increased prices. (*Panis eiusdem naturae est in Hispania et apud Indos, sed maiori hic pretio venditur quam im Hispania, propter indigentiam et argenti aurique abundantiam, quae causae augendi pretium.*)

This approach is far more advanced in comparison with its three aforementioned predecessors. It also totally covers the approach of Dr Martin de Azpilcueta Navarro expounded almost a quarter of a century before, and it even seems that he surpassed it. Actually, while Azpilcueta only takes into consideration the effect of abundance of money immobilizing the other effects with the hypothesis *ceteris paribus*, Matienzo adds to the abundance of money effect, the effect of the demand, in this case the scarcity of demand, as if he wanted to insinuate, in modern language, that for him, the level of prices is a direct function of the quantity of money and an inverse function of the volume of transactions. What seems true, however, is that Matienzo also bypassed Azpilcueta's point of view on the theory of money value and so lost another opportunity to resort to an authority at the highest level of Spanish scholastics. Additionally, Dr Azpilcueta's work was published twelve years before Bodin published, in 1568, his renowned doctrine on quantitative theory which made him well known to posterity, but which is in all aspects inferior in its approach to the works of Azpilcueta Navarro and Matienzo.

A more careful exploration of Matienzo's scientific production allows us to conclude that his quantitivist considerations are superior to those of Juan Bodin. Actually, if we read attentively his *Gobierno del Perú*, the writing of which was finished in Chuquisaca on 24 August 1567 – a year before the *Respuesta al Señor de Malestroit* by Juan de Bodin – we find that among other considerations of interest for the scientific researcher, Matienzo specially underlined the close relation, in his direct experiences, between the volume of currency and the general price level. Thus is how the subject is narrated by the judge from Charcas:

> There are opinions among those who are curious to understand the things of this land, about if it were convenient that gold and silver coins were made here – some say that land will decrease in value and that everything will be cheaper, because: who would want to give in 'reales' a hundred 'castellanos' for the making of a garment as they now give? Who would give for a head-dress, that is worth ten 'reales' in Castilla, a thousand or twelve hundred? It will be necessary, therefore, that everything decreases in value. But none of these inconveniences, in my opinion is enough . . . to say that land will decrease in value, and that things will lower their price is to guess; rather the contrary is seen everywhere by experience: where there is more money everything is more expensive.
>
> (Matienzo [1567] 1967: 99)

And what would happen if instead of being more abundant, money were less abundant? Matienzo's answer is drastic: 'and there being less money, it is clear that everything would be cheaper' (ibid.: 262). Therefore we can conclude that in the *Gobierno del Perú* also the variation of the quantity of money – if the other things remain constant – causes proportional changes in the level of prices. This would be tantamount to saying that within the typology of Hegeland – who differentiates three principal variants of the quantitative theory – Matienzo's quantitative theory would be localized in the second variant, because it adds the causality element.

Also, it is worth pointing out that the chapter of the *Gobierno del Perú* that has as a rather long title 'If it is convenient that there were farms (*de pancoger*) and that sugar mills, and cloth mills, and vegetable gardens and vineyards were made and that there were cattle . . . ', Matienzo gives an answer of great importance for the history of Hispanic-American economic thought. For that reason we transcribe it almost completely:

> All this is necessary for the conservation of this land [of Perú]; and even though some believe that it is better that there were none of these things, but that they were brought from Castilla, so with them to extract the silver and take it to Spain, I do not know how those who assert this is better, could found their arguments, nor that this should be coveted because the more silver is taken to Castilla and more goods are brought to this land, more expensive will everything be in Spain . . . and if we confess that due to this Spain gets richer, not because of it we should stop trying to make richer and greater this land and its natives because they are the cause of our being rich.
>
> (ibid.: 273)

In the paragraph, in addition to the seeds of the most diverse economic and social conditions, we find again the ample image that Matienzo reproduced in his *Commentaria* where he accepted the authority of Didacus Pérez de Salamanca, and in which we see together with the effect of the abundance of money that of the scarcity of and demand for goods, and at the same time aspects related to the international changes. But we find all this in a larger or smaller scale in the *Commentaria*. What is new is the consideration on the nature of the Hispanic inflationary tendency of this time, establishing that the historic cause of the increase of the general level of prices in Spain and through it also in the other European countries of its time, was due in the first place to the flux of the American gold and silver. With this Matienzo anticipated two other foreign authors, John Hales (also known as Thomas Smith or William Stafford), to whom is ascribed a work which is more or less similar and whose date is not very precise (probably 1581); and Noel du Fail (c.1520–91), whose work titled *Balivernes et Contes d'Eutrapel* was published in 1548, and of which it is affirmed that it would have anticipated the thesis of the price revolution caused by the American treasure – which is only true of the second edition, published in 1584. And Matienzo also anticipates in the quantitative theory of money his American countryman, Tomás de Mercado, who began gathering experiences accumulated in Nueva España in the same year as Bodin, and like Matienzo, with total independence of thought, formulated his quantitivist theory in identical terms.

Thus we have seen the important contributions made by the Hispanic-American scholars to the theory of value and the theory of prices as well as monetary theory and quantitativism, and from what we have examined, it is evident that the transfer of late scholasticism to Spanish America has been the object of careful refinement in Hispanic America for a much longer period than in the mother country itself. How, then, can one explain the economists' lack of interest in the contributions to economics of the theologians and jurists of the New World? It seems the explanation could be that the situation was similar to that in Europe until not long ago. As in the Old World, the Spanish-American scholastics considered it more natural to study the social and economic problems and to attempt to find solutions. But the posing of the problem, as well as the answer, followed the track of theology and moral philosophy, which for them were complementary. Scholastics followed the system of Hugo de San Victor (1096–1141), who divided the field of philosophy into four areas (theoretical, moral, logic, and mechanics). He also divided moral philosophy into three disciplines: ethics; economics; and politics. Once this three-way division of moral philosophy, which had an old Aristotelian flavour, was incorporated by Thomas Aquinas in his 'Treatise on Justice' in his *Summa Theologiae*, the joint or separate study of each of these disciplines remained as the guide for all writings throughout the centuries.

This occurs with the *Oeconomica* (1267) by Durand Pais, the *Yconomica* (1374) of Conrad von Megenburg, the *Iconomicas* (1553) by Gaggio, the *Economica Christiana* (1656) by Gio Stefano Menocio, and *La Economica* (1797) by Ramon Campos, which preceded the *Economics* (1879–90) of Lord Alfred Marshall by nearly a century. In this way, all the Hispanic-American scholars, theologians and jurists alike, worked intensively, though from different angles, in the field of economic science. Contemporary scholars have fallen in love with their classical, or better still, neo-classical inheritance. It was deemed unthinkable that in the notebooks, most often written in Latin, of the moralists of colonial times they would find any economic thoughts, unless these came by way of the *arbitraristas*, the name by which the authors of a mercantile persuasion were known. And if what happened to us is a mirror image of what took place in Europe, the way to recovery could be to follow the trail blazed by Schumpeter from 1950. In this sense, it is worthwhile noticing the difference between Schumpeter's and Alfred Marshall's stances as regards Adam Smith. 'All is already in Adam Smith' said a pleased Lord Alfred Marshall. But we can also say: 'All is already in the scholastic doctors' (Schumpeter 1971: 358).

5

THE QUANTITY THEORY OF
MONEY

From the beginning of the conquest the most important Indian industry was the extraction of gold and silver and draining it off to Seville. The impact produced by the flow of the precious metals on the level of Spanish prices and later, as the waves spread outwards, on the other European countries, was so great that during the last century the expression 'the revolution of prices' (Thorp 1957: 375) was born to describe it. Furthermore, towards the middle of the present century Earl J. Hamilton engaged himself in establishing a strict correlation between the flow of American treasure and the price revolution which took place in Spain between 1501 and 1650 and with these data to verify the quantity theory of money for this period. As would be expected, the subject stimulated the renewal of studies on the history of the facts as well as the economic doctrines. It was Hamilton who posed the question: 'Why did the prices rise? What answer did the Spaniards of the sixteenth century give to this question?' (Hamilton 1934: 299)

If we give a passing view on the answer given up to now we shall see that it is rare to find a reference to an author of Spanish-American origin (Sayous 1928: 289; Dempsey 1936: 174; Höffner 1941; 1955; Ullastres Calvo 1941–2; Larraz [1943] 1963; Grice-Hutchinson 1952; 1978; Iparraguirre 1954; Schumpeter [1954] 1971; Sánchez Albornoz 1959: 95; 1977; Sierra Bravo 1973; Gómez Camacho 1981: 7; 1985: 55; Baeck 1988). Philip II liked the title 'Hispaniarum et Indiarum Rex'. Today they are different worlds though they are united in a common faith, language and history. Therefore there remains the ineluctable task for the Latin American economists of our time to look back to these early times and be responsible for all the specific works. Among them, one of the first questions that stands out is: what was the understanding of the Spanish-American thinkers on the revolution of prices?

THE INDIAN SCHOLASTICS (1567–1791)

When the writings of the Indian (Spanish-American) scholastics appeared it was evident that all the basic pieces of their 'New Economics' were found already elaborated, with sweat and blood, by their predecessors, 'the West Indies mercantilists' and scholastics with the help of their science and their New World *'ispiriencia'*. Their principal intrinsic merit is to have known how to weld in a consistent theory the flux of Aristotelian-Thomistic contributions and those of the Spanish and foreign scholastics, together with the contributions of the New World mercantilists and scholastics, and to strengthen and to polish them.

The starting point of the quantitivism of Hispanic-American scholastics is monetary theory and this, in turn, is a chapter of the general theory of value and of prices. In respect of the theory of value, its considerations revolve around two subjects: the labour theory of value and the subjective theory of value. The attitude of the Hispanic-American scholastics is that of a total and unanimous rejection of the first, as we have already seen in the chapter on scholastic economics (Chapter 4).

As was the case with Tomás de Mercado, Matienzo reached his goal because he had the knack of combining his reading of the classics with a sagacious observation and analysis of American economic life. In addition to Matienzo's scholastic doctrinary sources, his considerations emerge from his observations as a magistrate in Chuquisaca. This hypothesis is further confirmed by the fact that in a brief signed by the president and two Chuquisaca magistrates on 1 February 1562, is collectively formulated – as if he wanted to leave a record of the birth of the School of Chuquisaca – the germ of the new monetary theory of Hispanic-American scholastics.

Finally, we must remember that Juan de Matienzo also left in his *Gobierno del Perú* a clear indication that he knew well all the writings of the Hispanic-American chroniclers of the time from the discovery onwards, and among them he quotes Cieza de León, who in his *Crónica del Perú* (1553) stated the considerations about American quantitativism.[1]

The School of Chuquisaca and the Audience of Charcas (1562)

A more detailed examination of the writings produced by the Courts of Chuquisaca (Charcas) allows us to verify that this doctrine began in Chuquisaca on 7 September 1561. The president and two judges of the Court of the Charcas – as if they wanted to mark the birth of a real economic school – stated the essence of their quantitative doctrine by means of a formal 'Letter to His Catholic Royal Majesty' dated in the city of La Plata, 1 February 1562. In this letter is made evident what anyone familiar with the province of Las Charcas could know, that is, the great difference in the level of prices between Lima and Potosí: 'In Potosí things ordinarily are four times dearer than in Lima' (Quiñones, López de Haro and Matienzo 1918: 66). This is established in the letter to the king of 1562, and the magistrates of Chuquisaca review two fundamental explanations for this anomalous gap of 400 per cent in the level of prices between Lima and Potosí. In the first place, they insist on the influence of spatial economy factors: distance, the means of transportation of the goods that came from Spain via Porto-Bello-Panama-Lima-Arequipa and their respective transportation costs. But at the same time they emphasize the decisive influence of the quantitative factor, in an environment towards which the irradiating forces of a real focus of development gravitate, the mountain of Potosí, the symbol of fabulous riches and also of the price revolution as far as the ultimate boundaries of the recently born capitalism.

It is the case – as the president and judges of Charcas argued – that 'Where there is more money always things are more expensive' (Quiñones, López de Haro and Matienzo 1918: 66). It is a brief and clear reply similar to the one given by Matienzo years later in his *Gobierno del Perú*, and much more precise than the classical thesis of Juan Bodin (1530–96), who 'will discover' in 1569 the loose nexus between the level of prices and the volume of precious metals instead of the volume of money[2] which the magistrates of La Plata (1562) stated, confirming exactly the thesis of the Marquis de Cañete (1556) and of La Gasca (1544) whose theories and reflections are superior to those of Azpilcueta.

The members of the Court of Charcas could deem their quantitativist thesis to be evident in an environment like Chuquisaca and Potosí, but they did not have great expectations as to the reception of their doctrine in the metropolitan world. They knew that their thesis could find opposition there. To counteract such a possibility they decided 'on demand of some officials of this Court', to gather testimonies of people learned in the affairs of Indian businesses and send this 'information' to the king together with the letter of 1 February 1562. We do not know the contents and the destiny of that 'information' but its mere mention is a clear sign of the popularity of the quantitavist thesis of the value of money and the attachment to it of the people of Chuquisaca and Potosí.

Here we transcribe in total this important text, a doctrine which will unite the magistrates of the Court of Las Charcas in their economic approach:

> they order [by order of the Viceroy] that in Potosí must be kept the fees of Lima: the zeal could be good but they have been misinformed because in Potosí things are four times more expensive than in Lima ordinarily and when they are cheaper they are the double than in Lima, and this is easy to understand as the goods are brought from Lima, which is three hundred leagues away, half by land and half by sea . . . and furthermore, where there is more money things are dearer as everything will be explained to Your Majesty by the information that goes together with this on demand of some of the officials of this Court.
>
> (Quiñones, López de Haro and Matienzo 1918: 66)

To all this another consideration should be added, which arises from a letter to the king from the city of La Plata, 22 October 1561. This is a letter signed by the President Pedro Ramírez de Quiñones (d. 1576), and the magistrates Matienzo and López de Haro, in which we find that the sovereigns of Castille had already been informed by the 'door keepers' of the court of the spectacular expensiveness of this land 'because in this city everything costs very high prices', and they (the sovereigns) demanded, by the Royal Decree of Valladolid of 15 July 1559, that the newly arrived magistrates of the court should send reports on the situation of the province so as to decide on salary policies. It is highly significant that the magistrates of La Plata answered the king that 'in fulfillment of Your Majesty's orders by means of [the decree] the information that adjoins this was gathered, and Your Majesty will see by means of it the "great expensiveness" of everything that is suffered in this Province' (Quiñones, López de Haro and Matienzo 1918: 21). Like the earlier 'information' mentioned above, this 'information' of October 1561 has not reached us, but we must be aware of the similarity of this information of October 1561 to the one mentioned in the letter to the king of February 1562. They may not be the same documents, but there is no doubt that the purpose of the documents, if not identical, is very similar: to verify and explain the reason for the 'great expensiveness' in the city of La Plata and the Villa Ymperial de Potosí.

Don Andrés Hurtado de Mendoza (Panama, 1556)

The record of how quickly the violent inflation that was experienced in Perú in the middle of the sixteenth century became apparent, is due to Don Andrés Hurtado de Mendoza, Marquis of Cañete, the third Peruvian viceroy, which at that time was the same as being South American viceroy of the Spanish province in the Americas. He entered the waters of Nombre de Dios in Terra Firma together with the fleet of Seville and a few days after landing and crossing the isthmus he wrote concisely to the king, in a long letter dated Panama, 16 March 1556: 'Only here have I understood what happens here and there' (Hurtado de Mendoza 1921: 261). The first thing that came to his attention, or better still, which he experienced personally, was when having to pay the expenses 'of having to move from his house in Nombre de Dios to Panama' with money of his own. He immediately underlined the phenomenon of the Indian high prices remarking with anxiety that he was sorry for the Spaniards in the Indies when he saw that land was so expensive. And immediately associating the high prices with the growing abundance of gold and silver of the Peruvian mines, our newly arrived viceroy offered his quantitavist explanation: 'Because as the land is rich, money is worth very little' (Hurtado de Mendoza 1921: 264). In the very short period of thirty days, Hurtado de Mendoza diagnosed accurately that the revolution of prices which was suffered, first in the Indies and later in Spain, was due to the opulence of its gold and silver mines and above all to the powerful mining centre of Potosí. And if this could be understood in only a month and in a site like Panamá – although in addition he would have had copies, at least, of the letters of his predecessors, and of course the correspondence of La Gasca, the 'Pacifier of Perú' – it can be assumed that the idea had been floating in the air for some time, especially in the field of mining exploitation, and that it was common knowledge to the people acquainted with business in Spanish America.

Pedro de la Gasca (Lima, 1549)

A predecessor of the Marquis of Cañete is Pedro de la Gasca who only remained for a couple of years in Spanish America, between 1546 and 1550, and they were years dedicated to pacifying Perú, an enterprise which ended with the defeat and trial of Gonzalo Pizarro in the valley of Xaquixaguana on 9 April 1548. But this short time sufficed for La Gasca to grasp without difficulty the effects of the flood of Potosinian silver on the general level of prices, i.e. that standard prices (except for those of gold and silver) were lower and more stable, the farther one was from Potosí. His understanding of this mechanism surpassed that shown by Azpilcueta. In fact, immediately after coming into contact with the American territories, in a letter of 12 July 1546 forwarded to the Council of the Indies, he shows that he was aware of the regional discrepancy of the system of prices within the same broad area, passing from the coast to the hinterland, when he stated that the road was long and painful (from Cartagena) to the New Kingdom (Santa Fe de Bogotá), and he believed that Armendáriz, President of the Royal Court in Santa Fé de Bogotá, not only would have a lot of work, but would spend more than his salary could afford: even if he does not say so explicitly, by 'hinterlands' he meant areas rich in gold and silver or emerald mines (Gasca 1921: 93). In a letter of 2 May 1549 he repeated the principle of the devaluation of gold and silver when new sources were exploited, as was the case with the recently discovered mines in the regions of Guamanga and El Cuzco: 'Such abundance is expected in these lands, that silver may be worth almost nothing, that it may be considered as unbelievable, because even now it is so for those who do not see it' (Gasca 1921: 181). In this last letter it is evident that La Gasca wanted to demonstrate – mentioning concrete cases of prices of many different products, goods and services – that in the mining areas, especially in the silver focal point of Potosí's highlands, prices were very high compared to those for the same products in Lima, precisely due to the greater abundance of silver in those areas (Gasca 1921: 181–3). We also find considerations of major interest for us in his letter to the Council of the Indies of 28 January 1549, in which he establishes his awareness of the great difference of the purchasing power of gold in the Indies compared to Spain: 'What in Spain may be bought with a "real" [is] not bought in the Indies with a gold peso' (Gasca 1921: 138) formulate with the abbreviation PPP (Purchasing Power Parity), is forestalled, as it makes us see that the parity of the purchasing power of a gold peso in the Indies is given by a 'real' in Spain. La Gasca establishes with this the foundation of the doctrine that will be assigned in 1556 to Dr Martín de Azpilcueta Navarro and the subsequent European and American constructors of the PPP, but whose ideas did not surpass the theories of La Gasca and the Marquis of Cañete, who were not mercantilist themselves but managed to grasp the realities of the American lands and their effects on Europe.

Chronicler Cieza de León (Popayán, 1547)

By May 1541 another young soldier, but one who this time was a chronicler, Pedro Cieza de León (1518?–54) 'the prince of the Indian chroniclers' had already departed from the City of the Kings towards Charcas, and was visiting the mining settlements of the Potosí highlands, the fabulous market of the 'Villa Ymperial del Potosí' which was accelerating in growth, and the noble and loyal 'Villa del Plata', a Spanish population in Los Charcas established in Chuquisaca (Cieza de León, no date). The impact produced on him by contact with the dynamic area of Potosinian development – as we would call it nowadays – and with the vast area of influence that was already appearing in Cuzco in the north and in Tucuman in the south, was vital, and his considerations emphatically confirm the quantitavist approaches of his predecessors Jerez, las Casas, Bernal and Valdivia. Cieza gathered information and wrote about it to enlarge the manuscript of his already bulky *Crónica del Perú*. Started in 1541 in Cartago, in the Valley of Cauca, it was at the point of receiving the final touch before being printed, once the last stretch of Cieza's itinerary had concluded. Actually this last part fills about twenty chapters of the *Crónica del Perú*, which run from Chapter 95 to Chapter 115, and it is in these chapters that Cieza's quantitavist considerations appear. This occurs in two instances, one in which Villa de Plata is described, and another in which the metal mines are described: the corresponding chapters according to Cieza's numbering are: Chapter 107 and Chapter 115.

Chapter 107 begins with the already mentioned paragraph in which a flattering presentation is made of the 'noble and loyal Villa de Plata', famous all over the world 'due to the great treasures that have parted from it to Spain'. Its situation was the optimum one, being located on the best site that could be found, which had already proved to have a good temperature in which to grow fruit trees, to sow wheat and barley, to cultivate vines and other things. This 'good temperature' must be understood in the sense that being located in the torrid zone and at a height of 2,700m its climate is really very pleasant, especially when compared with Mount Potosí, 4,800m high, very rugged and, being very cold and windy, was uninhabitable even for the natives. Unfortunately, as Cieza was in situ he did not bear in mind that his readers would not be able to follow him in his comings and goings. What is more, when he wrote about Potosí, although he admitted the weather was cold (Chapter 109), he nevertheless judged that 'it is healthy, especially for the Indians as very few or none of them are sick there' (Cieza, no date: 467). But the point of interest for us is understood completely only when we find out, through other sources that because of the intense cold and the strong winds

> for six leagues [measure of distance] roundabout Potosí from May to the end of August no fruit is borne, nor are there trees, nor is there grass in the mountain of the ground which is dark, red, and partially the colour of burnt ashes.
>
> (ibid.: 478)

Only when we have this information can we guess that for the Spaniards of Los Charcas the mountain and the Villa Imperial of Potosí were places of sweat and hard work, while Villa de Plata was used as an oasis of rest and family enjoyment, besides being the headquarters of all the political, administrative and religious institutions of the province of Los Charcas, and also the seat of certain activities that could not take place in Potosí.

Let us now examine the second paragraph of Chapter 107 of Cieza's chronicle. This is the first proposition, with which the second paragraph begins: 'The farms and country estates have nowadays a very high price, caused by the riches that have been discovered in the mines of Potosí' (ibid.: 461).

As the wealth discovered in the mines of Potosí is silver, not only is the relationship between the price level and the quantity of silver established here, but at the same time an order of causality is established: the increase of the volume of silver in the Potosí mines brought about the increase of the level of prices in the Villa de Plata. But such an interpretation comprises much more than what Cieza was thinking, as the relation he establishes does not include the level of all prices, but only the level of the prices of land or, still more precisely, of the farms and country estates, and only those in Villa de Plata. Other classes of properties and properties located in other places would not necessarily have 'high prices' because of the growth of the quantity of silver in Potosí. This remark, of course, is ours, not Cieza's, but we make it precisely to make clear and unequivocal Cieza's considerations in the sentence with which his second paragraph begins. It is probable that Cieza had borne in mind a real interpretation and not a monetary one, when he related the price of the country estates with the volume of mining production. Actually, it is probable that he might have had in mind the idea that, as the volume of the mining production increased (a larger number of labourers), larger amounts of consumption goods were needed, and consequently a higher valuation of the neighbouring farm lands, precisely due to the increase in the requirements for consumption goods. In such a case, it would be an effect of spatial economics or of localization or positional rent due to the vicinity of the mining developing area, of the same category as the one seen 2,000 years before by Xenophon (430–355 BC). When the plan of mining exploitation was being carried out, the localization of the workers' families in the mining settlement increased, the demand for consumption goods also increased and consequently the lands near the mining centre were incorporated in the production process according to the spatial economic order, increasing their rent and thus their prices too. It is evident that in this case, it can also be asserted that the price of the land rose due to the increase of the wealth of the newly exploited mines. Therefore, to the first quantitative interpretation of Cieza's ideas, a second interpretation of the spatial economic type is added. In which of these two interpretations should we place the first sentence of the second paragraph of Chapter 107 of Cieza's chronicle? The answer is not easy: but in the way it is stated in the context of Chapter 107, I am inclined towards accepting the real and spatial interpretation and not the monetary quantitative one. This question deserves to be more studied by more expert minds.

Chapter 115 is titled 'Cómo en esta parte deste reino hay grandes minereos de metales' (How in this part of this kingdom there is much metal mining). It is actually an attempt to synthesize all that Cieza had seen from Cartagena to Potosí, to arrive at the conclusion that in the Indies 'the greatest riches and treasures ever seen in the world and in many ages have been found' (Cieza, no date: 479). He continues numbering the different kinds of metal found. First it was the gold from the Cauca Valley region, from Popayan as far as Mompox village, as rich, if not richer, than Cuzco. Afterwards he states that in several areas such as Antioquia and Cartago in Nueva Granada, and also in all the kingdom of Perú there was gold and silver to extract 'for ever after': also determining that 'there is a great quantity of copper and more still of iron in the sand banks and the collars of the ridges that lower to the plains', as also 'there is lead, and this kingdom is well stocked with all metals that God created'.

Based upon this data he states his conclusion: 'And I believe that as long as there are men, there will be great wealth there: and so much has been extracted, that it has raised the prices in Spain in such a way, as never men could have thought.' This conclusion brings to mind similar ideas – as we have seen above – in Las Casas, and we will also find them later, in 1567, reproduced almost verbatim, but recognizing his debt to Cieza, in the *Gobierno del Perú* of Juan de Matienzo. Moreover, we must bear in mind that he had made that kind of remark even before Potosí was famous and even before it was discovered. But to localize them we have to look with greater attention at the part of the *Crónica* related to his days in the Valley of Cauca, in Nueva Granada. There we can read his remarks when he first came across the 'renowned and rich Mount Buriticá, from which great quantity of gold has been taken', which he describes in Chapter 14 of the *Crónica*. Cieza participated in its discovery when he was part of the army of Captain Juan de Vadillo en 1539, that is ten years before getting to know the other famous mountain, the silver mountain of Potosí, and he crossed it again towards the end of the same year, this time when enlisted in the army of Captain Jorge Robledo. It was on this occasion that he contrasted the 'great quantity of gold' that the Indians took from this mountain (that even nowadays occupies an outstanding place in the works of monetary history), with 'the very great need of supply of provisions' caused by the setting on fire of the village and of all the harvests produced by the Indians when the Spaniards entered. Cieza tells – in the part that corresponds, I believe, to the year 1542, that is, the same year that de las Casas was constructing his ideas that

> I remember that going to look for food, a soldier called Toribio found in a river (of the town of Buriticá) a stone as big as a man's head, full of gold veins that penetrated the stone from one side to the other, and when he saw it he put it on his shoulders to bring it to the camp. And climbing a hill he met a little dog that belonged to the Indians: and when he saw it he rushed to kill it to eat it, letting go of the gold stone which rolled back into the river, and Toribio killed the dog, having it of greater price than gold because of the hunger he had which was the cause of the stone staying in the river, where it at first was. And would it change into something that could be eaten, surely someone would go back to search for it, because we really have great need of food.
>
> (ibid.: 184)

Cieza's account is another version of the 'theory of the mouse' – as I called it elsewhere – sketched in the *Natural History of Pliny the Elder* (23–79 AD), but there is no doubt that here, still looking at the subjective approach to value, a subjective approach to the law of demand and supply is established, in a market in which one of the parts is represented by the precious metal: to the abundance and scarcity of any product, the abundance and scarcity of gold mining is opposed. In this case the abundance of gold was such that the man who let it go did not take the trouble to 'go to fetch it back'.

Once the objective taboo of precious metals had been broken, Cieza placed one after the other, in Chapter 2 of the *Crónica*, the three parts of the quantitative problem as he saw it, which reminds us of Jerez's point of view. In the first place, he stressed 'the very excessive prices of goods in the Cauca Valley', then he observed that 'for the glory of Spaniards', the conquerors of the Indies 'so low considered the monies that, even if they had needs they despised it'. And few lines below we find the confirmation of the remark that the Indian lands and rivers 'are very rich and there is abundance of this metal [gold]' (ibid.: 164). That is, in the same page he placed, one after the other, three ideas: (a) abundance of gold, (b) excessive prices, (c) low value of money. But the author does not deem it necessary to correlate them explicitly. This occurs when Cieza de León writes the chapter dedicated to the description of the Valley of Cauca, a valley which he travelled so many times between the years 1531 and 1547. As Cieza was in Cartago when he enlisted with the royalists who followed the summons of La Gasca in July 1547, it is probable that Chapter 2 was written towards the end of 1546.

From Chapter 30 onwards, Cieza describes the road from the city of Cali to that of Popayan, in which he confirms that he is actually marching speedily towards the place of encounter with La Gasca's troops in Túmbez. In Chapter 31 we read that Cieza already has 'reached the city of Popayan', and he finds that he has to give a last backward look, as he is practically in the Sierra of the Coconucos where the two great branches of the river Magdalena are born. The great hastiness in the drafting of the *Crónica* is notorious, as is the tight and very synthesized style, which makes the reading difficult. In the panoramic vision of Chapter 31 the subject of our interest is posed again. Here is the part of major importance for us:

> There are so many Indian provinces and towns from the birth of this river up to where it enters in the Ocean sea, and so much riches, rich gold mines and riches that the Indians had, and some still have, and so big is the trade of it that it cannot become dearer as it is much, it makes it become cheaper that the natives of those regions have not much reasoning, and they speak such different languages that it was necessary to take many interpreters to travel through them.
>
> (ibid.: 239)

In spite of the difficulty in reading this long phrase, and the quantity of subjects it contains, it is evident that Cieza again establishes the problem and is determined to give it a final solution. In the first place he underlines the great abundance of gold in Nueva Granada. In the second place he marks the importance of the great trade in gold, with which it seems he wants to emphasize that there is a great demand for gold in the market. In the third place, he establishes that, in spite of the great supply of gold – or as it is expressed in the text 'as it is much' – in the face of great demand – as it also says in the text 'so great trade in gold, the price in gold cannot increase' – it cannot become dearer. There is a fourth consideration, related to the possibility that the price of gold might tend to decrease, 'and it makes it be cheaper' because of particular reasons of the Indians, or rather, because of the knavery of the conquerors. But this question was later, in Chapter 46, cancelled by Cieza himself, when he says 'It is another time and they know well how to sell what they have and trade for what they need'; also, it has no interest for our purpose. If the interpretation of the long paragraph of Chapter 31 transcribed above is correct, we must admit that Pedro Cieza de León, following the way initiated in Chapter 14 (examined above), insists in

Chapter 31 on greater emphasis on the subjective view of the value of gold in terms of its abundance or scarcity. In conclusion, we can therefore affirm that Cieza de León's contribution to the theory of money has as a basis the thesis that with the abundance or scarcity of gold its value rises or decreases respectively. And as in the place and time in which he wrote, gold was used as money, it is possible that ultimately his thesis contains the germs of the quantitative theory, and as such it has surely been influential in preparing the way to the quantitative ideas in the Hispanic-American world, as well as in other countries in the sixteenth and seventeenth centuries. To these ideas, born during his sojourn in the Valle de Cauca, we must add those which emerged during his stay in the province of Los Charcas in 1549, when he visited the city of La Plata, the Villa Imperial and Mount Potosí. These ideas might have had a greater diffusion, even if their supporting arguments and coherence have certain formal deficiencies. In other respects it is certain that the *Crónica del Perú* has been known, appreciated and very frequently quoted by Juan de Matienzo, in his *Gobierno del Perú*, which will be the object of our research in the following sections of this work. It would not be too audacious to hint that Cieza's conclusions, together with those of his predecessors and contemporaries, are an important start for the awakening of the 'Second Scholastic Economics' both in Europe and in Spanish America.

Gonzalo de Bernal (Chuquisaca, 1545) and the discovery of Potosí

The discovery of the silver mines of Potosí at the beginning of 1545 is another event which would have had immediate repercussions in the debate about the theory of money value in the Indies. When he referred to the town of Armas (where he obtained a lot of Indians) Cieza de León exclaimed that it was 'plentiful of gold' and he firmly believed that 'for some time from its rivers gold would be drawn as in Viscay, iron' (Cieza, no date: 177; Quiñones, López de Haro and Matienzo 1918: 462).[3] But not even on this occasion did it occur to him to look deeper into the relationship between those two metals. This matter was reserved for one of the conquering soldiers, very obscure and ironically totally ignored in the history of the conquest. The only reference I find with which to rescue him from obscurity is owed to Garcilaso de la Vega (1539–1616). I refer to Gonzalo Bernal, who towards the last days of April 1545, when the fabulous silver mines of Mount Potosí had just been discovered, saw the beginning and the legal registration of the first vein, and exclaimed: 'The mines [of Potosí] promise such riches, that after a few years of working them iron will be more valuable than silver.' This event is highly significant. The discovery of the Potosí silver mine not only has a meaning in the history of quantitative theory – and as such is a powerful tool – albeit surely not the only one, nor the first to produce chain reactions in the field of the value of money theory. It is in this sense that this remark of Gonzalo Bernal must be considered, although the only thing I know about him is what Garcilaso de la Vega said: that he had been a steward of General Pedro Alonso de Hinojosa. Someone linked his remark with an event that happened much later, between December 1553 and 1554, that is, the uprising which started in El Cuzco, led by Francisco Fernández Girón, who ended by being executed in Lima. But this is a misunderstanding. Gonzalo Bernal made his remark before Diego Centeno (governor of the province of Charcas), a few days after the registration of the first vein in the name of Diego de Villarroel. 'Villarroel . . . registered it 21 April 1545, staking the vein . . . which is the same of taking possession of the yards that the law concedes, to those who find it so that they mine it as owners' (Garcilaso de la Vega 1968: 672). This is categorically affirmed by Antonio Vázquez de Espinosa (?–1630) (Vázquez de Espinosa 1948: 577). Though it was uttered as a prediction, there is no doubt that here we find an important milestone in the history of monetary quantitativism. And Garcilaso de la Vega (1968: 672) also understood it in this way in 1605.

In September 1545 from the city of Santiago, during the operation of the conquest of Chile, Pedro de Valdivia (1510–54) decided to send a messenger to Spain with news about his conquering and colonizing 'journey'. To finance this embassy he resorted to 'the gold that some Indians of mine had extracted and what the neighbours had, that all of them loaned it to me readily . . . making a total of almost sixty thousand pesos'. It was on the occasion that the vessel and those who sailed in it set sail from the port of Valparaiso, 'That the conqueror of Chile tried to grasp how much those sixty thousand pesos were worth.' Valdivia himself tried to evaluate them, making a difference between what they would be worth if the embassy went to Perú or to a different place. If the ship went 'to a place other than Perú it was evident that sixty thousand pesos was very much', it was a sum of very great value. And what would happen if this embassy were to Perú? Valdivia was well acquainted with the monetary effects of the discovery and the start of the exploitation of the silver mines of Potosí, and his answer was readily given: 'As that land has been and is so prosperous or rich in [silver] money, they would little esteem that amount.' That is, Valdivia gives the quantitative doctrine of money a citizenship card for Perú, as if he wanted to say that everybody knew this. And he made this remark when the messengers to his majesty 'set sail from the port of Valparaiso about September of said year of 1546'. What does this sum represent now for the conquerors of Chile? Valdivia asks himself again. And his answer was informed by the same reasons: 'Here [this 60,000 gold pesos] were very much for us because every peso costs us a hundred drops of blood and two hundred drops of sweat.' In other words, in Chile the value of money was founded on the costs of its exploitation (Cunninghame Graham 1943: 195).

Bartolomé de las Casas (1542)

The ex-conqueror and ex-*encomendero* (commissioner) Bartolomé de las Casas, later converted to the Order of the Dominicans, presented in 1542, by order of the 'Emperor king . . . in the City Halls of Valladolid', a work which he entitled *Remedios para Reformación de las Indias*, afterwards printed in Seville in 1552. In it he pleaded for the abolition of the system of *encomiendas*. The argument he uses to justify this measure is developed thus:

> As the privilege granted to the Spaniards to give them the Indians in *encomienda* has been so iniquitous and so damaging . . . and has borne such very enormous and irretrievable evils to God and to royal crown of Spain, and has destroyed those kingdoms and lands and killed so many people and devastated so many settlements. And even these kingdoms of Castilla are flagellated by God every day: and there is great fear that He should plunder them because of the great sins that the Spanish people have committed in the Indies, of which we see an evident punishment, that everybody sees it and says everywhere, that with it God afflicts us and shows that He is very offended with us in those parts due to the destruction of those nations: and it is that of so infinite treasures have been brought from them, that never King Solomon nor other king of the world owned, nor saw, nor heard about so much gold and silver, nothing has remained in those kingdoms, and even from what there was in Spain, little before the Indies were discovered, there is nothing at all. Because of this everything costs thrice the price they were worth before, and poor people suffer great poverty and need, and to Your Majesty, who so well employs his life in the increase of the Catholic faith, it becomes necessary and impossible of carrying out great heroic feats in the service of our Almighty God, as you really could achieve if so great disorders, due to said damaged *encomienda* and to what precedes it which are the unjust wars, would not have happened in the Indies: therefore it follows that that privilege is so iniquitous and evil and that so great damages and mischiefs it has caused, though at the beginning it did not seem bad but good. . . . Therefore it is true and just that the Indians take it away from the Spaniards . . . because it is iniquitous and tyrannical and against our sainted Catholic faith . . . against all natural law and of enormous damages and grievances and the finishing of all those kingdoms, and matter of provocation of the terrible wrath of God, who He will spill over us in vengeance for our sins we committed on them [the Indians].
>
> (Casas 1974 : 763–5)

In a work of mine in 1984, examining the *Remedios* of las Casas I observed the deep metaphysical frame in which the economic subject was established. De las Casas feared that God would punish his homeland, due to the slavery of the Indians, and one of the signs of this punishment that was already taking place he saw in the escape of the American treasure towards other kingdoms and the accelerated increase of prices in Spain. In his still more famous work: 'Brevísima relación de la destrucción de las Indias', written in Valencia also in 1542, edited in Seville in 1552, he repeated that he acted so to 'drive away hell from the Indies . . . and from pity towards his country which is Castilla, and God would not destroy it because of so great sins committed against His faith and honour' (Casas 1952: 13).

With the analysis limited to the quantitavist subject imbued in de las Casas' mysticism, the course of reasoning of the correlation among the different variables was not very clear. Likewise, it was possible to think that de las Casas related the revolution of prices in Spain more with the flight of money from the treasures brought from the Indies than with its abundance. But in spite of the inaccurate terminology, it could be supposed that de las Casas could have thought of a causal relation between flux of metals and price revolution.

Finally, it is most important to consider that Casas was well acquainted with the first quantitavist experiences that took place in the Antilles on Columbus' first voyage. It was de las Casas who knew of the navigational journal drafted by Columbus which he transcribed in the first book of his *History of the Indies* and which constitutes the basic source of the primitive American quantity theory as we shall see further on.

The ransom of Cajamarca (1533)

The conquest of Perú shows the other side of the contact between the Spaniards and the natives. The violence and the ferocity of the struggles were widely exploited by the enemies of Spain. The triumph of the Spanish expeditionaries, which sometimes seemed almost miraculous, filled the conquerors with well deserved vanity, while in the mother country the astounding news about the Indian treasure, which instead of being unfounded, as happened in the Columbus enterprise, were absolutely confirmed, because the magnitude of 'the ransom of Cajamarca' (*el rescate de Cajamarca*) surpassed all estimates.

If in the prowess of the discovery made on the first trip the names of Guacanagarí and Columbus are outstanding, in 'the ransom of Cajamarca' the major characters are Francisco Pizarro and the Inca Atahualpa. And in spite of the course of forty years that separate them, there is a strong bond between them in respect of their monetary ideas. The Inca Atahualpa plays in the development of American quantity theory the same role played by King Guacanagarí forty years before. In one of the first accounts about the ransom of Cajamarca sent to the king by 'the Governor of Panamá and other trustworthy persons' in 1533, we are surprised with the clear quantitavist approach. The same account reports that after Governor Pizarro had advanced, on foot and on horseback, with 200 Spaniards, they reached the place where a chief, great lord, called Atabalique, brother and General Captain of the Sovereign of those lands: that after peace was offered to him, as he resisted they fought him and he was imprisoned and they took from him more than fifty thousand castellanos of gold and more than twenty thousand silver marks . . . that said chief promised to give Pizarro and the Spaniards a piece of land as extensive as the courtyard of a castle, or more, and from it they had already taken more than four hundred thousand very large pieces [of gold], and of strange shapes; . . . and that after said battle, native people brought fifty thousand castellanos of gold, so they had already received from the chief more than two million twenty carat gold: and the duty of ten percent, corresponding to what would be brought, would be of more than four hundred thousand castellanos . . . and those who write this believe that the ships are detained for a long time to load and bring the aforesaid gold that they expect it will be a marvelous quantity.

(Carande 1977: 82)

This is the principal idea of this casual report that would reach the king's courts and the markets of Europe with the same speed and spread of Columbus' first letter about the voyage of the discovery of the Indias. Its authors are unknown, but there is no doubt that there can be only one source: some of Pizarro's people who participated in the conquest of Perú and who, already satisfied, returned on the first ship that carried part of the Incas' treasure, on 5 December 1533, or on the second, on 9 January 1534. Today we know that this news was spread almost simultaneously in French, German and Italian, so that we can say that at the beginning of 1534 it had rounded the world.

But what has this news, the data of which are common to almost all latter accounts and chronicles, related to the conquest of Perú, to do with our subject? It is precisely due to its clear quantitavist approach that it attracts our attention. Actually, when it is stated that the Incas had already delivered more than 400,000 pieces of gold, the writer was surprised to see that the Spaniards immediately broke them up to store and load them.

Seeing this, said Indian chief asked them why they did so, as he would give them as much as they wanted. And he also had his subjects bring more than sixty thousand marks of pure silver and he told them that, in his country, there was also cinnamon, of which they could order ten thousand loads to be fetched. He also told them that to have the silver they wanted it sufficed to put fire to a rock he showed them and from which they could extract as much melted silver as they wanted, ready to be hammered: so that there is as much gold and silver in this

71

kingdom as there is iron in Vizcaya, and that is why they do not think it is important.

(Carande 1977: 83)

This mention of putting a rock on the fire is not untruthful, as the Incas referred to the melting method, which means melting the metal veins in small furnaces which they called *guairas* and of which there were a great number on the slopes of the mines and which were seen at night as if they were festival lights.

The fundamental thing for us is the general awareness among the conquerors of Perú of the enormous abundance of gold and, especially, silver mines, due to which these 'precious' metals had so little value among the Incas that 'they give them no importance'.

Francisco López de Jerez (1534)

The conquerors, who used gold and silver as a means of payment, became immediately aware of the deterioration of the value of those metals. This is proved in the *Relación* by Francisco López de Jerez, who, after the victory over Atahualpa in Cajamarca, in which he participated as secretary to Captain Francisco Pizarro, and when he returned to Spain on 3 June 1534, had the *Relación* printed the same year. Francisco López de Jerez tells us that on 13 May 1533 the melting of all the gold and silver was started and the metal was allotted. In fact, after taking his majesty's fifth and the foundry rights, all the treasure of the Incas was distributed among the conquerors, who earned it as follows:

> eight thousand eight hundred and eighty gold pesos and three hundred and sixty-two silver marks corresponded to the cavalry men, and four thousand four hundred and forty gold pesos and a hundred and eighty-one silver marks to the infantry men, and to some more than to others in the measure the governor thought they deserved it, the quality of the persons or their work. A quantity of gold that the governor separated before the allotment, he gave to the neighbours who had remained in the town of San Miguel and to all the people who came with the Captain Don Diego de Almagro and all the merchants and sailors who came after the war had finished, so that all [the Spaniards] who were in that land obtained a part.
>
> (Le Riverend no date: 110)

We now see the sudden appearance of a society of the newly rich whose members could not yet believe that this were true. Francisco López de Jerez himself was beneficiary of a booty of 'a hundred and ten good silver arrobas (twenty-five pounds each)', earned in only one of the twenty years spent there: 'nineteen in poverty and in only one the riches I brought here'. We can foresee the price revolution that this historic allotment would produce, in the first place in the region of Cajamarca and San Miguel. López de Jerez himself described the madness of prices and stated that suddenly they have become 'so high, and I can say it truthfully, as I saw it and bought some things'. What is more, after having registered a list of the highest prices in the land that had been paid in those days, he expressed the view that now that everyone knew that they were acquainted with it in Panamá and from there spread by the conquerors to all Europe, it could be understood correctly. In effect, writes Jerez, many things should be said 'about the increased prices at which everything has been sold, and the little value given to gold and silver'. We already know that among the Incas those 'precious' metals had an unimportant value. And now that the Indian treasure had changed hands and it was in possession of the Cajamarca conquerors the depreciating effect accompanied its new owners. López de Jerez himself says:

> if someone owed something to somebody else, he gave him a piece of gold without weighing it: and even if he gave him twice what he owed he gave nothing: and from house to house went the debtors, with an Indian loaded with gold looking for the creditors to pay what they owed.

(Le Riverend no date: 110)

Formerly, in the 1533 *Relación* we only knew of Indians who rejected 'precious metals', but in this 1534 account of Francisco López de Jerez we learn that gold 'was held in contempt both by the Spaniards as by the natives'.

The navigational journal of the first voyage of discovery (1492–3)

This navigational journal contains the bases, the foundations of American quantitativism and proves that Columbus' reflections on the effects of the American gold and silver surpass Copernicus' ideas as well as Azpilcueta Navarro's.

The same day that the explorers landed the first fair took place between the admiral's people and the crowd of natives of the Guanahaní islet of the Bahamas who witnessed the landing (Fernández de Navarrete 1825; Ballesteros Beretta 1945; Sanz 1962).

> Because I desired that they were friendly towards us [Columbus said], because I understood that they were people who would free themselves and convert to our Sainted Faith by means of love, and not by force, I gave some of them a few red bonnets and some glass beads which they hang to their necks and many other things of little value, which brought them great pleasure and it was marvelous how they were ours. . . . Afterwards they came swimming to the boats of our ships

73

where we were, and brought us parrots, balls of cotton thread and
spears and many other things, which they bartered for other things we
gave them, such as little glass beads and hawk's bells [brass timbrels],
finally, they took all and gave of the things they had.

(Columbus 1971: 30)

This was a good start towards establishing a free trade market between the
Spaniards and the Antillian Indians of the Taino nation of Guanahaní, chris-
tened with the name San Salvador. Columbus never stops stressing the
increasing demand, or as he states in his own words 'the want of our things'
that the Indians showed.

At the next day's market the admiral ponders:

I was alert and trying to know if there was gold and I saw that some of
them brought a little piece [of gold] hanging through a hole in their
nose, and communicating by gestures he could know that going South
or coming back to the Island by the South way, there was a king that
had big vases of it, and that he had a lot.

(Columbus 1971: 31)

That was very important, a real event which would be taken into account
in the rest of the exploring trips. From San Salvador the chosen route goes
to the Santa Maria de la Concepción Islet and then to Fernandina Island,
which they reached on Tuesday, 16 October. The news of the discoverers
'who came from heaven' had already reached Fernandina's population,
producing natural wonder among the pacific Tainos. It was so that the first
night

there was no lack of canoes aboard the ships [Columbus states] that
brought us water and what they had. I ordered that everyone should
be given something, that is to say some little beads, ten or twelve of
them of glass on a thread, and some brass timbrels that in Castilla are
worth a maravedí each, and some laces, all of which they had in very
great esteem.

(Columbus 1971: 37)

The marketing also went on the morrow. The people were all of the
same condition, and they gave of what they had in change of any thing
given to them: and here I saw that the crew changed little pieces of
broken bowls and glass for spears. And two other sailors found an
Indian who had in his nose a piece of gold that was about half a castellano, in which they saw letters engraved and I scolded them because
they did not bargain for it and gave whatever they demanded in order
to see what it was, and whose money it was; and they answered that
they did not dare to bargain for it.

(Columbus 1971: 40)

The news was not very encouraging for the admiral, but a few days later another event would change his mood.

In the navigational journal of 22 October we read that even if most commerce with the Indians took place through the already mentioned spears and balls of cotton thread, this time a novelty occurred: 'some of the Indians brought pieces of gold hanging from their noses which they readily changed for a hawk's bell suitable for the foot of a sparrow-hawk, and for little glass beads' (Columbus 1971: 44). This established a great novelty in the bartering market of the Fernandina Tainos. Gold that was only to serve as an ornament and indirectly to be treasured, lowered in value and became a means of exchange like the rest of the Indian goods. This change shows us clearly, in economic terms, of a change in the level of gold value in the market of Fernandina. However, the change in the value of gold was not only not general, neither was it very accentuated, as gold was only accepted in exchange for one of the most treasured Spanish products, the hawk's bells, and only secondarily for the glass beads. Anyway, the gold from Fernandina kept the admiral pondering for several days, until 1 November, when he took a dangerous decision. At that time he was near Cape Las Palmas on the island of Cuba. The Indians of the place neared the ships with more than sixteen canoes full of spun cotton and other things and great was their surprise when they were told the news that 'the Admiral ordered nothing should be taken because they had to know that the only thing that the Admiral looked for was gold' (Columbus 1971: 51). The decision of limiting the interchange with the natives only to gold, suddenly stopped the flux of commerce. For a month and a half the discoverers' explorations were pursued successfully in Cuba and in La Española, but there is a complete silence about the gold exchange. They were already in Haitian land in front of La Tortuga Island in Paradise Valley when after two timid attempts, the expeditionaries unexpectedly renewed their demands for gold from Monday, 17 December. There was good news to be had everywhere. The attempt at bartering in the nearest village where Columbus sent several Spaniards was satisfactory: 'They change glass beads for some thin pieces of carved gold' (Columbus 1971: 92). Due to the avalanche of sailors onto the village after this attempt, the chief of that village had the natives carve the first small gold tiles (*tejuelos de oro*) of the Indies, breaking a sheet of gold as large as a hand: 'and he made little pieces of it, and bringing one small tile he bartered it (in the plaza)' (Columbus 1971: 93). The same day Columbus received a visit from a chief of La Tortuga Island who came with forty men in his canoe. Columbus was told by Haitian natives that in La Tortuga there was more gold than in La Española Island 'because it was nearer Babeque'. Babeque Island (the Great Inagua), had been known about by Columbus since 12 November when he had tried unsuccessfully to find it, as he had heard 'that its inhabitants picked up the gold by candlelight at night and they said that they made bows with it with hammers' (Columbus 1971: 57).

Facing these first considerations of space economics in the New World, the admiral remarked that more important than the distance, or at least on the same level of importance, it was fundamental to take into account what we, nowadays, call the volume of transactions, which was very low in La Española and in La Tortuga. In fact, the admiral said

> I do not believe there were gold mines in La Española Island or in La Tortuga, but that they brought it from Babeque, and they bring little because they have nothing to give for it, and the land is so rich that they do not have to work much to feed themselves or to dress as they go naked.
>
> (Columbus 1971: 93)

Columbus did not know that by introducing the volume of transactions into the discussion he contributed the first brick to Irving Fisher's 'change equation', but he records that he affirmed it in La Española Island on 17 December 1492.

The riches in gold of Babeque Island were confirmed by the young king of La Española Island who lived in the Haitian area, today called Gros Marne, and who visited the expeditionary ships for the first time on 16 December in the gulf between La Tortuga and La Española. In this first visit, the young king, accompanied by more than 500 men, watched the bartering market in the morning, in which 'some brought some grains of very pure gold in their ears and nose, which they gave readily', and (the king) ordering all of them afterwards, to honour the admiral. The second visit of the king of Gros Marne took place on 18 December and followed a more formal pattern. More than 200 men accompanied the king and four men carried him in a litter. Of course, there was no lack of food and drinks offered by the Spaniards in the ceremony. But the most interesting item was the interchange of gifts.

> I saw [wrote Columbus] that he liked a drapery that I had over my bed and I gave him it and [added] some very good amber beads that I had on my neck and red shoes and a flask of orange flower water, of which he was so happy that it was a wonder.
>
> (Columbus 1971: 95)

As the Indian king already knew that the discoverers' expedition was in search of gold and wanted to go to Babeque Island, we can guess his opinion. Columbus' remarks in his journal were:

> the king gave me also two pieces of carved gold which were very thin: and I think they obtain very little of it here as I believe that they are very near from where the gold is born, and there is a lot (*el rey me dio dos pedazos de oro labrado que eran muy delgados, que creo que aquí alcanzan poco de él, puesto que tengo que están muy vecinos de donde nace y hay mucho*).

76

In spite of the ironic tone of the comment there is no doubt that we are faced with remarks of great interest for our subject. It is a clear thesis of Columbus that the value of gold decreases ('they obtain very little of it here' – 'aquí alcanzan poco de él') with the nearness of its place of extraction ('if they are very near from where gold is born' – 'si están muy vecinos de donde nace') and of its abundance in the market ('and there is a lot' – 'y hay mucho') (Columbus 1971: 95). This happened at Puerto de Paz in La Española on 18 December 1492.

In the ceremony given in homage to the king of Gros Marne, the admiral learned from a principal of the sovereign, a person of great age and experience,

> that there are many islands near at a hundred leagues in which there is a lot of gold, and even one of them is all gold, and in the others there is so much that they pick it up and sift it with some sort of sieves and they melt it and make bows and a thousand other things.
>
> (Columbus 1971: 96)

Immediately Columbus decided 'to go there'. On the night of 19 December they left La Tortuga Gulf and on 20 December the expeditionary ships entered Acul Bay were they discovered a big settlement whose inhabitants, seeing the ships, ran towards them. 'So many came that they covered the land' to bring them bread and water

> and all that they had and knew that the Admiral wanted: and it must not be said that because they gave liberally what they gave had little value [said the Admiral] because the same did those who gave pieces of gold and those who gave the gourd of water.
>
> (Columbus 1971: 99)

More than 120 canoes also visited the vessels on 22 December: and the great Chief Guacanagarí who was in his village of El Recreo, sent the admiral the most valuable present they had seen up to then: 'a belt that, instead of a bag had a mask with two big ears of hammered gold, and the tongue, and the nose'. On 23 December the ships were visited by about 1,500 persons: then the admiral received the very important news that among the sources where gold was found, was the region of Cibao, that is located in La Española Island itself, and that people came to it to buy gold from other parts 'and that there is as much gold as one would want' to be found: 'and that in finding the place from which it is obtained he would get it very cheaply and as he imagined, even for nothing' ('y que hallando el lugar donde se saca habrá gran barato de ello, y según imaginaba, que no por nada') (Columbus 1971: 104).

In the meeting with Guacanagarí, in the Niña Caravel on Wednesday 26 December Columbus could ratify again his thesis that his gold trade was more prosperous because of the major quantity of gold in La Española.

When the king from Recreo had just arrived, a canoe that carried a chief from another province appeared, and they 'brought pieces of gold which they wanted to change only for a hawk's bell, because nothing they wanted more than hawk's bells' (Columbus 1971: 110).

The canoe had not yet reached the vessel where they called and showed the pieces of gold, saying 'chuq chuq' meaning hawk's bells, so they were about to go crazy for them. So we would not be mistaken if we stated that from then on, gold became a type of money-merchandise of the American Tainos, while the hawk's bells played the role of merchandise-money among the discoverers of the Indias, together with the Spanish monetary system. The Chief Guacanagarí did not lose the opportunity to link his name to the new parity of the two pre-money standards. A hawk's bell was equal to four pieces of gold as big as a hand. Once the exchange operation with the chief was closed, King Guacanagarí approached the admiral to suggest that 'he ordered a hawk's bell to be kept for him until the next day, because he would bring [in payment] four pieces of gold as big as the hand' (Columbus 1971: 110). Competition was also working wonders in the market economy established by Columbus in the Indies.

But the meeting between King Guacanagarí and Admiral Columbus has a special interest also for the history of economic doctrines. While the interchange of pieces of gold as big as a hand for a Spanish hawk's bell took place, it was evident that an increase of the value of the hawk's bell in relation to the purchasing power of 'the piece of gold as big as a hand' was also taking place. Undoubtedly this was satisfactory for the Spaniards: 'The Admiral was glad to know about this'. To which the response on the Indian side was quick:

> The king was glad to see the Admiral happy and understood that he
> [the Admiral] wished to get a great amount of gold, and he told him
> by gestures that he knew where they could find a lot of it near where
> they were: and to be optimistic because he would give him all the gold
> he would wish, and that he informed him that there was a lot especi-
> ally in Cipango, which the Indians called 'Civao', where there was so
> much that the Indians there consider it nothing, and that he would
> bring it from there, but that in this island, Española, called Bohío and
> in that Caribata province there was much more.
>
> (Columbus 1971: 110)

And as if to insist in the formulation of the quantitavist doctrine of the Indian king of the island of La Española, in the navigational journal of 1 January 1493 we find the following remark:

> The Admiral believed that King Guacanagarí might have forbidden
> everybody to sell gold to the Christians, so that all of it should pass
> through his hands. But as I told the day before yesterday, he knew the

places where there was gold in such a quantity that it may not be considered to have a price for them.

(Columbus 1971: 116)

Today Christopher Columbus would tell us that the abundance of gold in Cibao was such that its value was null and so it entered into the category of free goods. In not more than three months of the 'honeymoon' between the Spaniards and the American Indians he could verify empirically an observation that he transcribed daily in his navigational journal and that sometimes rendered the opportunity to ponder upon economic doctrines: that the value of gold could oscillate from an almost prohibitive level of purchase power, as happened in the experiments of the Guanahaní islet, and with very rare exceptions also in Fernandina and the island of Cuba; to a moderate level of esteem, as he verified in the region of the chief of the Valle del Paraíso who saw the necessity of 'creating' a sort of small tile to make the transactions easy; to the third stage, which took place in the region of the Chief Guacanagarí who will accompany Columbus in the history of American quantitativism. In the Acul Bay during the last days of December 1492 and the beginning of January 1493, we find Columbus remarking that the acquisitive power of gold 'is enough for little' if it is abundant, that is 'if there is a lot', and, of course, 'nearer it is from its source' its abundance will be greater and with this 'lower will be its price', and an extreme situation may come about, as he thought had happened in Cibao, that 'there was a great quantity of gold', making it 'extremely cheap', and because of this decreasing its worth 'to nothing', meaning that it could be bought with almost nothing or 'that it may not be considered to have a price' (Columbus 1971: 113). Here, we are essentially presented with an advanced quantitavist idea.

It is important to add that the optimism about the success of the enterprise of discovery would incorporate in Columbus' doctrine of quantity the equally optimistic expectations that in a very short term exchanging pieces of gold that equalled two *castellanos* for a needle would be nothing compared with what would happen in a month from then (26 December): or, as Guacanagarí had told the admiral that he had sent for gold and that he (Guacanagarí) would cover him (the admiral) up in gold before he left. This reminds us of an analogy that exists with Azpilcueta for he said that the American gold and silver had covered Spain up in them. Thus this suggests that Azpilcueta knew of these facts. Returning to our case, the Admiral said,

I hope in God that on my return from Castilla, I will find a barrel of gold that those who stayed will have bargained and they will have found the gold mine and the spicery, and this in such quantity that before three years have passed the King and the Queen can start and prepare the conquest of the Sainted House [of Jerusalem].

(Columbus 1971: 113)

Looking closer into Columbus' reflections on expectations, our attention is aroused by the relationship he establishes between the price level and the quantity of money; that is to say, between the price of a needle that on 26 December was not worth more than two *castellanos* and the price it would reach in a month's time as the quantity of gold in circulation would be much greater, which proves that he was establishing a relation between the increase in the quantity of gold and the increase in the price of needles. We have found similar examples on previous dates in Columbus' navigational journal. Thus in Fernandina on 17 October 1492 the price of a little bell was set at half a *castellano*, that weighed 2.30 grams of gold because then gold was rather scarce, but when the Spanish went to the fair on the Acul Bay on 23 December 1492, the bell was worth, due to the increase in the quantity of gold, 'four pieces of gold that were as big as a hand'. This shows that Columbus thought of the relation between the quantity of money and the increase in the price level, and though he did not state precisely how much it would be worth, it can be deduced that this would be a large multiple, and Guacanagarí himself was convinced that in a month's time he would get to cover Columbus up in gold. I accept that this interpretation can be questioned but if it is right we could then affirm that here we are, essentially, at an approximation to the quantity theory of money which is very close to that of our European predecessors and which even surpasses some of their ideas.

The inclusion of the expectations in his theory is also useful as a bridge between his quantity theory and his Christo-hedonist theory – in their essence evidently antagonistic – whose evocation of gold as the higher symbol of wealth reaches notes of bullionistic lyricism in the admiral's letter on his fourth trip, which reads:

> Genoans, Venetians and all people who have pearls, gems and other valuable things, all of them take them to the end of the world to change them into gold. Gold is most excellent, with gold treasures are made and with it he who has it can do whatever he wants in the world and even send souls to Paradise.
>
> (Columbus 1971: 200)

6

INDO-AMERICAN DEVELOPMENT DOCTRINES

If the belief that the question of development concerns only contemporary thinkers can find some justification in other parts of the world, it has been proved to be totally false in the history of the American doctrines. Actually, the conquest of what was originally known as the West Indies (called the Indies because Columbus mistakenly believed he had discovered a shorter route to India) and their incorporation in the system of the Iberian mother country has brought up, besides problems of other types, many and very complex economic issues. It was not only a matter of directing the economic process in a vast space with a very different culture and located far away from Spain, although this alone, considering the knowledge and the state of technology at the time, was a difficult problem for the central administration. In fact, it was not an easy matter to have a permanent migratory flow for the productive process or an administrative apparatus in the execution of the imperial economic plans. Nor was it easy to guarantee a system of cargo and trade for the Indian production via the metropolitan economic system if one keeps in mind the emerging smuggling activities, carried out on a large scale, as well as the competitive interference of the other imperial powers, on the one hand, and, on the other, great dislocations due to the process of economic exploitation in the new region, particularly the increasing flow of metals from the mines in Mexico and Alto Perú in the same metropolitan economic circuit.

But besides dealing with an experiment on a continental scale, in space, and of plurisecular dimension in time, the peculiarity of the 'mar océana' operation lay in the fact that it dealt with a development plan inspired by the social doctrine of the Church, and as such its economic objectives had to be compatible with the priority objectives of Christian social philosophy. In the famous papal bulls of 3 and 4 May 1493, by means of which Pope Alexander VI donated to the Crown of Castille the lands discovered or to be discovered in the Indies, the fundamental objective was that the aforementioned lands and islands, and their inhabitants and residents, would have to be civilized with the help of the divine clemency of the Catholic faith. This objective would be repeated and put into practice by the Catholic rulers and their successors in Spain, and would serve as a supreme guide for development plans in the Indies.

In the instructions dictated for the second voyage of Columbus, which began on 25 September 1493, it is ordered that

> Their Majesties desiring that the Holy Catholic Faith be increased and advanced, send and entrust the said Admiral . . . to treat very well and affectionately the said Indians, without enraging them whatsoever, procuring that much familiar conversation take place between the one and the others; making the best works possible.
>
> (Sierra 1944: 15ff)

Even clearer and more categorical is that this objective is circumscribed in the testament of Queen Isabel, in which she feels that the main goal for her successors should be the conquest of the Indies by means of Christian evangelization, since

> our principal intention was, at the time in which we entreated Pope Alexander VI as a reminder, that he made us the said concession of procuring the inducement and bringing to the people and converting the people to our Holy Catholic Faith, and sending to the said islands and lands, prelates and religious men, clergy and other persons devout and fearful of GOD, in order to instruct the neighbors and residents of them in the Catholic faith and to indoctrinate and teach them good manners, which accordingly are more largely contained in the letters of said concession.
>
> (Pereyra 1938: 208)

Despite the insistence of the Catholic Kings in innumerable instructions, orders, royal seals and provisions which led to the voluminous Recollections of the Laws of the Indies, what is certain is that the deficiencies of the missionary enterprise in the Americas were evident from the very beginning. Though the extremes reached by other imperial powers, such as the systematic extermination of the native population, were not practised by Spain, the quest for gold and the weakness in controlling the increasing alienation from the mother country resulted in unacceptable behaviour, as much among the colonists as among the agents of administration and even at times among the representatives of the Church delegates in the Indies.[1] Christopher Columbus was certainly not immune: his moral behaviour and administrative capacity deteriorated rapidly, and it was said that the Genoese was a calamity as a ruler and concurred in serious disturbances and legal offences.

It appears that the first protests which arrived at the Spanish court were written by Buil (today identified as 'Bernal Boyd, religious hermit, author of a Spanish-Aragonian book, vicar in Spain of San Francisco de Paula, and the first man who announced Christ and His law in the lands of America' (Sierra 1942: 22)) who clashed with Columbus and for this reason returned to

Spain. We know that Buil harshly censured the actions of Christopher Columbus, and his reflections contributed to the court intensifying its zeal for sending of more clerics and religious men to the Indies (Sierra 1942: 36). A protest sent from the Spanish colonies, in 1508, calls the attention of the Crown to the activities of certain immigrants which were injurious to the Christian objectives in the enterprise of the Indies, and requests the prohibition of the entrance of descendants of the infidels and heretics up to the fourth generation. The king's reaction was to provide supervision and control of the men coming to the Indies, including those belonging to religious orders.

Shortly afterwards, on Christmas Sunday 1511, there arose a vigorous protest against the exploitation of the Indians, pronounced by the Dominican Friar Antonio de Montesinos in a celebrated sermon, the text of which is reproduced in the *Historia de las Indias* (History of the Indies) of Bartolomé de Las Casas, who was eyewitness to this transcendental event in the cathedral of Santo Domingo. The thorny problem of the treatment of the Indians, which had been brought to the attention of the mother country since the beginning of the conquest, was set in this way. When, in 1495, Columbus tried to sell some natives he had sent to Spain as slaves, the Crown, after a brief hesitation, ordered the natives to be set free, arguing that they were vassals capable of adopting the Christian faith and as such could not be enslaved, nor treated as slaves. When, in 1499, Columbus arranged the distribution of 300 natives to the Spanish residents in the colonies, due to economic reasons, Queen Isabel had reacted, sending him a message: 'By what authority does the Admiral dispose of my vassals?' But Columbus' distributions, forerunners of the famous *encomiendas*, were finally confirmed by the Crown, assisted by the suggestions of governor Nicolás Ovando, who considered them 'a lesser evil' to the service of evangelization and the economic prosperity of the Indies. The royal order said in effect:

> Due to the great liberty that the said natives enjoy, they flee or move away from conversation and communication with the Christians, so that . . . they wish not to work or to lead a wandering life, and less can they be brought to learn the doctrines of our holy Christian faith . . . I order that you compel and oblige these said natives to deal with and talk with the Christians and work in their buildings, and collect and take out gold and other metals . . . paying them daily what you appraised: that which they do and comply by as free people, as they are, and not as serfs, and you make the natives to be well treated.
>
> (Hanke 1949: 29)

In this manner, the colonies, by taking advantage of the ingenuity and good faith of the Crown, gained the concealment of the almost unchecked exploitation and the de facto enslavement of the natives under the cloak of jurisprudential protection. Horrified by the daily acts of barbarity of his compatriots, Montesinos invited the upper crust of the colony of La Española to mass in the Cathedral of Santo Domingo, on which occasion he preached the historic sermon, written with the intention of horrifying the colonials. He stated:

> So as to let you know I am the voice of Christ in the desert of this island, and it is convenient that with all your attention you should all listen to what this voice has to say ... which will be the hardest, toughest and most dangerous voice you have ever heard. .... So that it is made known to you, all of you are living in mortal sin and you live and die in it, for the cruelty and tyranny which you use against these innocent people. Say, by what right and by what justice you maintain those innocents natives in such cruel and horrible servitude? By what authority have you carried out such horrible wars against these people who were meek and peaceful in their lands, where such an infinite number of them, by death and havoc never before heard of, you have consumed them? How can you keep them so oppressed and exhausted, without giving them food or healing them of their illnesses, that they incur from the excessive work you put upon them and they die for you, or better said, you kill them in order to remove and acquire gold everyday? ... Be sure that in the state in which you are, you cannot save more than the Moors or Turks who do not share and do not want our Holy faith.

> (Casas 1951: Book 3, Chapter 4)

The preaching of Montesinos, which was repeated the next Sunday even more passionately with the threat of not admitting the colonials any longer to confession, was received as a real scandal not only by the inhabitants and the Crown officials of La Española, but also in the royal court. Nevertheless, Montesinos was neither beheaded nor incarcerated; the court was satisfied with a simple reprimand and even this not so much for having spoken angrily against the colonials for the inhumane exploitation of the unprotected indigenous populations, but because it almost openly planted the question of the so called 'just titles'. On the other hand, the repercussions caused by the protests of Montesinos have been very profound and far reaching. In fact, through reprimanding Montesinos, Ferdinand the Catholic began to doubt the legitimacy of the titles that allowed the *encomiendas* and with these doubts arose one about the whole spirit of the conquest. Due to this, the question of the 'just titles' was made the order of the day, passing from government meeting to government meeting, with enormous repercussions in the colonies and Spain alike, and even spreading through all the courts of Europe, eventually leading to the new doctrine formulated by the Dominican Friar Francisco de Victoria of the University of Salamanca, by which not only was a forerunner of the Monroe Doctrine advanced, but implicitly the bases of international rights were elaborated (Victoria 1927; Barcia Trelles 1931).

84

However, more interesting are the repercussions which arise in the social and economic areas. In this case the dispute was also displaced from La Española towards the royal court, where the Dominicans and the conquerors sent their own defenders: Antonio de Montesinos and the Franciscan Alonso de Espinal, respectively. Even if we do not have any testimony as to the criterion maintained by Espinal, it is not difficult to get a sufficiently representative idea of the opinions maintained by the majority of the conquerors as regarded the natives. These opinions were moulded through two attitudes which at first glance seem contradictory: the heroism of the faith; and the heroism of profits. In the words of the chronicler Indias Bernal Díaz del Castillo, the Spaniards had arrived in the New World invoking that they did what they did 'to serve GOD and his majesty, and to give light to those in the darkness, and also to have riches' (Díaz del Castillo 1943: II, 394). This is more easily understood if one takes into account that many of the first colonists were merely ruined noblemen or licentious ex-soldiers dominated by their thirst for riches, and that the natives belonged to a cultural world which had a different set of values.

It should therefore not be surprising that these residents confronted the doctrine of Montesinos with their own doctrine which tended to view the natives as noble savages, according to which they were nothing more than hogs, lazy, given to vice, divorced from reason, incapable of understanding any doctrine and from whom no results from studying should be expected (Hanke 1949: 27, 59, 95). Montesinos had to face a collection of theologians and royal functionaries and a smattering of royal preachers, such as Bernardo de Mesa and Gregorio, who attempted to reinforce the thesis of the residents with allegations based on Aristotle which they extended to the natives, in order to establish that they were slaves due to their nature. Still, Montesino's vigorous defence managed to win favourable opinion on the Indians' side.

As a result of the more than twenty meetings of the royal assembly, a special commission published the famous Laws of Burgos, promulgated by the monarch on 27 December 1512, which constituted the first code of social legislation in the New World. Even if it were accepted that the natives were inclined to laziness and evil vices, therefore approving as 'fair' the system of *encomiendas*, the Laws of Burgos strictly prohibited those who lorded over this system to mistreat the natives: they should not be beaten or placed in chains or even insulted, and the lords were obliged to guarantee them humane labour conditions. Thus, it was prohibited to use the natives as beasts of burden, it was ordered that pregnant women be exempt from all types of work and it was determined that the natives who laboured in the search for gold would work a maximum of five months and have a mandatory rest period of forty days. The lords were obligated to build the natives adequate shelter, and to feed and clothe them in an adequate manner. In addition, they were obligated to build the natives churches and to indoctrinate them in the Christian faith. What is more, it was established that it was obligatory to teach at least one son, chosen from the most capable, to read and write, when the *encomienda* was made up of more than fifty natives. For the sons of any chief, older than 13, education was obligatory for four years, and thus they were given to the Franciscans in order that they remain with the order all this time and that they learn doctrine and how to read and write (Altamira y Crevea 1938a: 1–24; 1938b: 5–79). In this manner arose the first traces of the development of human capital formation in the New World.

And it was these educational measures from the Laws of Burgos which made up the starting point of a long line of famous centres for the education of the aboriginal people, founded and directed by the Franciscan fathers; for example, the Colegio de San Francisco founded in 1523 by Pedro de Gante as part of the same project as that in Mexico City, in which the children learned basic Spanish, religion, Latin and music, while the adults received classes in the arts and trades; also the Colegio Imperial de Santa Cruz, in the village of Tlatelolco, today a suburb of Mexico's capital city, founded in 1536 by the first bishop of Mexico, Juan de Zumárraga, and to which only the Indian nobility entered in order to

> learn Latin grammar, rhetoric, philosophy, music and Mexican medicine, so that they were teachers of the religious Spanish youth and taught them the language of the country, its history, its rites and customs; . . . secondary school from which the greater part of the higher classes of the Indian evangelists: the translators, amanuensis, typesetters and readers of the missionaries.
>
> (Pereyra 1930: 142)

The clamour for social justice launched by Antonio de Montesinos found a fervent follower in Bartolomé de Las Casas, a young man with a degree in law from the University of Salamanca. Las Casas had arrived to the New World in 1502 to dedicate himself, like all the adventurers who came to the Indies, to trading in slaves for the mines, and the farms of Indian settlements for rural exploitation. Although he had taken the sacred vows in 1510, the preaching of Montesinos left him as uninterested as it did all the other bosses of the *encomiendas* who heard it. What is more, a year later we find him participating in the conquest of Cuba and receiving as a reward new lands and natives as an *encomienda*. But his reaction, albeit slow, reached the point that in 1514, after examining his conscience, he resolved to abandon his prosperous dealings, set free the natives under his *encomienda* and place himself in the rank and file of those who defended the rights of the natives. As a simple clergyman, as a Dominican friar from 1522, and finally as bishop of Chiapas in New Spain from 1545, Bartolomé de Las Casas would make himself, by his writings and his vehement and untiring action, a champion of the social question in the Indies.

An apostate of half a century, undertaking a marvelous activity, with the resources of a voluminous theological knowledge, with the weapons of a dialectic firmness and with the fortification of an admirable heroism, makes of Las Casas one of the highest summits of human history. His work transcended from America to Spain, and from Spain to the entire world.

(Pereyra 1930: 297)

Unfortunately, his activity has been exploited in France and the United Kingdom as an instrument of anti-Spanish propaganda, due to which there arose in the past century and the beginning of the current century a reaction in Spain, condemning Las Casas to the point of viewing him as an enemy of the fatherland. But lately it is noteworthy that there has been a resurgence of positive criticism of his work, it being correctly argued that his doctrine 'was not of national, but human content, deeply religious in its origin and social in its projections' (Pereyra 1930: 299).

Completely convinced that the *encomienda* system had transformed itself into an instrument of enslavement and exploitation of the natives, Las Casas in 1515 sailed to Spain together with Montesinos to begin the battle of his life for the abolition of the *encomiendas* and for their substitution by an economic system compatible with the goals of evangelizing the natives. Beginning from this moment, he would elaborate an entire series of projects which he presented to the royal court, accompanied with calculations of cost and sometimes including the incomes which would enter into the royal treasury, if his plans were put into action. Thus, in a project in 1517 presented to the king by various religious figures, evidently including among them Las Casas, a policy of systematic colonization and integration of the Indians with Spanish settlers was advocated. These colonies would consist of forty farmers accompanied by their wives and children for every town to be founded, so as to serve as a dynamic element (could this be the antecedent of the big push of Rosenstein-Rodan?) for the Indian population which would be united as the integrating elements of the new towns. The Indians would not be given to the Spaniards as such, but would be reunited in communities in every town in which they would be common possessions.

The responsibility for the evangelization and the economic and social development of the Indian communities would fall upon the entire Spanish community, provided with a wide administrative apparatus consisting of religious figures, teachers, doctors, artisans, etc., whose cost was estimated to be 6,600 *castellanos* per year. The construction of schools, churches, and particularly of hospitals in the shape of a cross, with an altar in the centre, was foreseen for every town, each one of the works accompanied with its expense budget. With the objective of stimulating the cohesion of the Spanish colonists with the natives, it was equally foreseen that each Spaniard should be given five Indians, with their families, to live under his tutelage,

87

working and sharing the fruits of their efforts and the destiny of this new life and in this manner laying the foundations of a new society in the New World.

> And so, shall multiply the land of people and fruits . . . and all Your Majesty will be served, and its incomes will grow and will be increased, and the islands made noble, and as a consequence, the best and the richest of the world.
>
> (Hanke 1949: 161)

This idea of colonization by farmers reappears in 1518, this time signed by Las Casas, to whom is added the title of 'procurer of the Indians'. While in the Memorial of 1517 he is limited to emphasizing that he wants the Spaniards who come as farmers to be people who had never been in the Indies before, in the 1518 project, following a suggestion of Pedro de Cordoba, the releigious provincial leader of the Dominicans in Spanish America, Las Casas demands the reservation of lands for the new colonies far out of reach of the conquerors, so that the friars can preach the faith without any type of interference.

He proposes that he be given the concession of 1,000 leagues of land on the northern coast of Colombia and Venezuela, where he will found ten forti-fied towns, 100 leagues apart, proposing to colonize each one of them with 100 Christian farmers, ruled by a captain, and supervised by Dominican and Franciscan friars and a bishop. When faced with the problem of counting on skilled farmers, he suggests the stimulation of the recruitment by means of promises of good lands, reduced tributes and awards for those who dedicate themselves to the cultivation of silk, pepper, cloves, ginger, wine and wheat, and in addition, great ease of credits and special permissions to introduce twenty black men to work in the sugar industry, widening the possibilities of recruitment of workers to beyond Spain.

In a 1519 project, Las Casas conceived the idea of forming a new order of gentlemen, 'The Knights of the Golden Spur', whose members, to number fifty, provided with white habits, marked on the chest with a red cross (to differentiate them from the other Spaniards in the eyes of the Indians), would be in charge of the colonization of the Indies. The favourable system would not only carry out the goals of peaceful evangelization of the Indians, and by this comply with the objective of a socially just order, overcoming the difficult problem of the exploitation of the natives, but in addition and as a consequence of complying with the goals of social and spiritual develop-ment, it would guarantee a simultaneous growth of the economic activities in the Indies, bringing with it increasing revenues for the Crown's treasury.

Anticipating by many centuries the projects of modern development, Las Casas made an estimation of the progress of his plans for ten years in advance, foreseeing that in the first year, from the moment his plan of colo-nization is put into practice, the Indians would be pacified in the entire given area; in the second year, there would be a guarantee of 10,000 Indians paying tributes; in the third year, guaranteeing a sure level of income for the royal treasury, estimated at 15,000 ducats that was to be maintained during the fourth year; in the fifth year, the level of income would have reached 30,000 ducats, the same amount as for the sixth, seventh, eighth and ninth years of the plan, so that finally, from with the tenth year, the royal rent would be 60,000 ducats annually.

Despite the enormous difficulties that arose at every step of his path, Las Casas managed to overcome one after another the resistances of the court in favour of his plan for colonization with Christian farmers. A royal order of 10 September 1518 provided a series of advantages for the emigrant farmers, such as free journeys from their homes in Spain to the New World, free lands, animals, seeds and medicines and all that was necessary for their subsistence until the first harvest, tributary exemption for twenty years and awards for the workers in the ways shown by Las Casas. Another royal order of 20 September 1518 authorized Las Casas to establish towns of free Indians and finally on 19 May 1520 the king made the concession of some 260 leagues of land in the New World to colonize a coastal zone from the province of Paria (now in Venezuela) to the province of Santa Marta (Colombia), with extensive rights all the way to the Straits of Magellan, with the obligation of founding within the next five years three Christian towns with their respective fortifications and all the rest of the obligations foreseen by Las Casas in his propositions of 1519, the Spanish Crown committing itself to place at his disposal twelve religious men of the orders of San Francisco or Santo Domingo, plus fifty men of Las Casas' choice, those who

> we must arm them and we arm the Knights of the Golden Spur, so that they and their descendants be Knights of the Golden Spur of our kingdoms, to whom we shall give and assign arms so that they and their descendants bring with them their emblems and shields and armour decorated with their coat of arms forever.
>
> (Quintana 1914: II, 419)

As is well known, Las Casas' development plan ended up as a total failure. Despite his specific virtues and the fact that he enjoyed the support and patronage of the Spanish Crown, the greediness of the conquerors and the extraordinarily attractive power of the gold and silver mines of Perú proved to be much stronger, as even the very 'Knights of the Golden Spur' brought in by Las Casas to direct the agricultural and industrial exploitation of the Indies could not resist the temptations of greed and wealth. Human nature continued along the path of least effort.

Deeply depressed, Las Casas took the habit of the Order of Preachers and retired to a monastery near Port au Prince in La Española for almost a decade. But his idea of development brought on by the systematic colonization of the Indians by Spanish farmers, and to which he returns with a new plan in 1533, will find fertile ground much later, when the greed for gold has been reduced, after three and a half centuries of oversight. His shining knight will be Juan Bautista Alberdi, who, without knowing of his predecessor, will formulate the famous phrase that 'in America increasing the population is to extend welfare 'in America to govern is to populate' (Alberdi 1921: 114).

Overall, the failure of the colonization plan allowed Las Casas to learn the great lesson that while he could not count on favourable circumstances and colonists with sufficient spiritual fortitude to resist the attractive magnet of the exploitation of the Indians instead of the exploitation of the lands, the work of developing the native communities could only feasibly be carried out by peaceful means if the work were entrusted to religious men, and even in this case, only to carefully selected religious men.

The idea was not new, as it had been applied even before the time of Christ by the saint of India, Asoka, and in the time of Las Casas it had been applied with success by a Franciscan monk, Jacobo de Testera, who managed to pacify the Indians of Champoton in the Yucatan in 1533. Still, the merit of Las Casas consists in having laid the doctrinal foundations of this idea which he put forth in a voluminous writing entitled *Del único modo de atraer a todos los pueblos a la verdadera religión* (Of the only means of attracting all peoples to the one true religion), written in Guatemala in 1536–7, of which only Chapters 5, 6 and 7 of the first book have been discovered to date.[2]

Utilizing methods of scholastic argument, Las Casas attempts to show that peaceful evangelism has priority before all other political objectives and that its success depends upon the spiritual fortitude of the missionaries. Even if he restates the necessity of counting on reserved areas, completely isolated from the traffic of the conquerors, so that the missionaries may dedicate themselves calmly to the conversion of the Indians to Christianity, Las Casas centres his preoccupation on the quality of the missionaries. Preaching is a difficult art which must be systematically studied. Of course, the missionaries must possess a solid theological background, just as it is an imperative requirement that they possess moral tidiness and total lack of interest in wealth or personal matters, but the fundamental necessity is to know how to preach, that is, to know how to persuade in a persistent and convincing manner, both by his words and by the exemplary life a missionary should lead.

Faced with the mockery of his treatise by the Spanish residents of Santiago de Guatemala when he presented it as a sermon from the pulpit, Las Casas decided to put his ideas to the test. Accompanied by a group of Dominican friars, he went into the province of Tuzutlán, inhabited by Indians so cruel and fierce that the conquerors called the area the 'War Land', and within the period between 1537 and 1539, these Indians were in settlements and Christianized.

This rousing success of Las Casas produced a loud impact not only among the conquerors, but also in the royal court, and among its immediate effects was the creation of the New Laws in 1542, which although in effect for a very short time, mark the culminating point in the struggle against the *encomienda* system. The settling of the Indians of the province of Tuzutlán, whose name was officially changed to 'Land of the True Peace' after the success of Las Casas, persisted for some fifteen years, and was followed by many other similar experiments like that of Marcos de Niza in Tuliacán (Mexico), Hernando de Arbolancha in Amatlán (Guatemala), Armenta and Lebron in Santa Catalina (Brazil), etc. (Cuevas 1921–8; Sierra 1942: 135; Hanke 1949: 202).

These initial experiments served as raw material to widen and deepen the knowledge of what the missionary doctrines in the Indies would be made up of, all beginning with *Del único modo* by Las Casas, and displayed in works on the theory and practice of the missions in America, which were progressively more complete and systematic. This would all lead up to other more successful and longer lasting experiments, among them the 'hospitals' in Mexico and the Jesuit settlements in the Paraguay region.

The 'hospital towns' of Mexico are the fruit of the singular effort of Vasco de Quiroga, jurist at Vasta Cultura and Bishop of Michoacán. A graduate in canonical law from Spain, where he later worked as a magistrate in the Court of Valladolid, Vasco de Quiroga went to Mexico in 1530 in the position of magistrate to the Second Court of Mexico. Although he belonged neither to the secular nor regular clergy, Vasco de Quiroga possessed a religious and charitable temperament, and was deeply disturbed by the sad situation which resulted from the confrontation between the conquerors, cruel and thirsting for gold, and the defenceless Indian society, whose simplicity and humility reminded him of the way in which the apostles lived, barefoot, long haired, their heads uncovered.

Encouraged, no doubt, by the Archbishop of Mexico, the Franciscan friar Juan de Zumárraga, whose friendship and trust he enjoyed from the first, Quiroga resolved to elaborate a plan of economic and social organization very similar to the one proposed by Las Casas. The solution would consist of founding in every territory towns in which the natives, under the tutelage of the friars, would be settled into agricultural communities:

> where working and breaking the land, by their work maintaining themselves and being methodical in their order, with all in good order by the police and with saintly and good and Catholic ordinances; where there would be a house of friars, small and with little expense, for two or three or four friars, which would not be at hand for them until a time after they make the habit of virtue and they convert themselves to the naturalness.
>
> (Zavala 1941: 45)

In this manner, it would end, with the help of God 'by putting and planting a type of genuine Christians, as a primitive church, since GOD is as powerful now as then in making all that be in His service or was in conformity with His will' (Zavala 1941: 45).

The following year, Quiroga expanded his opinions in a *Parecer* (Opinion), sent to the Spanish queen on 5 July 1532, which to date still has not been found. From the allusions that he makes to this work in his later writings, we can state that it was on this occasion that he expressly mentions the *Utopia* of Thomas More,[3] which he had read in the personal library of Archbishop Juan de Zumárraga, and whose opinions he accepts immediately and incorporates as the backbone of his own thoughts. Actually, in his third piece of writing, the long and interesting *Información en Derecho* (Information on Laws) elaborated on 4 July 1535, in which he completes and recasts his earlier projects, Vasco de Quiroga reiterates his ideas that he took 'as a model the work of Thomas More, illustrious gentleman and of more human ingenuity' (Zavala 1937: 56). Quiroga also read the narrative of Luciano about the Saturnalia,[4] translated by Erasmus and More, in which the thesis of the Golden Age of humanity and the pre-Rousseaunian theory of the noble savage are defended, and these ideas are referred to in his plan of 1531. It is at this point that Quiroga's doctrine reaches its methodological peak.

As a faithful adherent of the Christian humanism of the Renaissance, Quiroga is very concerned with the social question just as was Las Casas. However, while Las Casas is hopeful as regards the fruitful transplantation of the European socio-economic order, Quiroga doubted the solutions of the Old World's model – which possessed a culture labelled 'grown old and shaken by the evils proper of the Iron Age in which it had fallen' – and turned his sight to the Golden Age, filled with humane love and virtue, social justice and moderation, which he finds as the perfect model for the New World. If this model could be seen as chaotic for the European nations, it was not so for the innocent, generous and simple societies of the New World. The one problem was to lead the Indians from their natural simplicity to the goals of primitive Christianity, thus avoiding the distortions in which the European Christian society had concurred. Therefore, to reach an adequate level of socio-economic welfare and of ideal political order in temporal matters which was needed to guarantee the evangelization and institutions of the Catholic order in spiritual matters, it would be necessary to guide the cultural life of the American peoples towards the path of More's ideal republic.

In order to achieve a utopian republic for the peoples of the Americas, Quiroga proposed the installation of More's political, economic, and social order in the Indies, indicating step by step the principal measures; the distribution of the cities, the corporative organization of the families, the gravitation towards agriculture, complemented with craft activities, the institution of collective ownership of the goods of production, the elimination of currency from the national traffic, the equitable distribution of production, the limiting of labour to six hours a day, and intensive and growing spiritual activity, especially of a religious nature.[5]

The inventory of Quiroga's ideas would not be complete without mentioning two other later writings: the *Reglas y Ordenanzas* (Rules and Ordinances) for the governing of the 'hospital towns of Santa Fé', written at a date yet to be established; and the *Testamento* (Testament) of 1565. In this way, the unbreakable faith and persistence of the Mexican humanist in his ideas is shown. But the specific message of these two final writings is constituted by his empiricist viewpoint, since the objective pursued in these works was to serve as a guide for the setting in motion and the administration of the plans of organization and social development.

Actually, Quiroga undertakes almost simultaneously and with equal success the role of reformist doctrinal writer and social engineer. Before the prolonged silence of the royal court, he resolved in 1532 to put into practice his ideas. Digging into his own savings, he bought some lands near Mexico City, on which he established a first village for Indians. A year later, while travelling as an official visitor, he established his second school in the province of Michoacán.

The success of these first two 'hospital towns of Santa Fé' earned the speedy recognition of the Council of the Indies, who proposed to King Carlos V that Quiroga be named as Bishop of Michoacán, because he has

> very good life and exemplary relations, and because he has been and is very inclined to the conversion and good treatment of the Indians and their instruction in the matters of our Holy faith, in which he has spent a large part of the salary Your Majesty has sent him; it appears to the council that it would be very providential to name him as Bishop.
>
> (Zavala 1941: 42)

Promoted to the prelacy in 1537, Quiroga intensified his zeal and proceeded to establish an entire series of 'hospital towns' in the diocese. It was for these human nuclei that the pious reformer elaborated his *Reglas y Ordenanzas*, mentioned above, in which he repeats the fundamental principles of More, not forgetting to adapt them to local circumstances and specific goals in the crusade for the evangelization of the Indies. The backbone of the new social order is the principle of the community of goods, but real estate earnings are in certain cases and under certain rules private, and even hereditary. There are private plots of land in which the peasants and the urban folk have their specific crops, but the large agricultural tracts are held in common.

Political organization was in the hands of the Indian magistrates, but at the head of the 'hospital towns 'was always a Spaniard (in the *Parecer* and in the *Información en Derecho* this involves a Spanish magistrate appointed and under the control of the court, while in the *Reglas y Ordenanzas*, this principal position is held by the rector, a supreme chief who should always be a

93

Spanish priest). Slavery is totally abolished and the supreme objective of the towns is the evangelization and welfare of the Indians. But in all other aspects there are no variations from More: the social structure remains established around the widened family nucleus; the biennial rotation between rural and urban folk continues; the agricultural sector persists as the fundamental economic activity and as such is obligatory for men and women alike, with a complementary dedication to certain crafts; the work day is ratified as consisting of six hours; there is equitable distribution of the social product based on need; and the creation of a chain of local institutions, from the infirmaries, the temples, and the schools, to the dispensaries, public general stores, and the coffers of the social treasury (Zavala 1937: 7–15; Reyes 1942: 162).

The social experiment was much more successful than that of Las Casas. After nearly thirty years of jealous supervision, Quiroga demonstrates in his *Testamento* the satisfaction with the fruit harvested and upon referring to the compliance with the *Reglas y Ordenanzas*, he pleads for it to continue onward and that 'it should not give up in anything' (León 1903: 100).

It appears that the 'hospital towns' survived their zealous founder. According to Moreno's *Vida de Vasco Quiroga*, the 'hospital towns' lasted until the eighteenth century and the Indians of Michoacán held in great veneration the name 'Tata Vasco' even during the nineteenth century (Moreno 1939; Reyes 1942: 162).

Still greater veneration was given to Quiroga in the cultural circles of Mexico. Praising his extraordinary success, Lombardo Toledano suggests that this model of social organization should become the pilot for contemporary Mexican social development, before searching through foreign doctrines and experiences; and he continues, stating: 'Only the lack of preparation of the directors of public education can justify, truthfully, the oblivion of the only Mexican experiment of schools for our Indians' (Lombardo Toledano 1924: 19). The ancient Valladolid of Michoacán, which transformed its name to Morelia, in the desire to perpetuate the memory of this great spirit, founded a university which carries his name, the Vasco de Quiroga University. It is that what is actually

> amazing about Vasco is the radical nature of the eagerness and the security of his carrying things out; such a wide feeling of the ideal and so sharp of what is real: a rare consortium of virtues that usually do not go along together.
>
> (Junco 1940: 101)

Vasco Quiroga, like Las Casas, was convinced that the secret of success for his plans of reform were above all dependent upon the qualities of their direct collaborators. The government sending religious men to direct the communities was a great step, but certainly not the whole solution, since what was necessary was a special category of religious men, like themselves;

more than contemplative, combative; more than monks, warriors of the faith disposed to fight everywhere and in any order. But such elements were not only very scarce in the New World, but in Europe itself. It was precisely with the end of raising a militia of religious men with a pure missionary sense, to which men of mediocre calibre could never be accepted, that the Society of Jesus arose, founded in 1534 by Ignacio de Loyola (1491–1566). Actually, the Jesuit order arose as an army of missionaries which from the first moment had to distinguish itself from all the other religious orders.[6] It should then come as no surprise that the first call for Jesuit missionaries for the Americas was made by Vasco de Quiroga and his agent the Canon Negrón (Cuevas 1921–8: 68, 80, 21).

But destiny decided things in a different way. The first Jesuit expeditions were directed to the Indias in 1541, to Japan in 1546, and to the Congo in 1547. After their first experiences in Asia and Africa, the Jesuits began missionary work in Brazil in 1549, and in the no smaller area of the Viceroyalty of Perú in 1567. Over time, they would extend to Mexico, California, New Mexico, the Philippines, Canada, Alaska, but the gravitational centre of their activities was in South America and above all else, the well known Jesuit province of Paraguay,[7] founded in 1604 by order of the General of the Order, Claudio Aquaviva, and organized and put in progress by Diego de Torres Bello, 'one of the most noted superiors which the Order has had in South America, director of almost all the colleges of Perú, founder and first provincial of the Jesuit provinces of the New Kingdom of Granada and Paraguay' (Furlong 1962: 28).

Even more, there are those who believe that the Jesuits had been inspired, like Quiroga, in their projects of social organization by Thomas More. But when dealing with this matter, other models soon come to the surface and have been widely advanced by scholars. So, Gothein considers the *Civitas Solis* model of Campanella to be more adequate (Gothein 1885). Espinosa, surely influenced by the work *La República de Platón y los Guaraníes* of the Jesuit José M. Peramás, placed more faith in the ideal state model of Plato (Espinosa 1935). Cunninghame Graham opts for the model of *Arcadia* by Philip Sidney (Cunninghame Graham 1901). And the instances in which a parallelism between the *New Atlantis* of Francis Bacon and the *Telemaque* of Fenelon has been found are many. Neither has there been a lack of attempts to find a parallelism with the Incan model, like the works of Abate Raynal in 1771, repeated in 1874 by the author of a memorial presented at the Academy of Dijon, and in 1934 by V. Buffo Della Scaletta, and supported by the authority of Louis Baudin (1962). There is no doubt that the Jesuits knew about all these models, if one remembers the high level of their preparation and their rich libraries, and it is possible that they assimilated one or another idea into their projects (Furlong 1946: 186). But to start from this point and arrive at the supposition that the Jesuits framed their ideology upon these singular moulds at a time when the cultural horizon of their epoch was crowded with sources of direct, immediate and royalist inspiration, would be evidently a proof of historical blindness.

We should ponder also the ideas scattered among the Papal Bulls of Pope Alexander VI, in the testament of Queen Isabel, and in the innumerable royal seals which successively came to swell the volume of the Laws of Burgos, the New Laws which would finally end up, much later, in the *Código de la Gobernación Espiritual de las Indias* (Legal Code for the Spiritual Governance of the Indies), compiled in 1571 by Juan de Ovando, president of the Council of the Indies. It must likewise be pondered, in equal measure, the valuable individual experiences collected by the members of the other religious orders and secular clergy in the same American territories, like those of Las Casas, Vasco de Quiroga, Pedro de Gantes, Luis de Bolaños, and many others.

Besides these writers we have Jean Foucher, Diego de Valadés, José Acosta or Tomás Díaz Dávila, and the Constitutions of the Jesuits, approved by Pope Paul IV in 1540, in which fundamental principles related as much to the form and organization of the missionary work as to its own substance are established. In this final order of ideas, it is apposite to remember the principle established by Ignacio de Loyola, that even if the final objective of all missions is evangelization, its basic requirement is the fostering of economic and social progress, and as such its most powerful instrument is education in all its dimensions: spiritual and secular; rural and industrial; primary, secondary, and university (Granero 1930: 7–8; Sierra 1942: 23). One must not forget that the simple ideas expressed in these Constitutions later took on a more scholarly look in subsequent works by the Jesuits.

For example, let us look at how the principle of education blossomed into a fundamental instrument of the Jesuit missions.

Diego de Borda, missionary in Goa, was, according to Granero, the father of the idea which over time would yield great results. That illustrious clergyman considered the convenience of a school, where children selected from diverse provinces prepared themselves in the Christian doctrine and the necessary knowledge, in order to later be the fine yeast which would improve, by their actions and their example, the towns from which they had left. The school was built . . . and was such a success for the order that Ignacio de Loyola understood the necessity to multiply the numbers of such schools. From Africa, the idea passed to Brazil, and from the schools of primary instruction it went on to departments of humanity. In this manner was finalized, by the dominion of experience, the realization of one of the most expensive ideas of the founder of the company of Jesus. The school, the studies of humanities, the superior education, the technical training in the mechanical and manual arts, recommended and urged

by Ignacio de Loyola . . . by the conviction that in order to maintain
the faith, it was necessary to also educate the generations in its virtues
(Sierra 1942: 122)

Anticipating by centuries the empirical social research, the Jesuits created
true pilot projects of experimentation and training, in order to proceed later
to large-scale applications. This was the principal role of the order's first
major universities of Bahía in Brazil and Lima in Perú. A similar role was
undertaken by the first towns founded by the Brazilian Jesuits and especially
in the Indian settlement of Juli, located on the edge of Lake Titicaca, where
the Peruvian Jesuits led the first missionary experiment in evangelism and
economic and social organization of the Indians of the Andean tableland. It
was in the Indian settlement of Juli (Hernández 1913: I, 432–6) that Diego
de Torres Bello was trained for years; he later initiated the great work among
the Guaranís of the Paraguayan territory in 1607, a model which would later
serve as a guide for the foundation of other sets of Indian settlements: in the
eastern grasslands of Colombia in 1626; in the high plains and valleys of the
Amazon and Marañon rivers in Ecuador and the north of Perú in 1637; in
the grasslands of the Chiquitos in the southeastern sector of Bolivia in 1692;
in the grasslands of the Mojos in the northeast of Bolivia in 1700, etc.
(Furlong 1962: 116).[8]

But the originality of the Jesuits is due also to their administrative
genius. The missionary teams, carefully selected, well prepared and trained,
vigorous in both the moral and physical senses, disciplined and obedient,
made up the driving element of a continuous and efficient hierarchical structure, 'of such a style that all was geared toward perfection, and upon moving
a wheel, all the rest was put into motion' (Furlong 1962: 185).

True masters of the tasks we now call 'technical assistance for underdeveloped peoples', the Jesuits knew to integrate their teams over a wide
inter-disciplinary and international base. Under the religious habit of the
order were hidden skilled technicians in the most distinct specialities:
educators and psychologists; engineers and architects; metal workers and
agriculturists; artisans of many different trades; doctors and pharmacists;
and even painters and sculptors. No less balanced was the composition by
nationalities of the missionary teams in the Indies: Frenchmen, Italians
and Englishmen, and especially Germans abounded, besides native
Spaniards and Portuguese (Furlong 1946). This operation could today be
compared with the technical missions sent by the United Nations to
Latin America. The Jesuits in 1748 numbered 1,913 men in service in
South America alone. Faced with the metaphysical nature of the
Franciscan missionaries and the critical disposition of the Dominicans, the
Jesuit missionaries, without diminishing the importance of the holiness of
some and the scientific abilities of others, stood out because of their prac-
ticality, of a kind that had not been seen before in the enterprises of

spiritual or secular development of the people of underdeveloped nations (Furlong 1946: 308).

Cultured men, coming from the most advanced university centres of Europe, the Jesuits in the Americas could not avoid the attraction of exploring and studying the phenomena of the new lands. From their laborious and patient hands came hundreds of manuscripts, the majority today still covered in dust in files, if not lost forever. An extremely rich fortune of voluminous monographs in the areas of geography, history, ethnography and linguistics, and in the fields of flora, fauna, and the mineral wealth of the Americas, became a testimony, not only to the intrinsic value of the Jesuit contributions in the areas of the sciences and the arts, but to the fact that these works all contributed to the structure of a first approximation of an inventory of the human and natural resources in the New World.[9]

But their greatest desire was concentrated in the formation of the elite class of the New World and on the fostering of cultural, economic and social development for the great mass of the Indians.

The impact produced by the Jesuit schools on the natives has no precedent. In Portuguese America, their influence has been decisive since the early days in the effective colonization of the country, maintaining their educational monopoly throughout the colonial period, with its echo lasting until today. This influence is so strong, that historians say one must first write a history of the Jesuits before daring to write on the history of the Indians or on the culture of Brazil.

Although in Spanish America there had already been a relative tradition in the education of the native elite, fed by the university and school centres of the Dominicans and the Franciscans,[10] the impact produced by the Jesuit schools was equally powerful (Abecia 1939: 171; Barreda Laos 1955: 95). Directors' positions were reached by their major universities in Mexico, Lima and Sao Paulo,[11] and soon thereafter were followed by the famous universities, San Ignacio de Loyola in Cordoba (Argentina), San Francisco Xavier de Chuquisaca (today Sucre, Bolivia) and the Xaverian university in Bogotá, Colombia.[12]

> The Jesuits assumed the role of directors of the conscience of the selected classes and the instructors of the youth belonging to those same classes. From that moment, the Fathers of the Order had within their hands the highest attributions of moral power in the new societies. There was no cause which laboured with such efficiency for the separation of the provinces on the other side of the high seas as did the expulsion of the Jesuits.
>
> (Pereyra 1930: 143)

The Jesuits' efforts toward the peaceful civilization of the Indians culminated in the foundation of a vast belt of settlements from California to the Argentinian Pampas, progressing slowly but surely from the state of tribes who in many cases were gatherers or nomadic hunters, until, at the end of 150 years, they attained the level of prosperous and educated communities which were at the same social and economic levels as many medieval European towns.

This was indeed the case with the group of thirty Guaraní towns, known collectively under the name of the Settlements of Paraguay. This group, with its centre in today's Argentinian province of Misiones, extended its prosperous settlements over a quadrilateral area whose sides, covering parts of Brazil and Paraguay, were 650 kilometers from north to south, and 600 kilometers from east to west. Although the majority of the settlements were more like hamlets, some achieved urbanized status.

Each settlement formed an independent economic unit with a Jesuit priest in charge, but with the assistance of a group of Indian collaborators. Among the settlements there was an intensive economic and social traffic, such that the settlements took on the appearance of a national economy, with its central focus in Candelaria, the seat of the father superior of the settlements.

The economic life was based partially on private family exploitation and partially on collective exploitation of just one town or even of many, such as was the case with the cattle breeding cooperatives. In the missionary economy, there was a strong solidarist and supportive spirit. The traditionalist mentality of the Indians found a strong antidote in the rationalist spirit spread by word of mouth and by the deeds of the Jesuits. It dealt with an economic order with a central administration of an aristocratic nature, and with an agricultural and cattle breeding economic constitution, yet with a substantial artisan base. In each settlement, almost next to the church, were the yards of the workshops in which the Indians exercised their specific trades. Even the fathers themselves were surprised at the craft abilities of the Indians. The education of these Indians formed a substantial part of the programme of activities, making schools and libraries available in each town, and the number of Indians attending school was more than satisfactory (Popescu 1952: 121–5).

In general the Jesuit settlements had reached a high level of economic, social and cultural development, surpassing even the Spanish centres in the Americas. The population increased rapidly, as the Paraguayan Indian settlements went from 28,000 in 1647 to 141,000 by 1732. In these times, the population of these settlements was greater than the civilian governed areas of the Río de La Plata, Paraguay and Tucumán combined. If to the numerical superiority, the organization, the discipline, the technology and the relative abundance of capable and willing teachers are added, it is not difficult to deduce what the missionary culture would have been (Furlong 1946: 229).

Beginning in 1733, a sharp drop in the population figures of the Guaraní settlements is observed. The crisis originated in part for exogenous reasons, especially due to the viral epidemics which ravaged the settlements for many years, but simultaneously for a noted relaxation in the religious fervour of the Jesuits, this relaxation being too noticeable for true historians to ignore. But an energetic intervention on the part of the general of the order put an end to the crisis. Beginning in 1739, when the population had reached 74,000 souls, the recovery began slowly until the population figure reached 100,000 souls by 1768, on the eve of the Jesuits' expulsion from all the Americas.[13]

With the expulsion of the Jesuits, Spanish America, at a time when it had only a fistful of capable men available, lost in one blow a total of 2,158 experienced and skilled technicians: 562 Mexican Jesuits; 201 Colombians; 229 Ecuadorians; 413 Peruvians; 316 Chileans; and 437 Jesuits in Argentina (Furlong 1942: 272).

> The expulsion of the order was one of the most insensitive acts of which a Spanish government could be held responsible, as on the one hand it alienated the good will of the superior classes and it surrendered to the dangerous temptation of a frivolous imitation, and on the other hand, it drowned the entire area in a pool of savagery on a continent that just began to see the results of a secular action.
>
> (Pereyra 1930: 144)

The disintegration of the Guaraní settlements continued, and today all that remains of them are the ruins of churches and their famous workshops.

But the scholar interested in the problems of people undergoing development would find it worthwhile, nevertheless, to emphasize that despite the disintegration of the secular work of the Jesuits in the Americas, their work cannot be considered as a failure. And this for the simple reason, as Louis Baudin so rightly observed: '*les réductions n'ont pas decliné, elles ne sont pas mortes, elles ont été tuées*' or, roughly translated, 'the settlements have not declined, they have not died, they have been destroyed' (Baudin 1962: 51).

The most serious aspect was that they were destroyed prematurely for, as many scholars have observed, this experience

> has been too brief to be decisive, yet this does not neglect it being the sole persistent effort, for nearly two centuries, of western men dedicated to civilize the savage, so as to lead them step by step to the notion of the dignity of work.
>
> (Capitan and Lorin 1948: 342)

Even a Marxist, José Mariátegui, admits the advantages of this attempt:

> Only the Jesuits with their organic positivism, showed in Perú as in other American lands capabilities for economic creation. The large fields given to them were fruitful. The vestiges of their organization remain as a lasting print. Whoever remembers the vast experiment of

the Jesuits in Paraguay, where they usefully exploited the tendency of the Indians towards communism, cannot be absolutely surprised that this congregation of sons of San Iñigo de Loyola as Unamuno calls them, were capable of creating upon Peruvian soil the work and production centers that the nobles, doctors and clergymen wrapped in an easy life in Lima never cared to create.

(Mariátegui 1957: 11)

7

CAMERALISM IN GASPAR DE ESCALONA Y AGÜERO

There is no certainty as to the birthplace of Escalona. In various biographical dictionaries, authors such as Mendiburu, Alcedo y Ceballos write that he was a native of Riobamba in Ecuador, while Echave remembers him as being a native of Lima. Nevertheless, Mariano Moreno, Valentín Abecia and finally, León M. Loza maintain that he was born in Bolivia. The arguments of this latter group of authors appear to be convincing. Actually, on the cover of Escalona's book, it is indicated in Latin that he was an 'Argentinian Peruvian', which, directly translated into Spanish, means that he was a native of the city of La Plata in Perú. This thesis is confirmed by the concession of the right to print the work, given by King Felipe IV on 7 July 1647, in which it says: 'For as much by your part the Licentiate D. Gaspar Escalona y Agüero, native of the provinces of Peru, lawyer before our royal audience of the city of Lima . . .'. It seems the most correct version is the one given by José Toribio Medina (1852–1930) and accepted by León M. Loza:

> Gaspar Escalona y Agüero, son of the licentiate of the same name, native of Riobamba, who was magistrate of Potosí and lawyer of the prisoners of the Holy See of Peru, and of Isidora de la Torre, born in Chuquisaca [La Plata, today Sucre, in Bolivia], and after having completed his studies in Lima, where he was a schoolmate of the famous León Pinelo, undertook the positions of magistrate of the province of Tarija, governor of Castro-Virreina, attorney general of Cuzco and inspector of the royal coffers, going later to Chile as a magistrate, a position to which he was appointed 9 May 1649, and which he exercised for a very short time, as he died 21 January 1650. He was married to Elvira Tello de Guzmán.
>
> (Escalona y Agüero 1941: xii–xvii)

Escalona wrote various works: *El Gazofilacio Real del Perú*, *El Oficio del Virrey*, and *Apelaciones en Derecho de los Virroyos a la Audiencia*. The last work was seen by León Pinelo (d. 1660), but has since disappeared. As regards *El Oficio del*

Virrey, it only dealt with a manuscript, which according to appearances, even if it had been seen by León Pinelo, was never printed.

The only work which can be found today is *Gazophylacium Peruvian Kingdom*, in English, which Gaspar de Escalona y Agüero titled in Latin as *Gazophilacium Regium Perubicum. Opus sane pulcrum, a plerisque petitum & ab omnibus, in universum, desideratum non sine magno labore, & experientia digestum, provideque, & accurate illustratum. In quo omnes materiae spectantes ad administrationem, calculationem, & conservationem jurium regalium Regni Peruani latissimé discutiuntur, & plena manu pertractantur.* The work was published in 1647 in Madrid, in two parts which dealt with preliminary comments and indexes (the first part), and appendices referring to the Royal Ordinances for the Tribunal of Account for the Indies, along with an alphabetical index (the second part).[1] In 1675, a second edition was published, and finally a third edition in 1775. The Editorial for the State of Bolivia incorporated in its *Biblioteca Boliviana* an extract of the principal parts of the *Gazofilacio Real*, published under the auspices of León M. Loza, in book form, in La Paz in 1941, containing a total of 291 pages. In the National Archives in Sucre, I have been able to pore over various editions of the original work, in the 1775 edition.

The first part of the work was written in Latin, with documentation in Spanish; the second part was edited entirely in Spanish.

The title of the work draws attention, not for its length, as this was in vogue for authors of that time, but more for the fact of using such a rare vocabulary as *Gazophilacium*. The author hastens to explain the meaning of the word, in the preliminary parts of the work: 'name which corresponds to erario, cámara, y archivo, where are guarded or deposited not only the wealth but the titles, scriptures, and rules by which the incomes of that "eceptro" are administered'. Actually, *Gazophilacium*, which is the Latin version of the Greek word *Gazophylakion* and comes from the words *gaza* (treasury) and *phillax* (guard or custody), means the Administration of the Exchequer or of the Treasury of the King. The word in ancient times was widely used, since *Gazophylakion* was at the same time the site where the alms and riches were collected in the Temple of Jerusalem. With the passing of time, this same name was given to cultural treasuries or deposits, especially books and dictionaries. Even today, the word can be found in the Latin languages of Italian, Portuguese, and Spanish (*Gazofilacio* is found in the dictionary of the Royal Academy of the Spanish Language). Nevertheless, in the body of the book, Escalona uses only words from the usual Spanish lexicon, such as 'Royal Treasury', 'Royal Exchequer', and 'Public Treasury' (Escalona y Agüero 1941: 7, 73, 82, 85, 110, 146, 233).

The idea of elaborating this work arose from the necessities imposed by everyday life. Escalona not only had been occupying very high positions of general administration, such as attorney general of Cuzco and *corregidor* of Tarija and governor of Castro-Virreinae, but also undertook the position of

Visitatore Arcarum Regalium, Inspector of the Royal Coffers, a position, as León M. Loza correctly observes, which was the equivalent of something like 'totalitarian governor of whatever concerned the financial movement of the colonial empire of Spain' (Escalona y Agüero 1941: xvi). It was on this occasion that it became clear that the royal officials needed to have on hand a treatise that would permit them

> the teaching of a science and art that was so needed by the princes and the vassals that are chosen by them: and in order that it be known that those who profess with firmness which they should, make themselves deserving of great mercies and awards.
>
> (Escalona y Agüero 1941: 74)

The work in itself is typically mercantilist, and to be even more precise, cameralist. Its fundamental objective lies in describing the physical structure of the colony, and in the presentation of the practical rules for action in conformity with the Indian laws for royal officials. It is a synthesis of the financial administration and legislation of the colonial period. And for being destined for the royal officials of the colony, the aspect that most interests us is that related to the Royal Revenues, and not to the Expenses of the Public Treasury. Consequently, we can say that we are considering a Treatise of the Tributary Administration and Legislation of the Colony. This is probably the most valuable aspect of this work. In the first part, which could have been titled 'Administration of the Fiscal Personnel of the Colony' and which occupies seventy-four pages of the work, a detailed examination of the higher level personnel of the Royal Exchequer is made: Accountant; Treasurer; Commissioner; Supplier; Payer; and Overseer 'who had and conserved the title of Royal Officials', describing in a systematic form the task of each one, the method of recruiting, the bonds that should be consented to for each position, the individual and joint responsibilities, as well as the 'prohibitions of diverse things for royal officials'. The second part is divided into two sections: the first in more than fifty pages describes extensively the calculations and accounts of the Royal Incomes and the functioning of the famous Tribunal and Audience of Greater Accountancy, known and conserved in the majority of the Hispanic-American countries up till today as the Tribunal of Accounts,[2] and the second part is dedicated to the analysis of each of the forty types of Royal Taxes existing in the Colony, and takes up nearly 150 pages. For the history of the facts and the ideas of the Colonial Public Treasury, the work of Escalona is really a first-class source of information and documentation, and as such, knowledge of it and permanent consultation with it is imperative.

As a faithful interpreter of the rationalist spirit that spread throughout the New World, Escalona sees in the calculation and the accounts the most powerful instrument for the progress of the financial administration.

The account is the shadow of the administration, spy of its steps, checking its excesses, and taking care of its proceeding. It is its so needful introduction and censure in the administration of that treasury, principally of the king, which obligates by divine right to adjust itself to the owner and satisfy by calculations the least well administrated, and pay the balance of the charges and discharges which are in its favor, which is the target and terminal stone of any account; . . . in royal officials arises this necessity with more squeezing; because the area of the Prince's patrimony is wide and divided into regions and diverse cash boxes, and all remote and distant from his presence, it is desired a greater collection, which is not only useful to its benefactor, but advantageous to the same administrators, who have so much relief and liberty in own goods, when they overcome the situation in which the cash box and that of the king is found, which communicate by way of the account, that is what distinguishes one from another.

(Escalona y Agüero 1941: 75)

For Escalona, 'the accounting of the Royal Treasury is such an arduous work and of such importance' that he insists, in the cases that for reasons of distance, as in the Indies, it is not possible for the Prince himself to take matters into his own hands, the need for 'individual and necessary intelligence of versed Ministers and men of science'. For him, 'the account is worth more than the income', although he warns that the management of the Public Accountancy is a very difficult matter: 'because without doubt in the numbers are the dangers without number'. For this, he considers 'fortunate the Monarch who would have in his assistance Accountants of the necessary expertise'. And to reinforce his opinion, he turns to quotations of the testimonies of authors from ancient times to his own day in which are brought to mind not only the names of the great accountants of Spain, the 'Most Rational and Accountant of Africa', etc., but at the same time he raises a true ode to this ministry so 'marvelous', so 'dignified', and so 'inexcusable' (Escalona y Agüero 1941: 118–19) in the management of the Royal Coffers.

We could not hope that Escalona y Agüero, who 'was animated by a first class monarchist fanaticism', would raise objections to the multitude of taxes which oppressed the person and the goods of the communities of the New World. His attitude is due to the nature of his important positions, even more so as a defender of tributes, invoking for this, like the European writers, arguments of imperious public necessity. So, in the case of the *alcábala*, he emphasized: 'the necessity to form and maintain in the south sea a sufficient naval presence to assure the treasury and the vassals against enemies and to keep them in peace and quiet', and although in the Kingdoms of the Castillas its imposition was around 10 per cent, in the Indies it was established at 2 and later at 4 per cent. But Escalona's obedience is not without limits. When dealing with the natives, he not only considers it just not to pay certain tributes 'for reason of people being miserable', but also he vehemently attacks the institution of the Yanaconas (an Indian tribe of Peru bound to servitude to the Spanish noblemen), as a 'new species of slavery' (Escalona y Agüero 1941:1 68). Also in the case of the port taxes and those of turnpike tolls, of the salt pits, metals, iron works, fishing,

> are of the Emperors, and of the Kings, as they were granted all these things because they wanted to honorably maintain their dispatches, or by which they could protect their kingdoms, and battle the enemies of the faith, and because they could threaten the people with undertaking dangerous actions or to do them other grievous harm.
>
> (Escalona y Agüero 1941: 131)

Although conceived with exclusively practical objectives, the work of the doctor from Chuquisaca is characterized nevertheless by a refined scientific spirit. Each one of his basic concepts is the object of a detailed semantic study and its essence is determined with total caution. Some examples will be sufficient to illustrate this fact. Let's look at the concept of 'Royal Officials':

> These officials have had different names and titles in different times and under different governments. The general and primitive one as regards the effect of the ministry and what could have been necessary in guarding the treasury in its charge and inquiring as to its growth, was that of the Questores in the Roman Empire, as referred to by Pompinio in the history of law. Notwithstanding that they were differentiated by more particular names later, and were referred to as Procurers of Caesar, Rationales, Susceptores, Provosts, Collectors and Chargers of Tributes, because they charged for the treasury of the Empire, took care of it and guaranteed its coffers and sent it to the Prefects of Treasuries which were in every province; and the latter to the superior ministry, entitled Comes sacrarum largitionum.
>
> (Escalona y Agüero 1941: 5)

To begin his study on the different classes of taxes, Escalona proceeds in a correct manner to clarify the diversity of names that the public taxes have received throughout history.

> Before entering in this area, and the explanation of every part of the treasury, it is presupposed by its most illustrious intelligence, that the particles that make up the mountain of the Royal Exchequer . . . have different names . . . although all are well . . . included under one same generic name and are entitled in law sometimes with the name of 'Tributes', others with the title 'Intribuciones', perhaps they are called Fiscal Functions: Ulpiano called them 'Fusions'. The emperors used to indicate them with the word 'Cannon', and also with the word

'Staciones'. No less, they use the words 'Sacras Largiciones', or 'Titulos Largicionales', which is from collations and loans. And finally, with the word 'Vectigalia', they usually indicated all that referred to the rest of the titles, in this manner to include the 'indictos' and 'superindictos', ordinary and extraordinary illations, and the same ones were embraced by the word 'Regalia', with allusion to the origin which the Royal Sovereignty gave them. Corresponding to this definition in English, we call it royal taxes, members of the exchequer, goods and treasuries of the Prince, tributes, impositions, royal rights, services, contributions, etc.

(Escalona y Agüero 1941: 128)

Referring to the duty on exports and imports (*almojarifazgo*), Escalona determines its essence in an unencumbered and clear formulation:

This word is Arabic, and comes from the word 'almoxarife', which as is stated in a law, means 'official who makes the charges for the rights to the land of the King, which are collected by means of a turnpike toll, and from the census of the lands'. It is founded on passage and navigation, which is made sure and free of any enemies of the Prince, while defending the coasts and the seas.

(Escalona y Agüero 1941: 165)

The same clarity is found in the determination of the Government Liquor Monopoly of Solimán

In the matters of pomp, superfluity, and vice, or to banish them from the Republic, or to dissimulate correction and fine on those who use them it is political advice to impose rights and duties: this was the reason for which there was imposed a poll tax of 5 per cent on coca by the Viceroy Francisco Toledo. And Cato the Censor, in order to cut expenditures on extravagant galas and of high costs, sent all to be registered, and by the same motive in some provinces where wine is drunk to excess and ravage by the vassals, the Princes have become accustomed to increase the duties on its sale. . . . In the Kingdom of Peru, if not with the same intention, in order to extend the Royal Patrimony it was resolved by Viceroy Count de Chinchon to have the government liquor monopoly of Solimán.

(Escalona y Agüero 1941: 260)

Even a matter such as the calculus, which could escape the notice of the most scholarly, is an object of clarification by Escalona: 'The account is called calculus, as it has been used in ancient times, with a variety of pebbles, as the Indians with their quipus, which are branches or threads with larger and smaller knots of different colours' (Escalona y Agüero 1941: 114).

For Escalona, the forty types of taxes and tributes established in the colony have as a final objective: 'the sustenance of the empire, the defense of religion, and the protection of the vassals'. Put in another way, Escalona emphasizes the political character of the tributes, a character which is centred on the idea of protection, defence, and security of life, as well as of people's creeds, within the new social configurations of state life.

Although the state, to complete its objectives of defending the vassals and religion, is obligated to impose this range of tributes, Escalona insists, however, that the duty of the contributions lies ultimately in the understanding, the spirit of imperial solidarity, and consequently in the willingness of the tax-payers.

The forty types of taxes seem to be very numerous. Nevertheless, compared with those in place in other empires, Escalona considers them moderate and in no manner too many, and he adds

> In pursuit of a style so laudable, being able to join very great treasuries of various means and manners, that they are determined as worthy by the rest of the Monarchs in their Kingdoms, only insisting on the ordinary ones, those which have style, not excesses; good will, not hatred, the affliction is deviated and not the ruin of the Kingdom, the exorbitance is abominable, greed is condemned; and equality and justice are exercised with dignity; it is not allowed, that the tears of the subjects be a tax, that the Exchequer be the spoiler and the cavern of the subtracted goods.
>
> (Escalona y Agüero 1941: 274)

In his ardent monarchist sympathy, Escalona considers it useful to note that even in the temporary dimension, the Hispanic fiscal system was characterized by justice and equality. In the final chapter, which can be better considered as a first attempt at a history of tributes, Escalona presents sixty-five examples, well collected from ancient times, of the different tributes and tributary techniques used in those times, as 'abominable note' for the style in which they had settled 'illicit rights, inhumane arbitrages, and execrable charges'.

But for us, the most interesting point to emphasize is that Escalona, in a time in which the Public Treasury was dealt with as a singular chapter within political, philosophical, or theological works, gives us a truly systematic and at times very scientific treatise, in which he unites in one the three great divisions of Modern Public Finance: Administration of Fiscal Personnel; Financial Organization and Institutions; and the Tributary Administration and Technique.

It is without a doubt, if not the first, then the most important financial treatise of the colonial era, produced by the efforts of a son of these American lands, a doctor from Chuquisaca.

8

JOSÉ CARDIEL

Cardiel was born in La Guardia, Rioja, on 13 March 1704. He studied in the Jesuit schools of Victoria, together with two of his brothers who entered the order. Of these three, two later went on Jesuit missions in the Indias. Pedro Antonio went to the missions in Quito and for a third of a century worked without rest in that area. José, who was the youngest of the brothers, entered the order on 8 April 1720. He made his novitiate in Villagarcía and studied philosophical and theological sciences at Medina del Campo. In 1729, when Cardiel arrived in Buenos Aires he was already a priest, and shortly thereafter he was working in the Guaranian Indian settlement around Paraguay, first as deputy parson in 1731, and from 1735 as parson. After a short period at the Colegio de las Corrientes, in 1743 he was designated to cooperate in the foundation of the Indian settlements of the Mocobies of San Francisco Javier, Abipones, Charrúas, and Guaraníes. Cardiel learned the local languages, especially guaraní, which he highly esteemed, and learned to perfection. Between August 1745 and August 1746, Cardiel explored the Patagonian coasts, and immediately afterwards went into the interior of this region, arriving at the Sierra del Volcán, and later at the Claromecó river. In 1747, he returned to the Abipones, and this time he founded, together with other brothers of the order, the Abipone settlement of San Jerónimo, which later would become the city of Reconquista. He stayed there for two years through the arduous and difficult beginnings of this settlement.

Shortly afterwards, Cardiel founded the town of Concepción upon the right bank of the Dulce river. Between 1749 and 1754, Cardiel was assigned the responsibilities of consultant, house confessor, and missionary. It was in this period that stunning events happened in the history of the Guaranian missions. Based on a border treaty of 1750, Spain, in an attempt to maintain its colony of Colonia del Sacramento (Uruguay), turned over to Portugal an immense and rich zone of land with seven Guaraní villages settled by the Jesuits in the Province of Paraguay. Cardiel's actions at this time have historic importance, for he risked his position, even that within the order, in a paper in which he maintained that the precepts of the General Jesuits do not obligate to urge the transfer of the seven villages and that it was not necessary to know anything more than the Christian doctrine to know that what the Kings did by their divisory line was unjust. . . . [This concerned a] paper where are placed with peculiarity the exorbitant damages and enormous inconveniences which ensue upon the Indians, and even upon the Crown of Spain, by the surrendering of the villages: with the origin of the new division of lands and states, and two maps.

(Cardiel 1953: 90)

Cardiel had to submit himself to the Commisar of the Order, Padre Altamirano, and participated intensively in the work of moving the seven villages. In 1757, we find Cardiel at the village of San José, at the end of 1758 in the town of San Miguel, of which he was named parish priest; in 1762 he marched overland along the Río Grande with the designation of chaplain of the Spanish army for Cevallos' expedition, and due to the harshness of this expedition, we finally find him, living his last years in the Americas at the Concepción settlement.

Later came the expulsion of the Jesuit Order by the Royal Decree of 1767–8. On board the frigate San Nicolás, Cardiel arrived at Cádiz in April 1769, after forty years of intense and endless dedication

in the conquest of the souls of our Indians as in the exploration of the most remote regions of our national territory. Having arrived here at the age of twenty-five, just as he was beginning his long productive trajectory, and was expelled, by order of the King, at the age of sixty-five, when well into the autumn of his life. All of his existence was given to the service of our lands. And even after settling in Faenza, until his death, coming to pass on 6 December 1782 in the same city, he continued with quill in hand to labour over his valued writings, letters, and above all else, his maps related to his beloved Río de la Plata lands, which remember him and whose name is given to a lake and one of the peaks of our Argentinian lands.

(Cardiel 1953: 7–53)

Cardiel's vocation for economic problems was stimulated by his long years in managing the affairs of the Guaranian missions, related not only to the spiritual field, but also to matters of a secular nature. And his writings are nothing less than demonstrations of this permanent interrelation between reflection and action, be it as an assistant to the parish priest with specific tasks and responsibilities of spiritual government, or as parish priest of the settlements, in which role the secular and spiritual functions were carried out equally. His 'Carta-Relación' of 1747 and his 'Declaración de la Verdad' of 1758 are rather like snapshots of the structure and economic process in the Guaranian settlements which cut through the historical current. His

'Breve Relación' of 1771 provides a vision of the whole of the most interesting experiment in development realized in the indigenous communities along the Río de la Plata basin in the light of the Church doctrine during its 150 years of existence.

Although his favourite theme is the economic and social life of the Guaranian settlements, it is noteworthy that Cardiel's interest is much wider. On the one hand, he attempts to enlarge the objective of his studies to a continental level, even if at the centre of them were the efforts made by the order in its great work of founding the missionary settlements. The best testimony to this is found in his unedited writing of 1757, whose long title serves as a short summary of the subject dealt with

> News from the Americas; of the population and extension of its inhabitants; of its political and civil order; of the ecclesiastic state in general and of our order in particular; of its Provinces, number of subjects; the extension of its missions among the heathens, and the particular way they are undertaken among the Spanish; and finally, what came to pass on the occasion of the dividing line between the two Crowns.
>
> (Cardiel 1953:7)

On the other hand, the study of the economic life of the civil governments of Buenos Aires or Río de la Plata, Paraguay, Tucumán, and Santa Cruz de la Sierra held a special interest for Cardiel. The administrative limits of these areas were almost superimposed upon the boundaries of the Jesuit Province of Paraguay, with its capital in Córdoba, and comprising a massive territory, in which were also included the Jesuit missions of the Guaraní people, which covered all of what today is Argentina, Paraguay, Uruguay, the southeast part of Santa Cruz de la Sierra in Bolivia, and for some time the territory of Chile also. And Cardiel's attraction for these lands was due to the fact that they were known by direct observation, and because he had explored parts of the territory in his role of pioneer discoverer.

Let's look at the title of Cardiel's 'Carta-Relación' of 1747, in the first part of which he makes note of the economic features of each one of the civil governments. He emphasizes the features held in common by all the civil governments: first, the spirit of the population seems excellent

> The people are of a docile, bland, and peaceful temper. They do not burst out like those of Spain in votes, words of anger, cholera, and boasts. Those of Buenos Aires show somewhat more haughtiness. And those who come from Spain, years later become of the same character, but not so much so.
>
> (Cardiel 1953: 15)

Cardiel did not waste the opportunity to express his attachment to an anthropo-geographic theory which would have great weight among scholars of the nineteenth century, by stating: 'Great is the force of food and the

111

influence of the stars, in altering geniuses and temperamental people.' The second factor is that in general it seems that he thought it was not worth the trouble to mention the differences between the Spanish and those born in the Indies, particularly regarding the reactions of those in the order:

> concerning the fathers of the land, who some call 'criollos', though they say that this name does not sound pleasant, there are various sentences and opinions; I say that in eighteen years of continuous dealing with them [he writes in 1747], I have found little or no differences with those from over there in virtue and letters.
>
> (Cardiel 1953: 17)

Another factor is the service of slaves and mulattos, which also characterizes the social life of these civil governments, including in the religious orders. He accepts as a generally received fact, as if it were very much in agreement with the natural law and it is not necessary to ponder that it deserves a more attentive and speculative consideration: 'The mulattos and black slaves serve us, like anyone else outside (the order), both secular and religious men, even those of San Francisco, that here there is no other way' (Cardiel 1953: 19). He does, however, insist that one of the most constant social policy measures of the order, the fight 'against the personal service of the natives has been the cause for hatred among the "encomenderos" and even the cause of the banishment of the order' (Cardiel 1953: 11). Yet another factor is how he observes with thoroughness the inverse relationship between the extension and abundance of the land of the ranches and their profitability:[1]

> Here there is nothing more than land to spare, so that there are Spaniards who have more land than the entire Kingdom of Murcia or Navarra, populated with all breeds of cattle; and with all that, hardly will it have an income of 1,000 pesos per year; the few being, the pawn and care of the service people, the rest are slaves, for the work of driving the cattle and the cheap price for the cattle is the cause of gaining so little profit.
>
> (Cardiel 1953: 16)

The fifth factor we shall call the great enterprise. The secret of becoming rich lies in commerce, above all in the commercial business dedicated to the intra-provincial transportation, but, Cardiel observes, this activity is only practised by those who come from other lands:

> the Spanish people from here, do not enrich themselves very much; those who come from Spain usually do enrich themselves in a very short time; all are merchants, which here is not a disgrace for the nobility; we see various transformations; a cabin boy, a caulker, a sailor, a construction worker, or a warship carpenter comes; here he begins to work as he did there (what a fright for the land lumbers who are not so

112

developed), making houses, ships, carpentry, sawing all day, or inserting himself as a barkeeper, which here we call a 'pulpero' or a tender; within a few months, he sees how with his industriousness and work he has put together some money; he makes a voyage with herbs or cloths from Europe to Chile or Potosí; now he comes as a man of fortune: he makes another voyage, and after this second trip, we see him as a gentleman, dressed in silk and braids, rapier and wig, of which here there exists an excess in luxury; this occurs every day; and later we see him as a Royal Official or Exchequer, Mayor and Lieutenant in the government.

(Cardiel 1953: 8)

On touching this point, Father Cardiel stated that he was stepping onto slippery ground, and tries to excuse himself

having a greater laugh than I thought possible with my intent; I go abbreviating, leaving out many things, to come quickly to the religious matter and that of the missions, on which I shall further expand, for this is the target of this paper; . . . more because perhaps this will fall into the hands of people who will want to know the conditions of the outsiders and the lands, it seemed I should touch on this subject.

(Cardiel 1953: 8)

Finally, as his sixth factor, he points out that the local Spanish people not only 'do not enrich themselves very much', but among them is also cultivated great laziness, partly caused by climatic factors, 'the force of alimentation', and 'the influence of the stars', but also on the other hand, by economic factors: 'due to meat being so cheap, nobody lacks food, and this is the reason for having so many loiterers' (Cardiel 1953: 6).

Among the economic peculiarities which differentiate the governments, he calls attention to the fact that money only flows in Buenos Aires and Tucumán, while in Paraguay, and also in the city of Corrientes which belongs to Buenos Aires, 'no money flows, they manage by means of barter' (Cardiel 1953: 4), even when it does not appear to be so, since 'there they have imposed the prices of everything, as if it were money'; what happens, Cardiel clarifies, is that upon knowing that a cow is worth six pesos in Paraguay and the *yerba mate* is two pesos for twenty-five pounds, they make the exchange without the intervention of money, 'and so with a cow are purchased seventy-five pounds of mate' (Cardiel 1953: 7).

Another economic factor in the governments through which money flows, observes Cardiel in his 'Breve Relación', 'is that there are no "vellones" [copper coins]; the smallest coin is the silver half real; and due to the great abundance of this metal found here, a peso is valued as a real in Spain', or 'a silver real in the Americas is valued as two or three quarter pesos in Spain' (Cardiel 1953: 11).

Furthermore, the governments of Tucumán, Santa Cruz, and Paraguay have a rural and agricultural character, while that of Buenos Aires is more of a commercial and urban type, whose swift growth gets the attention; it is worthwhile to repeat this detail, just as it was written in the 'Carta-Relación' of 1747:

In all of those governments (of Paraguay, of Tucumán, and part of Santa Cruz de la Sierra), there are more people living in the country, in straw cabins, which here they call 'ranchos', tending to their cattle, than people living in cities. These, in the buildings and the outlook of the people, are like hamlets in Spain, though with greater number of neighbours. Buenos Aires is the exception to the rule; because fifty years ago, all the buildings were low and almost all of them were of straw, it has grown so much with the arrival of various ships, even after I arrived here, that its inhabitants are more than sixteen thousand, the majority from Spain, not counting the service people, who are mulattos and blacks from Africa, and some Indians. And as to the buildings, now all are of brick and tile, and many of two floors, with railings and balconies; and the city has one league in length and almost half a league in width. . . . It is rich due to the great trade. There are there many fortunes of 100,000 pesos and some of much more.

(Cardiel 1953: 4)

To complete the overwhelming image of our city, Cardiel adds in some later paragraphs:

This city has what is novel more than the rest, a Castle of lime and brick, which the Indians from our missions made; and in Montevideo they are finishing another of lime and mortar; and between the two they possess sixteen companies of soldiers, whose wage is greater than overseas, eight pesos a month. There are neither more castles nor soldiers arranged together for a distance of one thousand leagues, until Lima.

(Cardiel 1953: 9)

The only thing that Cardiel pities is that this process of development was not accompanied by the corresponding cultural process, as he states, displeased:

In Buenos Aires and Paraguay Departments of Philosophy were opened after I arrived here, but with such small student bodies, that the one in Buenos Aires, such a large city, just finished this year with only three disciples. More modernly, Departments of Theology were opened in these two cities, and for lack of students, they were closed. People do not concern themselves but to trade and cattle raising. There are no more departments than these.

(Cardiel 1953: 19)

114

Evidently, the city of Buenos Aires was suffering from 'bullionist' fever, not very compatible with the teachings of theology and philosophy. Over all, Cardiel did not stop emphasizing that, at the school level, in which besides reading and writing, courses of grammar were taught, Buenos Aires was then equal to Cordoba as both had forty schools.

For a quantitative orientation of the economic history, the 'Carta-Relación' is raw material of extremely high value. It is sufficient to look at three examples. First, the price level in a given market in Buenos Aires:

> the cattle, as large as those of Castilla, are worth a peso, and because here the money has not changed, this is eight silver reals. The mares are at four silver reals. Tamed horses, two pesos, sheep bought in great quantity go for two reals, and sometimes for one half real.
>
> (Cardiel 1953: 6)

Second, Cardiel looks at the prices for the same product in different markets. In Buenos Aires, cattle 'are worth a peso', as we have just seen; 'in Las Corrientes the cattle are worth three pesos'; and in Paraguay 'the cattle . . . are worth six pesos' (Cardiel 1953: 7), 'the mules that here [in Buenos Aires] are worth two pesos, and at times only one, are driven in droves, like cattle, to Salta and Potosí, where they are worth sixteen and eighteen pesos'. The final example pertains to cattle in a given area:

> The countryside of the district of Buenos Aires, and those of the juris-diction of Santa Fé, Corrientes, and Montevideo were in years past full, not of thousands, but millions of cattle on one side and the other of the Paraná river for a space of two hundred leagues (this will seem exag-gerated to those who have not seen it); all were wild, without owners, which are called Cimarrones. But, so great has been the disorder in slaughtering them only for the leather, tallow, fat, and the tongues, leaving the meat to go to waste, that now the number of 'cimarrones' is small. Almost all are tame, with owners: and here in Buenos Aires is where most of them are.
>
> (Cardiel 1953: 8)

Cardiel estimates the number to be 400,000 cows for the decade of the 1740s. What is most interesting is the method used to make this estima-tion:

> According to the 10 per cent tax [diezmo] of each year, which is usually between ten and eleven thousand veal, there would be in the jurisdiction of this city some 400 thousand cattle: because if the tenth part is ten thousand, there are 100 thousand veal; and as we see in the great pasture lands of cattle, the live births being usually the fourth part of raised cattle, the mentioned number arises.
>
> (Cardiel 1953: 9)

The fifteen years of acquired experience in the administration of the Jesuit settlements, not only in a spiritual but also a secular sense, what today is called 'farm or agricultural enterprise administration', was the greatest source of his witty quantitative economic observations.

And it is this group of agricultural and cattle breeding activities, and above all else, the art of its good administration, which in Cardiel's lexicon of 1747 bears the name 'economics'. In four places in this work, we come across this word. First, to emphasize that the Indians of the Jesuit settlements generally sow corn, manioc, sweet potatoes, and vegetables, adding that

the most capable and hard working sow besides all this melons, watermelons, pumpkins, and other species that abound here, sugar cane, without having the patience to make it into sugar or honey, and it is very rare that they do this, and some wheat and barley. But, it does not come to their economy to make it into bread, but they eat it cooked or half cooked in water only; even though some of them have been or are bakers in the house of the fathers, so they well know how to make it and how to eat it.

(Cardiel 1953: 50)

Of course, observes Cardiel, it cost a great effort to accustom the Guaranís to undertake at the right time the harvesting of the crops sown, and even more to collect the fruits; these experiments were generally done in the privately sown plots, the *Abambaés*; an experiment lasted almost one year with the gathering of lima beans, which he inaugurated in the first years of his priesthood, without achieving the desired results; and

it was not due to them not being lovers of this vegetable, or for being far; . . . but, for a lack of economy and an incredible laxity. The following year they were made to reap, divided into groups as when they sowed, and in this way, the beans were harvested.

(Cardiel 1953: 54)

The third instance of using the word economy occurred when Cardiel examined the condition of the missions of the Chiquitos of Santa Cruz de la Sierra, and he related that 'at the present, there are seven towns of 300, 400 people, and it adds up to 600 families'. These were plainly expanding and showing very promising and even more accelerated results than those obtained in the Guaranian settlements; and this, because the Chiquitos who 'have a very distinct language from the Guaranís . . . are more provident and economic than the Guaranís' (Cardiel 1953: 161).

Finally, to strike a balance between the missionary activities of the order and a comparison with the other orders in terms of the number and progress of the Indian settlements, Cardiel agrees with some secular people who affirm that the secret lies ultimately in 'the great economy that there is in

116

our communities, and the great work and eagerness that the Associate Brothers have on the farms' (Cardiel 1953: 182).

In the 'Declaración de la Verdad' of 1758, the expression 'economy' appears more frequently, but on this occasion, it is placed neatly on display to indicate that for Cardiel, this term implies a certain specific type of conditioned activity of the dominant cultural system, and that it stands out especially when it is contemplated in comparative terms:

> There are some nations [of Indians] which have the economy to acquire and keep the necessary for life; there are others who sow and gather, their economy reaches no further for the entire year; in their lack of not knowing how to prepare themselves, they supplement this with hunting . . . there are other nations in which they do not work, they do not till, they do not sow, nor prepare things . . . these live by hunting, fishing, and stealing . . . of those economic nations of the Kingdom of Mexico and of the Incas of Peru, not one is found.
>
> (Cardiel 1980: 269)

It is evident that in this demonstration, Cardiel insinuates the idea of 'economic stages', since he clearly distinguishes between the stage of the nomadic people, the stage of the semi-nomadic people and that of the sedentary people. Among the nomads, Cardiel counts the Serranos, Abipones, Mocovís, Charrúas and many other Indian nations from Patagonia. Among the semi-nomads, he mentions the Aucáos of his time, 'who live in the Andes mountain range between the Araucanos of Chile and the Serranos' of the pampas of Argentina, as well as the Guaranís, who were semi-nomadic in their life before their conversion and settlement by the Jesuit missionaries. Among the sedentary people, he mentions the Guaranian settlement people of his time (Cardiel 1953: 197, 202; 1980: 270–1).

The morphology of the 'economics' of Cardiel not only has speculative ends, but is an important instrument in the service of economic policy. Actually, he observes in his 'Declaración de la Verdad', that if it is true that in the Jesuit mission the primal objective is to attend to the spiritual needs of the people, the secular order also requires special care. Still, the degree of intensity of the secular activities depends precisely on the economic system or situation existing in the native communities.

Consequently, Cardiel gives three points to emphasize this idea. First, he states that: 'When the Indians of our towns have the sufficient economy for their maintenance, the Fathers take little or no care of secular matters, as it happens in some town in Peru and Mexico; all emphasis is on those things of the spirit.' Second, he continues

> When their economy is something, but not sufficient, they take great care to exercise the labors of bodily suffering, caring for their ranches, of the common possessions, etc., directing themselves in the deals,

teaching themselves all the republic's charges; and if it is not done in this way, there will be no attendance at church and the Christian obligations ... then, if the secular matters go well, the spiritual ones advance a lot; if the secular is bad, the spiritual goes very poorly.

(Cardiel 1980: 270–1)

Finally, 'when they are of [a] vagabond horse riding nation, the care is much greater for the secular world, so that they can subsist' (Cardiel 1980: 271–2).

Besides the generic expression of 'economics', we find two other specific expressions: 'domestic economy'; and 'political economics'. With the expression 'domestic economy', Cardiel designates the set of activities related to the private ranches of each family (the 'Ababa'), with the 'tradesmen of the republic', or the artisans and mechanical officials who in the Jesuit missions belong, as we would say today, to the public sector, on the one hand; on the other hand, we have the common garden plots, or 'Tupambaé' (Cardiel 1980: 285).

The use of the expression 'political economy' occurs on the occasion when Cardiel takes into consideration the question of whether the missionaries could defraud the Indians. Cardiel replies that

this suspicion is born in the ignorance of the less malign. The Jesuits do not make tax lists. They do not enumerate the taxpayers. This is left to the Governour, by the royal laws and seals. In the beginning, after initiating the political economy, the Viceroy made the enumeration of the taxpayers. According to that number, tributes were paid for more than fifty years.

(Cardiel 1913: 84)

It appears that here the expression has the meaning of state, or of an economic system that corresponds to civilized communities. Actually, it would seem that the text intends to tell us that the Guaraní Indians were counted in a census and began to pay tributes to the King, after having left their savage or natural economic stage and passing to the civil or political economic stage.

The principal subject of Cardiel's writings is that of the Jesuit settlements for the Guaranís. In this matter, he already counted on secular experience, and he is a true virtuoso at diagnosing the situation of the settlements at their origins, following the process of development and making an evaluation of the political economy practised at the settlements during more than 150 years of persistent missionary effort. The basic objective of the settlements, with which Cardiel not only identified himself but to the achievement of which he had also contributed more than thirty years of his own life, was pacific evangelization. With this eminently Christian objective, there corresponded appropriate methods of the Christian concept of life. The missionary requires a special pledge of virtue and denial, but to convert towns, observes Cardiel:

> not all make the pledges like in secondary schools, and for them saint-liness is not enough; and even those who make the pledges, not all raise villages, which in pestilence or other unfortunate happenings are falling to pieces.
>
> (Cardiel 1953: 36)

This serves as a maxim when dealing with semi-nomadic peoples, such as the Guaranís, for whose conversion the secular means are equal to or outweigh the spiritual ones.

> The Jesuits committed themselves to winning over this kingdom from hell. Obtaining this with only the cross for a weapon, it cost them much sweat, anxiety, and continuous dangers to their lives. . . . Their conversion lasted forty years . . . and with a very powerful assistance from the All Powerful, they managed to bring civilized life, and Christian life, in villages of more than one thousand families, imposing upon them tasks or institutions which greatly conformed to their genius and capability.
>
> (Cardiel 1980: 273)

What have been the methods employed in political economy in what Cardiel calls the 'portage and secular government' of these communities of Indians, after their settling into sedentary towns? Basically, only two, one being the aforementioned 'activities of the republic':

> In the second patio of the house of the Fathers, are all the activities: weavers, carpenters, sculptors, gold workers, makers of lathes, hat makers, rosary makers, those who work in all types of glass, ox lances, dyes, combs, etc., and other classes of artifacts.
>
> (Cardiel 1980: 285)

In the Jesuit settlements, the artisans enjoyed a high esteem: 'There is no lowliness among these mechanically skilled people whatsoever, but nobility, even if it be the position of cobbler; on the contrary, he who had none of these positions was considered a vile person' (Cardiel 1953: 101). This method, consequently, yielded good results.

But what of the other method? The other method is that of the 'domestic economy', which is not very satisfactory for Cardiel, due to its slow process of development. Actually, after demonstrating the features of the policy of crafts' development, Cardiel makes the following reflections:

> It is not as difficult to apply them to these trade occupations in the republic as it is to the domestic economy; because in these positions they can be visited quite often; but in the economy of their families,

one can not stare over their shoulders. There is no way to make them make provisions for the future, to keep the sustenance the whole year, and if this is achieved by some of them, it is hardly the tenth part of the people.

(Cardiel 1980: 285)

Of course, the question is susceptible to a solution, as it actually was resolved, falling between two evils, the lesser evil and that which constituted the third fundamental method of political economy practised among the Guaranís: the complementing of the economy of the 'Abambaé' with the common economy of the 'Tupambaé', which has created so much confusion among many critics and historians up to the present (Popescu 1967: 108).

Besides the Guaraní Indians, Cardiel is interested in the Indian communities with a lesser degree of development. His contacts with the Mocoví and Abipon Indian groups, and with the Charrúas and Serranos tribes made him understand that the failure of all the attempts at conversion was due to the fact that the same method was applied to these people who do not sow, but live off hunting and robbing, who 'go roaming like the gypsies, the tartars, and the alrabians', who 'do not have more house than two or three mats, which the women carry on their horses' (Cardiel 1953: 163), and are therefore very different in their cultural values from the sedentary Indians. He remarks that his success with the Abipones was due exactly to having proceeded in the inverse manner from what was usual, and maintains that among these nomadic peoples, the secret of initial success lies in allowing the secular matters to have priority over the affairs of God: 'If this is not done, there is no hope for their conversion, because as they are people who do not reason, the faith must first enter through the mouth and only after this through the ear' (Cardiel 1953: 177). He emphasizes that this does not mean that all things spiritual should be abandoned but simply delayed until much later, since 'the medicine should be applied over time and with relish, when an advantage has to be taken; outside of its time, even if it is very good, it is poison' (Cardiel 1953: 177).

It was precisely by this contact with the Mocovís and Abipones that Cardiel elaborated a first approximation to the 'Particular means by which to convert these nations', which in economic terminology comes down to:

It is necessary to give them food and clothing, without forcing them to work in this, since there is nothing more abhorrent to them than work, for as short a time as it be, even though it is for their own good.

(Cardiel 1953: 178)

And in the following line, he discusses the duration of the programme:

It is necessary to do all this in the first and second years. By the third year, they are undertaking some type of trade or craft, they respect and

120

obey the Father, and do some work in their houses and garden plots; and so they march forward in all things every year.

(Cardiel 1953: 179)

But, we observe immediately, that such a plan of operations cannot be carried out without counting on complementary financial planning. The good Father Cardiel surprises us with what today we call the 'elaboration of investment projects'. Actually, after reiterating that this is the only way to convert such a savage people, he observes, with a certain amount of anxiety:

The difficult part is in such exorbitant expenditures on cattle, corn, salt and other foodstuffs; in clothing for everyone; in a salary for the labourers, to whom is given five, six and even to those who are more dexterous, seven pesos or eight reals; and in purchasing wood for the town, the church and house for all this.

(Cardiel 1953: 179)

And, continuing with his fine quantitative vocation, he estimates the annual financial budget of each town as 3,000 pesos or more for the first three or four years, so that after five or six years, the expenditure may drop; but that with all included, a budget must be considered for ten or twelve years, until these towns of horsemen find themselves at the level of development of the towns under the Guaranian settlements.

Cardiel reinforces the figures of his financial budget with data taken from similar projects: one undertaken by himself with the foundation of the settlement for the Mocovís, in which within four years, 12,000 pesos had been spent. For another settlement, for which he even drew up a map, Cardiel observes

in the lands of the Pampean Indians in the south of Buenos Aires, forty leagues in distance, as can be seen on the map, in the six years since it has been started, has spent close to 18,000 pesos; although this settlement is now in an arrangement where the Indians work to eat and dress themselves; and from here on, little shall be spent.

(Cardiel 1953: 180)

Therefore, the financial budget seems to be correct, especially if one considers that for this project, Cardiel was thinking of establishing three villages in more or less the same environment as mentioned above: one village in the lands of the Abipones, neighbours of the Mocovís; and two in the land of the Serranos, neighbours of the Pampas tribe and also at almost the same level of development, although he does recognize that the Serranos, besides assimilating some of the bad customs of the Spanish

are notably persistent in begging: they come asking with haughtiness, as if all this was justifiably owed them: they become angry rather easily when they do not receive what they ask for, and later they say:

'How can you want me to become a Christian, when you do not give me all that I ask of you?' They are not thankful for what they do receive, rather, they are continuously mumbling that no one gives them anything, no matter what they are given. If we want to buy a horse or a poncho from them for the use and payment of our labourers, they are so expensive, so haughty, such hagglers, and such is the malice of their treatment, that besides always bringing the worst, the worst horse, lame or maimed or old, etc. and the worst poncho, it costs an unbearable bother to close the deal, because it is necessary to take out of the store and count all the bells, vanilla, or glass beads to choose; and one by one tempting them, registering, sounding, tossing aside this one for having a bad colour, the other for bad sound or bad soldering, the other for being thin, etc.

(Cardiel 1953: 201)

We should admire in passing, not only this notable characteristic, which today we would call 'marketing technique', of the now-vanished Serranos Indians who inhabited the Sierras de Volcán, but above all else the deep spirit of observation in the smallest, but at the same time most typical details, with which Cardiel painted, with so many brush strokes, the essence of an entire economic system.

What is certain is that Cardiel knew that within the environs of financial possibilities for similar projects or programmes, the sources of new financing had run out. He could count neither on more alms from the pious laymen, nor on any help from the schools, and even less on help from the missions to the Guaranís, since they were already overloaded by financial obligations in the existing settlements. Cardiel knows that he is rubbing against the edge of utopia:

This is the greatest difficulty, and we run around roaming all over to take what is necessary to carry these three towns forward. Then, we see all the other means which for more than 100 years have been taken to convert these vagabond people, have had no effect, this is the only one that has had it. If we find money for so many expenses, without any doubt it will reduce to a rational and Christian life so great a multitude of vagabond nations which surround us near and far. This is why for all the others, there are no difficulties.

(Cardiel 1953: 27)

And what is worse, when Cardiel comments on these projects to the other fathers of the order, the image of his own personality begins to be weakened. It is not surprising that in various of his superiors' letters things are said such as 'Father José Cardiel is full of ideas only . . . and . . . everything is in extravagant ideas'.

The beginning of a solution, thinks Cardiel, could consist in absorbing some of the funds given by the Crown as defence expenses, as was happening in Chile with the settlement of the Araucanos.

> Now with the exception that the king has granted by a petition made to the kingdom to remove two companies from the fortress at Valdivia, and give their salaries, which is 24,000 pesos, to found villages of Spaniards dispersed in their farms, just like the Indians, giving to them already made houses, lands designated for vegetable gardens, plots, and cattle; and 150 pesos the first year, 100 the second year, and 50 pesos the third year to purchase cattle and exempt them from duties; and with the mission of the Spanish and German fathers who go to convert them and are foreseeing a journey to Mendoza, detained in this college, it is hoped to put down this rebellion. GOD will carry it forward by his infinite mercy and give us here similarly such powerful and absolutely necessary methods for the conversion of these Sacramentos, Toelches, and in all the area of Magallanes, where, beginning from the Sauce river, we hope to found missions like those for the Guaranís.
>
> (Cardiel 1953: 27)

But it is clear that the settlement of the Araucanos was of a high priority interest for the mother country, and Cardiel, although he does not say it, perceives by intuition that his suggestion will not find any support among the government media of the Río de la Plata.

There remains no other solution than to launch an appeal for financial and technical help to all of Western Europe, in order to achieve his objectives:

> Here I would like to proclaim, with a voice louder than a trumpet, which resounds throughout Europe in the hearts of the princes, in the universities, and in my Jesuit brothers. To the princes so that they wake up to leave no stone unturned in moving through secular means for the conversion of such miserable people. To the universities, so that the hearts of the individuals, moved to pity and compassion by such a loss of souls of our kin, redeemed by the blood of Jesus Christ, could procure a seat in the militia of the King of the Heavens by helping them. To my brothers who are already soldiers in this militia, that they instantly procure with prayers, pleas, and begging to our Captain of the Heavens and Earth, to accomplish that the rescue of so much loss comes, by conquering the common enemy who has usurped so many ranches from the true Lord and Redeemer.
>
> (Cardiel 1953: 203)

And, Cardiel continues

> Come here all ye of apostolic spirit. . . . Here you shall find very large

fields for their militia, very abundant fruits for their labour and harvest, even though there are very few standing and working infidels and with people, such as were the Guaranís and the Chiquitos, for having converted all or almost all . . . you shall find very numerous nations of another kind who work with even more merit and prize . . .

(Cardiel 1953: 204)

Cardiel's clamour to obtain European financial assistance, was raised just at the moment in which, in Europe, at the zenith of the Enlightenment, the French 'Encyclopaedia' was getting ready to publish the famous article on the Jesuits, which was the prelude to their banishment from the American lands. Cardiel's clamour was raised to save the Indian communities of the south and centre of present day Argentina from destruction, a destruction that took place a century later with the well-known campaign called 'Conquest of the Desert'.[2]

From everything we have examined so far, in which we have only allowed the same author to speak, it seems evident that the reflections of Cardiel carry sufficient weight to be taken into account in the history of Latin American economic thought, and more specifically, that of Argentina. To locate him more comfortably in the position that he deserves, it is necessary to consider that, principally, Cardiel had views which were amplified by his writings.

His fundamental concern was to give a global view of the history of the culture, in the widest sense of the word, along the Río de la Plata basin. In this, as Father Guillermo Furlong emphasized in the prologue to Cardiel's 'Carta-Relación' of 1747, besides writing history, Cardiel made history. It is within this multi-faceted framework of cultural history that it is necessary to integrate his economic reflections, as it was in exactly this way that he interpreted and configured them.

Still, there is no doubt that the socio-economic problem has a very defined weight, not as much for its size as for its intrinsic quality; it is probably for this reason, that Cardiel's restlessness was not always agreeable to his brothers in the order. It was always felt that his predilections for problems and lucrative activities marred the figure of the apostolic and renowned missionary. We have already seen that, right up to the present time, the mercantilist attribute found in more than one of Cardiel's writings, has not been retained, not even by those with such a fine critical spirit as displayed by Furlong. Nevertheless, this same Father Furlong pays him the highest homage, and this undoubtedly he did without having it suggested to him. It is enough to review the index of authors found in Furlong's great work *Misiones y sus Pueblos de Guaraníes*, published in Buenos Aires in 1962, to see that of all the authors whose works are listed at the end of the documentation, those of Cardiel – and more precisely, those of his works dealing with the clarification of social and economic problems – surpass any records of citations. This is important, because Cardiel's economic reflections are a very important source for economic historians.

Cardiel himself had this vocation as an economic historian and very specifically within this – so much the fashion today – in the area of quantitative economic history. We have already had the opportunity to examine his talent for taking global estimations within a horizon of statistical poverty.

It would also be fair to emphasize that due to his double focus, as an author who writes history at the same time that he makes it, Cardiel not only left us a valuable economic history, but that superimposed upon this, he left us the legacy of some of the first contributions in the economic and social geography of our lands, and all that is now missing is for one scholar, with sufficient preparation in this field, to proceed to make an inventory and analysis of all his works.

Equally present are his interesting reflections on sociology, especially if we remember his ability to focus on cultural life through various prisms, making and remaking his system of social communities, be they as Indian or Spanish republics in general, or as specific communities. This he does on the one hand from a political or civil disposition, and on the other from an ethnic or religious perspective. He also contemplates the cultural process as a function of climate, nutrition, 'influence of the stars', race or education, in a word, his work is a mine of high-carat quality which awaits an explorer who is not only well prepared, but who has an independent mind, and is able to overcome the barrier of value judgements and the plague of ideological deformations of our time.

In addition to being a superb author, Cardiel was a missionary. Furlong stated that Cardiel was a truly apostolic missionary who set out to do great works for the glory of God and the saving of souls. In addition, he claims that Cardiel was one of the most prominent missionaries that the Jesuit order had in the eighteenth century. Contemporaries of Cardiel said that his words and writings breathed fire into the missionary movement, and that Cardiel used the same honest language with the Indians as with people of high levels of economic interests in the New World. In addition, Cardiel made the great effort to learn the Guaraní language so as to be able to preach to the Indians, an effort which resulted in his complete mastery of this tongue. These eulogies of Cardiel may seem exaggerated, but Furlong affirms that they are the least that he deserves, given his personality, scholarly works, and untiring efforts at being a missionary first and only second an economic historian (Cardiel 1953: 5).

Now it is time to look more closely at what Cardiel labelled 'economics' in 1747 and 'political economy' in 1771. The mere fact of his having arrived at these labels is something worth noting. Deep within the dark jungle which obscures our cultural past, we have yet to find another writer who managed these terms as Cardiel did in our lands; a valid excuse may be that such terms were not common even in the European economic writings of those days, since Montchrétien's *Traité de l'Oeconomie Politique* of 1615 had already been forgotten, just as Hutcheson's *Principles of Oeconomics* passed unnoticed, and only in 1755 did the article on 'Political Economy' become well known. The few European writers who had looked at these terms before Cardiel only add honour to his name. And for this reason, any serious work on the history of economic thought for Argentina, Bolivia, Paraguay, Peru, Uruguay, and other countries should include Cardiel's name in a prominent place.

If we continue to look at economics as a three-way order of economic philosophy, economic theory, and economic policy, we may feel that Cardiel's 'political economy' is in total disorder. Yet this same criticism can be made of the works of Hutcheson, Du Pont, Rousseau, Muñoz, and even Verri. What is important is to see if Cardiel confronted the specific questions of our science in his writings, and where this is the case we shall review his ideas on these topics.

CONTRIBUTIONS TO ECONOMIC PHILOSOPHY

Due to the nature of the problems dealt with in the writings of Cardiel, it would be difficult to find anything related to economic philosophy in them. Yet it is evident that as much in his laying out of the empirical problems, as in their solutions, Cardiel shows his open adherence for the scholastic tradition. The starting point for all this is the problem of how to convert the Indians, of their peaceful settlement by use of the cross as a weapon, and by placing into communities of Christian living the various tribes, separated by circumstances of place and time, and most importantly, by their cultural differences. Consequently, the fundamental objective to be pursued is that of spiritual happiness, economic development and social progress being mere instruments in the service of Christian conversion and perfectionism. As Cardiel stated before, 'if the secular goes well, the spiritual is advanced; if the secular goes poorly, so does the spiritual'.

The postulation of the common good (Cardiel 1953: 8), the just price (Cardiel 1980: 464), justice in the system of contributions expressed by affirming that the king should not treat the Indians as beasts of burden, but 'as sheep, seeing them so poor that there is no wool to shear from them' (Cardiel 1980: 446), the protection of the Indians against *encomiendas* and personal service, which made up the backbone of all the Jesuit Indian schools (Cardiel 1980: 441ff) – all these are defended in explicit form by Cardiel, although he feels such problems do not merit any explicit formulation, as they are covered by the moral study which took place every day among the Jesuit missionaries (Cardiel 1953: 44).

In his works, a small Aristotelian cloud settles in, as Cardiel is seen with his arms crossed when confronted by the problem of black slavery, so common in those times, yet so prohibited in the Guaranian settlements. On

126

the other hand, it is comforting to hear that due to the apostolic zeal of the missionaries in the Indian settlements, the mechanical tradesmen were held in very high esteem. The trajectory of his life shows Cardiel to be not only a defender of Christian philosophy, but an untiring labourer in and intrepid zealot of the undertaking of God's great works and saving souls among the Indians.

CONTRIBUTIONS TO ECONOMIC THEORY

Let's now examine Cardiel's contributions to economic theory. The concepts of 'economics' and 'political economy', even if they do have a certain Aristotelian flavour, take on with Cardiel a much wider sense of economic order.

The method used by Cardiel for understanding the economic process is empirical inductivity with a clear historic and comparative tint, and contributing antecedents to the procedure of bringing out concrete points, all of which is quite similar to the methodology praised by Walter Eucken and called by him 'isolating abstraction' as counterpoint to the traditional methodology of generalized abstraction.

In the area of price theory, we find some of Cardiel's reflections which deserve mention: one related to the analytical concept of the just price compared to the current price, that is to say, for what it is worth in the market; and the other, through which he establishes a certain relation between the abundance of foodstuffs, their cheapness, and the propensity towards leisure.

In his monetary theory, Cardiel surprises us with the allusion to the relation of the value of money and its metallic quantity or abundance, also collected in a purely empirical manner.

But the strength of Cardiel lies in the historical vision of the economic process. What Werner Sombart was for the capitalist system, so was José Cardiel for the economic system of the Jesuit missions: one of its best biographers.

Cardiel, after delineating the history of the Jesuit missions in Argentina, wrote out a type of morphology of the Indian economic systems: nomads (Serranos); semi-nomads (Aucáos); and sedentary (the Guaranís of the Jesuit settlements). In addition, his other thoughts related to the economies 'in which money circulates' and the barter economies are of interest for the history of the morphology of the economy of the Río de la Plata, although in this case we would be hard pressed to state that these writings deal with the traditional economic pairing of monetary economics and the natural economy.

Actually, if in the barter economy pointed out by Cardiel for Paraguay, including Corrientes, 'there is no money circulating whatsoever', money did complete the function of a unit of account, since Cardiel also indicates to us that there were 'fixed imaginary prices on things' (Cardiel 1913: 49) in that economy. Therefore, the distinction to be made is between two kinds of monetary economies: one in which money serves both as a medium of exchange and a unit of account (Buenos Aires, Tucumán, Santa Cruz de la Sierra); and the other where money serves only as a unit of account (Paraguay, including Corrientes). This distinction is much more refined and is more difficult to perceive.

Of equal interest are Cardiel's incursions into the conceptual apparatus which today we call economic development and planning theory; the conceptual pair formed by development (sedentary agricultural communities) and underdevelopment (nomadic communities which live by hunting, fishing, and stealing) obsesses him (Cardiel 1953: 162–82, 195–205).

In addition to this obsession, Cardiel has clear ideas on short- and long-run development (Cardiel 1953: 180), gradual development (ibid.: 179, 202), plans of development (ibid.: 75–9), investment projects (ibid.: 188–9, 202), foreign technical and financial assistance (ibid.: 203, 208), and even urban growth (ibid.: 4), in his writings. The ideas as presented by him add up to a rustic apparatus, but he did lay the foundations for later research, and this in itself is of great importance.

CONTRIBUTIONS TO ECONOMIC POLICY

The bulk of Cardiel's economic reflections lie in the area of economic policy. Nothing less would be expected of a man who undertook secular and spiritual labours in the Guaranian settlements. His methodology is very correct: the first thing one expects of an administrator is a knowledge of the realities in which he works; his 'Relaciones' are a testimony that he was truly a great expert not only in the economic life of the Jesuit settlements, but also in the vast area of the Río de la Plata basin. Later, he proceeds with the diagnosis which covers almost all of his writings, together with the economic policy measures proposed in plain congruence with his determined objectives in light of his Christian morality. This concerns two quite distinct areas: the entrepreneurial economic policy; and the national economic policy.

The entrepreneurial economic policy, or as we call it today, business administration, was Cardiel's forte, as well as his speciality. It was in the administration of the Guaraní towns in which he proved his entrepreneurial ability and genius; it could not be conceived of in any other way by the one responsible for the economic governance of a Guaraní town, if we remember that it was necessary 'that the Fathers are charged with the great weight of teaching them everything, to attend to all, to be master of all, and to make them do everything, even against the ingenuity of the Indians' (Cardiel 1980: 283–4).

In sharp contrast with the economic administration of the missionary enterprises, which was carried out like clockwork, is the administration of lay enterprises. Neither the agricultural nor the cattle breeding enterprises responded to the model that Cardiel had in mind when he had calculated a very low income for these types of exploitation and also diagnosed the principal source of the failure. The only enterprise which seemed to him to be very profitable was commercial enterprise, but this was also a failure in that the enterprises were not managed by native sons. Nevertheless, despite his determined observations germinating in the reflections of a theoretical character, mentioned above, these objects were not of great interest for his preoccupation with economic policy.

It was in the area of national economic policy that his active efforts are to be found. The immense area of the 'kingdoms' of Tucumán, Paraguay, and the Río de la Plata basin were still practically in the hands of nomadic Indians on horseback. Attempts had been made to settle these Indians by the same means as those used for the sedentary tribes, but to no avail. The local Spanish population wanted to submit the Indians to a bloody war, but Cardiel went against the grain and proposed other methods for dealing with these tribes. He developed a long-run plan for the settlement of the nomadic Indians, including a call for a type of experiment to be made by setting up three settlements for them and allowing the settlers to work with the Indians for a period of ten or twelve years. He estimated the costs to be invested in each town, and elaborated a project for their financing, along with an investment plan for attracting financial and technical assistance from Europe. Of course, his ideas were not well received over there, but they are the seeds of modern programming techniques for great cultural areas.

These are briefly the ideas of 'economics' or 'political economy' of José Cardiel, missionary and explorer of these lands, so admired in other disciplines and so ignored in our own. In our belief, Cardiel was an important forerunner of empirical analysis and administration in the economic life of the Río de la Plata and well deserves to hold a position in the history of Argentine economic thought.

9

COLOMBIAN ECONOMIC
DEVELOPMENT

INTRODUCTION

For almost twenty years, the question of economic development has been a priority of the scholars of social sciences.[1] This phenomenon was closely followed by the growing conviction that the surest instrument for acceleration was planning, and the idea of planning development attracted wide attention not only in the developed countries of the Western world, but also in the environment of the developing nations.

As with the rest of Latin America, in Colombia the question of planning is the order of the day and threatens to become a taboo word for many people (Rodríguez Garavito 1967: 169–70). The beginning of the planning spirit in Colombia was on 20 December 1961, when the president of that nation presented his 'General Plan of Economic and Social Development', designed to assist the organs of planning for ten years. The impact produced by this document need not be emphasized, but what is important is the effect it had on the spiritual and cultural order of Colombia.[2]

Very frequently, this orientation towards planning in Colombian society is connected with a series of previous studies conducted by various foreign missions, especially the Center of Economics and Humanism, the Economic Commission on Latin America (CEPAL), and the International Bank for Reconstruction and Development.[3] This is a correct assumption, as these previous studies connected development planning with quantitative methods of programming. In this sense, we should support the thesis of Alvaro Torres Contreras, that 'the first appearance of any concept of planning in Colombia arose in 1949, as a derivation of the activity carried out by the International Bank' (Torres Contreras 1967: 25).

Of course, one need bear in mind that in each of the aforementioned missions, not only were Colombian national organisms involved, but also many of the nation's finest economists, sociologists, engineers, educators, and medical doctors. And this efficient collaboration is honoured by being mentioned in the first few pages of each mission's report. The special confluence of the international missions, and the decisive and fruitful collaboration of the best elements of Colombia in the work, shows that in Colombia there already existed an underlying predisposition in favour of the planning current, and consequently, the terrain was widely prepared for the reception of new ideas. Our task, therefore, is to attempt to identify the trail of this endogenous current and delineate its path.

A REVIEW OF COLOMBIAN ECONOMIC DEVELOPMENT (1811–1948)

Searching through congressional records, the researcher discovers that in 1948, planning was being discussed under a plan of development called the 'Plan Gaitání' as it stated in the 'Anales del Congreso' of 29 July 1948. If we go back two years, we find that it was a Colombian who defended the idea of planning on a world scale. Before the First Assembly of the United Nations, Carlos Lleras Restrepo maintained that

> we shall be able to avoid for a time the pitiless game of concurrence, or the application of unilateral and discriminatory measures which gave the interwar period an arbitrary and selfish character . . . certainly, just realizing a process of integration for the world economy, an integration directly sought and planned in order to succeed in the essential goals which we still mention. . . . The international economy requires even more the national economies, the application of a modern criterion which gives to an organism of research, planning, and coordination the essential position in the development of a work of wide projections.
>
> (Lleras Restrepo 1965: 287)

The Colombian cultural environment was impregnated with ideas related to planning for several years. We know that it was due to this new inspiration that in the Legislative Act No. 1 of 1945, through which the Magna Carta of 1886 was being reformed, the constituents incorporated planning, or the fixation of plans and programmes for economic development as a governmental norm.

But already in 1944, Jorge Cárdenas Nannetti, in his work, *Teoría de la Economía Colombiana* (Theory of the Colombian Economy), had dedicated an entire chapter to the problems of planning, with brilliant personal critiques. This should come as no surprise, as the Liberal Party convention in 1942 had put forth planned and responsible industrial development as one of its platforms of emphasis.

This change of attitude did not just appear out of thin air. In 1940, the then Minister of the Treasury, Carlos Lleras Restrepo, had stated via decree number 1157 of 1940 that

the government, by way of the Ministry of Economics, in agreement

131

with the studies issued by the department and those to be done in the future, adopts a general plan for the fostering of the economic activities of the nation . . . and to facilitate the development, the plan shall be divided into three parts: a plan of agricultural promotion; a plan for the promotion of cattle breeding; and a plan for the fostering of manufacturing.

(Colombia 1940: Decree 1157)

Not only the Liberal Party aspired toward a new social order. Beginning in 1931, when the encyclical Quadragesimo Anno appeared, a growing interest in a state intervention doctrine was noted, even when limited to just the social question. Likewise, the Conservative Party in 1939 pleaded for a more active and direct intervention by the state in commercial and industrial movements.

In preparing the grounds for the sowing of new ideas, professionals from real life and from academia have cooperated. Among the first who should be mentioned is Carlos Uribe Echeverri, who, while serving as ambassador to Brazil and Spain, had the opportunity to know personally the insistent planners overseas; and also Joaquín Vallejo and Alfredo García Cadena, who in the same period of 1930–40 loosed a permanent criticism of the economic policy of the country.

Uribe Echeverri's *Nuestro Problema: Producir* (1936) as well as Vallejo's 'Planeación Económica' (1959) and García Cadena's *Unas Ideas Elementales sobre Problemas Colombianos. Preocupaciones de un Hombre de Trabajo* (1956) are characterized by a vigorous defence of planning as an instrument of development, at the same time containing various outlines of 'plans of action', 'general working plans', 'plans of development', and 'quinquennial plans' for the most representative sectors of the Colombian economy.

In addition, many academic economists had pushed for a national plan of development. In this group was Nicasio Anzola, who in his *Conferences on Political Economy*, placed national development along the same lines of rational behaviour for businesses: 'Work, as an essentially rational act, demands a determinably simple plan to support it. On occasions, this plan constitutes a truly gigantic labour, as we have observed in great works' (Anzola 1936: 56), and only when it has been duly elaborated, does it suit the plan to be put 'in full force for the realization of the true labour, which is, all that intervene should have to submit themselves to the plan already formulated, the only resource to impede the failure of the undertaking' (Anzola 1936: 55–6).

This correct derivation of the planning principle is produced exactly at the time as the constitution of the same year, through Legislative Act No. 1, consecrates the jurisprudential ruling that

the State can intervene by means of laws in the exploitation of the private or public industries or enterprises, with the objective of

132

rationing the production, distribution, and consumption of wealth, or of giving the labourer the fair protection to which he has the right.

(Colombian Constitution 1936: Article 11)

As a faithful adherent of the principles defended by the historical school, Nicasio Anzola did not trust the auto-regulating and driving mechanism of the market and he considers that 'free competition at times is dismal for the national economy' (Anzola 1936: 120). From this arises the necessity of the growing participation of the public sector in directing the economy and this not only for fiscal objectives or as an economic topic, but above all else as an expedient of common good:

> The modern economy demands and clamours for intervention by the state in all that is said to be related to social well-being, tending through this to equally favour and protect the private capital, which will not be seen as having been sacrificed for the absolute freedom of industry and free competition, gospel of [the] individualist school.
>
> (Anzola 1936: 218)

But, it was actually Esteban Jaramillo who contributed more to the enlightenment of younger generations on the imperative of the active participation of the state in economic life. His position defines itself in a substantial essay, 'La Intervención del Estado en la Economía de los Pueblos' ('State Intervention in the Economy of the Nations'), published in 1935. This work was written with the objective of refuting the thesis of economic liberalism, which had just found a new and vigorous defender in a book by US ex-President Herbert Hoover (Hoover 1934).

On this occasion, Jaramillo wrote:

> Nothing is more beneficial and fruitful than liberty when within it all the economic activities of the people unfold in a harmonic and balanced manner, procuring justice, tranquillity, security, and welfare for them. But, that liberty is harmful and sterile when it contributes to the aggravation of social ills, when it makes economic inequalities more notorious and irritating, when it creates odious situations of privilege, or when depriving the less skilled of their sustenance. The freedom of industry, the freedom of commerce, the freedom of exchange, are excellent; but when the exercise of those liberties brings with them the unjust exploitation of the workers, attempts against the future of the race, the crisis of overproduction, unemployment, the monopolization of foodstuffs, or the ruin of the currency, the state is not performing its essential duties of intervening to bring to bay that enemy of public good. Absolute freedom is a social utopia, for the simple reason that it is conceivable within the reign of another utopia, economic equality, since in this case the contenders fight with equal arms.
>
> (Jaramillo 1935: 268–9)

Nevertheless, Jaramillo warns, if it is easy to demonstrate the interventionist thesis, then it is very difficult to put it into practice. This is not only due to the nature of each country, its traditions, and the fact that the level of social, political, and economic culture create different problems, but above all else because the public sector is not prepared to carry out the interventionist policy: 'The great difficulty of interventionism consists in the very frequent lack of truly capable technicians among the government functionaries. To form those capacities, to create true organizers, is a long and difficult task' (Jaramillo 1935: 268). Unfortunately, this correct observation has not been properly considered neither in its time nor in our era of development. And, without a doubt, it is the insufficient skills of the public administration to which the failure of planning in the majority of developing countries should be attributed (OECD 1966).

Another interesting contribution to the theory of planning corresponds to Guillermo Torres García. To him is owed the judicious reflection that one of the greatest difficulties in spontaneously producing a balanced development arises from the sectoral inter-dependence of the economic structure.

His point of view, shown for the first time in the 1929 edition of his *Nociones de Economía Política* (Notions of Political Economy), was reformulated and made more precise in the 1942 edition in the following manner:

> The development of industries in a country should be adequately and proportionally based on their conditions and must be developed simultaneously within that proportion. The simultaneity of the development of industries is explained very clearly by the interdependence which exists among them, as if each one is an indispensable element of one and the others. . . . An imperfect knowledge of the nations or an erroneous notion about the proportional and simultaneous development of the industries, can force governments and particulars to commit regrettable errors. Industrial development in a nation demands, consequently, prospects or plans conceived and carried according to the principles of economic science.
>
> (Torres García 1942: 25ff)

A valuable contribution to the theory of Colombian development planning is due to José Camacho Carreño. In his book, *Reflexiones Económicas* published in 1929, he makes a detailed analysis of the transformations emerging in the contemporary economy and its consequences for economic science (Camacho Carreño 1929). His interest is concentrated above all else on the transition from the individual enterprise to the large or collective enterprise, and he emphasizes that 'the collective forms have planted methods of industrial economy known by the name of Scientific Organization or Rationalization of Work' (Camacho Carreño 1929: 47) whose success as an instrument for the increase in efficiency in the enterprise has been widely confirmed by historical experience.

If this is so, why are the same principles not applied to even greater enterprises, to the entire national economy? Camacho Carreño did not doubt the validity of this idea:

> Despite the idealism of many, the state, in substance, jointly with other categories, assumes the role of supreme regulator of economic life, that of the enterprise of enterprises. Work has become a public concept. The collective economy does not obey natural laws, as certain theorists have fancied, and so it is being demonstrated that in the enterprise the empiricism that delivers the production arbitrarily without intensifying it or coordinating it by rational methods fails; in the State, the trusted and deterministic criterion fails so that there is no anticipation, no order, no distribution, no concertation, no synthesis of efforts and results. An economy, whether it is private as the enterprise, or social as the state, is no mischievous group of phenomena, it is a system of productive and consuming forces. And a system is a unit of principles.
>
> (Camacho Carreño 1929: 47ff)

Of course, this unit of principles is set in the practical life of the enterprises in a plan or a programme of action. From this comes the theory that to generalize the idea of order, it is necessary to extend the planning to all the national community. In fact, Camacho Carreño observes:

> to conceive a plan of enterprises raised within rational methods of labour, where units are trained to uphold the principle of greatest economy and not to coordinate their production with a directive from the state, that it worked as a nervous system within the economic regime, is to nullify the task. To perfect one aspect of the creation of wealth so that another of its facets deteriorates, makes no sense. A program of action that aimed at economy in individual production and that by application of physiological and psychological laws inferred the greatest human yield; but that it stopped the plan at this point without elevating it to the enterprise level for the collective organization of labour by the adoption of directives, to which the individual result in effective yield flocks with benefits, would be an attempt against reason. No less nonsensical would it be to organize enterprises, but not to organize the state, that is to say the social economy.
>
> (Camacho Carreño 1929: 164)

Camacho Carreño does not worry that he will be labelled as an interventionist, a reformer, a state socialist or a statist, as all these doctrines concentrate on applying the same principles of rationality for the individual enterprise to the social enterprise level of the state. All have the same common denominator: 'the rationalization of social labour'. It is just that it is necessary to determine correctly the sense of this principle:

It does not deal, as many believe, with the state only intervening to repress the social conflicts arising from labour, or to avoid them, or be it to exercise the checking and prediction functions, it is also necessary that the state creates new productive resources, that it increases the economic capacity of society, that it perfects the methods and that by its intervention it accounts for all possible types of riches. To check, to prevent, to create and to perfect, here are the four faces that make up the modern state, under which joint reflexes the human being acquires his maximum expressive power and the ability to cast himself in time and space.

(Camacho Carreño 1929: 165)

Camacho Carreño does not limit himself to studying the fundamentals of the 'doctrine of the state whose motive is to coordinate the productive forces of society' (Camacho Carreño 1929: 189), but at the same time to formulate a concrete and executable programme to solve the Colombian problems and whose centre of gravity is built upon the problem of its scarce and barely skilled human resources: 'If man is always necessary, let's dignify, let's revere and let's exalt his human value, let's get a worker out of an "Indian", as the first step of the program' (Camacho Carreño 1929: 234).

Our author ends his study with an administrative suggestion for development, which he considers of interest for the Colombian Minister of Industries:

The national organization of production should count on an Economic Council comprised of delegates of different organized professions (landlords, technicians, employees, labourers) and some lawyers and economists. This is actually the most probable way to unite the necessary competent people. The role of this council should not be to direct the production but to counsel those who do direct it and convince them by persuasion to orient their activity in the sense of general interest. It could also indicate to the government about the necessary measures of authority to guard and promote public benefit.

(Camacho Carreño 1929: 235–6)

Laureano Gómez not only designed a most worthy methodological plan, but at the same time a vigorous anthropo-geographical theory as a foundation for Colombian development. His work, *Interrogantes sobre el Progreso de Colombia* (Questions about the Colombian Progress), is a collection of the papers of two conferences held in the Teatro Municipal de Bogota, on 5 June 1928 and 3 August 1928 (Gómez 1928), which provoked a true scandal in the cultural circles of the time.

His starting point is the thesis that in order to be able to structure a strategy of development, one should begin with a correct and clear diagnosis, as we would say today. Without the knowledge of the structure of the respective economic system, without 'having an exact idea of its own state, of the progress already achieved, and those which need be made, without this knowledge, the nation drives itself to disaster' (Gómez 1928: 9). Once the study on the direction of and the elements in the system is completed, then the widening of the vision is imposed with the objective of 'seeing the beginnings of societies which came to be illustrious and gigantic and pondering the factors that give them their prosperity' (Gómez 1928: 12–13). By comparison with the societies already developed 'the question marks and the doubts' shall arise and the necessity of formulating principal and governing ideas will be imposed upon the nation.

Laureano Gómez is not content with formulating methodological reflections. These only serve him as a reference point to dedicate himself towards a deep and very original diagnosis of the underlying factors in Colombia's progress. The major obstacle to Colombian progress is found in the location of the country within a tropical belt. 'The first observation which arises is that in this latitude . . . there does not exist any territory which throughout all history of the human species, has ever been the seat of a true culture' (Gómez 1928: 14). Evidently, the accent on 'culture' could not have been received without leaving a deep wound in the spirit of his critics. But if we substitute the word 'culture' for 'economic development', his observation is an exact one. Even today, the lowest levels of development are concentrated within the tropical belts.

Laureano Gómez does not limit himself to diagnosing the economic stagnation of the tropical zones, but proceeds to explain this phenomenon.

> Where tropical nature obtains complete domination by humidity and temperature conditions, she imposes her greatness with such characteristics of uncommon and charming efforts that the human spirit is disturbed and depressed. The domination of man's monstrous adversary transforms terror into deification. The soul is drowned, it is dissolved in the ecstasy of that immeasurable and devouring beauty; it embraces the uselessness of the struggle of the tiny intelligent being against the infinite sons of the marriage of the humid earth and the sun. That is the origin of the metaphysics of India. . . . That primitive metaphysics has a forced consequence which we can observe in ourselves in some territories of the Bajo Magdalena and other tropical rivers. From such consequences comes the state of immobility in which the souls of men remain, submitted to that geographical median. It is a profound inertia for culture, an invincible lethargy. The animal habits dominate the animal human.
>
> (Gómez 1928: 17)

Happily for Colombia, he observes, 'thanks to a morphological accident, the rising of the Andes mountain range', the inclemency of the tropical environment could be partially checked. What is more

137

a thinker who analyzes the basis of greatness of the modern states, based on the material aspects, points out four pillars upon which every building of economic and industrial prosperity should rest. They are the possession of iron, coal, petroleum, and waterfalls. By immense fortune, in the division of the earth, we have been decidedly favoured with the very abundant distribution of these four factors of national enlargement.

(Gómez 1928: 40)

But despite all this, it is still necessary to have an availability of skilled and endowed human resources with a correspondent entrepreneurial spirit.

The diagnosis performed by Gómez on the quality of the Colombian human resources is extremely depressing, and this not only as regards the native and African descendant populations, but also those of Hispanic origin: 'It suffices us to know that neither for those of Hispanic origin, nor those of African and American influences, is ours a privileged race for the establishment of a fundamental culture, nor for the conquest of an independent aboriginal civilization' (Gómez 1928: 56).

The pessimism becomes worse when the author contemplates the gravitation of external economic forces on Colombian economic life, which by their potential superiority and their interests corresponding to diametrically opposite objectives, accentuate even more the distortions and structural deformation of the national economic process.

We find ourselves in the presence of a biological conflict. The groupings formed in capable natural boundaries, tend to overflow into those others in which the man, worse installed, does not dominate; before he is dominated by exuberant nature, which upon indulging it, yields him an easy, although miserable, life, like along the banks of the Magdalena river, with fish and plantain, make him very bland and subordinate to those who strengthen themselves in rough battles, by the conquering of a positive welfare and were favoured by other circumstances, such as blood, economic position, and contacts with the universal culture. It is frightening to think that the ending is already written in the book of destiny of the Americas. . . . The biological struggle, slow, but without alternatives, devouring and fatal, is in motion. Every day which passes, we lose something. Every day something of ours is acquired by the most capable, the richest, the strongest.

(Gómez 1928: 64)

This unsettling diagnosis, as difficult as it is irritating, explains the storm of fury which it had raised, but the author's objective was quite distinct.

His goal was to spark the mobilization of the conscience of the nation's elite towards a vigorous policy of systematic and persistent economic development, since 'our territory is not a spontaneous and decidedly favourable natural area for the fruitful establishment of a human culture' (Gómez 1928: 39). Faced with the lack of these factors of spontaneous growth, the only available alternative is that 'the progress which is here based, must be a work of intelligence and craftsmanship, of zeal and vigilance, which minute by minute collects the favourable elements and separates the adverse ones' (Gómez 1928: 64). He later returns to the idea of a planned economic order, with even more emphasis:

> Under these threatening circumstances, we cannot have the luxury of ineptness. Only an intelligent, vigilant and wise direction for the affairs of state can intervene efficiently to sway the course of events which appears sure. Only in a struggle of every minute against the adverse factors and in the detailed usage of the favourable ones, based on science and knowledge, on labour, and untiring energy, shall it be possible to just check the categorical imperative of the influences of the surroundings, which so closely threatens us, which now shows us the principle of its effectiveness and discovers from a distance the results of its fatal end.
>
> (Gómez 1928: 66)

Laureano Gómez is clearly conscious that the national elite is not sufficiently prepared to confront this problem. Nevertheless, it seems that he concluded his writing with the intention of jolting the Colombia elite, emphatically warning:

> My thesis is that this land is not the spontaneous natural boundary for a human culture; that that culture can base itself here, but only by great efforts of intelligence, labour, and money. That the nation is fundamentally wrong in the appreciation of the resources it has available and the methods it has in use to achieve this culture. And that if the country does not change its criteria or its conduct, it will perish. Irrevocably it will perish.
>
> (Gómez 1928: 95)

While Laureano Gómez faced the problem of Colombian development from the vast socio-cultural optic, Alejandro López , in his 1922 work *Problemas Colombianos*, limited the focus to just the economic realm (López 1929). But the preoccupation is the same, as López makes an effort to find the 'forces or doctrinal errors which might be stopping our progress' (López 1927: 9); and equally, to also consider that 'what is important is to arrive at a certain diagnosis of the forces retarding our progress, and localize them in such a concrete and unmistakable manner that the solutions suggest themselves as ideas-efforts' (López 1927: 10).

In his thinking, the main obstacles which hinder the nation's progress arise from 'the lack of investment values which inspire certain confidence and that disrupts all national activity', 'the multitude of jobs with which every individual is busy', 'the disease of debts', and 'the necessity to obtain greater labour productivity'; and these restraints converge and are summarized into one: 'the problem of education provided that we include in this denomination the reeducation of itself' (López 1927: 11). Nevertheless, observes López, whichever were the obstacles that will be identified, what is important is to localize them and define them clearly, so as to serve as a concrete guide to the government's policy.

> I dare to suggest that this method of uniting defined objectives and that other centers of interest should be formed, is the road to overcome our difficulties of diverse order. Less sterile than the constant incrimination of the government, because it does not make the people happy, as they said before, would be to settle it and reclaim concrete objectives.
>
> (López 1927: 14)

Of course, this means forgetting the philosophy of '"laissez faire" that prevails in Colombia' (López 1927: 175) to embrace bravely a conception of the world in which

> one could consider the state as the super enterprise which governs and controls all enterprises and the government of the nations as the attorney, procurer or agent of demand for that which it is incapable of organizing and is characterized by all that which has to function as an organism endowed with objectives, as it is with means to satisfy them.
>
> (López 1927: 239)

To better illustrate his ideas, he suggests that 'an official plan of action be studied, duly seconded by the private initiative' tending towards the labour of reconstruction and reorganization of the agricultural industry. The manner in which to proceed would lie in 'dividing that action into successive periods, of, let's say, five years, in each of which should be concentrated the effort toward determined objectives' (López 1927: 253). In the same manner, he insists on the necessity of a generalized plan of railroads, whose features he studies painstakingly.

But the most fundamental and durable part of his work lies in the profound study which he undertakes on the Colombian human resources, as much in general as in the principal sectors and levels of economic activity, and which occupies practically all of his book.

Another author worthy of mention is Juan Manuel Pabón, who wrote *Fundamentos de la Ciencia Económica* in 1922. Although, as the title states, this is a general book which also deals lightly with economic development, Pabón attempts to show the principles of the economic process through the focus of mathematical analysis. This work would seem to be the first book in all of Latin America to deal with mathematical economics.

During the 1880s in Colombia, economic planning was often talked about and very seldom acted upon. General Reyes attempted to develop a national plan of development to lead Colombia out of the suffering inflicted by a civil war. Five years earlier, Rafael Nuñez, on assuming the presidency, had called for better education, a reform of customs duties, and some industrial protection to help Colombia in its time of need. Carlos Martínez Silva had usually shunned any type of planning, unless it was the divine plan from providence. Antonio José Santiago Pérez maintained that the basis of any good political system was a good economic plan. This economic plan was always to be based on education, morality, and wealth, as these were the main factors of the republic; but he always maintained that any economic plan with a total absence of cultural education, was doomed to failure.

Sergio Arboleda claimed that changes in the structure were to blame for the lack of development in the Americas. In 1857, he presented a paper on the measures needed to develop industries in the south of New Granada. His was one of the first stabs at this problem by a native to the region. In his book *La República en la América Española*, Arboleda said that these industries were native to his region, and that all sociological factors, Colombia's climate, location, and the types of national industry involved, combined to make it best not to interfere and protect the domestic industries from foreign competition (Arboleda 1951).

Around the same time, José María Samper called for a 'combination' of laissez-faire economics and state intervention. He was in favour of letting individuals produce what they were best at, but that the government should intervene to guarantee efficiency. Samper would go one step further and call for a series of Latin American trade blocks, as he felt that having an inter-American trade agreement would only lead to all countries in the Hispanic world becoming overly protective to keep their national industries from being harmed by competition (Samper 1861).

Manuel María Madiedo was basically a liberal thinker who disliked government intervention in daily economic life. He proposed that instead of direct government intervention in the industries to break up monopolies, the government regulators should be replaced by independent professionals who were to make sure that the masses did not suffer in the manufacturing sector from unfair competition from the national industrial giants. Failure to do so would mean many men would lose their jobs, and they and their families would starve to death. The best testimony to the truth of this last point is any report on the miserable living conditions of Colombia's poor in the 1860s, whom he wanted to see as owners of the lands they worked (Madiedo 1863).[4]

Simón Bolívar, the famous liberator of a great part of northern South America, also attempted schemes for economic development. His main ideas were to promote and improve agriculture, improve literacy and education concerning agriculture, stimulate trade as much as possible, and award those who develop new goods for industrial manufacturing. Bolívar believed that the best way to carry out these measures was to form a Patriot Society, which would be in charge of these measures and the establishment of universities to grant higher education to those interested in all branches of science, agriculture, commerce, and arts.

The roots of service organizations for economic development in Colombia are much deeper than usually thought, as they go back to the colonial days of this country. The starting point for all this was the Sociedad de los Amigos del País (Society of the Friends of the Nation), founded in Vergara, in Guipúzcoa (Spain), in April 1765 by the Marquis de Peñaflorida, Sir Javier Munive e Idiaquez, with the expressed objective of 'improving the peoples' education, promoting and developing agriculture, the arts, and commerce'. The spreading of the idea in Spain is due to the decisiveness of Pedro Rodríguez de Campomanes, who in his *Discurso sobre la Educación Popular de los Artesanos y su Fomento* (1775) demonstrated the benefits of establishing 'Economic Societies' in all the provinces of the kingdom. By the royal decree of 9 November 1775 the Royal Economic Society of Friends of the Nation was created, placing Antonio de la Cuadra as director, and the Marquis of Valdelirios, as sub-director.

In a few years, the number of these economic societies that had been created in Spain, reached more than fifty. Valencia, Seville, Segovia, Mallorca, Zaragoza, and Tudela were the first ones to follow the example of Madrid, and soon these societies began to appear in all the most important population centres of Spain (Sempere y Guarinos 1797; Lafuente 1858: 407; Labra 1903). As the name of the societies emphasized the ideas of patriotism and love of the country, and the motto was to promote social progress as a way of learning, it is understandable that soon the success in the mother country was echoed in the Indias. Thus arose in La Habana the Economic Society of the Friends of the Country, in Guatemala the Economic Society of the Lovers of Guatemala, in Lima the society known as Lovers of the Country, in Buenos Aires the Patriotic, Economic and Literary Society of the Country, and in Quito the School of Concordia. Despite the variety of the names, all had the same aim as the society in Madrid: to develop industry, the arts and professions, agriculture and the breeding of cattle, and establish patriotic schools throughout the kingdom.

Of course, in the New Kingdom, the opportunity was not lost for opening up. Moreover, it seems that it was here that the first economic society arose. In La Habana, which figures as one of the oldest societies, a society was established in 1793, but the first economic society of the New Kingdom of Granada was created in 1784. Actually, Antonio Espinosa de los Monteros, in his work 'Extracto de las Primeras Juntas Celebradas por la Sociedad Económica de Amigos del País', stated that the General Assembly of the Constitution of the Society was created on 12 September 1784 in the town of Mompox, in the house of the lieutenant colonel of the royal armies, Gonzalo José de Hoyos, who was elected director, and that the statutes and the working plan of the society were determined on 19 September 1784. A charter was approved by the Viceroy and Governor General Sir Antonio Caballero y Góngora on 17 August 1789 (Espinosa de los Monteros 1784). Later, Pedro Fermín de Vargas relates in his *Pensamientos Políticos* that 'in the year 1787 an attempt was made to establish in Cartagena an economic society, with the name Society of Friends of the Nation of Turbaco' (Vargas 1944: 42). And finally, Abel Cruz Santos mentions in his 'Economía y Hacienda Pública' that the Patriotic Society of the New Kingdom of Granada was founded in Santa Fé in 1801 by the initiative of Jorge Tadeo Lozano (1771–1816), in which congregated around the wise Mutis, a group of the intellectual elite of this time, and among its principal objectives were to 'put into practice the most adequate means for the development of agriculture and cattle breeding, industry and commerce, the sciences and the liberal arts in the New Kingdom' (Cruz Santos 1965: 224).

The preoccupation for development planning and projecting can be found even among the authors of the young New Granadian economic literature, and among these writers, the works of five stand out: José Ignacio de Pombo (1810); Jorge Tadeo Lozano (1801); Antonio Nariño (1797); Pedro Fermín de Vargas (1790); and Antonio de Narváez y la Torre (1778).

From the letters which José Ignacio de Pombo (1761–1815) sent to the wise Mutis, we discover that the former was undertaking a plan for the reform of the kingdom since 1808, and though he recognized this as an affair superior to his efforts, he was confident that his plan could be advantageous for all of the Americas: 'I hope it is useful to the Kingdom and to all America' (Mendoza 1912: 252). In his voluminous 'Informe del real Consulado de Cartagena de Indias', published in 1810, Pombo (1965), after having performed an excellent diagnosis of economic and social life, clearly determines as objectives of his plan not only the increase of economic activities in general, but also a firm occupational policy. The development of agriculture, the arts or industries and commerce are in plain agreement with the first objective, but the development of just any industry is not always in tandem with the second objective.

> Under this respect, the advantages to the general and ordinary factories should be gradually increased, for even though it appears that each one of them only employs a small number of men, their consumption is multiplied, and also that of those who maintain them; and so their usefulness is more real and effective than those of the fine or luxury goods factories, which only produce for the rich who, with all due respect, are only a very small number of the inhabitants everywhere.
>
> (Pombo 1965: 193)

143

A great variety of classes of activities and factories is indicated in the 'Informe' to guide the country along the path of progress, but Pombo observes:

> the factories which we truly lack are those that are capable of taking us out of the present misery, those which could remedy all our evils, and which could proportion us the industry that we desire, they are the Factories of knowledge.

Without good and sufficient first class schools, drawing and mathematics schools, schools of the natural sciences, medical school and astronomical observatory, 'university departments of public law and political economics', of printed materials and newspapers, including 'a society of friends of the nation', adds Pombo, 'there would not even be fine customs, nor permanent wealth among them, that is only obtained through the cultivation of the arts: they are therefore of the most absolute necessity' (Pombo 1965: 191). So that, 'indicating the true way, or we should say, the only way to promote and develop industry is the improvement of education', Pombo understands he is giving high priority to educational development but knows that to carry out his plan, 'time, men, ways, and above all a lot of energy and constancy by the government will be needed'. As a first step, he calculates that 'sixteen or twenty thousand pesos in cash and the same in credit' would be enough to acquire the equipment needed for educational goals, printing presses, books, laboratory equipment, etc., including the wage of the professors (Pombo 1965: 191–2). Simultaneously, he suggests a complete programme of agricultural extension, plus a plan of colonization and foundation of new population centres with the objective of repairing and putting into order the distortions of development in the kingdom, produced by its peripheral position to the mother country, all of which should be financed through a deep reform of the tributary system (Pombo 1965: 192–271).

Upon critically examining Pombo's report, Rafael Gómez Hoyos came to the conclusion that it deals with

> a work of capital importance in the economic history of Colombia. Many of the topics, of his observations and suggestions, of his principles, continue to be relevant for the present, after so many foreign missions and international organizations have indicated the path for leaving the poverty of an underdeveloped nation. Did Pombo perchance propose a plan for our rudimentary economy that anticipated by many years the experts of today? Because the planning which he makes for the economic problems has an impressive sense of modernity in it.
>
> (Gómez Hoyos 1962: 299)

In the 'Correo Curioso, Erudito, Económico y Mercantil de la Ciudad de Santa Fé de Bogotá', which he edited jointly with doctor Luis Azuola, Jorge Tadeo Lozano published in 1801 a series of short essays in which the problems of development, or as they were known at that time, of the 'public happiness' were given top priority (reprinted in Lozano 1937: 1–43). Intrigued by the fact that the previous attempts made in the kingdom to make the inhabitants happy had failed, Lozano resolved to elaborate a project which appears to be 'more equitable, less costly and more attainable for the achievement of these important ends'. The starting point of all this was constituted by the diagnosis that in the kingdom abounded a 'great number of idle men and women'.

The explanation of this fact is simple: in 'a country where the arts do not flourish, it can be no less than full of beggars and licentious people'. But the lagging in the arts is due in part to the ignorance of the masses, which impedes the birth in them of 'a taste for the arts, agriculture, and commerce', and also in part, to certain distortions in the mentality of the leading class, above all else in its scorn for economic activities.

> The useful arts are taken for scornful things and those who practice them are treated with almost contempt: the motive for which few opt to practice them; to die of hunger and to educate the children in those same principles is preferred to make them learn a trade or to work in the country side; and there are even those who blush at making them learn the science of commerce. This undoubtedly arises from the scorn in which the arts and agriculture are held, and from the vanity with which a birth is boasted, qualified on a piece of paper, which is characterized by 'executive letter', and there is no shame in employing all that is most vile, licentious, and odious and despicable in the Republic.
>
> (Lozano 1937: 32)

In addition, Lozano says that an artesan, no matter how humble his craft, should be held in higher esteem than a nobleman who lives in shameful laziness.

To all of this is added the absence of the entrepreneurial spirit and the propensity to treasure money derived from a false concept of the essence of money and its dynamic role in the process of development. Jorge Tadeo Lozano surprises us with an admirable vision of the monetary flow taking as an analogy the fields of biological and physical sciences, in which their dynamic natures become evident.

> Money, like the blood of a body, gives life and shares with each and every one proportionally the movement and robustness that it needs to freely comply with the action that it must complete as a member of society. Businessmen are like the cysts and receptacles of it, to go

145

introducing it through the conduits which serve its circular movement; and that which in the blood is the chyle which mixes the blood, is in the businessmen the earnings they have reported. This instrumental motive of wealth can not be hushed, if it is to produce an effect. It is a mill of any factory that should not rest in its usage, for the owner and the exporters to use; it is a spring of rich waters which has the precision of having a current so as not to become stagnant . . . which in the manner of electric flow which passes through bodies, leaving them with a glowing heat, also enlivens the arms and hands through which it passes . . . by the continuous circuit of the superabundant transit . . .

(Lozano 1937: 5, 8, 14)

To leave this vicious circle, to achieve the movement of the abundant and varied natural resources of the country, the first step to be taken is the change of the spiritual structure of the population, and for this the only path is the constitution of an Economic Society of Friends of the Nation.

As the effects have not corresponded in times before, despite the careful attention with which this kingdom attempted to make them flourish, it is with fear that the same comes to pass again in the future; if a capable method is not established, which is a patriotic body that, dedicated to the reform of customs by way of a good education, and to introduce the fine pleasure of industry and the arts, it can later extend the knowledge and care to the indicated branches and to become useful to the common society.

(Lozano 1937: 31)

And in the presence of 'the fermentation that has excited the European economic societies in this capital and even in all of the kingdom' and taking into account that 'they have made the people happy wherever they were founded and have made mendacity and misery unknown', Lozano has no doubt as to which path to choose.

What other means could be adopted more efficiently than a society of friends of the nation? . . . The establishment of a patriotic society should be watched as one of the first announcements of the happiness of the kingdom. The great personalities who could foster it would have no doubt as to its great success.

(Lozano 1937: 37–8)

But proceeding now to the eighteenth century, we find even greater surprises. On the 16 November 1797 a document was presented to the viceroy to send to the king. It was entitled, 'Ensayo sobre un Nuevo Plan de Administración en el Nuevo Reino de Granada', and its author was none other than Antonio Nariño (1765–1823). In reality, it deals with a draft of plans, and it was Nariño who insisted on this aspect.

My idea has been only to present my thoughts in one glance, limiting myself to that which I have believed to be absolutely necessary in order that its utility be known, without entering into details or reflections, which many times cloud the basis of the principal matter; but if one should believe that they deserve all the attention that I think they do, I am quick to raise the difficulties which occur and to give a detailed plan of each point in particular and all in general, with all necessary assistance.

(Nariño 1946: 16)

Second, Nariño observes, the plan only refers to determined aspects related to the taxation and monetary policies of the kingdom.

I have not thought it convenient to mix in this paper the other equally useful points, although they are not as important, and which can be seen in part as belonging to the policy of the kingdom, such as governmental measures to increase one's own income and for the construction of roads; the way to give an exit to certain particular staples, and to encourage others not to enter into commerce; the establishment of a factory of porcelain in Pamplona; the methods of providing the kingdom with highly necessary utensils; the labour in the platinum and metal mines; the funds to maintain and to advance the missions, etc., etc. About all of this I shall speak, if what I propose is adopted, and it has served as a basis for these minor objectives.

(Nariño 1946: 87)

But, this 'new plan' has one more peculiarity. In a time in which fundamentally the objectives of the mother country were taken into account, Nariño, despite the fact that he wrote 'in an enclosure, destitute of assistance', dares to give the same priority to the objectives of the colony as to those of the mother country

It is necessary to keep in mind that I speak of a colony, and I keep to the principles ... that continue in the reciprocal interest of the colony with the mother country ... I do not propose anything that establishes factories or manufacturers which would make the national commerce decline, and which would damage them in an infant colony, abundant in fruits and scarce of arms; I do not forget that the wealth of a colony should be different from that of the mother · country, and that this difference is what should make the reciprocal trade less troublesome.

(Nariño 1946: 87, 91)

His starting point is a judgement of indisputable context:

No matter how rich a country may be in mines and other productions, if its inhabitants are poor, the state can not gain great advantages; that which has nothing to contribute, and the only means by which it contributes is to apportion them means of acquisition.

(Nariño 1946: 67)

Where it results that the interests of the mother country coincide with those of the colony, the surest road to satisfy the objectives of both parties in the optimal manner is to increase the wealth and welfare of the inhabitants. Upon examining the tributary system existing in the kingdom, Nariño finds that while some types of contributions are compatible with the process of development, others on the contrary are a true obstacle.

Among the 'contributions which are more costly for the obstacles that oppose the progress of the vassals . . . are in this kingdom the domestic sales taxes and the state brandy stores' (Nariño 1946: 69). It is against these two that Nariño's attack is most concentrated. As a substitute, he proposes a type of poll tax, which not only seems to be easy to execute, but besides will contribute in a substantial way to the development of industry and to the increase in the productivity of labour. The taxation measures are complemented with monetary measures.

In the presence of the chronic unevenness between the volume of metal money and the volume of transactions, Nariño suggests as a remedy for combating the scarcity of metal money the introduction of paper money. And he is clearly convinced that 'the paper money being introduced in a just proportion, the increase in the signs will facilitate the exchanges', and by this the economic development will be stimulated, so that 'the paper, which at first sight seems as if it will destroy the kingdom, will make stronger, let's say, the kingdom's prosperity' (Nariño 1946: 82).

His arguments taken in detail, sharp and reinforced with empirical backing and at times supported by authorities in the material, are not always convincing, but nevertheless we cannot deny his intuition for incorporating tributary policy and monetary policy as instruments for servicing economic development, and this at a time in which everyone was taking different paths and had distinct objectives.

Worries similar to those of Nariño are put forth in the writings of his friend and companion in the struggle for independence, Pedro Fermín de Vargas (1760–1807). But the ideas of the latter not only anticipate in date those of Nariño, but are much wider, deeper and better documented. Parting from the assumption that the nature of the viceroyalty of the New Kingdom had been completely liberal, and convinced that in order to 'see the kingdom flourish in a few years', it is only necessary that 'one wise hand . . . be applied with firmness in promoting the branches of agriculture, commerce, and mines', Fermín de Vargas decides to make himself the party responsible for this task. His love of country, his acquired experience, he affirms

in the highest office of the kingdom, the journeys by which I have crossed the country almost part by part and the observations that these

148

have suggested to me, put me in a state of speaking with greater knowledge than many others, of the inconveniences there are to overcome, the branches to cultivate, and the foresight which should be given to achieve the prosperity of this colony.

(Vargas 1944: 7)

Of course, the viceroyalty is an integral part of the mother country, and as such a similar undertaking should be carried out by 'interweaving the interests of the kingdom with those of the mother country, as every good citizen should calculate' (Vargas 1944: 47), especially if it deals with the first officer of the secretariat and later magistrate of Zipaquirá. It is for this same reason that the development of industry was not included in the general announcement which serves as the prologue to the study, a fact which leads some authors to believe Vargas had overlooked the problem. But in the body of his studies the important role which industrial development had in his concept is proved. It is enough to remember the allusion de Vargas makes to the province of Quito, where the manufacturers are abundant: 'This should serve us as a model toward which we should always tend, by means of the economic societies, to establish some factories, throughout the wide extension of the kingdom' (Vargas 1944: 104). Fermín de Vargas speaks timidly of only 'some factories', but does not take long to indicate the reason for this limitation: 'The kingdom can for now only aspire to certain rough manufactures, which will serve to dress the people up, and not being fabricated in the mother country, cannot enter into the prohibition of the laws' (Vargas 1944: 103). Far from some unilateral development based solely on agriculture, his plan opts for a balanced development of all the branches of activity, agriculture, industry and commerce, and this as much for economic reasons as for social reasons. The development of industry not only brings 'abundance to the people in those villages', but also stimulates activities in the other economic sectors, due to the 'mutual assistance that agriculture and commerce receive from this so brief an occupation', and above all else, because it has the virtue of checking the tendency towards unbalanced social growth

We know that the arts and manufacturing, giving work to the citizens who do not have rural land property, and elevating perhaps their industry to an immense value, balancing the classes of the State, containing the preponderance of the proprietors or the owners of the livelihoods.

(Vargas 1944: 103)

But Fermín de Vargas gives us many new focuses in his plan for the development of the kingdom. In the foreground, his regional optic juts out. He attacks with vehemence the insensitivity of the government for having forgotten the interior lands, which is exactly what happened in the days of the galleons. It is also because of this that he insists on the industrial development of the nation, because 'if the rough manufactures are not stimulated, the interior of the kingdom shall always be a vast desert because its distance to the coasts opposes an invincible obstacle to its commerce' (Vargas 1944: 102–3).

The necessity for a vigorous infrastructure policy arises, especially in regard to roads to unite the interior and the coasts. And in this aspect, de Vargas' point of view is imperative: 'If we do not attempt to make the interior of the kingdom communicable with the coasts, it is better not to even think of developing it' (Vargas 1944: 25). The means to realize these works should be different from those used up to this point, as for example:

> the collection baskets, which reduce the people to opening the roads on their own; similar measures do more harm than good; when the workers are taken out of their houses, they abandon the sowing of crops and this sets them back for some time; besides which by this method, the poor man works as much as he can, while the rich and the merchants do not contribute anything, being those who take the greatest advantage of similar operations.
>
> (Vargas 1944: 35)

The solution lies in incorporating the armed forces in service to the development policy. Actually, Fermín de Vargas surprises us with this very modern concept, suggesting that the 1,600 men of the garrison of Santa Fé 'would spend their time better and live healthier lives if they were designated to the opening and construction of roads', making them even more useful for society (Vargas 1944: 36–7).

The motto 'agriculture, the first of the arts', is a formula that is better used as a smoke screen to make his compatriots and the officials of the government aware of the necessity for a harmonious regional and sectored development policy, and above all else to call attention to the fact that together with the free cultivation of the primary sector equal encouragement in the prohibited sector of manufacturing is needed.

But there is more. Alongside the economic planning, de Vargas presents a wise and beautiful outline for human resources. Convinced that the greatness of a town lies in the number and quality of its inhabitants, he suggests a series of measures, such as: the stimulation of immigration; the stimulation of marriages through agrarian reforms and development of industries; and checking mortality by means of campaigns against diseases, especially leprosy and smallpox, fostering of medicine, and hospitals, and vigilance of the cities of the low lying areas, with the objective of increasing their populations; and stimulation to make the Indians more 'Spanish' through an adequate policy of racial mixing; stimulations for fundamental education through local school districts in the interior of the country; stimulating the efficiency of the work force by reducing the number of holidays and the

150

giving of lands to soldiers when they complete their tour of duty, with the objective being the improvement in the quality and productivity of labour (Vargas 1944: 99).

But it is not sufficient to elaborate plans of development, no matter how complete and well studied they could be. The fundamental point is to have a body of capable directors who are competent to carry out these plans. Unfortunately, observes Fermín de Vargas, the situation is not very encouraging.

> The ignorance of the Viceroys in politics and economics contributes in no small part to this disgrace. . . . What would it cost our ministry to designate those who have displayed their talents in foreign embassies these positions? The men, accustomed to dealing with affairs of government and politics, could have much education and sagacity in all that is related to commerce, treaties, navigation, etc.; instructed in the politics and economics of cultured and industrious nations, they could endeavor to develop the same ideas in the Americas.
>
> (Vargas 1944: 78)

Fermín de Vargas does not neglect to confide his worries about studying and carrying out the plans of development in a special institute, and it should come as no surprise that he also thinks of the Economic Society of Friends of the Nation:

> The patriotic body of which I speak should be founded under the same rules as for Madrid and Vizcaya . . . considering this to be the only chance for the development of the kingdom. . . . Of the knowledge of all, then, and also of the relations which could be requested, or could be directed by the institution of the corresponding members, factual records could be formed which would serve as an assurance of the correctness of the objectives for the economy, which are exclusive to the kingdom and should be promoted. From the funds of the Society would be taken that which is necessary to purchase in Europe the models of those machines which are indispensable for the perfection and advancement of agriculture and suitable industries for the nation. . . . In a virgin country like this one, such a vast area for the investigations and experiments of a body composed of intelligent and zealous men of the kingdom. The protection by the government that it should enjoy would place them in a state of obtaining the purest news about the affairs of their institute, and of executing their plans without opposition. The government itself should be interested in its advancements towards glory by seeing the kingdom prosper, having an educated body which facilitates the official news from various points of their particular economy, whose weight could be relinquished to the Economic Society.
>
> (Vargas 1944: 15–19, 96)

As we can see, the functions suggested for the society of friends of the nation actually correspond to the offices of planning: the elaboration of plans based on special studies; the determination of the priorities of investments; vigilance of the execution of the plans; and assessment by and representation in the government for all questions related to economic development.

And if we contemplate the enormous distance in time which separates the planning of the development by Fermín de Vargas, and modern planning, we should receive with approval the comments of Rafael Gómez Hoyos

> With more than enough justice Grisanti observes that the Studies of Vargas constitute a small Currie plan, prepared by a native of Colombia, with one hundred sixty years of great foresight. Actually, more than the observations of a singular person, these seem to be the conclusions of a study carried out by a mission which was contracted to realize socio-economic investigations and to present plans for the development of the country.
>
> (Gómez Hoyos 1962: 279)

Historical research has identified an even earlier economic writer from Colombia. It deals with a report on the 'province of Santa Marta and Río Hacha of the Viceroyalty of Santa Fé', elaborated by the governor, Antonio de Narváez y la Torre (1753–1812), in Río Hacha, on 19 May 1778. It is sufficient to read his subtitle to realize the interest he has in the history of planning for Colombia's development

> Narrative, or report on the Province of Santa Marta, and Río Hacha as regards the current state of its Commerce, Cultivations, Ranches, and Fruits; which manifests the few that are gathered now, and those that can be cultivated, and which coincide with development in order to increase Trade and Agriculture, the causes of their decadence and the methods considered opportune to advance these important objectives with benefits for the Province, of its neighbors, and the entire Kingdom.
>
> (Narváez y la Torre 1965: 17)

The writing is also of interest for the fact that it plants the problem of developing an area which is characterized by backwardness in freighting, and with a society practically in a primitive state, since 'there is nothing in all of the province, except some ranches and cultivations', and of the more than 70,000 inhabitants, some 40,000 were 'gentile' Indians and the rest were composed of 'white men, subdued Indians, mulattos, free and enslaved blacks, and the other castes of people' (Narváez y la Torre 1965: 20, 36). And the author of the work is completely conscious of what should be confronted, with a very peculiar situation

> To force a province to go from average agriculture and a reduced

commerce to a flourishing state, there are only steps to take and by which can be obtained development, the doing away with impediments, stimulation, protection; but to go from no agriculture and almost no commerce as is the case of the province, to establish and found the latter, there is an infinite space, the immense distance that exists between nothing and being; and a creative spirit which yields it is necessary.

(Narváez y la Torre 1965: 18–19)

The author accepts that the 'dilated extension and the fertility of the lands' of this province is a stimulating starting point; and to this was added the fact that 'the kindness of the king has liberated by law various of its fruits by diminishing the others, and has conceded finally to free trade with a view toward developing the province and making it flourish' (Narváez y la Torre 1965: 18–19). And due to this, Narváez y la Torre predicts that the area could be susceptible to the development of various branches of agriculture, such as tobacco, sugar, cotton, Brazil wood, etc., without counting the exploitation of the pearls, which already enjoys certain natural privileges.

He even takes into consideration the establishing of some manufacturing. To stimulate the cultivation of cotton and its processing among the Indian population, Narváez y la Torre affirms, 'I have sent off to Barcelona for four little machines of the ones invented for both uses, to introduce their employment and to make them work at my own cost'. What is more, the author does not miss the opportunity to make several insinuations in favour of a more extensive manufacturing policy

My first thought about this was to go sponsoring and preparing for other factories of greater extension and importance; because . . . if these same conditions as under which cotton is gathered are established (bringing masters and machines for it), for the factories of gaudy ornaments, handkerchiefs, shawls, and other such articles which are made from it, avoiding the costs and shipping of this raw material from Spain, and making the finished product here, along with the risks, insurance, and money prizes, corresponding to the time which by two round trip voyages and the detention of the goods in our ports would be invested, and stopped from the time of the purchase of the cotton until the sale of the finished product, saving time, cost, and labour (which can be employed in other useful areas), all could be given here at much lower prices and would give greater utility to the King and to the Vassal: and I had thought it to be convenient to propose and promote the idea.

(Narváez y la Torre 1965: 21)

Nevertheless, the author, as if frightened by his own dangerous conclusions in this prohibited field, tempers his enthusiasm

> But upon reflecting further the matter, I find it inconvenient that as the principal attention of the government in these countries should be the development of agriculture in what makes our neighbors of the foreign islands flourish, with the incentive of the greatest usefulness and more rest they dedicate the factories to them, the people, principally the men who are apt for this work in the fields that would be left without workers, which even today are very scarce and in no manner corresponding to the extent of the land, consequently there would be no cultivation or use for land as immense as it is fertile, and in Spain, where the land is not as fertile nor as abundant for all its workers, there would be many left without employment if the factories shut down or if the materials from the government were scarce or lacking, in this system, in which the Americas provide Spain the materials of their fertility and immense extension that this country produces, Spain rewards us with manufacturing, that the industries and the application of its craftsmen work, in order to employ in this manner everyone with regards to the nature of both countries, and to maintain reciprocal connections, linkages, and dependencies with one and another part of the Monarchy.
>
> (Narváez y la Torre 1965: 23–5)

Our author renounces industrialization not because he considers it inconvenient for the nation, but for reasons of convenience for the mother country. If the author had been a true believer of the dogma 'agriculture, first and only one of the arts', or a physiocrat as he often is branded, for what reason does he show fondness for industrial development, in such precise terms, only to later retract them? Is it not more obvious to think that the author applauded such development from the bottom of his heart, only to retract for fear of a government? For the remainder, Narváez y La Torre puts forth the question, reserving the decisions for his hierarchical chiefs: 'Nevertheless, the Ministers of His Majesty with more brilliance, and knowledge could be able to examine and weigh one and another reasons, and then determine the most convenient for the happiness of both parties' (Narváez y la Torre 1965: 26). And once the question is issued, the rest of his study is limited to the problems related to agriculture and cattle and mining development.

Once the objectives of economic development were formulated and identified within the development of agriculture, cattle and mining, the author Narváez y la Torre realized:

> But as it is that without agriculture, there is no commerce, neither with little population can there be agriculture. Commerce, agriculture, and population are like three links or rings of a chain which in order to

154

be put together it is necessary that the three unite and be interwoven; or as the three sides of a triangle, when one is missing, there only remains an angle, or open space, which does not completely form a figure . . .

(Narváez y la Torre 1965: 35)

Nevertheless, of all three sectors, population reaches a priority position in the thinking of Narváez y la Torre:

The basis of every building, and the prosperity of the state should always be the increase of the population, and even more so in the colonies, or Provinces of the Americas in which the primary objective should be to give worth to the immense extension and fertility of its lands . . .

(Narváez y la Torre 1965: 41–2)

Narváez y la Torre is an enthusiastic populationist. To reinforce his doctrine, he resorts as much to empirical proofs, alluding to successful experiments of migration policy in the foreign colonies and in the Spanish colonies, as to the testimonies of his forerunners. In relation to the latter aspect, he brings the memory of years ago when the governor of this same province, Pérez, had suggested the settling of the towns with people from the Canary Islands, who, by being working people, would take advantage of the fertility of the land, and would influence emulation and love of work in others, and that 'His Majesty by the Royal Decree of 7 September 1769 approved the project, sending off for polls to see if there had been someone or some people who wanted to make the settlement' (Narváez y la Torre 1965: 44). In addition, he brings a curious testimony of the migrations market of those times, indicating that every captain of a ship who carries any man who could not pay his passage to the Americas, will receive money from the public trust, and that

from the same fund they would give a compensation of seven and a half English pounds for every person who transported from England or Scotland, of six pounds for those from Ireland, three and a half pounds for those from the Americas, and 2 pounds for people from the Caribbean islands.

(Narváez y la Torre 1965: 42)

After all these and other testimonies in favour of his doctrine of attracting immigrants which 'influenced emulation and love of work', we should hope to hear a concrete proposal for the province of Santa Marta y Río Hacha, with high quality immigrants from England, Holland, or Scotland. But he disappoints us. The Caribbean environment and the history of the colonization has a greater pull on its decisions than the ethereal conclusions of reasoning. His order of priority is another thing:

Although the populations of the Islanders, and the other Spaniards, or free people, for the given reasons, I think it is convenient for them, yet I consider it more useful and absolutely necessary and should be solicited and developed in this province, is that of black slaves because only with them can the ranches be worked upon . . . and not earning a wage, or causing other expense, after first purchasing for them their maintenance and wardrobe, which is very limited, they do work in a less costly manner, and are thus more useful.

(Narváez y la Torre 1965: 44)

As proof of the priority of the slaves in the process of development, he invokes the inclusion of 'the principal attention of foreigners has been to increase as much as possible the number of slaves' (Narváez y la Torre 1965: 46). And now that the king had granted so many classes of raw materials free passage for objectives of economic development, concludes our author, there is even more reason to ask for the policy that 'makes it easy by all means possible the entry of blacks, looking at them as the raw material of all the raw materials that should be produced in the Americas' (Narváez y la Torre 1965: 51).

Despite any discrepancies with the goals of the plan, we cannot lose sight of the meticulousness of the budgeting for the expected costs and benefits which Narváez y la Torre presents in support of his project for importing black slaves (Narváez y la Torre 1965: 61–5). It is possibly in this aspect that his most durable point of union with the contemporary efforts of planning is found.

The scholars of the colonial era in Colombia will find that in the records of this era meticulous diagnoses and multitude of plans and projects of development of the Viceroyalty are united; resources are found in the Jesuit missions of Orinoco and Casanare, which left a vast experience in Indo-American development using techniques and procedures, anticipating by centuries the thoughts of our contemporary thinkers (Popescu 1967); the writings of Bartolomé de las Casas, who elaborated in 1518 the first plan for agricultural colonization in the Indias, precisely in the area of the provinces of Santa Marta and Paria, and whose plans are accompanied by ten years' of balance sheets of incomes, are thus a treasure for economic historians (Popescu 1967: 57).

10

THE ECONOMIC DEVELOPMENT OF ARGENTINA IN THE THINKING OF MANUEL BELGRANO (1770–1820)

INTRODUCTION

In the last decades, the interest of those who study political economy has been the object of great and repeated mutations. The first jolt produced the Keynesian revolution, which brought to fashion once again macroeconomic analysis and the calculations of national income. Shortly thereafter, the centre of gravity was displaced by input-output analysis, which was introduced with great success by Wassily Leontief, for the benefit of inter-industry and inter-regional analysis. At almost the same time, the mischievous mood that razed the fields of this science, made the study of the problems of economic development a fashionable pursuit.

While the interest in the study of Keynes was principally concentrated on the study of the short-run effects of economic phenomenon from the focus of economic development, the long-run effects are of primary interest. In this way, along with the short-run analysis, there began to spring up analysis of longer periods ('secular dynamics' and 'grand dynamics').

As with all long-run movements, the centre of interest of the new discipline was built upon changes in the structural order: the mentality of the consuming and producing masses; the volume and quality of the population; the economic organizational form; the proportions for the distinct branches of activity; the economic order; the state of technology; the principal institutional categories; etc.

Because man always becomes interested in the problems of development with the intention of applying his principles to the growth or progress of the economy, it should be no surprise that the labels 'theory of economic development', 'theory of economic growth', and 'theory of economic progress' were used frequently, and without distinction (Popescu 1959).

It is very understandable that when one speaks of economic development, our first concern is to search for information and inspiration in the centres of research in Europe and North America. This is due to the progress made in these places by specialized research. Nevertheless, I believe that foreign scientific research can present itself alongside domestic sources of information. In effect, no matter how surprising it may appear at first sight, the study of the problems of economic development has preoccupied many of our thinkers of the past century. I will mention as an example Esteban Echeverría, who presented a 'plan' for national economic growth in his works (Popescu 1954; and see Chapter 12 of this volume). But it appears that the roots of such modern anxieties can be traced beyond this to our very first economists. I am thinking in particular of the work of Manuel Belgrano. The objective pursued in the present chapter consists precisely in selecting, placing in an inventory, and presenting in a systematic format the multitude of these early ideas for a theory of Argentinian economic development which is produced throughout the writings of Belgrano, the founder of our national identity.[1]

ECONOMIC DEVELOPMENT AS PART OF SOCIO-CULTURAL DEVELOPMENT

Reform of habits

For Manuel Belgrano, economic development is a wide-reaching process, which, transcending the strict limits of economic phenomenology, extends its roots to the deep web of education, as 'the most solid foundation, the base, let us call it that, and the true origin of public happiness' (Belgrano 1810a: 18). Material progress in Belgrano's thinking cannot be conceived separately from social progress, and this must in turn go with cultural progress.

> How is it willed that man has love for his work, that habits be arranged, that there be lots of the honorable citizens, that virtues put to flight the vices, and that the government receives the fruit of its charges, if there be no education and if ignorance is passed on to generation after generation with larger and greater increases? There was a time of disgrace for humanity in which it was believed that the people could be kept in ignorance, and by consequence in poverty, in order to conserve the highest degree of obedience, but that unjust maxim of the people was prescribed as a production of the most cruel barbarity.
>
> (Belgrano 1810a:19)

In order to lead towards progress, that which most requires immediate action is 'to amplify and diversify the establishments and to shape the moral man' (Belgrano 1810a: 20) indispensable for the growth of the industrial arts.

This policy, according to Belgrano, was to be imposed in a pressing way if that was what was wanted to pull our populations out of their stagnation. 'I have seen with pain, without having left this capital, an infinity of idle men in whom one sees nothing but misery and nudity' (Belgrano 1973a: 60).

One of the principal mediums to conciliate in order to unite this state of being

> are the free schools, where the miserable could send their sons, without having to pay anything for their instruction; there fine principles would be dictated and inspire in them the love of work, because in any village where this does not reign, commerce languishes and misery takes its place. . . . In order to make men happy, it is necessary to put them in the precision of labour by which to prevent the indolence and idleness that are the origins of the dissolution of customs.
>
> (Belgrano 1973a: 61)

Equally, there should be

> free schools for girls, where they will be taught the Christian doctrine, to read, to write, to sew, to embroider, etc., and principally to inspire in them the love of labour, in order to separate them from idleness, as injurious or more so in women than in men.
>
> (Belgrano 1973a: 62)

Accepting as a general axiom the principle that 'interest is the only motive in man's heart and well managed, it can provide infinite utilities' (Belgrano 1973a: 48), Belgrano recommends making usage of awards and honourable mentions as the 'means more [fitting] for the purpose that the spirit of man does not sleep, in whichever state man be in' (Belgrano 1973b: 101). Belgrano thought

> Never shall I tire in recommending the school and the award as means for the prosperity of the state; nothing can be attained without these; and our labours and searches would always remain without any effect if this principle is not adopted as a maxim for educational policy.
>
> (Belgrano 1973a: 64)

Belgrano was convinced that the traditionalist mentality would be one of the most powerful obstacles to social progress. Therefore, the inexorable attack that he carries out against the empire of customs can be explained.

> What a heap of things customs have not authorized without at least allowing us to make the smallest analysis to see if they conform to the rules of equity and reason. We blindly follow the stale path that our fathers opened for us, and we dare not take our eyes off the path for fear of finding a cliff at each step. Because of such a lack of resolution, they make the most trivial things impractical for us, and we place ourselves at the level of those barbaric people, blind worshippers of the ancient maxims. This detestable servitude, when just touches on opinions, can make us superstitious and unpolished; but, when this servitude interferes with our interests, with our comfort

159

and subsistence, it does not stop until it makes us wretched and unhappy.

(Belgrano 1810b: 197–8)

Only now, one can clearly see that the principal aim of the general illustration recommended by Belgrano is that of rooting out the sources of the traditionalist spirit in order to impress upon the spirit of the masses a rationalistic mentality, favourable to progress, allowing in this manner

> that the lights illuminate everyone, that everyone receives instruction, that they acquire ideas, that neither the labourer nor the businessman nor the artist ignores that which pertains to each person; that one and another endeavour not to stick so closely to the thinking of their ancestors, which they should only adopt when it is convenient for them; and when it is not convenient, do away with and abandon it: that which was useful in another time now is injurious, the customs are changing as are their uses, and as everything from time to time changes, there being no more mystery in all this than the vicissitude of human matters.
>
> (Belgrano 1973b: 106–7)

The promotion of technical schools

As regards the establishment of schools of agriculture, if it is to be taken into account that 'the wealth of all men has its origin in that of the men of the fields', then for Belgrano, there is no alternative. There will have to be founded a

> school of agriculture, where young labourers will be made to know as much the general principles, as the practical lessons of this excellent art, so well awarded by how much in their exams they prove their progress; granting them instruments for cultivation and encouraging them as much as possible; making them the primitive advance allowances which will enable them to buy a proportionate plot of land in which to establish their farm, and the seeds they need for sowing, with no other obligation than that they return the same quantity as that which they had been issued for their establishment in the term in which it is considered sufficient to, without causing them neither overcharge nor discomfort, allow them to undertake their works.
>
> (Belgrano 1973a: 46–7)

The establishment of business schools is another urgent task in the educational plan of Belgrano. The science of commerce is not to be reduced to buying for ten and selling for twenty; its principles are more dignified and the extent that these principles embrace is greater than can be imagined. This is the reason why it is indispensable to establish

160

first, an entitled school of commerce, where the youth can go to learn arithmetic to be able to keep accounts, reason, and keep the books; in calculus and rules of exchange; in the rules of merchant navigation, of insurance, etc.; in the method of establishing and maintaining merchant correspondence, in the laws and rules used between negotiators, etc., where at least they are taught the general principles of geography and the products that abound or are scarce in countries, so that they can with these principles make their speculations with the greatest possible knack, and if they dedicate themselves to commerce, it will provide advantages and furtherances to those who engage themselves in this work.

(Belgrano 1973a: 65)

The schools of commerce should be attended by 'all those who dedicate themselves to this career, having those who have not undertaken courses in them so that they should not be admitted to our respectable syndicate' (Belgrano 1810c: 150).

But by far the most urgent, seeing the particular location of the country on the edge of the Atlantic Ocean and the Río de la Plata, is the creation of a school for the merchant marine. Actually, Belgrano states

I say that it is necessary to put equally, as a measure of protection for commerce, a nautical school, without whose principles, no one could be owner of a ship on this river; and for which, besides, there would be young men capable of joining the ships that come from Spain, in case the country found without pilots or pilots' mates. The utility and the advantage that this establishment will provide, even for those who wish to pursue the career of navigation, cannot be measured, nor may I make one see more clearly than by calling attention to the progress that has been made by the young men in schools of this type.

(Belgrano 1973a: 66)

And when, as fruit of this determination, six years later the Nautical Academy celebrated the act of the granting of diplomas to its first graduates, Manuel Belgrano could say with pride: 'My quill is weak, I recognize it, but the satisfaction that attends me is great, as I have been one of the engines for the realization of these ideas in benefit of our youth' (Belgrano 1973c: 116). And directing himself to those in attendance, among whom also figured Viceroy del Pino, Belgrano added:

You know it, yes you do, that from here will leave individuals useful to the whole state, and in particular to these provinces; you know that you now have among you whom to resort to so that they may conduct your ships; you know that with the principles that they are taught, you have excellent military officers; and you also know that in them you will find young men, who with the principles that they have acquired, as accustomed as they are to calculations and meditation, who will be excellent professors in all the sciences and arts that are applicable, by carrying in their hands the master key of all the sciences and arts, the mathematics, they will display for the universe, from one pole to the other, the immortal stamp of our patriotic fervour.

(Belgrano 1973c: 117)

The promotion of economic science

Where Manuel Belgrano most successfully laboured was in the area of the diffusion of knowledge of contemporary economic science. In this field of study none of his contemporaries had better preparation or wider knowledge. In effect, when in 1794 he returned to his country with the title of lawyer and the appointment as Secretary of the Royal Consulate in Buenos Aires, Manuel Belgrano brought with him not only the memory of the ideas of the most illustrious Spanish economists of the era (Pedro Rodriguez de Campomanes, Melchor Gaspar de Jovellanos, and José Alonso Ortiz), but also the fresh knowledge of the dominant ideas of the epoch from the economists of the school of François Quesnay and the writings of Genovesi and Galliani, whom Belgrano read in their original languages (as he read and spoke in both French and Italian). In addition, Belgrano familiarized himself with *The Wealth of Nations* by Adam Smith, learning of the great work through the *Compendio*, which was a book of Smithean ideas put forward by Condorcet and translated into Spanish by Carlos Martinez de Irujo in Madrid in 1792. Finally, in the same year as Belgrano's return to Argentina, he had been made aware of the direct Spanish translation of Smith's work by José Alonso Ortiz.[2]

Only two years from the date of his return, the first work on political economy appeared in Argentina, *Principios de la Ciencia Económica-Política*, translated from French by Belgrano in Buenos Aires in 1796. This work is the best witness to Belgrano's adhesion to the physiocratic doctrine. The first part of the book contains a free translation of paragraphs III to XXI of the work 'Origine et Progres d'une Science Nouvelle' by the French physiocrat Dupont de Nemours, published in 1768, while the second part incorporates the Spanish version of 'Abrégé des Principes de la Science Économique', attributed to Margrave de Baden, which was published in French in 1772 (Gondra 1923: 73). Nevertheless, this adherence of Belgrano's could be interpreted as a reaction against the fact that agricultural activity had been strangled by the monopolistic practices of the Spanish merchants along the Río de La Plata basin. What remains certain is that Belgrano, despite his appreciation of the physiocratic doctrines, had a point of view that was superior to the said doctrines.

In that same year of 1796, Belgrano begins his series of 'Memorias Económicas' (Economic Records) read publicly at the consulate, where he worked as a secretary. As is now known, the primary reason for the four-yearly reports was to serve as an instrument of programming and projection of development, that is to say, as the vehicle for the promotion of economic prosperity in agriculture, the arts, and commerce along the Río de La Plata, in an imitation of the economic societies in existence in the metropolis.

The third instrument of scientific diffusion, this time designated for informing the masses, was the publication of the newspaper, *Correo del Comercio* in the first number of which (10 March 1810), was published a summary of the first part of the chapter 'On the Principles of the Merchantilist System' from Smith's *The Wealth of Nations* (in Spanish). In the dedication to the workers, artesans, and businessmen that headed the first page, Belgrano highlighted that the goal of this organ was to raise consciousness regarding classes, which should be united and proceed as equals, because it is not possible for one without the other to achieve more than ephemeral advances.

Promotion of statistics

Besides the exhibition of the works of the most important economists of his time, Belgrano thought about the pressing need to know the true state of the country's economy. In a policy of economic development, or to express ourselves as did Belgrano in all the dispositions that are directed towards the economic order in effect to promote agriculture, to encourage industry, and protect commerce, nothing was more important than to undertake a calculation of the national resources:

> nothing more important than to have an exact knowledge of the wealth and strength of the states . . . without any knowledge as to the public fortune, of the necessities and resources of these provinces, it is not possible to dictate the most inspiring foresights to the general happiness. The same ones who project and submit themselves to, by being carried away by the most refined public spirit, the arduous workers of the motherland, will not know to take a step without exposing themselves to prejudicial errors, lacking the statistical reasons.
>
> (Belgrano 1810d: 49)

And what was the situation of the calculation of the country's resources? Belgrano answers with total bitterness:

> We lack the geographical and topographical plans of the Provinces of the Viceroyalty, elevated with the perfection and exactness that science requests. . . . We ignore the surface of the territory we occupy and its extension, the forests that exist, the quality of its resources, the climates we enjoy; the nature of the lands, the state of agriculture, the

production of animals, minerals, and vegetation that nature presents us, the population we have, of which we still do not have knowledge of births and deaths.

(Belgrano 1810d: 50)

To fill this serious gap, Belgrano tried to take a first step, distributing by means of his secretary a printed form 'the objective of which, with the smallest possible disturbance, was aimed at those in charge, to obtain the useful information that was demanded by so considerable and advantageous an undertaking' (Belgrano 1810d: 50). As could be imagined, the result of this first undertaking of a statistical survey was not very successful. A year after the distribution of the forms and despite having been validated by the most respected persons, and taking the necessary precautions so that this would be undertaken with the utmost zeal, Belgrano bemoans with evident disgust:

> Until now not one plan has been returned, not even of the poorest parish, where it could have been completed with just a little bit of curiosity; even more than the formality, this plague has worked to detain the course of this great, necessary, and useful work.

(Belgrano 1810d: 50–1)

ECONOMIC DEVELOPMENT IS A HARMONIOUS PROCESS

The branches of economic activity and inter-dependence

It was not easy for Belgrano to take an original attitude as to which of the principle branches of economic activity should be given preference in his plan of economic development. This was due in principle to the fact that Belgrano's favourite professors disagreed fundamentally upon this point. In his first 'Memoria' for the government meeting of 1796, the branch of activity that has a privileged position is agriculture, 'as it is from the fertile mother that provides all the raw materials that give movement to the arts and commerce'. The influence of physiocratic thinking cannot be more evident. Belgrano edits this 'Memoria' in the same year in which he translated into Spanish the two physiocratic writings attributed to Dupont de Nemours and the Margrave of Baden. So it is explained by Belgrano:

> agriculture is the true destiny for mankind, it is without contradiction the first art, the most useful, the most extensive and the most essential of all the arts. . . . It is the fertile mother and the true wet nurse of its vassals . . . the only absolute and independent source of wealth.

(Belgrano 1973a: 41–3)

It may be, as we already mentioned above, that these favourite ideas of Belgrano were connected with the situation of agriculture at that time.

164

Whatever the explanation, Belgrano's attitude is decided. In his thinking, it is 'obligatory to attend primarily to agriculture'. And notwithstanding this, in this first 'Memoria', which carries the heaviest physiocrat stamp, far more advanced ideas are profiled. In the title it is clearly underlined that it deals with the general methods of 'the promotion of agriculture, the encouragement of industry, and the protection of commerce' (Belgrano 1810d: 49). As is mentioned in the third paragraph of the same paper, these 'are the three universal sources of wealth'. The idea of economic inter-dependence of Genovesi and Smith is felt from the first, ending the enthusiasm for the unconditional acceptance of the physiocractic doctrine. As the years pass, this idea of inter-dependence of the distinct branches of economic activity will take even greater weight in the thinking of Belgrano. Therefore, in his third 'Memoria' read to the government gathering of 1798, we discover the reflection that 'the wisest legislation never separated agriculture from commerce, to both they dispense equal protection'. In plain concordance with this thinking, Belgrano reports that the government gathering will be composed from then on 'of farmers, men of commerce in equal number, in order to avoid any type of superiority between two professions that equally contribute to prosperity'. This time the principle of order is that 'the mutual dependence that exists between agriculture and commerce is such, that one without the other can not flourish' (Belgrano 1973b: 97).

Belgrano reflects:

> agriculture only flourishes with great consumption and this, how can this be done in an isolated country without commerce? this is the way the economists clamour for commerce; that foreigners are to be attracted to the ports of the agricultural nation, then the prosperity of the ports should contribute to that of commerce.
>
> (Belgrano 1973b: 97)

But, on the other hand, commerce also depends upon the flourishing of agriculture:

> Because, which would be the objectives of commerce without agriculture? Perhaps the manufacturers, and these to whom are they indebted for their raw materials? Is it not agriculture who furnishes them? Yes, gentlemen, she is the womb of the arts and commerce.
>
> (Belgrano 1973b: 97)

In the same manner, the economic progress of a nation depends on the degree of connection and harmony between its branches of economic activity:

> Mutually helping themselves, consulting their respective interests, they reconcile them by reflecting upon the most efficient means to contribute to the welfare that should result as the common good of

these provinces. Working each one for himself, the general good will be reached.

(Belgrano 1973b: 99)

Years later in an article about this, in the *Correo del Comercio* published in issue number 27 of 1 September 1810, Belgrano stressed the same process of the inter-dependence of agriculture and industry. The union between agriculture and industry is such, Belgrano said, 'that if one weighs more than the other, it comes to destroy itself. The fruits of the land without industry have no value; if agriculture is negligent, the channels of commerce will remain stopped'.

The gradual development of industrial activities

Another fundamental principle that is at the base of Manuel Belgrano's doctrine of economic growth is that of gradual development.

The vast land and maritime coasts of this Viceroyalty, comprise within themselves such riches that the most exact calculation could never be done; but to make them worthy, I shall not say all, but a good portion of them are reserved for other times, so that as the population grows, there are hands in abundance for the dedication to these objects; it is precisely why we go by degrees toward the purpose of general happiness, beginning to promote and dedicate ourselves to improve the same fruits that we now possess until carrying them to their greatest perfection.

(Belgrano 1973c: 131)

Among the industries, besides the common agricultural activities of cultivation of cereals and the breeding of cattle, which according to Belgrano could have greater importance for the economic development of the country, and which therefore should enjoy special protection by parts of the government, are: the development of the wool and cotton yarn industries (included in his 'Memoria' of 1796); the industrial cultivation of flax and hemp (to the promotion of which is dedicated his 'Memoria' of 1798); and the leather goods industry (promoted by his 'Memoria' of 1802).

In his fondness for textile activities (cotton and wool yarns and the cultivation of flax and hemp) and for that of tanning, Belgrano has shown himself to be highly correct. We know today that the affirmation of industrialization of almost all advanced nations took as its starting point the textile and leather goods industries.

Due to his spirit of moderation, Belgrano preferred to speak in a low voice when dealing with his own industrialization projects. In order to avoid any suspicion whatsoever, Belgrano clearly let it be established that, rather than putting in danger the industrial monopoly of the metropolis, he thought that his policy of economic development should be limited to the promotion of an elaboration process of semi-industrial products. These were the yarn and leather that would in themselves serve as raw materials for the factories located in the metropolis.

Even so, the most Belgrano could propose for the promotion of such industries was that there be brought from Europe 'the necessary spinning wheels and teachers' to guide the yarn, wool, and cotton industries, likewise to bring back from Ireland six master tanners, the most excellent that could be found, or, this not being possible to

> send six or eight young men to the countries of Europe where they will most benefit from all the operations and learn so many notions and if there should appear one or another thought of difficult achievement, we should resort to Viscaya in search of some good teachers and capable tanners.

> (Belgrano 1973c: 133–4).

ECONOMIC DEVELOPMENT IS IN ACCORDANCE WITH A FREE MARKET

Economics

Individual property

Shaped by the ideas of Quesnay and Adam Smith and the political ideology of the French Revolution, Manuel Belgrano thought and acted only within the framework of liberal philosophy. So powerful had been this philosophical base that Belgrano, despite belonging to a family of merchants (who had enriched themselves through the monopolistic system), did not vacillate in qualifying these same monopolists, as men 'dispossessed of all love for their fellow men', and the principal party to be held responsible for the peasant class to 'live in misery and nakedness' (Belgrano 1973a: 56).

As a consequence, economic progress should also be realized, according to Belgrano's concept, within the framework of private property and free competition in the market.

The root of all the evils that devastate the miserable life of the working classes need not be searched for, according to Belgrano, in the lack of agricultural instruments, in the inadequate system of cultivation, in the lack of roads or an inefficient system of transportation, in the high level of taxation, or in other causes of this kind. 'All the evils are caused by the principal one, which is the lack of ownership of the lands that labourers work: this is the great evil from which come all their unhappiness and misery.' Advocating the principle of individual property, Belgrano proposes always 'that they be given properties' as long as it does not imply throwing the owners off their

167

properties, since 'there exists no right to take away from those who have the lands'.[3]

Belgrano thinks of another procedure, that later will make Rivadavia famous for having put it into practice.[4] Where it would not be possible to give labourers lands as property, Belgrano solicits:

> at least give them it in emphyteusis . . . that we all understand to be a type of almost direct dominion, so that the workers become attached to the lands and work them in their own house, which they know could be the sustenance of their family for a very modest pension.
>
> (Gondra 1923: 269)

The order of the 'complete freedom of competition'

Manuel Belgrano is a passionate defender of the principle of economic freedom. His unshakable faith can be explained by the very facts of the country's economic life. The manoeuvrings of the Spanish monopolists to impede the free trading of our cereal crops with the outside world are well known. As a consequence of such arbitrary bans, the price of wheat suffered spectacular drops, which led to the ruin of agriculturalists. This fact was very worrisome to the population of the viceroyalty, and was part of daily discussions everywhere, from the town hall and government gatherings to the conversations in people's homes.

In 1793, a representative of the labourers placed a petition before the king, a petition that would grant the labourers their freedom to conduct commerce. In 1794, the ranch owners of Buenos Aires and Montevideo presented another petition asking for the promotion of trade in meat and meat products. Luis R. Gondra has powerful motives for considering Belgrano as not only an inspiration but also as an editor of a portion of this last petition.

In his first 'Memoria' of 1796, Belgrano shows clearly his adherence to the principle of free trade:

> The fast and easy sale of products can be verified whenever the extractions of the production will be free. Not for having a reasonable price for the production in the cities, should the labourer be subjected to sell the production at a certain price, said price placed therefore by a man without the intelligence or knowledge as to the expenses, the care, or the labour to which the cultivation is subject. . . . Neither should the labourer be prevented from going to sell where it is most profitable for him, as the labourer should enjoy all the freedom in his sales and extractions that, providing the profits that he had intended, motivates him in his work; thus the cultivation will be increased.
>
> (Belgrano 1973a: 48–9)

In the record of 1798, Belgrano returns again to this particular theme:

> Many people believe, that by concession of complete freedom for the extraction of production, that the country will remain poor and miserable and that everything will become expensive; . . . as a counterpoint, I am content to quote the seventeenth and twenty-fifth maximums of Quesnay, that say: first, 'that the free trade of products not be hindered, because accordingly as is the extraction so is reproduction and the increase in agriculture'; and second: 'that full freedom be granted to commerce, as the surest, most exact, and advantageous policy for domestic and foreign trade consists in the simple freedom of agreement'.
>
> (Belgrano 1973b: 100–1)

The 'Memoria' that most fully developed Belgrano's arguments for the complete freedom of trade in their most exhaustive forms has unfortunately been lost. It deals with a writing given to Viceroy Liniers in July 1809, shortly before his being replaced by Viceroy Cisneros. Invoking the economic advantages for the same metropolis, Belgrano pleaded for the opening of the port of Buenos Aires to trade with the English. On these points a hearing was begun, in which were included the Cabildo (town council), the ranch owners and labourers, represented by Mariano Moreno, a young and prestigious lawyer who graduated in Chuquisaca, and was a disciple and enthusiastic follower of Belgrano. His celebrated paper, 'La Representación de los Hacendados' (The Statement of the Ranch Owners), is seasoned with all the habitual resources of legal dialect, and the ideals of economic freedom that the master of Buenos Aires had put in fashion years before (Gondra 1945: 9–35).

The doctrine of free determination of prices had been developed by Belgrano in an exhaustive manner in an article entitled 'Economía Política', signed 'Almada', drawn up apparently due to a decree on the control of prices by Viceroy del Pino. By this decree, the prices for meats were being fixed and intervention took place in the buying and selling of these goods by the 'loyal executor', and likewise for trading in wheat and flour.

The point of departure for the reflections of Belgrano is the question about the origin of the scarcity that was being experienced. The price levels, Belgrano affirms, can rise under two circumstances. In a determined moment, the increase in the amount of money in circulation can be the cause of the increase in prices. This had occurred in the past

> When the difficult war that had engaged our nation obstructed the channels through which the increasing amounts of currency should be circulating among us, this incident played no small part in making all the prices rise extraordinarily, due to that infallible maxim which

169

states that the value of things comes from the amount of currency that is in circulation.

(Belgrano 1810b: 200)

But the rise in prices could also be due to the disturbances produced in the actual circulation of goods. In the actual circulation, the disturbances can be due to variations in the productive factors: the exhaustion of the fertile properties of the lands; drought; pests, etc. or also to interferences in the self-regulating mechanism of the market. Belgrano believes that it is precisely the lack of freedom of the agriculturalist to sell his product as he pleases, which is the only reason that made the price rise.

Yes, my son, the lack of freedom for the seller discourages him to such an extent from continuing in his labours, that before long he will surrender himself to the most embarrassing laziness rather than subject the fruits of his industry to the whims of an appraiser; . . . and see, here one less seller, whose absence surely the public must feel, because it has these fewer fruits to consume; and, furthermore, because one more individual is missing from the concurrence of sales.

(Belgrano 1810b: 200–1)

The result will always be the same: the price will tend to rise above the fair price. And who determines this fair price? As a very assiduous reader of Galliani, Belgrano surprises us with a very modern answer:[5]

There is no loyal executor, nor better rate than agreement; this is what levels off and fixes the price between the buyer and the seller; no thing has an actual price, nor effective price by itself; it only has that price which we desire to give it; and this is linked precisely to the need which we have for it, the means by which to satisfy this inclination, the desires to achieve it, and its own scarcity and abundance; there is no other manner by which to continue assuring the public of the good rationing of the fruits for consumption than to let liberty and concurrence rate and level off prices by themselves.

Gondra 1923: 288)

Evidently, when he speaks of 'agreement', Belgrano thinks of the resultant price in the market called perfect competition, in which are present a very elevated number of suppliers and demanders. He affirms,

there exists no fear that the seller imposes any other price upon his output other than that which is precisely levied by its abundance or scarcity; for as he is not the only seller, he must conform to that price which others give him, and even moderate his price even more if he wants to expand promptly.

(Gondra 1923: 290)

Finally, it should be pointed out that Belgrano takes the mechanism of self-regulation and correction of the concurrence price as a process that implies reactions that are cast in the long run, and as such are incorporated as one more part in his economic development system. Temporarily, circumstances could give way to extraordinary profits, but in the long-run the self-regulating mechanism levels off all the circumstantial deficiencies and maintains the price at its natural level. As a result, concludes Belgrano, firmly convinced of his thesis, 'never will I grow tired of repeating to you, that agreement is the judge that can set the true price of things'.

FINAL WORDS

It is not difficult to anticipate that some readers may have doubts about one or another of the theses defended by Manuel Belgrano. But it also seems very probable, despite the divergence of details, that the majority of us remain truly convinced that we find ourselves presented with a systematic set of measures tending to promote the organic and harmonic development of the entire economic and social set-up of the budding national identity. The exalted father of independence, the creator of the flag, is also the founder of the first doctrine on the development of the Argentine Republic.

11

THE TREATISE OF DIEGO PADILLA

DIEGO FRANCISCO PADILLA

Diego Francisco Padilla was born 12 November 1751, in Bogotá. Following the vocation of his eight brothers, who all embraced the religious life, Diego Francisco, at the age of 16, entered the Monastery of San Agustín de Santafé, shortly thereafter to continue his university studies at the (no longer existent) San Nicolás Augustinian University in Bari, also known as the University of San Miguel, situated on the lands in front of the monastery on the north bank of the San Agustín river.

It was at this university that Padilla studied philosophy for three years, and later theology, while by his own efforts he learned history, jurisprudence, and politics. Much later, Padilla held professorships in mathematics and music, and gave courses in geography and geometry.

THE TREATISE ENTITLED 'POLITICAL ECONOMY'

Biographical background

This is not the moment to examine all the scientific works of Padilla. I only mention one political work[1] (ascribed to Padilla, his *Aviso al Público*[3] and *Tolerancia*.[4] What is of interest here is the writing which appeared as an addition to the *Aviso al Público* and is called 'Traducción Libre del Tratado Intitulado Economía Política Hecha por un Ciudadano de Santafé' (Free Translation of the Treatise Entitled Political Economy Done by a Citizen of Santafé).[5]

The title of this essay itself is enough to get the attention of economists. Even if for a long time, problems of a practical economic character had been expounded in works such as those by La Torre (1778), Pedro Fermín de Vargas (1790), Antonio Nariño (1797), Jorge Tadeo Lozano (1801), and José Ignacio de Pombo (1810) (Popescu 1968b: 85), what is certain is that the name 'Treatise Entitled Political Economy' refers to the treatment of economic problems from a general theoretical point of view.

172

Regrettably for the scholars of economics, the existence of such a work has passed unnoticed until relatively recently. The few who touched upon the subject have all been historians, and the number of these is very small. Although critiques of Padilla's works were published during the nineteenth century, it was only in the first decades of this century that authors began to remember this treatise.

The first mention of the treatise was credited to Eduardo Posada in 1917, and in 1925, Gustavo Otero Muñoz also touched upon this theme. On the other hand, the Samper Ortega collection of 1937 does not even mention it. In *El Periodismo en la Nueva Granada*, published in 1960, L. Martínez Delgado and Sergio Elías Ortiz make mention of the treatise. Finally, in 1962, Rafael Gómez Hoyos, surprises us with a compact synthesis of the principal problems related to the subject, at the same time trying to offer solutions. With this, the distinguished historian forges the first link in the chain of positive contributions, facilitating the way for later researchers. Even though one may differ in one or another insignificant aspect with the solutions proffered, what is certain is that economists should always demonstrate their debt of gratitude for the fundamental contributions of Gómez Hoyos in this field of study.

Date of publication

Of all the additions to the *Aviso*, that which contains the treatise is the only one for which the date of publication is difficult to determine. This may be the reason why the Pineda Collection assigned the treatise to the final edition of the *Aviso*.

Neither are historians in agreement as to which edition the treatise belonged, nor can they support their suggested dates with any reasons. Rafael Gómez Hoyos maintains that the treatise was included in the first number of the *Aviso*, which would give it a publication date of 29 September 1810. To support this theory, Padilla saw no reason to date the addition, nor mention it as an addition to his first edition of the weekly publication. Also substantiating Gómez Hoyos' theory is the fact that the page numbering is sloppy, as is common with first editions of newspapers published in those times.

As a counter-argument to this thesis, one may state that it would have been very difficult for Padilla to include an addition, much less one of forty-six papers, as was the treatise, to the first edition of the *Aviso*. Not only would this have incurred editorial difficulties, but also financial difficulties. Only once the newspaper was established with its market of readers, would it have been convenient to think upon enlarging its dimensions or making additions to it. For this reason, the rationale of Eduardo Posada, that the addition appeared on 22 December 1810, along with the thirteenth edition of the paper, or that of Gustavo Otero Muñoz who claimed that the addition was printed along with the twelfth, thirteenth, or four-teenth edition, seem to be more congruent. Also relevant is the fact that the main competition for the *Aviso*, namely the *Diario Político de Santafé de Bogotá*, presented a series of articles about political economy, beginning on 28 December 1810. Not only did the articles touch upon Padilla's subject of political economy, but they also seemed to follow his methodology and ideas. These facts would all seem to lend credence to the belief of Posada that the treatise was included as an addition to the 22 December 1810 edition of Padilla's paper.

Political economy as economic and financial administration of the state

Methodology

Due to its only containing forty-six pages, the title 'Treatise' seems preten-tious. We could not make the same statement as regards its contents. They deal with a systematic monograph of a universal character, based on an abstract methodology in which the inductive examples only serve to illus-trate the general principles inferred by the deductive route. Without a doubt, what draws attention is the focus of the author on the interpretation of economic science as a theory of public administration, especially in its economic and financial facets.

Looking at its essence, the treatise can be divided into four parts. The first part is of a methodical character, the remaining three are the backbone of the work. In the methodological portion, the essence of political economy is determined and its frontiers are drawn; both as regards 'private or domestic economy' (Popescu 1968b: 60) and political science.

For the author of the treatise, political or general economy, or public economics, is nothing other than the science of administration of the state. Given that between the administration of the family units and the adminis-tration of 'the great family that is the state' (Popescu 1968b: 61), there are differences not only in the suggested size, but also differences of substance, it is necessary to distinguish between public economics and personal economics. In sum:

> the paternal power rightfully goes toward a natural establishment, but in a large family like the state . . . the political power is purely arbi-trary in its instruction, and for this same reason it can not be based unless by contracts and pacts, not even the magistrate can order others unless by force of law.
>
> (Popescu 1968b: 61)

Of course, at the base of these pacts or contracts there is a strong propensity towards sociability, underlined by the author in future pages:

Look for motives which men united by mutual necessities from society have had to unite themselves even more with civil societies; and you will not find any other reason or motive for the protection of all than that of assuring the goods, the life, and liberty of every member.

(Popescu 1968b: 67)

It is that in its thinking, the political body is a moral being, which has a general will, which precisely aspires to the conservation and welfare of each and every part, and that is the source of public reason which in turn is the basis of law.

It is evident that between the private will strengthened by the principle of liberty, and the general will that gives sustenance to the principle of governmental authority, there arise difficulties in determining a common denominator. The author notes:

This difficulty that should seem insurmountable has been removed at the beginning by the most sublime of all human institutions, or even better, by a celestial inspiration, that teaches man to imitate here below the never changing decrees of the divinity; by what inconceivable art has it been able to discover a means to subject men in order to make them free, and to employ in the service of the state all the goods, the arms, and the very life of all its members but to unite them and to follow the judgement? The prodigies are the law's work. To it alone are men indebted for justice and liberty. This is the sane organism of the will of all that reestablishes the right and natural equality among men. This is that heavenly voice, that dictates to every citizen the precepts of public reasoning, that teaches to work according to the maximums of his own judgement, and to not be in contradiction with himself.

(Popescu 1968b: 68)

By imitating celestial decrees here on earth, the general will is man's will; in this way the voice of mankind is simply an imitation of the voice of God.

From where does the general will, which is the first principle of public economics and the fundamental rule of government, arise? It is not infrequent that those in the management of public affairs prefer to follow their own interests or those of their sub-chiefs, instead of consulting upon the good of the state. In light of this, it is suggested:

it would then be adequate to divide the public economy into popular and tyrannical; the first is that of every state where reign between the people and their chiefs the union of interests and of wills; the other will exist necessarily where the government and the people have different interests, and consequently, opposite wills.

(Popescu 1968b: 67)

But as the distinction between political economy and private economy is imposed, it is equally imperative to distinguish between political science and political economy (or public administration, as we would say today). The author implores:

> I beg my readers to distinguish well between the public economics of which I am going to speak, and that I call government, and the supreme authority that I call sovereignty. The distinction consists in that the latter has the legislative right and obliges in certain cases itself to the nation, and the former the executive power and can not oblige but the individuals.
>
> (Popescu 1968b: 64)

In order to be more precise in his thinking, the author uses an interesting macrocultural figure that implies concurrently a vision of the macroeconomic circuit.

> The political body taken individually may consider itself as an organized body, living and similar to mankind. The sovereign power represents the head; the laws and customs are the brain that is the origin of the nerves and the centre [of] understanding of will and feelings, whose organs are the judges and magistrates; commerce, industry, and agriculture are the mouth and the stomach that prepare the common subsistence, the public contributions are the blood that an economic sage makes it exercise, firstly its functions in the heart, sends it again for distribution throughout the body as food and life; the citizens are the body and its members that make the machine move, live and work, which cannot be injured in any part without the painful sensation making an impression in the brain, supposing that the animal is found in a perfect state of health.
>
> (Popescu 1968b: 64)

The object of political economy

In light of the strict structural inter-dependence of the political body, it is easily concluded that 'as the first obligation of the legislator is to make the laws conform to the general will, the first rule in public economics is that the administration be accordant to the laws' (Popescu 1968b: 69).

To said effect, it is necessary to begin with the government itself, which should be first in respecting the laws. If a minister has as his specific charge to make sure people respect the laws, this observance is imposed by him with greater reason. Of course, his example of observance shall be the best incentive to guarantee the success of the administration.

In order to enforce the laws, it is evident that there be a strong government, for even if it is the owner of the law, it must be the guarantor of the law and must enact it. It is from here that springs the true talent of government.

It is not always easy to comply with the objective of a good administration, especially if diversity of customs, places, and climates are present. But the administrator will complete his charge if he accepts as faithful guides the spirit of the laws, the general will as the source of and supplement to the laws, and that he follows the path of equity, that of justice, under any circumstances.

On the other hand, it must be known how to conquer the hearts of the people, so that they cooperate voluntarily in the work of public administration. It is not enough that they obey, but that they do it with love.

> If it is right to know how to employ men as they are, it is much better to know how to employ them as they should be. The most absolute authority is that which penetrates to the interior of man, and that is exercised no less upon will than upon man's actions.
>
> (Popescu 1968b: 70).

To accomplish this, it is suggested:

> Form then men, if you want to direct men. If you want laws to be obeyed, make them beloved, and in order to make what should be done, it is enough to think in what one should do. This was the great gift of the ancient governments, in those far away times in which the philosophers gave the laws to the people, and they employed their authority in making the people wise and happy.
>
> (Popescu 1968b: 70)

Consequently, the second rule of government is:

> Do you want the general will to be carried out? Then make all the individual wills agree; and as virtue is nothing more than the conformity of individual will with the general will, to say the same in other words, make virtue reign!
>
> (Popescu 1968b: 71)

In the same way that the first administrative imperative is to find men who know how to administer the laws, the second depends on people who know how to obey the laws. But the author says that the second imperative is much more important than the first, because where there are virtuous public habits, there need not be administrative geniuses.

One of the most powerful instruments in the service of public virtue, states the writer, is the love of country (Popescu 1968b: 74). The love of country is the most efficient instrument, because if the representative body of general will is held in high esteem, the good gained by the individual will be adjusted to it.

In conclusion, if we want citizens to obey the laws, we should endeavour

177

to ensure that they love the laws, or, what is the same thing, that they are virtuous; and if we want the people to be virtuous, we should try to make them love their country.

Instruments related to the people

To stimulate love of country, the people must enjoy civil security on the one hand, and a correct education on the other. One refers to present generations, and the other to future generations.

Civil security responds to the obligations assumed by the society so that the people abandon the natural state; this is the guarantee of individual life and social justice. The author writes on the history of the individualist doctrine:

> In effect, the pledge of the body of the nation, is it not to provide the conservation of the least of its members with as much care as the others have? And the health of one citizen is less of a common cause than that of the entire state? That it is said to us that it is fine that one man perishes for everyone, this sentence will be worthy of admiration from the mouth of a dignified and virtuous patriot who voluntarily surrenders himself to death, for the health of his country; but if it is to be understood that it will be permitted of the government to sacrifice an innocent to save the multitude, I find this maxim to be one of the most execrable that the tyranny ever invented, the falsest that could be dwelled upon, the most damaging that could be admitted, and the one most directly opposite the fundamental laws of society. Far from one person should perish for the others, all should pledge their goods and their lives for the defense of each one, so that individual weakness is always protected by public force, and each member by the entire state. That patriotism show itself, therefore, as the common mother of the citizens, that the advantages that they enjoy in their country always make them kind; that the government allow them enough portion of the public administration so that they know they are at home, and that the laws are not seen as anything else but the guarantee of common liberty.
>
> (Popescu 1968b: 75–6)

But at the same time, this author surprises us with a fervent defence of the principle of social justice:

> That which is most necessary and could be the most difficult in ruling is a severe integration to make justice for all, and above all else to protect the poor against the tyranny of the rich. The greatest evil is made when one comes across poor people to defend and rich people to restrain. Over the mediocrity one only exercises all the force of the

laws, they are equally impotent against the treasures of the rich as against the misery of the poor; the first eludes the laws, the second escapes the laws; one breaks the curtain, the other passes behind it. It is for this that one of the most important affairs of government is the prevention of the extreme inequality of fortunes, not taking treasure away from those who possess it, but taking away from everyone the methods of accumulating it: not building hospitals for the poor, but keeping the citizens healthy so that they will not fall ill. Men unequally distributed over the land and placing themselves in one place, while the others flee; the arts of pleasure and pure industry favoured at the cost of useful and hardworking occupations, agriculture sacrificed to commerce; in sum, the venality carried out to such an excess that consideration is counted with strong pesos and the virtues themselves are sold at the price of silver. . . . Such are the evils . . . that a wise administration should prevent in order to maintain by good habits the respect for laws, the love of country, and the vigour of the general will.

(Popescu 1968b: 77)

As we see, the work shows a complete programme of political economy destined to prevent and combat the social disparities suggested as the consequence of the inefficiency and passiveness of the public sector.

'But all these precautions will be insufficient if the matter is not taken further. The safety of the present generation being guaranteed, one must think about the future generations' (Popescu 1968b: 78). If it is certain that 'the country can not subsist without liberty, nor liberty without virtue, nor virtue without citizens' (Popescu 1968b: 78), it is precisely for this reason that the obligation of 'forming good citizens is not the affair of one day, and to create men it is necessary to instruct them as children' (Popescu 1968b: 78–9). The formation of human resources, as we say today, appears to be one more obligation, that belongs exclusively to the state:

If there are laws concerning the age of maturity, there should also be for infancy, that teaches one to obey others; and as the reasoning of each man is not allowed as the only arbitrator of his obligations, one should even less abandon the education of the children to the worries and inspirations of their parents, as this is even more important to the state than it is to their own parents because . . . the state remains and the family breaks up.

(Popescu 1968b: 79)

Of course, to comply with this requirement, inspired surely by Montesquieu,[6] a body of competent educators should be formed, as the education of future generations is a sublime function. The author believes that public education under the legislation set forth by governments and the

179

magistrates established by sovereignty is one of the fundamental tenets of any popular or legitimate government. It is worth noting here that the planning of human resources has as its principal objective political development before economic development.

Instruments related to goods

The two basic rules of public administration are that there be men who know how to administer the law and people who know how to obey these laws. It remains to examine the third obligation of the state, that of public income. To this area is dedicated the largest portion of the treatise.

Though the author recognized that property is the true foundation of civil society and the true guardian of the citizens' actions and states (probably influenced by Locke), that the right to property is the most sacred right of man (Popescu 1968b: 81), and even more important than liberty itself, he admits, however, that in order to maintain the government and the state it is necessary that citizens contribute out of their goods. In order to find a solution to this matter, Padilla concludes that Puffendorf's thesis, which claims that the right to property does not exist after the owner's death, due to the nature of this right (Popescu 1968b: 82), could expand the right rather than change it.

As regards public finances, the author closely followed the ideas of Bodin (1590). Before taxes, the author prefers as sources of public income the fees of the state. The fundamental principle of financial administration is centred on taking the major precaution of preventing public expenses rather than increasing taxes, trusting people to be honest, and affecting individual goods only as a last resort. The treatise highlights the role that grain deposits can undertake as a source of public income in times of scarcity. Equally, it insists upon the consistency of taxes, that they always be accepted by the people and that they be equitable.

The criteria of tributary justice leads to progressive taxation: he who has nothing pays nothing, but he who lives in opulence could be taxed on all that exceeded the necessary. But besides the distinction between necessary and superfluous, the principle of progressive taxation finds a reinforcement in the daily inequalities of the social community, that 'strongly protects the immense possessions of the wealthy and leaves the poor with hardly the miserable enjoyment of the hut that he built with his own hands. Are not all the social advantages for the rich and powerful?' (Popescu 1968b: 89) The poorer classes always find the door closed, even when they have the right to open it. But there is more: 'the losses by the poor are much less recoverable than those of the rich, and the difficulty of acquisition grows in proportion to the necessity' (Popescu 1968b: 90). Finally, it should be taken into account that everything the poor spends ends up in the hands of the rich, and as it is only those who have a part in the government who receive sooner or later the results of the taxes, their interests in seeing taxes increased is explained. Therefore, any taxation system must not only look at the private wealth of taxpayers, but also consider their different conditions and the superfluous nature of their goods.

As regards the types of taxes, the author of the treatise is an irritated adversary of taxes upon land, considering that they cause depopulation, and consequently the ruin of fields, because the worse scarcity in a nation is a scarcity of men. On the other hand, the author admits that

> the rights concerning the import of foreign merchandise for which the inhabitants of a country are anxious without the country really needing them and those concerning the export of the products of the lands of the country and of which there is an abundance, and without which the foreigners cannot pass over to the products of very lucrative and useless arts, over to the admissions to the things of pure taste in the cities, and in general over all the luxury objects.
>
> (Popescu 1968b: 93)

This would complete the objectives of a tributary policy in agreement with the principle of social justice, and reactivate agriculture without harming industry. In this way, the policy would get closer to the fair intermediate point which 'is the true strength of the state' (Popescu 1968b: 94).

The author of the treatise

Diego Francisco Padilla

On more than one occasion it has been maintained that the true author of the treatise was none other than Padilla. This alternative is posed by Rafael Gómez Hoyos, as far as I know the only author who, besides analysing the treatise, has posed the question of its authorship. In fact, it is asked: is Padilla really only the translator of this work, or is he the author of it? The answer of Gómez Hoyos is the following:

> At first view and taking into consideration the cultural anxieties of the learned Augustinian, and even more the custom of the era to dissimulate and hide the true name of the owner of a writing, one could give an affirmative answer. Without a doubt, a test checking the work persuades us with certainty that it actually deals with a translation and not an original work.
>
> (Gómez Hoyos 1962: 315)

As we shall see later, Gómez Hoyos invokes a series of formal arguments, in order to maintain this opinion. Nevertheless, it is enough to read the treatise attentively to discover that the same author indicates his homeland as being Genoa:

181

In order to demonstrate the economic system of a good government, I have frequently turned my eyes toward this republic: happy to find there in my country the example of wisdom and proverb, that I wish to see reign in all countries.

(Popescu 1968b: 85)

It could be that Padilla had once passed through Genoa, but no one would dare to maintain that the illustrious Augustinian could have had any home-land other than Nueva Granada; it is here that he was born, educated, and died, and it is here that his parents, both from Santafé, were born and died.

Is Padilla the translator?

If dealing with just a simple translation, who is the translator? The names of Bernardo Alvarez and of Padilla surge to the forefront, but there is also the possibility of a third party. Regrettably, this topic has barely been touched upon by historians. When Martínez Delgado and Ortiz affirmed that Dr Manuel Bernardo Alvarez published his lessons on political economy in the *Aviso*, were they referring to him as the author or the mere translator of these lessons? And when Gómez Hoyos later put forth the alternative of Padilla as author/translator of the treatise, does the acceptance of this second hypothesis necessarily mean the rejection of the first? This is very probable, and this is enforced by other elements. First, in terms of Dr Manuel Alvarez: although maintaining that the *Aviso*, run by Padilla, reflected his political ideas, in reality his collaboration with the newspaper was only through poetry. Second, upon analysing the treatise, it is established that the prologue could be the work of a translator, with the prologue being assigned with certainty to Padilla. But beyond these theories of assignation, we find nothing more in the writings of historians. The question remains open until the time when historians give it the attention it deserves. If in the meantime the economist dares to confront it, he will have to be very cautious in his judgement, and even so, his judgement had better have a provisional char-acter. It is with these reservations that we try to pose the question of the translator.

The fact that in the title of the work it is indicated that the translation was performed by a citizen of Santafé is the first clue. More significantly, the introduction is preceded by a lemma in Latin, extracted from Seneca, one of the favourite authors of Padilla. The love of country, one of the basic ques-tions developed in this treatise, was also the central theme of all twenty-one editions of the *Aviso*. The translator dedicates the work to those who love their country, and declares that he was moved in his pledge for the same love of country, a point upon which he will not cede an advantage to anybody. And this requirement Padilla fulfilled in excess. 'Love the nation', said Castillo y Rada, 'as a son does his mother: delirium for liberty and never in its virtues has hypocrisy penetrated' (Martínez Delgado and Ortiz 1960: 340). These are sufficient indications that Padilla was the author of the introduction of the treatise, but was he also the translator of the treatise?

There is a paragraph in Padilla's introduction that could serve as the key to identifying the translator. It is said in the introduction that the translator, moved by his love of country

> has resolved to serve the country, and seeing that not by his own writings, by confessing in good faith that his few or no inspirations are not sufficient to serve do her dignified service, at least he wants to serve with the writings of another.
>
> (Romero 1960: 31)

This appears to this day to be the fundamental argument for assigning the translation to Padilla; not to affirm that he had 'few or no inspirations' in the field of political and social sciences, as Padilla in this aspect was quite the opposite. This is not a confession, but one more proof of the already highlighted humility, modesty and discretion of his scientific estate and his learning. He is aptly characterized by his first biographer: 'He was a wise man without ostentation, a patriot with no interest, a religious man without hypocrisy (Fernández 1829: 18). So, the question is of another type. If the version had been written by another person, it is evident that a man like Padilla would never have taken as a collaborator a person with little or no inspiration.

Is the author a disciple of Rousseau?

Guided by a certain intuition, Gómez Hoyos moves firmly towards the original text of the treaty. In the first place, he establishes that the original was edited 'in French, by the constant references made to the government of France, and above all for the various French tendencies that escaped in the version of Padilla' (Gómez Hoyos 1962: 315). Actually, Gómez Hoyos observes that twice Padilla uses '*sucesos*' in the same sense that it is used in French, that of success or a good result, not as it is used in Spanish to mean events.

In the second place, Gómez Hoyos analyses the treatise and establishes that it is saturated with Rousseau's doctrines. Even more so, Gómez Hoyos tries to limit the group of thinkers in which, later, the author of the essay will be found. He points out:

> The social pact of the rigid feeling of Rousseau, the general will as interpreted by his school, the transition from the natural state to the civil state, the popular or legitimate government, are the inspiring ideas in all the pages. The maxims and even the formal technique, the natural optimism, the romantic ideas, the continuous examples of

Greece and of Rome, unquestionably signal an advantaged disciple of Rousseau, who in physical material and in the rigidly individualistic concept of property, had strongly suffered the influence of the liberal school and of the physiocratic current.

(Gómez Hoyos 1962: 316)

It is here that the chain of arguments by Gómez Hoyos is broken, and it is for this reason that the illustrious Colombian historian could not identify the author of the treatise. To identify the author of a treatise written in 1810 as a post-Rousseau scholar with liberal and physiocratic tendencies, but who quotes not even Rousseau, nor Smith, nor Quesnay, who struggles for a strong state, strong enough to be able to defend the class of the poor from exploitation by the rich, and who in taxation material advocates a progressive fiscal system, with no tax upon land, is not an easy thing to do.

The mere fact of reviewing the most recent names quoted in the treatise, such as Bodin, Puffendorf, Montesquieu, Montaigne, and Locke would have served as a good indicator to look back in time, not to a post-Rousseau period, but to a pre-Rousseau one. The original version of the treatise appeared not only before the economic writings of Adam Smith, who as we know published his *Wealth of Nations* in 1776, but also before the writings of François Quesnay. Quesnay began his series of monographs in 1756 with an article about cereals, continued in 1757 with his thinking on taxes, and finally progressed to his immortal 'Tableau Économique' in 1758.

The treatise: translation of 'Économie Politique' in the French *Encyclopaedia*

The identification of the author would have been much easier if it had been taken into account that Padilla stated in his translation that the work was done by a foreign author. In further references to the original piece being part of a great collective work, Padilla steers us towards the French *Encyclopaedia*, begun by Diderot and D'Alembert in 1751 and published in twenty-two volumes, as being the source document.

In Volume V of the *Encyclopédie ou Dictionnaire Raisonné des Sciences, des Arets et des Métiers* . . . , which appeared in November of 1755, there is incorporated on pages 337–49, an article entitled 'De l'Économie Politique'. This article, which in 1756 was published in the form of a brochure under the title of 'Discours sur l'Économie Politique' and subject to various re-editings was precisely the object of the 'free translation . . . done by a citizen of Santafé, who offers it to the true lovers of the fatherland' and published as an addition to the *Aviso al Público* in December 1810.

That these facts are true can be confirmed by a paragraph by paragraph comparison of the Spanish translation with the original French. The translation by Padilla is very loyal to the original French, except for where

Padilla felt the original work was repetitive or included ideas not considered important.

The original author of the treatise is Rousseau

Finally, it remains to identify the author of the article 'Économie Politique', published in the French *Encyclopaedia* of 1755. As Gómez Hoyos reasoned, it deals with an original work in French, along the doctrinal lines of Rousseau. But, as Padilla had later refuted many of Rousseau's points, Gómez Hoyos decided that the original work had been that of a disciple of Rousseau. Yet we must remember that in that famous paragraph from the treatise, the author speaks of Genoa as being his homeland. But for a translation error it would seem that the original author was an Italian. In the original French, the author's homeland is written as Geneve, which is not Genoa, but Geneva. What is important here is that the translator in his defence could allege not only that he had read all of Rousseau's works, except the earlier writings, but that many of them were worthy of a Spanish version. It can be revealed that the author of the treatise on political economy under question here was none other than Rousseau himself, and that the version in the French *Encyclopaedia* served as the basis for the translation of 1810.

Was Rousseau translated in Bogotá in 1810, and Morillo, the great encyclopaedia hunter, allowed this large work to escape his notice? How can it possibly be conceived that the 'Discourse on Political Economy' of Rousseau circulated through the Americas, to be translated by the Augustinian Diego Francisco Padilla? So many questions run through readers' minds, especially since more than 150 years passed before we could even identify the original author of the treatise.

DIEGO FRANCISCO PADILLA A ROUSSEAUNIAN?

Encyclopaedism versus Suarezism

The discovery that the wise Colombian friar was the translator of the discourse on political economy from the Genevan encyclopaedist will be a strong position in the polemic between those of the encyclopaedist faction and the Suarezist factor in the independence of the American republics.

Will the myth of encyclopaedism in the New Kingdom of Granada be one no longer? What once seemed fact no longer is. To the translation of the 'Declaration on the Rights of Man and the Citizen', done by Antonio Nariño in Santafé de Bogotá in December 1793 (Vergara y Vergara 1946: 3–6) , is now added the translation of Rousseau's article, attributed to none less than Diego Francisco Padilla, of whom it was said, until only recently, that by his writings he smashed the Voltairian doctrines (Perez Gómez 1924: 6). Would it be a mere coincidence that Padilla is rated second in importance in

Colombian history of economic thought behind Nariño, and that Padilla's works continue to be undervalued and suffer the indifference of Latin American scholars?

It is foreseen that the 'Discourse' of Rousseau and the treatise of Padilla will be the objects of re-evaluation not only by historians, but also economists, politicians, and public administrators. A few lines need to be dedicated to seeing by what means, and where, it is possible to establish a bridge between the thinking of Rousseau and Padilla.

Rousseau as a pre-Rousseaunian

When speaking of Rousseau, his culminating work 'The Social Contract' (1762), is called to mind. Even though it is widely accepted that his 'Discourse on Political Economy' (1755) was an anticipator of his 1762 work, what is certain is that his thinking evolved and changed greatly over just seven years.

The respective position of religion is fundamentally distinct in the two works. In his discourse on political economy, Rousseau says men are driven to imitate the divine powers invested in earthly holy men, yet in his treatise on the social contract, he wishes to throw out the idea that the Church is the only way to salvation.

The respective position of the idea of natural sociability and the natural law is somewhat of a controversy. In his 'Manuscript of the Social Contract of Geneva', Rousseau has a chapter 'on the society of the human species' in which he explicitly refutes the idea of natural law. In the final edition of 'The Social Contract', this chapter was removed, with no reason given for this action. Yet, in the 'Discourse on Political Economy', even though posed in an indirect form, we discover the rudiments of the natural sociability and the natural law. Even more, it is observed that the ideas of natural sociability belong to a current of thought that dominated Rousseau's thinking before the 'Discourse on Inequality', edited around 1754. In this work, Rousseau rejects the idea of natural sociability.

The respective position of the institution of property also differs between 1755 and 1762. In 'The Social Contract', Rousseau states that property only exists under civil law, and is not a natural right. But, in his 'Discourse on Political Economy', Rousseau states that property is the true fundamental thing of civil society, and the true guarantor of the earnest desire of citizens; property is more important in certain respects than liberty itself. Also as regards the institution of property, it must be emphasized that the ideas of the 'Discourse on Political Economy' belong to a current of ideas preceding his 'Discourse on Inequality', both published in 1755. In the latter, Rousseau declares that the fruits belong to all, and the ownership of the land to no one.

Similar discrepancies arise in relation to fiscal and taxation policies. In the

'Discourse on Political Economy', this question occupies half of the text and is considered as a powerful instrument in the service of social justice. In 'The Social Contract', we read that the words 'public finance' are a sign of slavery; it is unknown in the Republic, because in a truly free state, the citizens do everything with their arms and nothing with money.

It seems that many of the principal ideas of 'The Discourse on Political Economy' have been extracted from the folder on 'Political Institutions', on which Rousseau was working, far from the influences of the encyclopaedists, around 1750. It is for this reason that we can not only affirm that the Rousseau of 'The Discourse on Political Economy' differed from the Rousseau of 'The Social Contract', but also that at former periods of his life, Rousseau was found to be in a stage of pre-Rousseaunian thinking![7]

Padilla and the new philosophy

The biographers of Padilla emphasize many of his virtues: the vastness of his learning; an exceptional memory; the brilliant oratory; and productivity in the field of science. But few remember his open spirit and receptiveness to new ideas. Of course, this does not mean that Padilla disowned his favourite masters. In his thirst for learning, Padilla read all valuable works attentively, without bias towards philosophical leanings, and took the most important points from such works, to re-elaborate and strengthen his system.

One of the most authentic testimonies of his progressive spirit is that, beginning in 1775, Padilla had begun to read in the faculty the fundamentals of the 'new philosophy', in which were examined the ideas of Descartes, Bacon, Newton, Locke, Montesquieu, and other contemporary authors. This 'new philosophy' had been introduced in the New World by means of the 'Teatro Crítico' and the 'Cartas Eruditas' of Benito Jerónimo Feijóo and later found an ardent defender in the philosophical ideas of Dr Félix de Restrepo.

If this were the spiritual basis of Padilla in 1775, what could it have been between the years 1784–6, on the eve of the French Revolution, when he stayed in the Eternal City and visited various other Italian cities and who knows what other metropolises? And what was his spiritual basis when the Revolution of 20 July broke out? The answer is given by Padilla's writings and by those who have dealt with them.

The roots of his Christian philosophy continue penetrating deep into his spirit. This aspect no one may deny. But at the same time, the extent of his spirit and his thirst for knowledge make him open the windows of his soul with generosity towards the new sources of learning. This was valued especially in politics and economics, which were called upon to perform a major role in the crystallization of the new order in America. And the *Aviso* reflected Padilla's new openness to ideas. In all issues of this newspaper, we find quotations from Pascal, Franklin, Montesquieu, and others, with scarce quotations from Saint Augustine and Thomas Aquinas. Padilla's incessant quotations of Virgil, Ovid, and other ancient masters led to criticism of his dwelling on the past.

In a reply to an anonymous criticism from Cartagena, Padilla qualifies the author of the anonymous letter as 'very poor' (Martínez Delgado and Ortiz 1960: 471) and defends his quotations as being both apt and in accordance with the points in discussion (Martínez Delgado and Ortiz 1960: 471). In terms of political economy, when satisfactory answers could not be found in Church sources, Padilla did not hesitate to look for them in the Rationalist philosophy. This should not be seen as treason against his Christian ideas or his Church, for the Catholic saints had also made reference to Cicero, Aristotle, Seneca, etc. when writing some of their most ardent defences of the Christian philosophy.

Actually, as we know that during his stay in Europe, Padilla perfected his studies in the monastery that his order had in Monte Casino, it would not be incompatible if, on this occasion, due to his open spirit and his quest for all things new, he may have had contact with the encyclopaedists and other European philosophers.

The direct translation and publication of the 'Discourse on Political Economy' from the French *Encyclopaedia* would not have been possible unless this work was available at the monastery's library or if Padilla undertook this great task twenty-five years earlier during his stay in Rome.

The simple fact of translating one of Rousseau's works in his newspaper is not enough to qualify Padilla as one of his disciples. Even though he greatly embellished the introduction to his translation with flattering adjectives for the original writer and held Rousseau in the utmost esteem, we see Padilla more aligned with the philosophy of the Rousseau that was in vogue in 1750. That is, of a pre-Rousseaunian Rousseau.

Padilla had always maintained the importance of political economy in his issues of *Aviso al Público* prior to his inclusion of his translation of Rousseau's work. In addition, Padilla defended his own ideas on love of country and the defence of his religion. He stated that 'America would never risk its loyalty and its faith' for 'we want nothing but to maintain the Church and the fatherland' (Martínez Delgado and Ortiz 1960: 427). Finally, he defends the cornerstones of the French Revolution: liberty, independence, equality, and the rights of the citizens. He reminded his readers that the French, by forgetting that their revolution should involve both lay and religious ideals, had now been enslaved along with the rest of Europe by Napoleon Bonaparte (Martínez Delgado and Ortiz 1960: 516).

On the other hand, when the Rousseau of the 'Discourse on Political Economy' transformed himself into the libertine or irreligious writer of 'Emile' or 'The Social Contract', Padilla displayed the same courage by qualifying Rousseau as an author of impudent and irreligiously seditious and poisoned writings. This is just further proof that Padilla, even if he did admire the political and economic ideas of the Rousseau of 1750, separated and greatly distanced himself from the ideas of the Rousseau of 1762.

PADILLA'S PLACE IN THE HISTORY OF LATIN AMERICAN ECONOMIC IDEAS

The economic thinking of Padilla

The basic problem that captured Padilla's attention was the liberation and the independence of the American republics, especially of New Granada. The American solidarism, the union of all available forces, and the love of country are his favourite and highest priority themes; all the rest, including economic problems, are relegated to a secondary level.

> Every man loves his country, and this love is so noble, so intense and inflamed, that in comparison with it nothing else is so loved of the earthly possessions; private interest, comfort, the most alive passions, life itself is despicable, when one deals with liberty and security for the fatherland.
>
> (Martínez Delgado and Ortiz 1960: 417)

Once the ideas of a fatherland and the common good are established as the basic objectives of Padilla's system, all the other goals, even if economic, should be formulated and structured in such a manner that ensures the achievement of these two basic aims. In his thinking, political economy should be perfectly synchronized with and subordinated to the higher purposes of national policy.

In his universalistic view, there are two groups of problems, one of internal order and the other of external order. In the internal sector, Padilla assails the businessmen who prefer the pursuit of personal interest over the objectives of the country: 'Even now there is no lack of those who love money more than liberty, and who think less of this fine sovereign than of vile interests' (Martínez Delgado and Ortiz 1960: 339). Even more, during the serious times that Colombia was going through, Padilla found that there had been a breed of men who worked directly for the enemy:

> These are tradesmen of the ports of America, whose interests lie in Cádiz. Their heart is where their treasure is found. They fear to lose the fortune or the favour that they have deposited in that market, and it seems to them that liberty from the kingdom is of less value than the utility of four tradesmen.
>
> (Martínez Delgado and Ortiz 1960: 341)

Luckily, Padilla observed, there were businessmen who placed the lofty national objectives first; these were the businessmen of Bogotá, who served as an example for those of the coasts:

Learn from the generosity of the sons of Santafé, who preferring the common good over their own profit, have renounced with pleasure the commissions on which they subsisted, for the freedom of the Indians: they have given their own houses where they live, using the return on their sale for the public cause; and they have done away with their profit to relieve the fatherland in its urgencies. Illustrious Andrades, Lastras, Manríquez, Umañas . . . present yourselves in the midst of America, give lessons of patriotism to those egoists, show them how to sacrifice their possessions and their persons to public liberty, and to prefer the well being of the country over all earthly possessions, invoke the assistance of the solicitors of the cities so that united, they rant with you against those men, who by their private interests dazzle the towns, they detain them in servitude and they hide the evils that it brings with it to the regency.

(Martínez Delgado and Ortiz 1960: 341)

The same universalistic viewpoint dominated the area of international relations. Among the national economies exists a strict inter-dependence, and consequently, this imposes cooperation and peace as economic principles before rivalry and war:

It is true that Providence divided the earth into distinct climates, and gave to each climate diverse products, but: to all climates it gave men of a same species, of the same will, with a same precept, to mutually love and procure all things good; and this same diversity of production makes some men need the others, that this necessity obliges us to intercommunicate and by this communication fraternity and alliance were tightened between us.

(Martínez Delgado and Ortiz 1960: 451)

Consequently, from this same fact of world inter-dependence it is derived that the progress of each and every one of the nations responds to the supreme principle of common good. Padilla goes as far as to state that in this world, all men should be happy, rich, peaceful, and wise; living in comfortable houses and enjoying tables well-stocked with food.

What has merit for the entire world, has equal merit for the distinct parts of a confederation of nations, such as the old kingdom of Spain. In fact, Padilla asks himself:

Why cannot one place be happy without making another miserable? Cannot one town be free without enslaving another? In one same kingdom cannot the profits, the wealth, the glory of one city be assured without the poverty, the lowering, and the misery of another?

(Martínez Delgado and Ortiz 1960: 450)

It is certain that the plan of the illustrious Augustinian friar anticipated by 150 years the principles of international economic cooperation defended as much by the United Nations as by the social doctrine of the Catholic Church.

Confronted by a policy of unilateral benefits for the mother country, Padilla counters with his programme of American economic policy. The people of these lands claim the right to be equally free

> to work, to undertake, to plant the seed of whatever they like, to establish the factory they fancy, to exercise the art that accommodates them, to work in the position and type that is useful for them, to do all that law does not prohibit, neither having contradictions between religion and society, nor with the state. This and much more involves the benefit for which South America fights and sacrifices, in imitation of North America.
>
> (Martínez Delgado and Ortiz 1960: 361)

Nevertheless, this will be a long process, even if political independence is attained:

> There are lights which cannot be suddenly presented to the eyes without blinding them; and as Tacitus says, to the people who have lived in servitude it is not fit to suddenly place them in total liberty, because this brings evil sooner than benefit; it is necessary to put them in possession of it by degree and little by little, so that it may benefit them.
>
> (Martínez Delgado and Ortiz 1960: 361)

Padilla is fully conscious that his generation will not see the American economic prosperity that will have the desired effect of political independence. 'But our prosperity will be seen and if we do not have the pleasure of enjoying these benefits, we shall have the glory of having deposited them as seeds in the soil of our fatherland' (Martínez Delgado and Ortiz 1960: 376).

Guided by this view of social, political and economic justice extended to all the people of the world and by this to all the people of the Americas, Padilla considered it useful to incorporate as additions to the *Aviso al Público*, among other things, two documents focused on the same criterion of justice and equality, the 'Letter directed to Spanish Americans by one of their Compatriots' by Juan Pablo Viscardo, published in Philadelphia in 1799, and the 'Treatise entitled Political Economy' of Rousseau, published in the French *Encyclopaedia*, Volume V, in 1755.

Padilla, translator of the treatise

Besides having anticipated a renovation in the socio-economic current of the Church, we owe Padilla the distinction of having spread to the New

Grenadine cultural elite, and thus to the other American centres, the ideas of one of the most famous encyclopaedists, who was the true source of *The Rights of Man*, translated for the first time by someone in New Granada.

The importance of Padilla's Spanish version of the 'Discourse on Political Economy' can only really be appreciated by taking into account that in the Hispanic world, only a few other works by foreign authors dealing with political economy had been translated. Until 1810, as far as is known, the ten works that were converted into Spanish included works by Cantillon, Smith, Condillac, and Belgrano's translation from the original French of *Principles of Political-Economic Science*. In this way, the translation of the treatise by Padilla became the eleventh writing of major importance translated into Spanish, at a time when the United States had not produced any translation[8] and in Spanish America there was only available the aforementioned translation by Belgrano.

In a certain sense, the work of Padilla had a similar destiny to that of Belgrano. Belgrano did not identify the original author of *The Principles*, he only mentioned Count C. as the author of the first part of this work, and SAS as the writer of the second part. One hundred and twenty-seven years were to pass before the Argentinian economist Luis Roque Gondra (1923), managed to identify the authors as Dupont de Nemours (1768) for the first part, and the Margrave of Baden (1772) for the rest. Equally, it took 158 years to determine that the basis of Padilla's translation was the 'Discourse on Political Economy' of Jean Jacques Rousseau.

CONCLUSION

Although the American continent was discovered about 500 years ago, its spiritual basis cannot be studied except step by step. Its documentary richness, which is worth more than all the gold, silver and gems taken to the Old World, is still mostly hidden in archives. As Alfonso Reyes wondered in *Ultima Tule*, we also ask ourselves, who said that America has been discovered?

12

ESTEBAN ECHEVERRÍA

INTRODUCTION

Esteban Echeverría was born in Buenos Aires on 2 September 1805, being the second of nine children of José Domingo Echeverría and Martina Espinosa. He began his university studies in Buenos Aires, learning Latin and philosophy, but soon, in 1826, we find him in Paris, dedicating a major part of his time to political science, philosophy, political economy, and law. Towards the end of 1829, he spent a month and a half in London, later to return to Paris to concentrate on his training in politics and economics. It was in this period that he had the opportunity to know the great writers like Montesquieu and contemporary writers such as Sismondi, Lerroux, Lamennais, Saint Simon and other thinkers who were confronting the ideas of the classical liberal doctrine. Fighting poverty, misery, and illness, Echeverría decided to return to his country. In June of 1830 he was back in the Río de la Plata basin.

With the establishment of the 'Literary Salon' in May 1837, he began his political and socio-economic activity, after having gained renown for his literary production. After the salon was closed, there began on 8 July 1838, under his direction, a group known as 'The Association of the Young Argentinian Generation'. In August 1838, he edited, with the consent of Gutiérrez and Alberdi, the 'Código o Declaración de los Principios', which constituted the social beliefs of Echeverría's beloved nation. In addition, on 10 January 1839, it was published unsigned in *El Iniciador* in Montevideo, and, when reprinted in 1846 under the title *Dogma Socialista*, would form the cornerstone of Echeverría's economic and social doctrine.

The last chapter of Echeverría's life begins with his exile to Montevideo in June 1841. His output continued at an increasing rate, and was concentrated more and more upon social issues. For example, we have 'El Àngel Caído' and the 'Manual de Enseñaza Moral' in 1846, and 'Avellaneda' in 1849.

By this time, Echeverría's health was delicate and in 1851 he passed away and was buried in a cemetery in Montevideo. The editor Carlos Casavalle published Echeverría's *Obras Completas* (Complete Works) as a five volume set in Buenos Aires between the years 1870–4. A critical and documented edition of Echeverría's *Dogma Socialista* was prepared by Professor Alberto Palcos and published by the Universidad Nacional de La Plata in 1940.

THE ECONOMIC AND SOCIAL PHILOSOPHY OF ECHEVERRÍA

The evolution of his ideas

In order to understand Echeverría's thinking as a whole, it is necessary to take into account the evolution of his ideas. Until the years 1832–4, Echeverría's thought is best characterized by a witty scepticism that can be attributed to the influence of Condillac, Tracy, and Bentham, the three being in vogue in the teaching at the University of Buenos Aires (Echeverría 1870–4: 6).

One of Echeverría's works that particularly reflects this spirit is represented by *Historia* (History), written in Paris in 1827. Echeverría developed in this work the thesis of the eternal struggle between the people and its eternal consequences, misery and evil. This thesis was being embraced a century later by Gumplowicz (1838–1909) (Gumplowicz 1928).

After the year 1834, in his later works, Echeverría seems to have cured himself of his juvenile scepticism. He substitutes this concept for another one that is more complete, that would impregnate all his works, and in particular all his economic and social doctrine. The framework of Echeverría's new philosophical concept can be compared to a pyramid divided into three parts: the imposing base, constructed with the elements of scholasticism; on top of it an almost impenetrable layer built from the arsenal of rationalistic philosophy; and at the top an attractive and elegant tower, constructed in the style in vogue at that time, that of the philosophy of history. Examined from afar and superficially, it is this tower which seems outstanding to us. But seen closer up and with more attention to details, it is discovered that within this structure there exist not only the fine lines of rationalism, but also the vigorous Christian basis of Echeverría's philosophy. Even though it may appear paradoxical, this combination, so unlikely and so antagonistic, constituted not only perfect harmony for Echeverría, but also what was necessary to satisfy his personal restlessness. Without a doubt, from a methodological point of view, this doctrine would be unacceptable today. But in Echeverría's time, the situation was very different, as only Kant could avoid the temptations of the philosophy of history. If one attempts to search for preferences in the philosophy of Echeverría, the result would be that the rationalist source serves him only as an accessory, while between the other two areas, the scholastic ideology prevails. The philosophy of history plays no other role than a scientific instrument.

Scholastic bases

In his 'Código' in 1838, Echeverría had already demonstrated his Christian faith. 'The gospel is the law of love, and as the apostle James says, the perfect law, that is the law of liberty. Christianity should be the religion of the democracies' (Echeverría 1940d: 168). The gospel is the law of God, because it is the moral law of the conscience and of reason (Echeverría 1940d: 167). The doctrine of Jesus Christ is our doctrine because it is the doctrine of health and redemption (Echeverría 1940d: 175).

The philosophical ideas dealt with in Echeverría's 'Manual de Enseñanza Moral' (Manual of Moral Teaching) present a universal Christian character:

> If the universe is the work of God, all the beings of the universe are subjected to certain and determinate laws, because the order and harmony of the universe can not exist nor be conceived without ruling laws. . . . In such way that the laws of God are the laws of order, so that every being in the universe, as an agent of the laws of God is destined to realize in his sphere the order and to concur by his part the demonstration of universal order.
>
> (Echeverría 1870–4: IV, 347)

Given that this order is the good, and that man being free and blessed with intelligence is held responsible for every violation of the divine law, the result is that for every man 'the duty of acquiring the knowledge of the laws of God has been imposed upon him as a condition of life, in order not to infringe upon them and to realize order or good' (Echeverría 1870–4: IV, 348). 'Every man is obliged to work so that others observe the law and to simultaneously agree on the progressive realization over time toward order or toward good' (Echeverría 1870–4: IV, 349). Besides, man should observe the 'laws of relations' (or the influence and communication of every being with the other beings and with God), which will be divided into four groupings: with his neighbour; his family; his country; and with all humanity. This arises from the precept to love 'thy neighbour as thou lovest thyself', which Echeverría later uses as a basis for his law of solidarity.

Bases from the 'philosophy of history'

Echeverría reviews in a scientific manner his philosophical ideas that flow in great part from his Christian faith. This is how he arrives at the philosophy of history. 'Nothing is invented in politics, everything is deduced logically from the studying of the past and an opportune application' (Echeverría 1940f: 86). Following his favourite teachers, from Pascal, Leibniz and Vico, Herder, Turgot, and Condorcet to Saint Simon and Lerroux, Echeverría believed himself to have found the keys to the destiny of humanity in the law of indefinite progress or the dogma of perfectibility. Of what did this law of progress consist? Echeverría agrees with Pascal that

> humanity is like a man who lives forever and makes constant progress. This with one foot planted in the present and with the other extended toward the future, marching without becoming fatigued, as if impelled by the breath of God, in search of the promised Eden . . .
>
> (Echeverría 1940d: 152)

It is here that we find, according to him, 'the great modern discovery and the supreme truth of philosophy'.

'Civilization itself is nothing more than the indelible testimony of humanitarian progress . . . because to progress is to become civilized' (Echeverría 1940d: 159). Only that the law of progress is conditioned upon the 'law of space and time'. Humanity does not develop uniformly.

> Every village, every society, has its laws or peculiar conditions of existence, that come about from its customs, its history, its social state, its physical, intellectual, and moral necessities of the same nature of the ground upon which Providence wanted it to live perpetually.
>
> (Echeverría 1940d: 160; 1940f: 185)

From all this comes the result that the nation is the true bearer of progress, or that nationality is sacred. From this arises the corollary of sanctity, independence, and sovereignty of every nation (Echeverría 1940d: 160, 194).

Rational bases

If the existence of nationalities is the guarantee of the realization of the law of progress, Echeverría reminds us also that before the human society existed, with its rights, the individual existed with his no less divine and by consequence, inviolable laws. His universal Christianity, like his adherence to the doctrine of perfectibility, did not impede Echeverría from consenting at the same time to the dogma of the rights of man, cornerstone of the rationalist philosophy. In Echeverría's thinking, romanticism did not yet exercise hegemony over classicism. To the idea of nationality, favourite daughter of the nineteenth century, was even more opposed the individualistic ideas of the eighteenth century. 'The individual, by the law of God and of humanity, is the exclusive owner of his life, his property, his conscience, and his liberty' (Echeverría 1940d: 200). Actually, towards the end of Echeverría's life, one can observe a rather lively reaction against this formulation of the rational philosophy:

> But human reasoning, drunk with pride and science and power that he himself created, he wanted to deify his own concepts and he got lost in

the chaos, because he lost sight of the bright traditions that revealed the genius in the past.

(Echeverría 1870–4: I: 348)

Nevertheless, this one anti-rationalist attitude does not allow us to suppose that Echeverría renounces the rights of man. The truth is that the rights of the individual as well as the rights of society are a major source of worry. By showing his Christian philosophical thinking, we have found the spheres of these two groups of rights (individual and social, of conservation and of relation) to be well defined.

The law of solidarity

It is here that Echeverría reaches the dilemma of the individual or society. Even if it were true that modern political science can have reservations about the procedure by which Echeverría could arrive at two groups of rights, this will not diminish his merit for having shown how to find a solution to this problem.

Echeverría cannot accept the domination of either one thesis or the other. If the sacred rights of the individual become the societal tasks, how does Echeverría reconcile the two principal antagonists? If man has his saintly and inviolable rights, it is no smaller truth that he must comply with the law of progress and therefore chain himself to the forward progress of his nation. This is man's law of being because 'man is not only a social animal, as the ancients defined him, but man lives in society and does not live without society' (Echeverría 1940g: 448). 'Society is a fact printed upon the pages of history and a necessary condition that Providence imposed upon man for the free exercise and plain development of his faculties, to give him patrimony of the universe' (Echeverría 1940d: 453).[1] But, if the will of the Creator is that the destiny of man is to

live in unending communication with his fellow beings, if this be not only a necessity, but also a law of his being, there is necessarily a natural and normal way of communion and association of man with man or of men between themselves . . . there is a law of mutual solidarity and participation that should preside over common social work and determine its objective.

(Echeverría 1940g: 448–9)

The law of solidarity is therefore 'the moral law, the law of duty' (Echeverría 1940g: 453) of every man. Here is the basis of the social philosophy of Echeverría. For Echeverría, this law of solidarity 'is no other thing than the evangelic gospel of charity, embraced and applied by the philosophy of a wider and more complete manner' (Echeverría 1940g: 453).

Nevertheless the acceptance of the law of solidarity for Echeverría is not only the fruit of a logical chain of events. There are also national circumstances that contribute to this result, the deaf struggle between the two tendencies in Argentina: federalism versus unitarism. Only a harmonious fusion between the two factions would have been able to spare the country from the internal struggles.

> A harmonious fusion, upon which rest without alteration the liberties of every province and the prerogatives of the nation, a unique and inevitable solution that results in all the application of the formula now called upon to preside over modern politics, which consists . . . of the harmonization of the individual with the general, or in other words, liberty with association.
>
> (Echeverría 1940d: 224)

To this intermediary position, considerations of geopolitical order are added. The geopolitical structure of Argentina opposes itself to the preponderance of centralism, the 'territory being divided in provinces separated among each other by vast deserts' (Echeverría 1940a: 417). The cornerstone of Echeverría's thinking is this law of solidarity, which he accepts without reservation. From this arose the categorical imperative for the statesman to work in such a manner that social interests and individual interests have no bias between them. In the harmonic alliance between these two principles lies the entire art of politics. This is the meaning of the principle of association, established by Echeverría as the first symbolic word of his *Dogma Socialista*: 'the perfection of association is in proportion with the liberty of each and every one' (Echeverría 1940d: 156).

The organic principle of society

Echeverría's society has an essentially organic structure. It has nothing in common with the atomistic philosophy of the eighteenth century. For Echeverría, society is not an agglomeration of individuals but a homogeneous and animated body of one particular life. Society is the result not only of the reciprocal relations of individuals in space, but also of time, due to 'the continuous incarnation of the spirit of one generation after another' (Echeverría 1940d: 212).

> The union, the fraternal reciprocity between the members of a family, that is to say the sons of the same earth, that have the same origin, equal customs, common interests, and whose confluence of action will have a same end, these are the ties which make up society. It is impossible that without such confluence and ties, there were peace among the sons of one family and so it is with the nation, nor could society, in such case, march freely and actively towards its goals.
>
> (Echeverría 1870–4: V, 348)

It is true that the individual in Echeverría's society is not tied in one absolute manner to society, but despite this, society does not lose its organic character. It is important that individuals recognize that 'the society is a fact stamped on the pages of history and the necessary condition that Providence imposes on man for the free exercise and plain development of his faculties' (Echeverría 1940d: 152). It is important that they feel they are part of this 'superior organism' and that they realize that life outside of society would be a latent life (Echeverría 1940g).

The principle of limited liberty

The term 'liberty', one of the most frequent in the work of Echeverría, is not always used in the same manner. If at times 'liberty' means 'independence' to Echeverría, or 'social emancipation', in most cases the usage is in the classical sense: 'liberty is the right that every man has without any obstacles to employ his faculties in the attainment of his welfare and to choose the means that can serve him for this objective' (Echeverría 1940d: 165). In this manner, liberty has, nevertheless, three limitations.

The first is of the same essence as liberty. Echeverría decides upon the strict concept of liberty, stripping its wide concept of its anti-social and anarchic characteristics. Echeverría's liberty is strictly complemented with the duty of Christian fraternity: without the fraternal spirit, liberty does not draw men closer, it only divides them. In the same way, liberty must be complemented with equality: 'for men to be free, they need to be equal, and vice versa, to be equal they need to be free' (Echeverría 1870–4: IV, 395). Naturally, Echeverría does not think of a mechanical equality:

there have always been high capabilities and low abilities in society, men only disposed for material work and men of superior intelligence. . . . All is hierarchical in the universe, and the order and harmony are provided by the connection and the necessary subordination of efforts and intelligence.

(Echeverría 1870–4: IV, 393)

It is in this sense that Echeverría employs the famous formula of Saint Simon: 'to every one according to his capability, to each capability according to its works'.

The second class of limitations refers to the exercise of liberty by the diverse social groups. The lower classes, although disposed of civil liberty, can not enjoy complete political liberty:

sovereignty is the greatest and most solemn act of a free people. How will those who do not know its importance be able to concur? . . . The masses have nothing more than instincts, they are

199

more sensitive than rational ... they desire to be free and do not know the path to liberty.

(Echeverría 1940d: 201)[2]

The final limitation refers to the exertion of liberty by the different groups. For Echeverría, civic liberty, freedom of the press, of religion, and of cults have no limits. The freedom of teaching, on the contrary, has a special limitation. Echeverría takes a decidedly anti-liberal attitude on this question. While liberalism in the area of education is translated as the state being neutral towards culture and schools,[3] Echeverría's opinion is that 'instruction without a given and recognized goal, without a look of morality and sociability, far from being useful, can be damaging, it can mislead spirits, relax customs, inseminate egoism, suffocating the seed of civic virtues' (Echeverría 1870–4: IV, 394–6; 1940a: 409). Especially as regards civic education, Echeverría praises a skilful and systematic approach.

The institution of property

The essence of property

Among the natural rights of man, Echeverría also includes the right to property. 'The individual, by God's and humanity's laws, is exclusive owner of his life, of his property' (Echeverría 1940d: 200). Given that the natural rights of man are holy and inviolable, since they existed before the establishment of society, not even the state enjoys the right to violate with tax legislation this natural law of divine origin. Echeverría rejects, albeit indirectly, all the theories of collective property, and openly opposes his beloved teacher, Lerroux.

The order of property

Even though he unconditionally supports private property, Echeverría does not agree with its actual distribution. One should not confuse the right with egoism, because in this way the principle of equality is violated. 'There is no equality where the poor class suffers alone social charges' (Echeverría 1940d: 163). Faithful to this concept, Echeverría takes as a motto for his political economy that 'industry (or economy) that does not tend to emancipate the workers and take them to equality, but tends to concentrate wealth among a few people, is to be abhorred' (Echeverría 1940d: 215).

> To fulfill the complete concretion of class equality and the emancipation of the masses, it is necessary that all social institutions be directed towards the aim of improving the intellectual, physical and moral condition of the most numerous and poor classes.
>
> (Echeverría 1940d: 216)

The idea of the social character of the economy, including property, is analysed by Echeverría. This idea first appeared in the writings of Saint Simon, and was later developed and widened by Wagner and Schmoller. The right to property should be adapted to the needs and interests of society. Even when Echeverría says that property is a form of oppression, he cannot be labelled as socialist. For Saint Simonian socialists, man's exploitation of man is a vice inherent in private property, because it is seen as receiving a product without working. But Echeverría's meaning of exploitation is similar to that of Sismondi. Like Sismondi, Echeverría never opposes the owners of the means of production, he simply says that sometimes property can transform itself into a method of oppression and tyranny.

Why can property transform itself? Because one sector of mankind believes itself to be destined to be placed in a position above the others. Therefore, the origin of the abuse is not in property, per se, but in those property owners who do not follow the divine law of solidarity. If they understood and applied the principles of solidarity, the struggle between the oppressors and the oppressed would be replaced by a true harmony of classes. The correct term then would be exploitation as in Sismondi and not exploitation as in Saint Simon. But also, without this interpretation of 'the exploitation of man by man', it would be very difficult to find in Echeverría support of the socialist thesis of the collectivization of the means of production. Even if Echeverría criticizes the distribution of the means of production, he does not follow Saint Simon's path of collective reforms. Echeverría would refuse to follow his proclaimed suggestions on inheritance, and has been incorrectly labelled as an agrarian socialist (Ingenieros 1946) when he actually worried about the progress of the Argentinian farmlands. To label him an agrarian socialist is to confuse his agrarian reform with agrarian socialism. Echeverría defended the right to private property[4] and wanted to see workers transformed into property owners, in order to stimulate and protect them (Echeverría 1940d).

The revolution and the struggle between classes

As Echeverría praises a transformation of the existing social order, it is interesting to know whether he proclaims a change by violent or peaceful means. The word revolution, which he uses very often, should not be interpreted in the sense of rioting mobs or the turbulence of a civil war. For Echeverría, revolution is progress and progress is civilizing action, which conforms to his idea that progress should come about within conditions that respect the law of time (Echeverría 1940d: 160). Echeverría considers his time to be one of transition and preparation, which would absorb life for two or three generations. He is against a struggle between classes. Echeverría mentions the motto of the workers of Lyon: 'live working or die fighting', which he takes to be a desperate solution to unchecked abuse by the landlords. Actually, Echeverría defends harmony between classes:

> the mutual solidarity of all men, morally and socially speaking, is the brotherhood or the mutual love that nears and unites them by means of an agreeable and necessary tie in communion . . . in a defined aspiration of all rational beings . . . .the beginning of the brotherhood . . . is destined to complete the synthesis of the individual and the social man . . . beginning without which liberty and equality are chimerical or misleading.
>
> (Echeverría 1940g: 454)

The denomination of Echeverría's doctrine

There is among Echeverría's works a text in which he expresses most completely the essence of his doctrine, by application of the principle of solidarity to all social sectors

> We want a policy, a religion, a philosophy, a science, an art, an industry [read economy], that concurs simultaneously to establish the harmony of hearts and intelligence or the strict union of all the members of the Argentinian family.
>
> (Echeverría 1940d: 216–17)

To that set of principles destined to 'come to terms with all the opinions, all the interests', Echeverría refers to as the 'social dogma', 'popular democracy', 'foundations or principles of all his social system', 'the social theory of the thought of May', and particularly, 'social dogma'. Although Echeverría uses the word socialist quite often, he uses it to express other concepts. He uses the verb 'socialize' to express the action of creating and promoting the spirit of harmony and social solidarity (Echeverría 1940a: 419). It seems that Echeverría is the first to have utilized the expression 'social democrat' (at least in the Latin world).[5] Nevertheless, there is no connection between this expression and the social-democratic political party created later by Liebknecht and Bebel. In the same way that the word socialism, invented by Lerroux, suffered a change in meaning, being monopolized by the collectivists, the term that Echeverría conceived of in a strictly solidarist manner, lost its acceptance when monopolized by the Marxists.

CONTRIBUTIONS TO POLITICAL AND SOCIAL ECONOMICS

Problems of methodology

A profound expert of the romantic movement, and at the same time an admirer of the works of Vico, Montesquieu, and Sismondi could never have remained indifferent towards the historic movement. Without a doubt, Echeverría's appreciation as regards the historic method are at the same time the result of the observations made of his own country, where culture, according to him, was deformed by the application of imported systems. But while the young German historical school reached an extreme point, our author stopped at a more reasonable and conciliatory position. Even though an ardent defender of the historic method, Echeverría does not think about the integral substitution of the abstract method. It would be better to unite the two, not to marry oneself exclusively with one method: to be eclectic is perhaps the best way. Reason can be conceived; experience rectifies the senses and reason once again works, until hitting the mark. When this has been accomplished, everything that is possible to man has been done: beyond this, his skills will not reach (Echeverría 1870–4: V, 372–3).

National system of political economy

The conclusion concerning methodology, united with its extraordinary sense of observation, should have driven Echeverría forcibly to opinions similar to those of Friedrich List, without letting it be known that his were developed many years before List's. The moving force of nationalism, his people having recently been liberated from Spanish domination, explains why this idea enjoys a dominant position in Echeverría's doctrine. But at the same time the young rebel does not go too far. Between the two extremes of individualism and humanism, Echeverría adds, like an outline of fundamental and organic union, the idea of nationality. It is true that the law of progress can not be complied with but in a national investiture, and that the national sentiment is a duty imposed by divine law (Echeverría 1870–4: IV, 397). Echeverría seems to say that without nationalism, there is no culture (Echeverría 1940f: 141), for him, universalism is the supreme purpose. As in the case of individuals, also 'there is, by the will of the Creator, by the law of human nature, a necessary communion among all people, and all of them are, within themselves, solidary' (Echeverría 1940f: 141). By this extension of the principle of solidarity, by virtue of which all peoples are reciprocally solidary and responsible, Echeverría is a precursor of the French economist Lucien Brocard (1870–1936), who is shown to give a solution to the antinomy of nationalism–internationalism (Brocard 1929–31).

Given the importance of the national ideal in his system, the principal worry of our author is to crystallize it, affirm it, and consolidate it by any means. If Echeverría goes as far as to give special attention to economics, it is precisely because it is the 'source of wealth and power of the nations' (Echeverría 1940c: 278). For identical reasons, Echeverría is convinced to enter the science, to build an economic system based upon the elements of Argentina's reality, and thus give life to an Argentine economic discipline. The methodology to follow is

Adopting and reckoning those general laws . . . that the philosophical economists have discovered, we should then endeavor to discover by way of observation of the facts, the local laws that our industry or our national wealth observes in its unfolding, in order to base on it a truly Argentinian economic science.

(Echeverría 1940b: 286)

This national economic science will be based upon statistical data.

As we see, Echeverría is not only a precursor of the national school of political economy, but is also the promoter of the Argentinian national school of political economy. It is true that others before had been concerned about the problems of political economy, but for them political economy always carried the stamp of physiocratic or Smithean.[6]

Economics, industry, and economic science

Echeverría uses the word industry as equivalent to economy. This lack of distinction has a historical explanation, for at that time in France, there existed the habit of designating as industry all types of economic activities. Conforming to the language of his epoch, our author also, probably following the terminology of Jean Baptiste Say, speaks to us about the manufacturing, mercantile, and agricultural industries. But if Echeverría confuses the words, he does not mix the notions. 'Do not ignore', he says, once again in the spirit and letter of Say, 'that political economy is the science which shows how to produce, consume, and distribute the wealth among nations'. We will see later on that Echeverría, like Sismondi, overcoming the political economy focus of the classical writers, grants special attention to distribution.

Economic freedom

Naturally, Echeverría adheres to economic freedom:

That which the industry requires in order to prosper, are not restrictions and binds, but fostering and freedom. The freedom is a natural right . . . what shall we ask for industry? Freedom, guarantee, protection, and promotion on the part of governments. Only under those conditions will our industry be able to prosper.

(Echeverría 1940c: 281)

Echeverría's concept of economic freedom differs from that of classical laissez-faire only by requesting some state intervention. It has already been seen in Echeverría's thinking that the concept of freedom is limited. The principle of economic freedom defined in his phrase: 'every man can exercise what appears right to him, and in his manner, as long as it does not harm the right of another to the same liberty', is valid with two limitations: first, if private initiative does not suffice, the state should intervene. The need for intervention is based, according to Echeverría, in the same essence of the economy, which is the daughter of necessity. Consequently, 'to increase the necessities of a people, to make them know the commodities, is to prod them into being industrious' (Echeverría 1940c: 279).

> The idea of intervention is also imposed upon national considerations. It is necessary to watch that all the individual efforts, far from becoming isolated and concentrated on egoism, concur simultaneously and collectively to a unique purpose: the progress and growth of the nation.
>
> (Echeverría 1940d: 15)

One must be careful of arriving at arbitrary conclusions from this and to consider Echeverría as an interventionist. For Echeverría, neither economic freedom nor interventionism are ends in themselves. The supreme objective is the welfare of the community, or the production of national wealth. Echeverría accepts or rejects intervention according to whether it serves or not the achievement of the supreme objective. The acceptance of one or the other depends upon the economic structure of each nation. If private initiative is insufficient or collides with society's superior interests, then it is the duty of the state to enter into action, in order to stimulate or moderate the initiative.

The second limitation to the principle of economic freedom has social policy purposes, that is to say, to prevent it being transformed into an instrument of exploitation of the weak. 'The industry that does not tend to emancipate the masses and elevate them to equality, but concentrates wealth in a few hands, we abhor it.' The policy of the state should be oriented towards 'the intellectual, physical, and moral improvement of the most numerous and poorest class' (Echeverría 1940d: 157). The state should possess a 'generous soul for all its sons, because it examines closely the moral solidarity of the destiny of all of them, because it professes the moral principle of solidarity of all its members' (Echeverría 1940g: 454).

The theory of work

Work as a duty

Echeverría grants special attention to the problem of work. There is a surprising parallelism between his ideas and those of Saint Thomas Aquinas, updated by the papal encyclicals. The supreme sentiment of work is identified with the feeling of life itself. 'There is no life then without work; or better, work is the first condition for the conservation and welfare of individual and social life.' It is necessary, consequently, 'to consider work not

205

only as a necessity, but also as a virtue' (Echeverría 1870–4: IV, 359). The same parallelism is proved by examining the immediate meaning of work:

1 It frees us from idleness and laziness, raising us over irrational instincts. 'He who does not work surrenders himself to vice, because idleness is the mother of all vices' (Echeverría 1870–4: IV, 330, 332, 359);
2 It assures us of the necessary means to 'to live and acquire personal independence . . . to furnish welfare to our family and to attend to the subsistence of our old parents and return them part of their love and care' (Echeverría 1870–4: IV, 360);
3 It allows us to complete the duty of Christian fraternity, that is to say 'assist the poor . . . to do good and exercise charity toward the next one' (Echeverría 1870–4: IV, 359–60);
4 Finally, it allows us to comply with our social duty, contributing to the progress of the community. 'As society is made up by families and men, it results that by the enrichment of the citizens by their work, society gradually becomes richer and prosperous, and the homeland gradually becomes rich and powerful' (Echeverría 1870–4: IV, 361).

Therefore, for Echeverría, work does not only have an individual character in its acceptance as a right, but better yet, a universal one, and as such it is a duty.

The dignity of manual labour

Echeverría also makes the distinction between manual labour, especially that of an economic character, and intellectual labour, which is needed to complete the former. While Aristotle, Saint Thomas de Aquinas, and Pope Leo XIII grant a great dignity to intellectual labour, Echeverría considers the two types of labour as equally dignified and courageous.

> One and the other labours are equally legitimate, because both tend to the welfare and conservation of the individual and society. Generally speaking, material labour by its production satisfies the physical necessities; and intellectual labour the moral necessities, such as education, science, spiritual enjoyments, etc.
>
> (Echeverría 1870–4: IV, 358–9)

Professional orientation and formation

By agreeing to give equal dignity to the two types of labour, Echeverría bears in mind not only the phenomenon of intellectual proletarianism, but also the lack of criterion for the authority as regards professional orientation and formation. This should be adapted to the conditions and means of local production (Echeverría 1870–4: IV, 332). Mentioning the occupations which best correspond to the socio-economic structure of the country, Echeverría praises a reorganization of public education (Echeverría 1870–4: IV, 361). Without worrying about the psycho-technological problems especially, Echeverría takes a favourable position towards the phrenological thesis, which begins to be in vogue again today in the examinations for professional selection.

> The physical powers reside in the body, the moral powers in the soul. . . . The manner in which these two principles exercise their action is an unfathomable mystery for man. The phrenological point of view appears to us in this respect to be the most luminous.
>
> (Echeverría 1870–4: IV, 351)

CONTRIBUTIONS TO ECONOMIC AND SOCIAL POLICY

Economic policy

Agricultural industrialization

Economic development, according to Echeverría, is the main element by which to carry out the supreme law of progress and consequently is the preferred among all the sectors of culture (Echeverría 1940e: 278).[7]

Given the nature of Argentina's soil and the lack of capital and labour, our author pronounces in favour of developing the agricultural sector. Naturally, Echeverría is not content with the actual development of Argentinian agriculture in his time. He insists on the necessity to complete the purely extractive aspect of agriculture with the progressive industrialization of its products (Echeverría 1940a: 408; 1940e: 279).

> Who doubts that the skin of cattle and horses could leave our market tanned and prepared? That the horsehair and wool could benefit and acquire higher prices than that which they enjoy at the present? . . . We do not find ourselves at the state of manufacturing cloth with our wool, but our industry could impress on them a greater value, raising their price before putting them in the hands of strangers.
>
> (Echeverría 1940c: 279–80)

To this end, Echeverría elaborates a true Economic Plan.[8] He proposes a series of measures, among which we emphasize: the development of the means of transportation; the struggle against drought and plagues; professional formation and orientation; and a type of scientific organization of labour (Echeverría 1940c: 280).

He demands a strict collaboration between science and economic practice. Echeverría recommends research of economic character as a priority:

Useful and excellent it will be to investigate the transformations that have suffered the value of rural and bestial property from the end of the past century until today; to calculate the number of animals that existed then in our fields, that which the civil war and the drought has destroyed without benefit, that which was consumed in this period and that today exists. Thus, we could also discover the population of then and of now, the value of the principal peninsular merchandise then consumed . . . to calculate . . . if today we reckon with more real wealth than in those times.

(Echeverría 1940c: 281–2)

Without a doubt, Echeverría did not only ponder the industrialization of agriculture. He figures a great extension of industrialization in the other sectors. But for the moment Echeverría considers it indispensable to encourage the agricultural branch, with the purpose of 'agglomerating the capital to carry in time our activity to another class of industry' (Echeverría 1940c: 279).

Rent dependent on position: Heinrich von Thünen and Echeverría

Completely independent of von Thünen and without needing the fiction of an ideal state, Echeverría arrived at the same conclusion. It is known that von Thünen explained the rent dependent on position beginning with the hypothesis of a great city located exactly in the centre of a plain with constant fertility. Under this hypothesis, the producers situated in the proximity of the city obtained a rent dependent on position, given that the transportation expenses were lower for them than for the goods from farther away. In order to compensate for the effects of the law of increasing transportation, the cultivators were obligated to undertake less intensive cultivation as they were situated farther from the city. For Echeverría, the driving force towards discovery of the rent dependent on position was the worry of finding an adequate solution to the problem of taxation. Echeverría thinks that the experience acquired by the Western European nations will be of no use: there the imposition is done on the basis of rent for quality, because its lands are divided between fertile and sterile, but in Argentina one could not make taxation be ruled by the same principle, because the land is of equal fertility in all parts, especially in the zone of Buenos Aires (Echeverría 1940b: 287).

Echeverría constructed a taxation system based on the criterion of the rent dependent on position. The similarity of the conclusions of Echeverría and von Thünen is surprising. Let us contemplate Echeverría's conclusion:

In order to establish a fair tax, it would be necessary to divide the province's land into zones, fixing the capital as the center of the areas. The first zone would be composed of the lands of the manor

208

houses destined for daily consumption. The second, the small isolated farms that we shall label as urban, to distinguish them from outlying farms, occupied with the planting of firewood and fruits, and with the sowing of cereals; the third group the lands for raising cattle on this side of the Salado river, whose value is maximum; the fourth the lands on the other side of the Salado river, whose value decreases gradually until coming to a minimum at the frontier where the desert begins. The lands of the small isolated farms where wheat, corn, potatoes are sown, should be valued according to the distance from the city, because the main expense of farming consists of transportation. This and much other data would be necessary to establish a tax based on the intrinsic value of the territorial properties.

(Echeverría 1940b: 287)

Echeverría proceeds, just like von Thünen, to divide the taxable surface by concentric zones. At first view, while von Thünen divides the territory of his ideal state into five circles: large vegetable gardens; tree plantations; cereals; cattle; and hunting grounds; Echeverría only has four. Examining more attentively the second circle of Echeverría, it is seen that it actually contains two circles: that of urban small farms; and the rural lands of forests, fruits, and cereals. All of this is not very important, as the principal idea is that Echeverría, like von Thünen, bases his theory on the expenses of increasing transportation.

The territorial tax

According to Echeverría, a sane fiscal policy should: guarantee to the state a fixed tax on solid and permanent bases; and assure the establishment of the tax in agreement with the principle of social justice.

Echeverría criticizes the Argentinian fiscal policy for not having respected these two principles. The war with Brazil and the blockade of Buenos Aires are two typical examples (Echeverría 1940a: 408), demonstrating the ignorance of the first principle. As concerns the second, it is sufficient to mention his observation that the customs tax was paid in the last instance by the poorest class (Echeverría 1940c: 283).

To remedy this evil, Echeverría proposes the implementation of the territorial tax, which, according to him, is 'the safest and easiest to establish, that which presents the least difficulty for its collection, and that which provides the state with a fixed income' (Echeverría 1940b: 287).

It would be a mistake to believe that Echeverría praises taxation on a progressive scale. He resorts to using an established proportional scale, as we just saw, in relation to the rent dependent on position. Besides, Echeverría said categorically: 'There is no equality . . . where contributions

209

are not shared with equality and in proportion to the goods and industries of each one' (Echeverría 1940d: 163). This is one more proof that he did not accept partiality in his policy regarding the treatment of the different classes.

Agrarian credit

Our fervent defender of the promotion of agriculture does not think only of the political measures mentioned above. He encourages, besides this, the organization of agrarian credit. Echeverría justly reproaches the 'unitary party' for not having introduced, in their clause to the statute of the Banco de Descuentos, that one part of its capital should be given as loans to agriculturalists and small investors, and that they would go towards encouraging industry and labour in the fields (Echeverría 1940a).

Social policy

The social question

In this matter also there is the divine law of solidarity which Echeverría takes as a starting point. Consequently, he rejects the exploitation of man by man or the poor by the rich. He did not engage, with hatred, in the class struggle, it was only the sense of justice that he felt was damaged, before the sad reality of which he was a spectator:

> The proletarian works day and night to enrich the idle class; he changes the sweat on his brow for the subsistence of himself and his family. The retribution for his labour is not equitable. . . . The owner of the means of production exploits him. The proletarian, in the meantime, is a man like any other and in virtue of the law of God and its nature . . . he has the same rights that others have.
>
> (Echeverría 1940g: 450)

We witness a case of very poor organization of labour, which comes from the lack of a principle of solidary spirituality by society, which should have to serve 'as regulator of the distribution and retribution of labour, or in the reciprocal participation in the uses of property' (Echeverría 1940g: 451).

The programme destined to resolve the social question could be summarized, according to Echeverría, by the following measures: taxation policy; social assistance policy, summarized by the phrase: 'The social dominion is not moral nor does it correspond to its objectives, if it does not protect the weak, the poor, and the needy' (Echeverría 1940d: 163); and the wages policy, which we will examine shortly. The executor of social policy is the state itself, and for its purpose, the state should abandon its classical neutral position.

210

The state, the visible head of society, performs the functions of the true social providence; cares for its members; knows the needs of all of them and pleads to satisfy them without any preferences; provides education to all with the aim of improvement and perfects and leads social progress.

(Echeverría 1940g: 45)

Wages theory

Of the three characteristics of wages (based on necessity, sacrifice, and efficiency), Echeverría adopts the last one, summed up in the famous formulation of Saint Simon: 'to each one according to his capabilities, to each capability according to its works'. Without doubt, Echeverría wants to apply it above all else in political and social life. As regards economic life, its application suffers from limitations. In the area of property, as we have seen, Echeverría has often abandoned the principle itself. Other exceptions to the principle of efficiency are made up of invalids and the poor in general, who even if they do not work, enjoy the protection of the Echeverrian state.

What is more, Echeverría affirms that the wage is not equitable if it does not give the worker the possibility to feed himself sufficiently, give education to his children, be protected from illnesses and unforeseen events, and finally, to assure him a peaceful old age (Echeverría 1940g: 450–1). Echeverría breaches the rigidity of the principle of efficiency. Actually, all he meant to say was that for a wage to be equitable, it should satisfy the elementary needs of the working family, or to use a modern expression, it should be above all else a family wage. Only when the level of a family wage has been surpassed, does the principle of efficiency that Echeverría adopted from Saint Simon come into play.

The social agrarian policy

Echeverría's attention is caught by the desolate condition of the agricultural worker:

The inhabitants of our fields have been robbed . . . they have been killed by the thousands in civil war. Their blood ran in the war for independence . . . and still they are overcharged by taxation, their industry is shackled, they are not allowed to peacefully enjoy from their work the only property they can count on, while the rich are at leisure. Equality has been proclaimed and the most frightful inequality has reigned, liberty has been shouted and it has only existed for a certain number; laws have been dictated and they have only protected the powerful. For the poor, laws have not been made, nor justice, nor individual rights, but violence, sabres, and unjust persecutions. They have been outside the law.

(Echeverría 1940c: 283)

Shocked by the ravages of drought, Echeverría overflows in a rebellious torrent, which at the same time constitutes his social agrarian policy:

Is it possible that when the harvest is poor, that half the population does not eat bread and the other half eats expensive and bad bread? Could not so such wealth as is consumed by vain businesses be employed in establishing regular emigration to the farm lands? Could not the workers who have no field of their own be stimulated and protected by giving them farm lots that have been sold at a low price? Could not the most diligent be awarded, giving them resources for harvesting, with public funds destined for this reason so that they do not waste nor pawn their labour, but accumulate savings?

(Echeverría 1940c: 284)

It is therefore seen that in the thinking of our author, the problems of distribution hold special importance. His ideas are very popular today, thanks to the influence exerted by the diverse intermediary and socialist doctrines (Gonnard 1952). In the days of Echeverría, the situation was different; except for some exceptions (Sismondi, Saint Simon, etc.) the economic doctrine was characterized by a spirit of neutrality, and not of interventionism by the state. Only in light of these considerations can one appreciate at their fair value his ideas and what is so revolutionary about them.

The reform of customs

The young Argentinian economist recognized that his ideas where unattainable in the Argentinian society of his time. We will enumerate the reasons: the lack of understanding and the ineptitude of the people to appreciate rights and obligations which their new social status bestowed upon them; because 'the American generation carries the habits and tendencies of another generation inoculated in their blood . . . based upon the inequality of the classes' (Echeverría 1870–4: IV, 214). It is true that the revolution brought political independence to Argentina, but the period of internal struggles that followed drove the nation to the edge of social anarchy, since the most solid and sane social institutions are those born from beliefs and customs (Echeverría 1870–4: IV, 344). For this reason, Echeverría considered it indispensable that before beginning the application of his economic programme, a reform of habits and customs must be attempted.

He considered that the business of reconstructing an adequate social medium for his economic programme, while difficult, was not impossible. In his thinking, 'a people is never perverse, the perverse and evil ones are those who trick and exploit their ignorance' (Echeverría 1870–4: IV, 214). He recognized that many abuses had taken place during this time of tyranny. 'They were misled because they were ignorant, and they were ignorant because no one educated them about the new social life inaugurated in May' (Echeverría 1870–4: IV, 357).

The task of education is imposed by another consideration. Our author did not believe in the native kindness that was preached by Rousseau and Mandeville. According to Echeverría, 'man at birth brings nothing but instincts for good and needs to educate those instincts, exercise them so that they are converted into regulatory beliefs of his life' (Echeverría 1870–4: IV, 357). 'Masses have but instincts: they are more sensitive than rational; they want good but do not know how to find it; they want to be free and do not know the path to liberty' (Echeverría 1940d: 202). This is the imperative of education.

Evidently, given that people 'do not change their habits as to the manner of seeing or feeling but after a long and laborious education' (Echeverría 1870–4: IV, 209), Echeverría considered it an inevitable obligation of Argentinian government to incorporate the principles of reform, primarily 'in the education, in the customs, in the intelligence of everyone' and only afterwards in the constitution and in positive legislation (Echeverría 1870–4: IV, 340).

The organs for the reform of customs were, according to Echeverría, the priest, the mother, and the teacher. 'The priest is a public position. The mission of the priest is to moralize, preach brotherhood, charity, that is to say the law of peace and love, the law of God' (Echeverría 1940d: 170). If Echeverría criticized the clergy, as he did, often enough and harshly enough to have been given the unfair label of anti-clerical, he did it precisely because he believed that they had not always 'sown in the conscience of the people the seed of moral and intellectual regeneration: the gospel' (Echeverría 1940f: 92). Still Echeverría was greatly disturbed by the insufficient number of teachers. 'What values the doctrine if there are no teachers to understand and teach it?' (Echeverría 1870–4: IV, 342). Thus he saw the need for a teachers' school, an idea he encouraged.

But if he entrusted intellectual education to the teachers, it was to the mother that he gave the education of feelings. 'What does it matter that the child learns good doctrines in school, if he hears not from his father's lip, and especially from his mother's, some word that fecundates them, or if he sees examples that contradict them?' (Echeverría 1870–4: IV, 344). Remembering Tocqueville's observation that the prosperity of the North American union was due to the superiority of its women, Echeverría wondered: 'Why cannot ours, as intelligent as beautiful, be the equal and powerful influence in the reform of national customs and the welfare of the fatherland?' It was for the ideal woman, the republican woman, that he wrote his famous poem 'El Àngel Caído', which is considered as a true family album. For Echeverría, the key to reform of customs was the family. 'Develop good mothers to have good sons, develop good citizens if you wish to have a homeland: herein lies the entire problem of education' (Echeverría 1870–4: IV, 345).

THE IMPORTANCE OF THE DOCTRINE IN THE HISTORY OF ECONOMIC DOCTRINES AND IN ECONOMIC HISTORY

Its importance in the history of economic doctrines

The ideas of Echeverría had the same destiny in his country as all intermediary ideas, while on the historical scene, the great dispute about hegemony between socialism, during its development, and the still powerful liberalism, was beginning. Considered by the liberals as infected by socialist ideas and by the socialists as reactionary, these doctrines that we label as solidary were the object of ridicule and harsh criticism by the two extreme schools.

But at the beginning of the second half of the nineteenth century a restructuring of the forces in the field of economic doctrines is shown. The interests of the economists in favour of extreme positions began to falter. The tradition of Sismondi started gaining ground. The German historical school, renewed by Roscher and Schmoller, the 'lecture room' socialism represented by Adolf Wagner, the interventionism begun by Dupont White, the idea of equilibrium between the individual and social sphere preached by John Stuart Mill, Henry George, and Leon Walras, the organic idea sustained by Christian doctrines, and that of solidarity defended by Gide and Bourgeois, all of these intermediary doctrines managed to capture the attention of economists. The immense merit of having given a frame to solidarism in a system and having attempted to restructure economic science in light of this system undoubtedly comes from Heinrich Pesch and Othmar Spann, even though the latter merely pretended to be a universalist.

Since the Second World War, the works and the representatives of solidarism have returned in great number. And with this, they also increased the different strands in the main current of solidarism itself. With the exception of the Christian group who maintain a line of more or less perfect equilibrium, these authors defend positions that oscillate at times towards individualism, as in the case of Ropke, the father of the expression 'the third road', and at times towards socialism, like the English Fabians. In the area of economic policy, there have been attempts to construct a system known as 'economic planning', which should not be confused with the centrally planned economy of the socialists, which enjoys great sympathy among Swiss, German, Austrian, French, and American economists.

214

Importance in the history of economic facts

In the economic life of states, one can notice a similar development. The highest point of the liberal state was between 1845 and 1876. In the seventh decade of the nineteenth century, a new mood of spirit started forming in economic life. The foresight of the socialists and solidarists is seen as though confirmed more and more by facts. Incapable of defending their position in the unequal fight of competition, the industrial and agricultural workers requested the support and protection of the state. The waves of economic crises ruined the finances of many countries. The generation of 1880 is not like that of 1840. In place of the declining liberal state, the social policy state arose. In truth, the reforms were always timid and found to be average; also the economic constitution of the states was still liberal. But in this constitution, two important gaps appeared, one in internal economic life, where the measures were of an eminently socio-political character. For example, the workers' unions obtained their legal status, social security was introduced, and the working day was limited, as well as the work of women and children, etc. The other gap was in external economic life, where states broke with the policy of free trade, which led to this historical period being called the protectionist era.

After the First World War, it seemed that liberalism was coming back. But the reality was different, as statesmen possessed by nationalism practised an intensive interventionism. This was the time of the interventionist state. The intervention did not limit itself only to the socio-political sector, but also extended to the economic sector. Intervention in one sector provoked intervention in the other. The Italian corporate policy of 1926, the development of German deflationary policy under Brüning between 1931 and 1933, the inconvertibility of the pound, and the initiation of the policies brought about by the agreements in Ottawa in 1932, the Farm Relief Act and the National Industrial Recovery Act by Roosevelt in 1933, and the policy begun by Leon Blum.

We lack the necessary perspective to examine the tendencies of economic policy of the different states from the last years of the Second World War to the present. But there are, without doubt, signals of a transition from the interventionist state towards the planned economy state. Naturally, it deals with multiple forms, according to the economic and social structure of each country, but the tendency is unquestionable.

THE CONFIRMATION OF ECHEVERRÍA'S IDEAS

We have reviewed the evolution of economic ideas and facts in the second half of the nineteenth century and the first half of the twentieth century precisely in order to show that all these new courses and tendencies in both ideas and facts were very familiar to our great visionary. Without attempting to identify the system of Echeverría with any system which came after him, it can be said that the latter systems were encouraged by and had already existed in the thinking of this great Argentinian. It does not matter whether his ideas are accepted or not, it is enough to know that his solidarist idea, for which he had fought, suffered, and died, was embraced by the majority of the economists and politicians of the Western world.

'Here is the destiny of human thought', Echeverría said, 'uniting man with man, village with village, generation with generation, in order to show itself lively and obvious in the practical and social life.'

13

A TREATISE ON POLITICAL ECONOMY IN 1823

THE DISCOVERY OF THE TREATISE

The Pineda Foundation collection (Volume 47) in the National Library of Colombia, contains a small work whose long title is: 'Observaciones y argumentos sobre el estado político de la República de Colombia, antecedido de un Tratado Sucinto sobre la Economía, con notas contra algunos de los principios de Juan Bautista Say y Jeremías Bentham' (Observations and discussions upon the political state of the Republic of Colombia, preceded by a brief Treatise on the Economy, with notes against some of the principles of Jean Baptiste Say and Jeremy Bentham), which we shall refer to as the 'treatise'. It seems that the work was planned to be written in four volumes, but in the Pineda Foundation collection, only the first volume is to be found.

A mere examination of the title catches one's attention. The contents are of great matter for the history of Colombian economic thought. This new 'treatise' is judged to be the third most important work in Colombia and the seventh overall in all of Latin America.

According to the title page, the work was published in Bogotá in 1827, printed by Imprenta de N. Lora. Nevertheless, from the dedication and a reproduced letter to the author from Pedro Gual, it appears that it was written in 1823 and presented to the Colombian Secretary of Foreign Relations on 3 November 1823. The manuscript later passed to others for inspection, as stated in Gual's letter dated 9 January 1824. The manuscript had probably been filed away for some time by Gual, due to the inclusion of arguments against Jean Baptiste Say and Jeremy Bentham. Possibly, the manuscript passed to the Secretary of the Treasury, or even to Francisco Soto, a recognized author in the area of political economy. Before the silence of his literary judges, the author was

> only intending to hold the writings in his hand without ever thinking that they could deserve the attention of his compatriots; but destiny wanted them to fall under the power of some of his friends who were deeply interested in his publishing them and finally he had to give in to the entreaty of friendship.
>
> (GPP 1827: iv)

The manuscript was published in the last months of 1827, with a dedication, added after it was printed, which says that the paper is dedicated to his excellency, President Simón Bolívar, by his obedient servant [the author], Bogotá, dating from 1 January 1828.

Even though the author makes no mention of the additions or modifications to the original manuscript, an attentive reader of the text would not doubt that there were such additions. It is for this reason that it would be desirable to locate the original manuscript of 1823 and also corresponding opinions of the authorities of that time. The work was discovered by Eduardo Posada, who has also added reflections on this treatise in previous works (Posada 1925).

THE AUTHOR OF THE TREATISE

The author of the treatise hid behind the pen name GPP, and remains anonymous to this day. Even though the identification of the author exceeds the limits of this present work, I believe it convenient to recall that Eduardo Posada insinuated that it dealt with a foreign author. The supporting reasons are given on one hand by the opening statements of the treatise by the author and by the letter of Pedro Gual, and on the other hand by the similarity found by Posada with two other booklets written by Luis Blanc in Cartagena (Posada 1925: 350).

An examination of these booklets leads to the conclusion that their only similarity with the treatise lies in that all contain problems related to Colombian economic development. But in form and in content, they propose different viewpoints. Luis Blanc is characterized by a refined and well connected style, but his reasoning is guided by common sense; to a· coarse and immature style, GPP adds a subtle and speculative reasoning. Luis Blanc is a liberal, GPP is a solidarist. The former is pro free trade, such as was practised with the Caribbean islands, the latter is an adversary of such traffic and would like to switch all trade to Europe. For Luis Blanc, internal trade is productive; for GPP it is sterile. Blanc believes the time is right for the development of national industry; GPP thinks that a manufacturing policy would not suit the Colombia of his time. Blanc has in mind the United States as a development model; GPP takes China as an example. Luis Blanc focuses his attention on the problems of foreign human resources; GPP to the internal human resources. One sees immigration as the solution; the other sees training. The former finds a great obstacle to development in the poor administration of customs; the latter sees it in mineral exploitation.

Furthermore, if Luis Blanc had had reason to hide behind the initials L. B. in his first booklet, in the second booklet he declared authorship of both publications by using his full name. In this way, if the treatise, edited a year later and with less conflictive content for the governmental censors, had been written by Blanc, he would have put his name to the work.

But this serves as no substitute for the doubt as to the real author of the treatise. In his introduction, the author asks for the readers' pardon as regards the defects of his Spanish. This could make one think that the author was a foreign scholar. Nevertheless, in the next line the author states that any defects are due to the nature of the matter under discussion. From these clarifications, it can be deduced that any eventual grammatical errors were due more to the poverty of economic vocabulary or the immature writing style than to an imperfect domination of Spanish.

The problem is complicated by the letter from Pedro Gual, then Secretary of Foreign Relations for Colombia, which was sent to the author of the treatise, and which says:

> My good sir: Your kind letter has arrived to my hands on the third of last November in which is proposed a plan which embraces many points, all related to making this country better. I have now passed it on to the people to whom it corresponds to examine this material. Meanwhile, allow me to present to you my most expressive gratitude for the interest you take in the good fortune and prosperity of my country. Your very attentive and obedient servant, Pedro Gual, Bogotá, January of 1824.
>
> (GPP 1827: i)

As we can observe, it is surprising that Gual makes the point of saying 'this country' and 'my country', giving credit to the belief that GPP was a foreign author. On the other hand, the author seems to insinuate just the opposite in the text of his treatise, often using the possessive pronoun 'our' when talking about Colombia. On page 11 of the treatise, there is a paragraph in which the author insinuates repeatedly that he belongs to the Colombian community:

> We have made a revolution of things; we have rejected the oppressors of our land, and we should give a start to the revolution of ideas, and establish others more dignified . . . that lead to our prosperity as a free nation.
>
> (GPP 1827: 11)

If the above mentioned letter of Pedro Gual dated 9 January 1824 could ever be found in the national or Venezuelan archives, it would be very easy to determine the author. Until then, this remains a puzzle. We can only say that the author was a knowledgeable and great defender of Colombian trade, as long as it took place with Europe and not the Caribbean islands. It is very probable that the author had dealt in export and import trade with Europe, and upon entering the autumn of his life, decided to dedicate his remaining days to writing a four volume set on economics and would only be stopped from achieving this goal by death.

METHODOLOGY

Political economy as economic policy

Although the author seems to know the works of contemporary writers, even disputing the ideas of Say and Bentham, his methodology relates more to earlier writers, like Montchrétien and Rousseau, according to whom the object of knowledge of political economy lies in the art of administering the national economy, with all its judicial and political implications. This focus can be seen in the title of the treatise itself, where the author very clearly expresses that the object of his research is the science of Colombian administration, above all else in the related aspect of economic and financial problems. Said in another way, our author has as his basic premise the investigation of the regulations to guide the economic system along the correct path, and not to understand the functioning of the economic mechanism. The anonymous author works on the problems of economic policy and not of economic theory.

The terminology employed also moves along old paths. When the author uses the phrase 'economic policy', he refers to economic facts. He also uses the expressions 'economic science' or 'science of political economy', but the meaning that he gives them is neither of economic theory nor of general economic science, as is usual from Smith onwards. For the author, as for his Colombian predecessors Friar Diego Padilla and Joaquín Camacho, economic science is simply limited to the field of economic policy. The role of the economist is simple, as his function lies in 'indicating the means of production and assuring the national wealth' (GPP 1827: 9). That to this end, the economist should understand the economic mechanism, which needs the assistance of a system conceptually called economic theory, the author never seems to take to heart. Still, he could not free himself of similar methods to prove the validity of his practical rules.

But the most surprising matter in this practical focus is the clear distinction between the problems of general economic policy and those of Colombian economic policy. Even if one accepts that there could be certain common norms of economic policy in all the nations, the instruments and methods of economic policy differ from country to country, due to the differences in cultural, social, and natural structures. Based on this criterion, the author rejects the maxims of economic policy written by European authors, as being inapplicable to a country such as Colombia, with such a different economic structure. He initiates a strong discussion with Jeremy Bentham and maintains that in a country of 'very little population, little capital, and much poverty', instead of stimulating economic progress, the existence of these factors is an obstacle to it. It is in this clear distinction between economic policies that our author surpasses all of his Colombian predecessors. For his persistence and systematic reference to a specifically Colombian

220

economic policy, the author rightfully deserves the title of the precursor of the Colombian national school of economics.

Equally worthy of attention is the fact that, while in the field of general economic policy the author establishes the maxims by a deductive route, in the formulation of his Colombian economic policy, he always utilizes the inductive method. In exploring this area, the wealth of statistical and count-able material is impressive; before this it had only been used in an equal manner by Narváez y la Torre (1753–1812) (Narváez y la Torre 1965).

THE CONCEPTUAL APPARATUS

Even though, as we saw, his focus revolved around the problems of economic policy, the author could not ignore a conceptual apparatus, which at times is delimited and defined in an explicit form. On a large scale, this conceptual apparatus has the classical economic literature as a source of inspiration. The author employs and defines some common concepts of his time, such as wealth, value, price, etc., but with less fortune than those who inspired him.

Let us take as an example the concept of 'wealth'. On one occasion, he employs it in the sense of actual capital: 'I understand on this occasion that wealth is whatever useful thing that already exists in the nation' (GPP 1827: 53). On another he limits it to just the notion of new capital or investment: 'the wealth of the members of one nation lies in abundantly possessing the things that should be consumed, or in their absence, other resources . . . that have some use, be them diamonds or common stones' (GPP 1827: 2–3); and finally, on another occasion, he gives a very wide definition of capital, as much actual as human:

> what resources remains to individuals who have no wealth? The other members of the nation that do not effectively have it, can, nevertheless, obtain it by means of their knowledge . . . putting into practice all they know or can learn that is useful . . . applying their powers, natural, mental, or physical of whichever mode. . . . According to this, the wealth of one nation consists in the wealth and means [knowledge] of its members.
>
> (GPP 1827: 4)

Fortunately, the author supports one of his principles of economic policy on the concept of wealth interpreted in the sense of actual capital and human capital, which will prove to be very beneficial.

The confusion of the classic writers as regards the nature of value and price, confused our anonymous author even more. He faithfully follows the distinc-tion between the concepts of intrinsic value, and value in exchange, with the difference being that he interprets the value in exchange in terms of current prices. Based on this concept of value, he is going to open an extensive polemic with Jean Baptiste Say on the role of domestic trade in production.

SOCIAL PHILOSOPHY

It is not easy to trace the philosophical background of the author of the treatise. At first viewing, it seems to be within the individualistic framework. Having defined the nation as 'a body of citizens who have their government', he states that the duties of this government are 'maintaining the rights and privileges of the nation, by way of laws that assure property and civil liberty of the associated members in general and of each of them in particular' (GPP 1827: 2). Nevertheless, when we investigate closely what the author understands by civil or political liberty, we discover that the he slips towards a decidedly solidarist tendency. He observes that

> when we deal with liberty, it is necessary to see it not as savage liberty, but as political liberty. Then we know that it exists to practice everything good, and not to do evil, or contrary to laws: some say they are useful, but to work against liberty is to be useless; and the disobedience in the practice of liberty is not a right, but an abuse. Liberty well understood is the blessing of men and to the contrary, taken out of its context, is the curse of them.
>
> (GPP 1827: 7)

In the same way, when dealing with the idea of equality, the author surprises us with an anti-individualistic attitude. Equality is worthy only as equality of national duties, set in the obligations of each and every one, with or without material resources to 'respect and obey the laws and contribute to the general expenses of the government' (GPP 1827: 2). And if the author accepts an idea of equality, this applies only to the legislative field, as 'all enjoy equally the benefits of the laws' (GPP 1827: 12). Possibly the best illustration of the author's anti-individualistic attitude is displayed in the following paragraph:

> The united forces of the members who form the nation, create an equality. Some will have greater fortune than others, but each one will always have something, which will be a link in the chain of general interests, which is the basis of all wealth and increases with security. This produces abundance, of such a condition that breaking one of the links of this chain, it is destroyed, and its base runs the same luck [sic], plainly that when it is lost, it is ruined.
>
> (GPP 1827: 8)

Therefore, the supreme objective of each government is to achieve the good of the nation (GPP 1827: 50).

If from the formulation of the general principles of his social philosophy, the author passes to contemplating the social, economic, and political structure of his own homeland, recently liberated from the colonial chains with musty customs with which it was born and had been created, then his adherence to national solidarism is even more rigid. The author observes:

> It is an undeniable truth, though very sad to remember, that half of our population is made up by worthless men, who have no stimulus to labour, that need the full force of the law to submit to it. If these are silenced and if the youth are allowed to follow the example of their elders and parents, within fifty years the republic would no longer exist, or would exist in the same backwardness as it is found today.
>
> (GPP 1827: 13)

For GPP, then, equality is worthy only among groups of the working population that contribute to public prosperity, but should not be extended to the idle population. What is more, from this inequality of contribution to the public prosperity, there also originates a public order inequality. The determining criteria of the number of representatives to Congress should not be simply a certain proportion related to the population of a department (state), but should be based on the people 'older than eight years of age who were owners of a property, substituting a lack thereof with the exercising of some profession or useful industry, even if they were day labourers or not' (GPP 1827: 17).

These reflections lead to the author's doubting of the usefulness of a system of representative government.

> For this and for the greatness of a people's representative government, of which I then admire the guarantees it offers to people and the protection for the citizens' properties; I desire that our present system increased the force of the executive power to accomplish public good, which is its objective. Then it will be certain that the useful citizens shall prosper; and that the indolent men will be needing to work for fear of the laws.
>
> (GPP 1827: 13)

Surely the author of the treatise was persuaded that this social philosophy was very nearly that of Bolívar of 1828, for only then could his dedication to his excellency, the liberator president, Simón Bolívar, by his obedient servant, be understood.

GENERAL ECONOMIC POLICY

Production, development, stability, and distribution

For GPP, the objectives of economic policy are universal, and as such, are worthy ones for any nation. In a first approximation, he reduces the objectives to industry, prudence, and foresight. We should observe that his terminology is uncommon, even more so if thinking that in the time he was

223

writing he could count on a fairly developed lexicon among the Latin American authors. We already have seen that when he spoke of the science of political economy, he was thinking of economic policy. What do industry, prudence, and foresight then mean? For him, they mean: '(1) Industry creates wealth; (2) Prudence increases it; (3) Foresight assures it' (GPP 1827: 1) Regardless of all terminological reservations, we cannot deny the sagacity of the planning. Today we would say that the fundamental objectives of every economic policy lie in the adequate usage of the economic resources for productive ends ('industry'), within a policy of economic development ('prudence'), and under the stability of the economic order ('foresight'). For GPP, industry and its growth are functions of the capitalists, natural resources, and human resources. But human resources should not be measured, he observes, in terms of the overall population, but only that of the 'industrious population', understanding by this the population that contributes the physical labour, and/or knowledge.

But next to the community of members who form any country, our author also grants a pre-eminent position to the public sector, both administrative and legislative. Although initially he maintains that the public function should be limited in principle to guaranteeing the stability of the economic order, later he grants it a larger role. In entering upon the question of budgetary disequilibriums, the author recommends diagnosing the economic situation with the following points:

> First, to observe the fundamental laws of government and to see if in its form some unnecessary expense has been created. Second, to see if the legislation fulfills the objective of assuring the existing wealth and endeavours that it not be diminished. Third, if that same legislation is directed toward creating new sources of wealth or increasing that which exists. Fourth, to examine how wealth is distributed, if it be generally or partially.
>
> (GPP 1827: 5)

We should observe also that in this treatise, the question of how wealth is distributed is incorporated as a new objective of economic policy. Nevertheless, the author here does not refer to the distribution of product, but the distribution of the population between working and idle. In attempting to explain the alternatives planted by the fourth of his questions, he observes:

> If the riches are generally distributed, then the defect is not in the nation; but if, on the contrary, they are distributed with partiality, there exists a defect; search for this defect and it will be found under the dark shadows of idleness and imprudence. If the defect exists in the administration or in the laws, it is very easy to solve it; on the contrary, if it exists in the nation and if it is caused by indolence, to avoid it is a

very difficult task. Legislation may decree law after law to generate industry, but in what way will the executive power make them compliable? Men invent a thousand ways to mock laws, and enjoy their idleness with ease, the same as the laborious people enjoy the fruit of their industry.

(GPP 1827: 5–6)

Domestic trade

The author is in agreement with his contemporary economists that the economically productive activities are agriculture, manufacturing, and trade. But this last activity, he emphasizes, is only productive when it takes place between countries. International trade is productive in the sense that the volume of national goods increases with a favourable balance of trade. 'Trade then is increased by the exports of general products in exchange for imports, which is one of the principal bases for creating wealth' (GPP 1827: 18).

The same cannot be said as regards the domestic trade of a community, and so it appears that the contrary thesis held by Say has no foundation. GPP observes that domestic trade

never creates new riches, it only distributes those already in existence. The truth is that it creates new enjoyments by its utility, and it increases the value of things by the cost of transportation from one place to another . . . but it does not increase the true wealth. Due to these facts, I have the temerity to be in opposition to Jean Baptiste Say, profound and respectable economist, whose opinions are generally accepted in this century.

(GPP 1827: 19)

He insists again with greater determination on this discussion over Say's ideas, in the appendix to his monograph.

In order for something worthwhile to be transported from one place to another, it is necessary that it exists before this transport. If this thing has a higher price in one interior location than in another, this is due to its scarcity. This thing is exchanged in the place to which it is carried, for another that is more abundant there, and so the nation maintains an equilibrium of wealth; but it is truly not increased. At the moment of exchange, each one enjoys something that he did not have before; but these things already existed in the nation before their enjoyment, so that the exchange hardly has given enjoyment, much less new wealth. . . . This transport, with its expenses, increases the price, not the intrinsic value, but does not increase national wealth. After the exchange each individual has new enjoyment that, without the exchange, he would not have enjoyed. As these new enjoyments have been caused by riches that existed before the exchange, after which there had been no increase in the wealth of the nation, then it is clear that domestic trade in no way multiplies national wealth.

(GPP 1827: 53)

On this point, our author commits an error. The root of his error lies in the conceptual confusion about the nature of value and price, that we emphasized above. This materialist attitude is curious, when at the beginning of the treatise he had observed with acumen that the foundation of productivity lies as much in the physical contribution of material goods as in the intangible services:

> and this is why the director of a work performs industry, like the craftsman, the businessman, and his employee: with the only difference being that the practice of the director and the businessman is mental performance, and that of the craftsman and the employee is physical.

(GPP 1827: 4)

But, if the author has lost the battle against the predominant thesis in economic doctrine, he has won another one. In a period in which our thinkers received any foreign thesis, even the most superficial, with a dogmatism and veneration that approached that for holy books, our author shows critical spirit and independence of criterion, which although objectionable, are to his credit. The author is a rebel against the principle of authority, which has done and continues doing damage to Latin American researchers. His reasoning has been shown to be erroneous; but before labelling it as either erroneous or certain, it is necessary to recognize that it does deal with reasoning. Anyway, those familiar with the history of our science will remember that in the majority of cases it has been a history of many errors and very few correct guesses.

NATIONAL ECONOMIC POLICY

Human capital

If the objectives of the economic policy have a universal character, the same cannot be said of economic policy measures. These are dependent on the economic structure of the respective country. Therefore, observes GPP, given that the Republic of Colombia is very different from other countries or the rest of the nations, because although having an immense territory, it has a very low population, few capitalists, and much poverty, it is necessary to limit the objective of the research to the economic policy measures for that country, and to set in this way the bases of 'economic science . . . of this republic' (GPP 1827: 9).

The first aspect of the economic structure is related to the population of the country, and this, as much in the quantitative as in the cultural aspect. The author is not content with emphasizing that a country with a low population is being dealt with, but he thinks it advantageous to elaborate a table of demographic movement from 1778 to 1827, which we summarize in Table 13.1.

The reader would expect that the stagnation of the total population over two decades would be the object of great consideration from the economic point of view. Lamentably, GPP leaves the question open and deviates towards eminently political considerations. He observes:

> Looking at this list, we have the provinces from Boyacá to Guayaquil in 1827 being comprised of as many people as had lived in Venezuela and New Granada together in 1778. And from 1808 until now, the population of New Granada has grown by 206,964; and on the contrary, that of Caracas for the same period, has decreased by 130,429. A representative is sent to Congress for every 30,000 inhabitants, and one more for a remainder of 15,000. Consequently, Venezuela has twenty-six representatives and New Granada sixty-seven, a favourable difference of forty-one. Also, there are four senators for every department: Venezuela has four departments, thus sixteen senators. New Granada has eight departments, it shall have thirty-two senators, sixteen senators in favour of New Granada.
>
> (GPP 1827: 49)

More satisfactory are the author's incursions into the qualitative problem of human resources, where he attempts to clarify two fundamental aspects: one related to the division of the population into four groups according to the level of participation in the global productive process; and the other related to the estimation of the volume of human resources in the industrial sector. Related to the global division of the population, estimated for 1827 at 2,776,535 people, GPP distinguishes four classes, which are divided in the following manner: 'One fourth part of no advantage for neither the society nor the government. Another fourth part of very scarce utility. Another, of more regular or better citizens. And finally, another of useful and intelligent

Table 13.1 Demographic movement from 1778 to 1827

Year	New Granada	Venezuela	Columbia Total
1778	1,279,440	728,000	2,007,440
1808	1,800,000	900,000	2,700,000
1827	2,006,964	769,571	2,776,535

Source: The census for the year 1778 was carried out during the government of the Archbishop Viceroy Caballero y Góngora; for 1808 and 1827, the censuses were carried out by Humboldt and the Secretary of the Interior, respectively.[1]

men' (GPP 1827: 15). Although the author does not clarify what he intends by these terms, it appears that he refers to the three categories that we are accustomed to using today as 'non-skilled labour', 'skilled labour', and 'human resources of average to high level', respectively. Anyway, the division of the population into four groups of 25 per cent each is neither realistic nor convenient. Even if we would accept that at the beginning of the nineteenth century, the labour pool was represented by high percentages of children over 8 years old and of women, it would be hard to accept that the labour force would be more than 50 per cent of the total population. We should have the same reservations about the relative volume of 'useful and intelligent men', fixed by the author at 25 per cent of the total. This type of population should have been much less, something on the order of 10 per cent of the total. But despite all the estimation imperfections, what we should emphasize is the fact that the author has been conscious of the need to contemplate the Colombian population from the point of view of the percentage which participates in productive processes. Even these estimations, which are more like a balanced occupational pyramid, produce many serious questions in the mind of the author.

> Will 694,133 useful and intelligent citizens be enough to maintain the dignity of the Colombian people? Will the 694,133 men who qualified for the third class be enough to assist in operations? Will this number of men of no benefit be a shameful ignominy for the nation? What will be the lot of these individuals? What about the nation of which they form a fourth part?
>
> (GPP 1827: 15)

His computation of the work force in the industrial sector is highly ingenious. The author estimates this sector's contribution to national income to be approximately 1,220,000 pesos. Besides, he establishes, 'I am very sure of the information that I have' (GPP 1827: 44), that the labour force in the industrial sector earns an average of one and a half reals.[2] He finally estimates that the number of working days per year (deducting Sundays and other holidays) comes to 245 days of work. On this basis, he determines not only the size of the labour force, but also the income per capita in the manufacturing sector, approximately 20,000 people with an average annual salary of 46 pesos. What is more, GPP surprises us with an estimation of the consumption of the manufacturing sector's income, distributed by region. The consumption of the 1,220,000 pesos would be shared in the manner shown in Table 13.2. Without a doubt, our anonymous author is a distinguished predecessor of Colombia's social accounting.

The research of GPP is not merely limited empirically to the diagnosis of Colombian human resources. His principal objective lies more in discovering solutions for its better and more productive employment. He is fully aware that the task is difficult and that he cannot resolve it in a few years,

Table 13.2 Regional distribution of the consumption of the manufacturing sector income

Region	$
Boyacá	300,000
Cundinamarca	400,000
Cauca	100,000
Ecuador	300,000
Asuay	100,000
Guayaquil	20,000
TOTAL	1,220,000

when all colonial history has contributed to establishing certain mental habits contrary to the ethic of hard work.

> Men who have lived like slaves for entire centuries and suddenly find themselves free, think undoubtedly that they have no other duty than to satisfy the nature of their most intense necessities, and surrender themselves right away to indolence and vagrancy; and if this is what they understand by liberty, they live shamefully deceived.
>
> (GPP 1827: 13)

To achieve a change in the mental structures, the author thinks of a series of indirect measures, especially in the areas of agricultural and fiscal policies. But in order to guarantee their success, he unpredictably figures them to work simultaneously with other measures of direct action. For those entirely lacking any stimulation to work, the author, in conformity with his social philosophy, suggests a type of obligatory service: 'The useless men who have no stimulus for work need the force of the law in order to surrender themselves to work' (GPP 1827:1 3).

Mining

Guided by the principles of a policy of active human resources, GPP condemns the mining policy initiated and developed under the Spanish domination, precisely for having been 'well calculated to encourage the indolence and promote the misery' (GPP 1827: 24) of the new kingdom. On the contrary, he maintains, the gold mines were 'the disgrace and the unhappiness of this country' (GPP 1827: 35).

To defend this thesis, he resorts primarily to deductive arguments.

> It is certain that the precious metals are products of the country, and by this it can be disputed that the consumption [of imported goods] is paid for by national products, and that this is advantageous because products of our lands are given in exchange; but this argument is absurd, because it is not adaptable to stimulating the people to work,

and putting a few men devoted to the washing of gold to pay for the entire consumption; the rest who lack this occupation or those in commerce or in the arts, would live in indolence and misery.

(GPP 1827: 25)

But this argument is reinforced with inductive arguments, taken from the economic history of Colombia and other mining countries. In Colombia, the author observes, 'only a small portion of the people are employed in the extraction of gold, and almost all of them work no more than two or three days every week, washing the gold in their gourds' (GPP 1827: 25). The qualitative deformation of the occupation pyramid and massive unemployment characterize all the countries dedicated to the exploitation of mines according to the author:

Before the discoveries of Christopher Columbus and Américo Vespucio, the European nations received gold from the coast of Africa, etc. From the mouth of the Senegal river to Angola, some 500 leagues in length, there are many different villages in all this extension and not one is civilized, where gold is found in abundance. . . . The Africans . . . in Senegal and Angola . . . have mines: they work them, they are slaves, poor and ignorant and for this they are found to be unhappy.

(GPP 1827: 39)

Meanwhile, the nations that do not possess precious metals 'cultivate the arts in order to obtain them, and to this end the industry has been practiced generally and new inventions have been introduced every day to facilitate methods in the factories and in agriculture' (GPP 1827: 36), as has occurred in Great Britain, France, and Germany; in the gold-mining nations not only 'many could remain necessarily inactive', but besides they would not have any stimulus to be active, intelligent, and industrious to forget and to ignore all the other branches of industry. Before these historical facts, his conclusion is decisive: 'Finally, wherever an abundance of gold is found, ignorance, slavery, indolence, and small population are also found' (GPP 1827: 31). The luminous conclusions of GPP are a little obscured by a paragraph shown a few pages before, related to Colombian mining activity: 'If all the people without other position are employed in metals extraction, this branch of industry would become universal, and the country would acquire fame as a mining nation, as other peoples acquired it for manufacturing, etc.' (GPP 1827: 25). This demonstrates that the principal worry of the author is not fear of mono-cultivation, but of national unemployment.

To break the vicious cycle, the economic histories of certain people serve once again as guides. The author remembers that 'the great China decreed the death penalty to whomever extracted the precious metals from the mines and only allowed this speculation one month every two hundred years, with the objective of stimulating the people toward a more useful industry' (GPP 1827: 38). The author would respond pleasantly to a similar instrument of economic policy, but he fears utopian measures. 'I know that it is impossible for the government to close its mines, as in China, and also to cut the practice of illicit trade in gold: but it is not impossible to diminish it' (GPP 1827: 40).

Industry

The characteristic feat of all civilized nations like Great Britain, France, and Germany, is and has been, observes GPP, the cultivation of arts and the development of manufacturing activities. Won't this also be the path which the Colombian economy should follow? 'Colombia has factories in Quito, Socorro, Vélez, etc. Now, if these factories are advantageous or injurious to the nation, this is a question of no small magnitude' (GPP 1827: 43).

To answer this question, the author contemplates the problem from various points of view: the fiscal aspect; the possibilities of international competition; and the regional structure of the country.

Seen from the fiscal point of view, the problem is susceptible of two solutions, depending on whether it deals with domestic consumption industries or export industries. The domestic consumption industries, even if they contribute to the exchequer the rights called sales taxes,[3] do not stop prejudicing it by the loss of 15 per cent of import taxes if these products had come from the exterior.

> For that reason, every 'vara' of the cloth manufactured in Colombia for domestic consumption (until there is a superabundance of people who cannot find what to do in the fields and forests) is very injurious and against the policy of the nation. The contrary would happen if the factories' output could be exported, as happens in Quito, because then there would be profits from trade and the government would take advantage of these profits by charging at the ports the rights of importation, on any product, whose profit and business expenses would be paid by the foreigners. For this, every 'vara' of the cloth manufactured in Colombia for foreign consumption, at any time or under any circumstance, is beneficial for the nation. But the same does not happen for the towns, which, like Socorro, cannot export their manufactured merchandise.
>
> (GPP 1827: 46)

The reader ought to be able to see that the author not only contradicts his principle of the harmonic development of all economic activities that he defended in his mining policy, but he also fails to realize that manufacturing is the most productive type of economic activity. Also, one could argue that the author's fiscal vision was too shortsighted and that for a policy of national growth one should consider the secular effects of public finances. But if we agree that the author was wrong on all this, we would coincide in that his thesis conformed very well to the interests of the importers and exporters, among whom we would surely count GPP.

In return, the contemporary reader would be very interested in knowing the author's reflections on the regional analysis. Where there exists little population and it is sparse over an immense territory, measures should be taken to gather it. The argument is both economical and political. The author might have been able to adduce that where the consuming population is small, there is not an adequate market to absorb the national manufactured products. But, instead, he only observes that in such countries, as in his Colombia, the workers in the factories do not earn more than a real and a half daily. He seems to give priority to a harmonic regional development policy over a sectoral one. In his thinking, for reasons of national economic and/or political integration, and of equality of income, regional development is to be stimulated. 'This can be executed solely by means of agriculture, since the ranches and prairies of one town will extend into another town' (GPP 1827: 43). On the other hand, if the workers who earn a real and a half in the factories 'can earn the same in the field, it is necessary that the government's attention be occupied in effecting this political change' (GPP 1827: 44). Finally, the author remembers that besides the scarce population, the immense Colombian territory suffered also from lack of capital goods. Before such a similar economic and territorial structure, his conclusion is decisive: 'In a country with a small population and few capitalists, I figure that it is not well estimated to assure the prosperity of society in general with factories' (GPP 1827: 43). The solution is doubtful, of course, but the reader will need to ponder it before rejecting it.

More proper seem the author's observations related to the competitiveness of nationally manufactured products in the world market. If his diagnosis of human resources is remembered, if the weak capacity of the national market is taken into account, and if it is not forgotten that simultaneously with their political emancipation the Ibero-American republics opened their ports to free trade, the author's sober comment should not surprise us: 'The nation cannot expect to compete with any country in manufacturing' (GPP 1827: 44). This 'any country' is simply a generalization for what was happening in Western Europe and the United States. But the diagnosis of GPP soon proved to be correct. A few years later, in a work entitled, *Observaciones sobre el Comercio de la Nueva Granada*, published in Bogotá in 1831, by another anonymous author,[4] it was confirmed that Colombian factories, especially those of Socorro, were dying. How could the national industries not have been dying when 'the same cloth that could be hand made in Socorro, is made in England with machines and with a fivefold saving?' (Wills 1831: 44). What is more, the nineteenth-century history of Ibero-America confirms the thesis of GPP. But that which was impossible to expect in the nineteenth century, to change the input (that is to say, improving human capital, widening fiscal capital, and assimilating technological progress), would allow this to be the hope of the twentieth century, throughout South America. But with this we cannot invalidate the clear-sighted observation of GPP that the Colombia of 1827 was not prepared to rival the factories of the Western countries. The author's realism was a severe warning to those responsible for the economic policies in Colombia.

Agriculture

Convinced that a policy of industrial development, by being premature, could be a chimerical business, the author turns all his hopes toward agriculture and foreign trade. If the country cannot hope to rival other countries in manufacturing, he says, 'it has much to expect from other branches of industry, in commerce and agriculture' (GPP 1827: 44).

Although it is surprising that the author did not dedicate a separate chapter to this problem, the reader finds at every step GPP's deep preference for agricultural activities. 'Many people could be employed in agriculture' (GPP 1827: 48), and it is 'by way of only agriculture' (ibid.: 43) that an economic and political integration can be achieved. Agriculture is the activity that serves as an antidote to the vices of mining.

> If the republic does not possess precious metals, I wonder, would the population not eat, drink, or dress itself? The business men should be looking for how to pay for consumption, and I say, not having gold, they could make agriculture flourish, and each province could be full of industry and each person employed. The labourer would not sow hardly for his consumption, but in abundance, knowing that he would have immediate sale of his product: then the brooks of the Atrato, Sinú, Cauca, and Magdalena rivers would not be used in illicit commerce, but in transporting to the ports on the coast the industry of many thousands of people. Will the government have seriously considered the difference this will achieve? Does the nation know it can soon rival its northern sister (United States) in some branches of commerce? Has not Providence treated this territory to a splendid profusion of trees and shrubs? Has not nature displayed its prolific powers in the rich variety of vegetation? Is here not the region in which an eternal spring and the fruits and flowers cluster the arms of millions of plants in a constant succession? What could be said if the hand of agriculture would have touched this immense treasure, this source of wealth? Nothing, absolutely nothing, can exceed the beauty, the variety, and the grandeur of the forests of this republic.
>
> (GPP 1827: 26)

Therefore, to elaborate a Colombian economic policy programme, one must know to search for appropriate models.

> In case that a nation wants to follow the example of others, it should choose those most similar in the point being dealt with. This way, if our government wants to imitate foreign peoples in this area, it should imitate China, forgetting the European nations in which, not having mines, have had to adopt a different conduct. The Chinese have closed their mines; they have dedicated themselves to agriculture, and by this have achieved the prosperity in which today they are found.
>
> (GPP 1827: 39)

Foreign trade

In GPP's economic system, agriculture and foreign trade are two levers of Colombian prosperity. Agriculture is the source not only to supply the domestic consumption, but to assure that there is a surplus. Foreign trade facilitates the movement of this surplus to other markets, where it is sold at good prices, and with the income from this, a like amount of foreign goods may be imported. Both are therefore the principal bases of the creation of wealth: agriculture increases wealth by elaborating national produce and foreign trade enables 'the increment by means of exchange or trade with other nation' (GPP 1827: 39).

The increment of wealth by foreign trade is demonstrated in a confusing manner. Sometimes it seems to be a direct effect of commerce, but even in this case the author hesitates between two positions. One is that foreign trade productivity always rises 'when imports and exports are equal' (GPP 1827: 18); the other position is that productivity rises only when the balance of trade is favourable for Colombia. But in the two cases, the author is right in understanding that the increase in national wealth or income is an indirect effect of foreign trade, as much for imports as for exports.

Actually, the author is conscious that due to foreign demand for Colombian goods, both old and new activities are stimulated and thus national income and employment levels are increased. Here is a testament to his vision of the open macroeconomic circuit:

> Our forests are full of useful trees; and in undergoing foreign trade, people are employed to cut them and to carry them to the coast. In order to export them overseas, ships and seamen are needed. The foreigners pay the industry of all these people, and if all are from our republic, it [will] lead to an increase in riches equal to the earnings of the agriculturists, carriers, etc., which will be paid by foreign peoples, as has been said.
>
> (GPP 1827: 54)

This observation is undoubtedly precise and correct. More deficient is his 'awareness' that the foreign supply may stimulate national demand of certain goods and services, that could in time foster the development of new national industries. In this aspect, the author merely refers to the advantages of foreign trade. Taking as an example the importation of raw cotton, he only says: 'The foreign nations would not bring to Colombia this raw merchandise, since, of course, it is in the republic, and at a lower price. But the foreigners will bring whichever other thing is missing here . . . ' (GPP 1827: 54).

Before the undeniable advantages of foreign trade, it remains to be asked: in what measure has Colombia learned to profit from these advantages? After a brief retelling of the history of grenadine commerce under Spanish rule, which he criticizes, the author diagnoses the situation of his time:

> The fatal truth is that the republic has not literal commerce (allow me the expression), it has only a species of domestic trade and resale of the goods. Everything produced is consumed inside of the republic, and there being no surplus to export, ships and seamen are not necessary, and all this is caused by trade with the islands.

> (GPP 1827: 27)

To overcome this commercial stagnation, the author elaborates an entire programme, whose principal points of view can be summarized by: (a) good roads and reservoirs from one side of the country to another (GPP 1827: 37); (b) storage warehouses in customs (GPP 1827: 32); (c) ships and seamen capable of making transoceanic voyages (GPP 1827:3 2); (d) private trade companies provided with large capital to confront the foreign competition (GPP 1827: 34); and (e) the diversion of trade away from the Caribbean islands and toward the markets of Europe (GPP 1827: 28, 32).

Money

It is surprising that the author did not call greater attention to monetary problems. Like other classic writers, he saw money only as a veil.

> We know that gold has no value in of itself; the only value that it enjoys is due to its usefulness; and that it is necessary to guard the precious metals in the country, only for the use for which they were acquired.

> (GPP 1827: 40)

The complex problem of international exchange rates is passed over. The author's major contribution lies in having contributed some details of the little researched history of the coin called 'macuquina' (Popescu 1968c: 40), a true puzzle for the monetary authorities of that time.

We know that the government has taken its measures to recast it and to gradually destroy it throughout the republic. But they could dictate law after law to extinguish this coin and it will never be finished, if by taking these measures it is not taken into consideration the principal source of this type of coin. In the Caribbean islands there is a great abundance of it. There it is called Bit, or royal macuquino, or even peseta macuquina; they do not distinguish between these two coins and this is why they are indifferently exchanged for three cuartillos, the royal or peseta macuquina. This is the reason that this island coin is brought here frequently, because in this commerce it has a profit of 25–225 per cent. And it is a well known truth that some of the merchants who come from Jamaica bring macuquinas to pay the import rights. This way the merchandise imported to Colombia, its rights paid for by this Jamaican money, do not suffer any loss.

(GPP 1827: 42)

To end with the macuquina, the author suggests adopting a copper coin and allowing exchange of the macuquina for the newer coin at the mints for a limited time.

Public finances

No nation can exist without a government whose principal duty lies in guaranteeing the security of property and civil liberty of the citizens. The nation must have wealth before contributing to the general expenses of the government; this wealth will come from the wealth of the citizens. Consequently, observes GPP, 'the public contributions are undoubtedly born of the contributions of the citizens who form the nation' (GPP 1827: 12). The formulation of the principle of taxes as the only source of public income is certainly a very advanced conception.

Following the classical line of thought, the author defends the idea of the balanced budget. In the cases of unbalanced budgets his first concern is to determine not only if some unnecessary expense has been incurred, but also to watch for the continued increase in national taxes as the only source of growth of the public sector contributions. The effort of maintaining or re-establishing a balanced budget is intimately linked to all the national economic system (GPP 1827: 8). The author's fundamental objective on writing the treatise lies precisely in analysing the Colombian financial system. But upon understanding the process of inter-dependence among the distinct economic sectors, the author is obligated to widen his field of vision until embracing the entire national economic system. This is due to his incursion into the areas of human resources, mining, manufacturing, agriculture, foreign trade, and money.

Accepting that the government is vigilant of the security and liberty of its citizens, the author formulates the obligation of the citizens to support the expenses of the government: 'It is necessary that each and every one of the individuals contribute to the national expenses, as all enjoy equally the benefits of the laws' (GPP 1827: 12).

Nevertheless, upon examining the situation of Colombia's public finances, the author observes that there is a very high percentage of citizens who contribute nothing to support government expenses. Half of the population pays nothing, and the other half, the working population, is burdened by unfair taxation. This situation is marked by the author's protest:

> Where is the workers' advantage, their security? On the contrary, they lose individually a portion of their wealth in contributing to the necessary expenses of the government, when by right and security, they should not pay more than half of what they pay.
>
> (GPP 1827: 6)

Moreover, the author believes that this situation disagrees with the spirit of social philosophy itself.

> Shall just one principle of political economy be found that justifies the burden of taxes placed by the state on the working part, while the other remains in idleness and laziness? But under our actual legal system, these destructive maxims are being practiced.
>
> (GPP 1827: 16)

This helps to confirm that 'the social philosophy' was *his* social philosophy. It is actually a socio-financial philosophy, born of the worldly concept of the business class, of which GPP was undoubtedly a member.

Our author realizes, nevertheless, that the fiscal derivations of his social philosophy are at odds with the ideas held by the great European philosopher, Jeremy Bentham, whose *Treatise on Legislation* was a mandatory textbook at Colombian universities. GPP assails the doctrine of utilitarianism:

> When the wise Jeremy Bentham wrote his principles of legislation, he had the European nations in mind; but if he had wished to write about Africa or Asia, he would have had to think on those countries. If we wish now to speak for Colombia, we should consider exclusively Colombia. Otherwise, it would result that Spain could very well legislate for us; but our legislation should be arranged to the circumstances of the republic, and not to the principles of European writers: for this same reason, the study of such authors in our universities should be reduced to only analyzing their doctrines, but never should study be subject to them.
>
> (GPP 1827: 51)

This criticism led directly or indirectly to Decree Number 427 sanctioned by President Bolívar, in which it is ordered that in none of the universities of Colombia will Bentham's *Treatise on Legislation* be taught.

The poll tax

The criticism of GPP pointed, nevertheless, against the thesis related to the tax known as the poll tax.[5] Bentham was a fit adversary of the poll tax, but our author felt that Bentham's stance was biased for Colombia. He observes that

> In Europe there is much indigence and little poverty, that is to say there are many people without means to search for their sustenance, be this due to physical or economic impediments. The great population and the lack of land greatly increase the indigent class in those countries. In Colombia and other parts of America, this class is very reduced, because there is an abundance of land relative to the population. The opposite occurs with poverty: all here are poor; that is, they possess enough to live, or have facilities to procure it. This makes one see the great difference there is between England, for example, and Colombia, in those two states of society. For this a poll tax in England and other European nations, would be an injustice totally reproached by humanity; as there is much indigence, for the motives expressed, which the people cannot avoid due to circumstances. But among us it is different, as there does exist indigents due to the indolence of men, and so it seems the best approach would be to stimulate men to work and thus shake them from the apathy in which they are wallowing. And in the England of Bentham, there is much indolence and every parish must support its own indigents, demonstrating that not only the most disgraceful men do not contribute toward public expenses. The others contribute what they can, so that Bentham is justified in fighting against the poll tax . . .
>
> (GPP 1827: 51)

Until Colombia was at least as well off as England, our author's defence of a national poll tax really cannot be justified. This doctrine would be of no service for Colombia. Against Bentham's argument that a man pays for a poll tax for no other reason than having a head, our author vehemently replies,

> I say that it is not only for that; it is because he has arms and hands. Any nation and whichever government needs man's arms and hands more than his head. A few heads in the government may assure the nation; but this also needs the effort of all the arms and hands that should make it sure, and it is maintained by the union of the endeav-

ours of the members: to God liberty, to God security, to God subsistence.[6]

(GPP 1827: 7)[7]

It is curious that GPP does not use the writings of his Colombian predecessors to support his theory. The 'Ensayo sobre un Nuevo plan de Administración en el Nuevo Reino de Granada' written in 1797 by General Antonio Nariño (Vergara y Vergara 1946) would have been an excellent source. Advocating the suspension of domestic sales taxes, and abolition of the taxes on tobacco and brandy, Nariño maintained that these could be substituted by a poll tax, which he considered to be of easy execution, useful, not costly, and of no danger, which 'will be received with open arms and which will spread for all parts contentment and happiness, that should guarantee tranquillity' (Vergara y Vergara 1946: 175). This and other decrees, including some signed by President Bolívar, should have served as fine ammunition for our anonymous author.

The poll tax is today regarded as being unequal and unjust by all Western financiers. The taxation policy is a function not only of the social philosophy of the legislature, but also of the level of cultural development of the respective society. In those societies positioned on the first steps of cultural and economic development, it has even been noted by Esteban Jaramillo (Jaramillo 1960: 191), that sometimes a poll tax is acceptable, and other times not. Today, thanks to the research of Ernesto Wagemann (Wagemann 1948: 132), we know that the reactions of the communities characterized by a spirit of sustenance are the exact opposite of communities with a spirit of profit. For the former, a poll tax that is well conceived and applied may be an instrument of economic growth; for the latter, it would only be an obstacle to development. The thesis of GPP about the poll tax, based on his time and above all on his social philosophy, would have complete justification.

14

THE LÓPEZ-PELLEGRINI SCHOOL

Carlos Pellegrini was born in Buenos Aires on 11 October 1846 and died on 17 July 1906. His studies were carried out in Buenos Aires, and culminated in a doctoral degree in Law in 1869. His professional career revolved around economic matters, which would interest him for the rest of his life. His career started in 1868 in the exchequer; in 1872 he was elected deputy to the congress of the province of Buenos Aires and in 1873, deputy to the National Congress. After performing his duties as minister and vice-president of the nation, on 6 August 1890 he became president of the republic, with the collaboration of Vicente Fidel López as minister of the exchequer. On 12 October 1892, Pellegrini handed over the presidency to Luis Sáenz Peña, but he continued participating in the public life of his country, be it in economic missions in Europe and the United States or as national senator, until his death. For the study of Pellegrini's doctrine one should resort to primary sources where his speeches and writings can be found (Carranza 1897; Muro 1910; Rivero Astengo 1941) and to studies done on his ideas (Newton 1965; Cárcamo 1971). There are two important studies carried out by members of the Argentine Academy of Economic Science: the first one done by Alfredo Labougle (1957) on the subject of the ideas and works of Carlos Pellegrini, and the second one, by Nicolás Repetto (1961), on Pellegrini's ideas on the topic of human relations in a labour context. Besides, there are also a few more works that will become mandatory readings for those interested in Pellegrini's ideas (Oca Balda 1942; Cuccorese 1985–6; Segovia 1989).

On the basis of the above mentioned sources and works, it is tempting to produce a synthesis of all these important writings, and this can also be found in Demaría's *El Pensamiento Económico del Dr Carlos Pellegrini* (Demaría 1966) which was done on the basis of Rivero Astengo's book, which I consider the best writing found on this subject up to now. It is fit then to remember some of the main currents of his views of Pellegrini's economic thought. Carlos Pellegrini was really a symbol of the creative force and a standard bearer of the firm faith in the Argentine destiny of greatness (Demaría 1966: 6–9). Certain of the potential of the country, Pellegrini pleaded for the fulfillment of all the compromises the country had assumed so as to stimulate a steady inflow of capital to the economic circuit. As regards the national debt, Pellegrini used to say that 'there was no possible credit for a nation without its religious fulfillment of its debt compromises' (Rivero Astengo 1941, IV: 105). Pellegrini ran ahead of his time as concerns the solution to the 'social question' by means of a system of proportional participation in the earnings of the firm (Rivero Astengo 1941, III: 124) while consenting to support 'industrial health laws designed to avoid the abuses and evils that threaten the health, vigour and destiny of the human race' (Rivero Astengo 1941, III: 120) which Pellegrini conceived as the best defender of the democratic principles and institutions (Rivero Astengo 1941, III: 134; Demaría 1966: 12–13). The axis of Argentine economic development should be the development of all the economic sectors. To the principle of sectoral development Pellegrini adds regional development, insisting on the imperative of 'the economic conquest of the whole Patagonia' and the localization of his industrial focus in Bahía Blanca, 'the great capital of the south' (Demaría 1966: 14–16). The government's role in the promotion of economic development adequately fits Pellegrini's organicist view of national life. In his own words, the government is to find 'the solution that draws the main lines along which the development of the country should occur, by means of the combined action of industry and commerce, and that provides the means of eliminating the obstacles that prevent its free dealings' (Rivero Astengo 1941, IV: 147). The points of his interventionist policy were made up by his protectionist policy for industrial development and the exchange rate stability maintained by the observance of the government's regulating institution (Demaría 1966: 17–18). Demaría remembers what Ezequiel Bustillo, the pioneer of Patagonian development, once mentioned to him: 'when Carlos Pellegrini died, the men of the time felt that the head of the country had disappeared' (Demaría 1966: 7).

But before the greatness of the economic thought of Carlos Pellegrini it seems appropriate to us to limit our essay to his industrialist doctrine, even more so when we add to the above mentioned bibliography the works of Néstor Tomás Auza (1968), Juan E. Guglialmelli (1984) and Arturo Frondizi (1987). Not much is known about the essence of Pellegrini's industrialism as a member of the Argentine school of political economy of Vicente Fidel López (1815–1903), and even less about his links to sources related to foreign influences, so we shall limit our task to these two topics.

Essentially, industrialism is a neutral concept, indicating the structure of a system as much as it refers to the aim of the respective economic order. It is known that during the nineteenth century, Smith's system was designated as an 'industrial system', to distinguish it from the 'agricultural system' of the physiocrats and the 'mercantile system' of the period from the sixteenth century until the mid-eighteenth century. Otherwise one should remember the systematic proposals brought about by Pellegrino Rossi (1865), Eugene

Daire (1845: 15–26) and Emilio Lamarca (1877: 46). What is more, if one accepts that the followers of the founder of political economy were free traders, and the mercantilists essentially were protectionists, it would be more appropriate to label the former group as industrialists. But soon it was seen that the least developed regions in the industrial field were obligated to take protective measures for their incipient industries to protect them against the impetuous competition of similar foreign industries.

The arrival on the scene of North American industrialism meant that industrialism changed its free trade attire for a protectionist one and inserted itself within the solidarist doctrine with nationalistic overtones (Hamilton 1791; Carey 1814). As the same took place in France and Germany, these ideas could not go unnoticed along the Río de la Plata. In a series of illuminating and excellent research done not very long ago, José M. Mariluz Urquijo demonstrated the growing interest by eminent Argentinians, from the Anchorena brothers in 1815, de la Valle in 1818, de Angelis in 1830, and certainly no less important, the governor of the province of Corrientes, Pedro Ferré in 1830 (Mariluz Urquijo 1952, 1963, 1965). Along with this, the impressive anticipatory work of the Argentinian industrialist doctrine by Esteban Echeverría can not be overlooked (Popescu 1954).

But seen from the classical liberal doctrinal point of view, these works barely deserve mention. And if they are examined, it is to show their absurdity, their reactionary attitude before the river of immense orthodox currents. What was worthy for the first decades of the nineteenth century cannot be repeated for the latter half of this century. The history of economic thought also has its time. And it was in this time, during which the trajectory of the political life of Carlos Pellegrini began (and would continue its course until the autumn of his life) that liberal classicism entered a cone of darkness, which ended with a process of decadence and disintegration, as much on the theoretical plane, due to the marginalist revolution, as on the political plane, with the emergence of two powerful schools which competed to displace the occupants of the edifice of political economy.

The more dangerous of the two schools was collectivism, but its time was not immediate. On the other hand, solidarism, even though less virulent, is nothing more than an image of protectionism. Both reactionary schools could also be labelled 'classical', because they continued building by taking as a raw material the orthodox classical idea of the objective value theory. Nevertheless, their structure is quite distinct from the orthodox classical thinkers. Along theoretical lines, the solidarist authors urge the usage of inductive historical methods, instead of the abstract deductive methods of the classical thinkers. Typical representatives of this orientation are those of the German historical school led by Roscher and Schmoller, and we should not forget the forerunners of this school in the first half of the century (Simonde de Sismondi, Friedrich List, Adam Müller, and Adolf Wagner), representing all the specific lines of the solidarist family. Also, there was Karl Marx, who was the undisputed head of the collectivist family.

Another substantial difference, particularly valid for the solidarist current, is the organic vision and the eminently solidarist conception of the world as regards economic life, as was shown in the social organicism of August Comte, or the economic nationalism of List: 'Between the individual and humanity resides the nation' (Popescu 1985: 52).

In such a framework, arose the Argentinian school of national industrialism, in the 1870s. Its undisputed chief was the Professor of Political Economy at the University of Buenos Aires, Vicente Fidel López. As a professor, he stimulated a whole generation of students to investigate the national economic problems, and as a director he surrounded himself with the best in the professional field from young graduates to the consular figures of the Argentina of his generation, who actively participated in the public life of the country.

A close study of the works of all these figures leaves the undeniable stamp of the existence of a vigorous Argentinian school of economics which acted in unison for the rest of the nineteenth century.[1] And López' right hand man in his struggle to give the doctrine of Argentinian industrialism importance was none other than Dr Carlos Pellegrini, who on becoming president of the nation in 1890 designated his beloved teacher as minister of finance. In this manner, the economic doctrine united as one the members of the school.

The most palpable example is offered by the 'Diario de Sesiones del Congreso' (Congress Records) with the memorable debates concerning the development of national industry on 14 September 1875,[2] 18–25 August 1876 and 12 December 1899 in the House of Representatives, and in the Senate on 28 September 1895 and 5 October of the same year. These debates are the best testimony of the existence of a unitary whole which we may call the López school, the first Argentinian school of economics, which scholars should use as a demonstration of a product of Argentinian economic science. For Pellegrini's intense, constant, and enriching participation at López' side, and because he reached the position of president of the country, the school deserves to be renamed the López-Pellegrini school.[3]

Of course there are slight differences among the members of the school, including differences between López and Pellegrini as to the extent of industrial protectionism. But there is no doubt as to who the leader of school is, as Pellegrini calls López his 'distinguished teacher and friend'. The same was said by Pellegrini's second in command, Miguel Cané, who in the House of Representatives claimed: 'I confess that I form part of the school that is called protectionist in my land, of which I recognize the honourable representative López to be the head' (Argentine Congress, Chamber of Deputies 1876: 35). For this reason we should pause to dwell upon the protectionist path of Vicente Fidel López.

In the first place, it must be remembered that since the beginning of the

1830s, due to the February Revolution in France, López, a young university student of the Department of Jurisprudence, was identified with the reform movement, or as he himself said, with the 'ardor for social revolution and the reign of new ideas' of one Santiago Viola, who 'employed some twenty or twenty-five thousand francs of his fortune in having sent to Buenos Aires all the currently famous books in Paris, translated in French, Italian, German', to quench the thirst for reading of the university youth, a group which included Miguel Cané, with whom he formed 'the nucleus with the objective of organizing an association of historic and social studies, according to the new French school'; or later, between 1835 and 1836, with Don Marcos Sastre, who

> taking the idea and the institution of Cané, put himself to the task of organizing the literary salon . . . with the support of an excellent partner with money [the German] Federico von Schentein, whose adherence went as far as to make books be sent here and to donate them to the salon.
>
> (López 1896: 345)

It was in this literary salon that López met and formed an intimate friendship with Echeverría, who worked between 1837 and 1838 to 'elaborate the program, the basis, the objects, and the dogma by which we were going to work' (López 1896: 36). As a result of the autobiographical testimonies, López was identified with Echeverría and the governor of Corrientes, Pedro Ferré. But the most significant point in his autobiography is that López began planning an economic school in this period. Actually, as can be substantiated by his own testimony to Congress years later, the same author remembers what occurred in his refuge in 1840:

> I was living then in Córdoba, and pleased to see the wool weavings that were made there, I dressed myself with elegance in the cloth that we sent to be made, in my taste, by the poor people of the little town, into what were called 'géneros guasos', and the young people who at the onset found my extravagance strange, ended up imitating me.
>
> (Argentine Congress, Chamber of Deputies 1873: 278)

Vicente Fidel López, upon beginning his professorship in political economy at the University of Buenos Aires in 1874, continued repeating his industrialist doctrine, as is noted in the doctoral thesis of one of his many students:

> in our university what is taught is political economics applied to the economic conditions of the Argentine Republic; and the erudite professor who gives this course is an ardent adherent to the doctrine of the protectionist school, and has brilliantly demonstrated to his disciples the advantages that would result from the application of those doctrines. The same gentleman has had the patriotic thought of

244

founding a protecting society. This society is composed of, for now, students of the political economy wing, each associate being obligated to buy once a year in the national cloth factory, the cloth needed for a suit and besides, to buy two pairs of gloves, made in the country. God wants that this society prospers and extends its ramifications throughout the province.

(Nevares 1874: 6)

The fundamental points of the industrialist doctrine of López were shown for the first time when he served as a national representative and member of a project related to the foreign trade policy of Argentina. It was on this occasion that he diagnosed that due to the principle of free foreign trade, a complete degeneration of our productive efforts and social advancement occurs.

Bearing in mind that all the young countries such as the United States and Australia are eminently protectionist of their own output to avoid their territories falling into dependency on the already developed nations, López warned that Argentinian history itself provoked serious thought about the industrial policy to follow.

If we take into consideration the history of our domestic and national production, we shall see that since the revolution of 1810, which began to open our markets to free foreign trade, we began to lose all those raw materials that we elaborated . . . and which we could call emporiums of incipient industry . . . today are completely annihilated and go progressively along the road to ruin.

(Argentine Congress, Chamber of Deputies 1873: 262)

López continued:

My project does not concern the categorical defense of the prohibitive system, because the protectionist system, as I propose it, is dedicated only to favor with internal expenses the industry of those raw materials of which we are producers with advantage over all other countries.

(Argentine Congress, Chamber of Deputies 1873: 264)

The central idea of his protectionism was regional in nature: it was the great work of domestic promotion. Attention must fundamentally be placed

on the miserable condition of our tropical products, like sugar, coffee, indigo, and so many others of the same class; in that which we can produce, in wool and cotton cloth, with territories such as Catamarca, La Rioja, and Córdoba, which have no superiors in the world.

(Argentine Congress, Chamber of Deputies 1873: 266)

And finally, recommended López, it is necessary 'to promote industrial labor which is the only one that can bring us the true organic transformation and constitute in that manner a rich and civilized society' (Argentine Congress, Chamber of Deputies 1873: 267).

Carlos Pellegrini had known López from infancy. His father, Carlos Enrique Pellegrini, was intimate friends as much with Vicente López y Planes as with Vicente Fidel López (Rivero Astengo 1941: I, 95, 109). The senior Pellegrini had decided sympathies towards protectionism (Rivero Astengo 1941: I, 88). It should be no surprise, therefore, that at 22 years of age, the younger Pellegrini formulated in his doctoral thesis the following: 'The protection of the government is necessary for the development of industry in the Argentine Republic' (Rivero Astengo 1941: III, 40).

Elected as federal congressman, Pellegrini participated in the polemic of the House of Representatives of 1875, formulating the goals of Argentina's economic development:

Every country should aspire to grant development to its national industry; it is the basis of its wealth, of its power, of its prosperity; and in order to attain it its establishment should be encouraged, over-coming whenever possible, the difficulties that oppose it.

(Argentine Congress, Chamber of Deputies 1875: 1123)

This goal of development, defended throughout his life, was baptized by the Uruguayan Angel Floro Costa as 'championing industrial protection, on account of the school of the illustrious Doctor López' (Floro Costa 1902: 69). To this, Pellegrini answered: 'Provisionally, the school honors me, but I doubt very much that it offers more guarantees than those of the illustrious statesman, who those of us dedicated to economic studies honor by calling him teacher' (Rivero Astengo 1941: III, 323). And then, Pellegrini rounded off his concept:

A nation, in its modern concept, cannot depend exclusively on cattle breeding and agriculture, their products submitted not only to the activity or ability of man, but also in great part to the mischievous action of nature. There is not today, nor there could have been, a great nation, that is not an industrial nation, that knows to transform the intelligence and activity of its population into value and wealth, by means of mechanical arts. The Argentine Republic should aim to be something more than the immense farmland of Europe, and its true power does not consist, nor shall it consist in the quantity of its cannons or its armor, but in its economic power.

(Rivero Astengo 1941: III, 323)

It is important to show his organicistic vision, that the protection of indus-trial development is nothing more than an extension of the principles that strengthen the development of life. Actually, Pellegrini observed:

Free exchange is the ultimate aspiration of industry that can only find in it its full development, as the plant searches for free air to grow and have a leafy crown. But, from the fact that the plant needs fresh air to achieve its greatest growth, do not deduce that we should not shelter it upon birth, because what is an element of life for a growing tree, could be an element of death for a newly-born plant. If free trade develops the industry that has acquired certain vigor, and permits it to achieve all the splendor possible, free trade kills the infant industry.

(Argentine Congress, Chamber of Deputies 1875: 1121)

It is important to emphasize the inductivist historical approach of Pellegrini. For the great-nephew of John Bright, industrialism required customs protection in the beginning only for the nations on the way to economic development, since the already developed countries only need the 'protection' of free trade. There is protection in both models of industrial development policy, only that their solutions differ as functions of protection's location in time or in space.

Pellegrini's spatial reasoning allowed him to understand situations found in the bulk of Argentina between the economic centre located in the federal capital and its periphery provinces. It is fitting to remember in this respect the reflections expressed before the national senate on the 28 September 1895.

In the Argentine Republic there are two tendencies, and one can almost determine the territorial region where one and the other operate. There is one faction that has its center in the small space that surrounds Plaza de Mayo of the federal capital, and there is another faction that has its center in the rest of the nation. One faction could be called commercial, the other industrial. At each instance the distinct tendencies of these two factions are displayed. One of them is the declared enemy ... of all protection and wants the absolute freedom of trade; the other demands protection as an indispensable condition for the development of national industries. . . . These two interests, that are not antagonistic, are those of commerce and of industry; commerce and industry are reciprocal complements . . . they are the two wings, the two wheels upon which the progress of the nation is supported and advances . . . but it is certain that between these two interests there are some that are original, that are preceding and perhaps could have priority to the others. I understand that the interests of industry are preceding and a priority.

(Argentine Congress, Chamber of Senators 1895: 505)

Is this historicist and inductivist vision of Pellegrini due to the influence of the German Historical School, as the connection has cropped up in some writings (Guglialmelli 1984: 23)?[4] Is it not that behind all this there is a far more subtle transfusion that only his professor knows about?

The López-Pellegrini school knew that in its time, the doctrinary knowledge was represented by two foreign authors, Friedrich List and Henry Charles Carey, the son of Matthew Carey. Emilio de Alvear, in a series of letters published in the *Revista de Buenos Aires* beginning with Volume XXI of 1869, establishes the tie with the head of the North American school of economics, converted after 1848 to the school of protectionism (Alvear 1869).

The contact of members of the school with Friedrich List is due to López, dating from the time of his discharge as professor of political economics at the University of Montevideo in 1864. The haste to find a contemporary text on the material led to a book in French, published a year before under the title of *Una Revolución en la Economía Política – Exposición de las Doctrinas de Macleod* (Revolution in Political Economy – The Doctrines of Macleod). The author of the work was Henri Richelot, who today has all but disappeared (unjustly) from bibliographies, including those of the French writers.

It was Richelot who wrote a history of the Zollverein in French; to him we also owe the debt of the translation into French of the *National System of Political Economy* by List, in 1841. Richelot developed sympathetically the attachment of Macleod to the inductivist methodology of Bacon, to the subjective theory of value, and his sympathy for the mathematical optic, but did not share his free trade philosophy. He remembered the corrections of J. S. Mill and Rossi and entered directly into an evaluation of List's work that he translated into French, saying:

> Nobody has demonstrated with such eloquence as List the advantages of the freedom of trade; but neither has anyone made the usefulness of such protection stand out, applied with discernment to the industrial education of a nation conveniently prepared. He has supported this unanswerable argument, that if it loses value in exchange, [it] earns productive efforts, whose growth matters more than a mass of values. The readers of this exposition would not have forgotten, that according to Macleod, a country is rich, not so much for the quantity of riches it possesses, but for the development of its productive efforts.
>
> (Richelot 1863: 170–1)[5]

Enthusiastic about this investigation as well as the great interest of Macleod in developing a credit theory of money (Richelot 1863: 317), Vicente Fidel López decided to use the work as a textbook and he annotated it well in the preamble to his course in political economy in 1864 (López 1864).

The enthusiasm of the López-Pellegrini school for Richelot's work kept growing, and the contemporary critics approved it (Schumpeter 1971: 1210),[6] so soon the miracle happened and Richelot's work was translated into Spanish and printed in Buenos Aires in 1876 (Richelot 1876: 244). This made the protectionists along the Río de la Plata content, since a few years before, in 1873, the native free traders sent away for translation and printing *The Treatise on Political Economy* in three volumes by Girolamo Boccardo, in whose third volume was published a critique of some fifty pages demolishing protectionism in general and specifically the protectionism of List (Boccardo 1872).

The great followers of López and Pellegrini in the twentieth century, Alejandro Bunge (1880–1943) and Raúl Prebisch (1901–86), also creators of schools, did not leave any record of having read the works of López and Pellegrini, but they clearly confirm the basic postulates of his doctrine. Please note the incorporation speech given by Alejandro Bunge to the National Academy of Economic Sciences on 19 August 1927, entitled, 'The Creative Forces of the National Economy' (Bunge 1927: 154–68). Equally, look at the long list of works by Raúl Prebisch, also a member of the academy, from his student days to his death. The López-Pellegrini school has left a profound mark on the political, economic, and cultural history of Argentina. Thus, studying and remembering their works always leaves a sense of profound spiritual pleasure in any researcher in the field of the history of Argentinian and American economic thought.

15

HUMAN CAPITAL IN BOLIVIA

INTRODUCTION

In the field of theory as much as in economic policy, and also in the area of national planning, the problem of evaluation and planning of labour, which includes all the questions relating to the rational usage of human resources and development, has provoked a sudden and growing interest.[1]

The reason is simple. Human capital is a factor which is at least as important to the process of economic development as are capital goods to production. Furthermore, including development plans that centre upon requirements of capital goods for production, it is necessary to implement them with explicit programmes on the volume and necessary proportion of labour by sectors, regions, occupations, and educational levels. This is done to achieve the objectives of the plan, and consequently, it is equally imperative to make forecasts as rigorous as possible as regards financial resources for the adequate and opportune formation of the necessary labour. But to the purely economic viewpoint needs to be added the social character of development planning. In fact, a policy of development which is not at the service of full employment or at least at a satisfactory employment level, not only contradicts the human objectives of the entire process of development, but at the same time will generate grave tensions, which in time will be translated into insurmountable obstacles for this same process of development.

It should not be surprising that recently the problem of labour planning and formation should be the object of many international congresses and be permanently incorporated in the agenda of almost all international organizations: UNO; UNESCO; OAS; BID; OECD; even some organizations such as the International Labour Office (ILO), which granted labour first priority in technical assistance policies.

The interest in labour problems reverberated immediately in Latin American circles, thanks to the uninterrupted series of meetings, seminars, and conferences, sponsored mostly by the same international organizations, in close cooperation with CEPAL (Spanish acronym for Economic

Commission of the United Nations for Latin America). And that which occurred on a continental scale also happened on a national scale.

In many Latin American countries new entities, committees, corporations, institutes, or centres of study arose, dedicated to the analysis and perspectives of the development of human resources. Almost simultaneously, in 1957, Argentina and Colombia left unmistakable testimony of the interest in these types of problems. Shortly afterwards, the seed was carried to the Central American countries, but where it put out its strongest roots was in Chile and Colombia, later to extend from there to the rest of the Latin American countries.[2]

Background

This tendency is also being made evident in Bolivia. In rigorous terms of technical programming, evidently, the beginnings of the interest in Bolivia date back some years, but it is interesting to note that the problem as such has always concerned the Bolivian thinkers. It had already germinated in the first Bolivian writing on political economy by Julián Prudencio (Prudencio 1845).[3] Prudencio not only perceived the close relationship between economic progress and professional formation, but also claimed that for a nation on the path of development, it is better to import capable people to stimulate national industries and employment, than to import goods that could ruin the existing industries and increase unemployment. But even more valuable seems to be the work of José María Dalence (1785–1852), *Bosquejo Estadístico de Bolivia* (Statistical Sketch of Bolivia), in which he undertakes the evaluation of the labour force in quantitative and qualitative terms, making use of a skilful technique quite similar to that in use today (Dalence 1851).[4] In the twentieth century, another Bolivian thinker, Néstor Villarroel Claure, surprises us with some substantial research on the economic fundamentals of education in Bolivia, initiating with this the current of economic education in Bolivia (Villarroel Claure 1929).[5] Among the great precursors of research on Bolivian human resources should equally figure the work of Asthenio Averanga Mollinedo, assiduous cultivator of demographic studies in general, and the first one who attempted to interpret and evaluate the figures of the 1900 and 1950 censuses concerning Bolivian labour and education (Averanga Mollinedo 1956).[6] But if from the general aspects he would have gone on to contemplate the contributions in the specialized departments, the inventory would have been even much wider.

A decisive step in the furtherance of research on human resources was taken at the moment in which Bolivia began to receive foreign technical assistance. The starting point was the so-called *Informe Bohan* (Bohan Report), which arose due to the technical assistance agreement signed with the United States in 1941. This document, which is actually a first approximation for a plan of unbalanced economic development, is based on the expansion of the infrastructure, agricultural development, and the creation of the petroleum industry, and contributes a line of qualitative references on the structure and the objectives of a labour policy in agriculture and mining.[7] Very valuable references on the subject are also contributed by the Report of the Mission of Technical Assistance of the United Nations carried out in Bolivia, under the direction of H. L. Keenleyside in 1950. It is in this document that the thesis that in 'Bolivia, like everywhere, the most important national resource rests on the energy, the character, and the intelligence of its inhabitants' is energetically emphasized. Although the twenty-two experts who integrated the mission did not know the results of the 1950 census, they nevertheless managed to make important contributions to the quantitative diagnosis, by areas and sectors, of Bolivian human resources. But its great and durable contribution lies in the profound qualitative diagnosis which coincided in many aspects with the *Informe Bohan* and the multitude of reflections and suggestions to implement the labour plan with that of economic development (United Nations 1951).[8]

The report of the US Department of State of 1956 by Cornelius Zondag in collaboration with Bolivian experts M. A. Valderrama and Rolando Kempff Mercado deserves special mention. In this document are examined the perspectives of Bolivian development within the new framework of the economic and social policies which arose due to the Revolution of 1952. The central idea of the diagnosis is that 'the Bolivian problem, is a social problem, a problem which dwells in the type, the composition, and the quantity of its inhabitants, on top of the complexity of its geography', and consequently, the chain of problems that the country had to confront in the following years are nothing but mere reflections of the distorted problem of human resources. Actually, the document harped on the fact that Bolivia suffered a tremendous scarcity of human resources, that had been aggravated, on the one hand, by the changes in the social structure since the revolution, and on the other hand, by the distortions produced by the economic diversification plans through the development of the petroleum reserves in Bolivia and the agricultural potential in the zone of Santa Cruz. The report trusted that with the return to a system of balanced development and the liberation of the economic controls, perfected by incentives and stimuli in the various areas and sectors, the country could reinitiate a stage of prosperity (Zondag 1956).[9]

This incisive report on Bolivia carried out by Zondag was soon eclipsed by the CEPAL study, performed almost simultaneously and published shortly after Zondag's report, which used in its elaboration the reports of Bohan and Keenleyside as valuable inputs.

The CEPAL study, which is still well known and deserves to be so, embraces the totality of the problems related to economic development in the country, as had earlier reports. CEPAL's report stands out, in its systematically formal aspect as a means of focusing on the problem. So, while the three authors mentioned before, presented in fragments the reflections in our field, without any formal order, dispersed everywhere in their voluminous reports (a fact which explains completely the utter disinterest of later scholars to explore, take inventory of, and critically analyse their contributions), in CEPAL's report, the basic problems of Bolivian human resources are reunited in a special chapter, facilitating rapid consultation and documentation.

But regardless of the purely formal aspect, the lasting value of this document arises from its substantial methodological aspect. The focus utilized to explore the field of human resources calls on our attention. Actually, it is a double focus, or if you like, a focus of two distinct dimensions: one of a wide interdisciplinary and qualitative vision, constitutes the focus on the sociological dimension; the other of a more restricted vision, but rigorous in its hypothesis on work and of a more quantitative character, represents the focus on the economic dimension.

Although the sociological analysis of the problem of human resources scarcely embraces the size of a reduced section and is even hidden in the interior of the voluminous document, it is without a doubt one of the most valuable contributions, above everything else, for a country like Bolivia, in which a transition between two very different cultural worlds is taking place. It is obvious that in this country many of the decisions about the measures to take, at the chosen time, like the form in which to implement them, are intimately intertwined with value judgements which demand a wide, but cautious, inter-disciplinary vision that can only be provided by the sociological viewpoint.

On the other hand, after the assumptions of the problem have been planted in a section which follows the sociological analysis, the quantitative analysis that 'obeys the desire to proportion a methodological standard which serves as a base for the Bolivian technical organisms in the elaboration of a development program', occupies practically the rest of the book. The model elaborated by CEPAL anticipated two fundamental objectives: economic growth, and the creation of jobs at least equal to the projected growth rate in the labour force. But what is even more surprising is that between the two fundamental objectives, the creation of jobs has high priority in the development model.

The remainder of the book is dedicated to the quantitative implementation of the objective of employment with the objective of economic growth and the description of the phases that should be covered in global production by sectors and areas to achieve the established objectives. Certainly the quantitative evaluations are estimates and the process of development is described in a very general manner, but notwithstanding this, it is certain that the effort realized marks an important phase in the technique of planning of Bolivian human resources (CEPAL 1958).[10]

253

Of course, the work by the International Labour Office (ILO) in the field of Bolivian human resources cannot be overlooked, although in this case only its principal contributions will be listed. For that purpose, it is important to remember the activity carried out by the Expert Commission for the Protection of Aboriginal Workers, beginning in 1926, and by the Conference of the Member American States of the ILO, beginning in 1936. We should also mention the participation of the ILO in the joint US-Bolivian mission of 1943, which investigated the working conditions in the tin mines in the Altiplano (Bolivian-United States Labour Commission 1943).[11] Finally, note should be taken of the activity developed by the Expert Commission on the Work of the Indians, begun in 1946 and finished in 1953. With the publication of this monumental work on Indian populations, numerous passages are dedicated to the life of Bolivian Indians (ILO 1953). Also important is the creation of the Andean Programme, whose first steps were to send various inquiry missions to the region of Santa Cruz precisely in order to study the possibilities of colonization with the Indians of the Altiplano, and the installation of the first base of action in Pillapi, on the Bolivian shore of Lake Titicaca (ILO 1958).

Similarly, the ILO has given direct technical assistance to the Ministry of Labour, sending successive missions with specific objectives in the distinct aspects related to Bolivian labour. Besides assessments, formation of counterparts, and the collaboration in the creation and institutionalization of special services, these missions have collected multitudes of impressions and realized special studies on each one of the recommended objectives, in which have been presented suggested ways and recommendations that tend to facilitate the work of the government in the area of labour. Among these studies, the following should be mentioned: the study on industrial hygiene in the mining centres by Angelo de Tuddo in 1952 (Tuddo 1952); the work of Fernando Demoulin, André Agnan, and Jean Guidel on professional formation, of 1955–61 (Agnan 1955–61); William H. Mason's work on the organization and programming of employment (Mason 1959); a report by E. R. Tichauer on industrial productivity (Tichauer 1960); that of Albert Lhoir on worker education (Lhoir 1962); and finally, that of Sanford Cohen on the evaluation and planning of labour (Cohen 1964).

With the creation of the National Junta of Planning (today, the Secretariat of Planning and Coordination) the problem of human resources is incorporated in the agenda of action and scientific research of the Bolivian public sector.

A start was made by the publication of a meritorious investigation into 'the problems of employment of the labour force' in the official organ of the junta. Its authors, apparently a group of national collaborators headed by Alfredo Eguino, took as a starting point for this study a project elaborated for it by the National Sub-Director of Statistics. On this basis, they elaborated a work on the principal aspects of the structure and the growth of the labour force, the occupational distribution by sectors and regions, and finally, the employment 'surpluses'.

This excellent beginning unfortunately had little luck. In the 1962–71 Plan Decenal, despite the fact that at each step the special interest for the problems of labour was emphasized, and many contributions were displayed, a great diminution of the technical rigour and a total absence of reference to the substantial contributions is noted, including its own aforementioned work, which was eliminated from the plan (Cohen 1964).

A recovery attempt was made in 1962, by the preparatory works of the first biennial plan of development, when Alfredo Eguino and José M. Illescas attempted an 'analysis of labour for the two year period 1963–4'. But this stimulating work in many aspects had even worse luck, since it remained filed away (Eguino and Illescas 1962).

Although later on special investigation groups were institutionalized within the Secretariat of Planning, including in the field of human resources, the contributions have been displaced by eminently educational matters. To date, there have not been contributions in the labour sector. This halting of research activities was solicited in certain measure by scholars of various organisms of technical assistance, like the US Department of Labour, the ILO, and the United States Organization for Cooperation in Development (USAID).

SUMMARY AND CONCLUSIONS

The problem of human resources has been the object of growing interest by scholars of the distribution of planning. But despite the efforts made to implement the planning of human resources into the general system, the results achieved have been only moderate.

Although in development plans elaborated to date objectives related to labour have been incorporated, in none has the adequate programming of the steps to follow for reaching the specific goals been achieved. The reason for this deficiency lies in the fact that there has not been realized a satisfactory diagnosis of the situation and perspective of Bolivian human resources.

The basic cause of the deficiency of the diagnostic attempts lies in the complexity of the subject, even more so when the focus and the methodology to follow in its study are only recently being developed, and even then the steps to follow differ from country to country. This situation is hampered on one hand by the scarcity of sufficiently capable and experienced Bolivian technicians, and on the other hand, by the great scarcity of specialized studies. As a crown to all these obstacles, we should add the fact that the last national census was undertaken seventeen years ago, and at that time clear ideas of the types of statistical series and variables that were needed for the objectives of labour planning were missing.

To overcome these obstacles, many national and foreign researchers have tried to estimate and interpret the course of events. This entails considerable efforts which could not be sufficiently pondered upon. Special circumstances forced them to realize estimations at whatever price and risk, to be used in the development plans. Therefore, when one has time to research the numbers presented, doubts arise. This is so without going into the problems of the numerous and confusing variants which are presented in distinct basic series of data. By looking closely only at the series available for total population, working age population, and the labour force, one sees the problems inherent in the data analysis.

The basic object of this work is to serve as a constructive criticism. Once the present situation is re-examined, on the basis of the same studies and collected observations, the incorrect or doubtful interpretations are thrown out. Then we may continue to construct our plans along the indicated lines as far as circumstances and data allow us to go.

Finally, one must keep in mind that the problems of Bolivia in undertaking a plan of labour are also the problems of Ecuador and El Salvador; that is, that Bolivia suffers the same inherent problems found throughout Latin America. This means that the cumulation of problems and obstacles which Bolivia confronts are more a sign of its specific level of development, than a national phenomenon. Within the spirit of continuous conquest that dominates the Bolivian elite, there are many sound reasons to trust that this level will soon be overcome and consequently the perspectives for the research and planning of human resources will also be more satisfactory.

16

SILVIO GESELL[1]

Silvio Gesell was born on 17 March 1862 in the city of St Vith, located at the confluence of the borders of Belgium, Luxembourg, and Prussia, which was exchanged many times between the three nations. His parents were of German descent on the paternal side, and Walloons on the maternal side. Therefore, Silvio Gesell spoke both French and German at home; and was formed both by Prussian discipline and French delicacy, by maternal Catholicism and paternal Protestantism.

The Gesells made superhuman efforts to bear the educational expenses of their nine children. But just as the seventh child, Silvio, was finishing his first year of secondary school, the father, who was quite well on in years, became very ill. This obligated the family to change its plans drastically. After three years of working as a clerk in the state postal service, Silvio took the advice of the eldest brother Paul and decided to work in the area of commerce. Silvio's first steps in this direction were as a clerk in Paul's dental supplies business. Between the years 1882–4, Silvio worked in Málaga, Spain as an agent for his brother's business.

After returning to Germany to do his military service, Silvio continued working in various enterprises in Braunschweig, and finally, in an international transportation company in Hamburg, which led to his arriving in Buenos Aires in the summer of 1887. Here he began his own business and his own family, for he decided to marry his fiancé, Anna Boettger of Braunschweig, in Montevideo. Soon both his business and family grew: in 1888 the first child, Ernesto Fridolin, was born; in 1889, Ana; in 1891, another son, Carlos Idaho; and in 1893, another daughter, Juanita, all Argentinians born in Buenos Aires.

The birth dates of his last two children coincide with the publication dates of his first works on monetary policy: *Die Reformation in Münzwesen als Brücke zum Sozialen Staat*, 1891a; *Nervus rerum Fortsetzung zur Reformation in Münzwesen*, 1891b; *Die Verstaatlichung des Geldes-Zweite Fortsetzung zur Reformation in Münzwesen*, 1892; and *El Sistema Monetario Argentino*, 1893. But these are merely the starting point of a long series of publications which were produced year after year, even after Silvio's death in Eden Oranienburg on 11 March 1930, by his students and his fifth child Hans-Joachim Führer, who was owner of a translation company in Freiburg, Germany. Recently a seventeen-volume set of Silvio Gesell's complete works was published, with a prologue written by one of his newer followers, Werner Onken. In this prologue, the importance of Hans-Joachim's financial assistance is emphasized (Gesell 1988–96: I, 16).

The question of just how Silvio Gesell entered into the world of publishing can be found in the collective experiences of his work in businesses in Argentina, Germany, and Spain. The rapid success he enjoyed in running his own businesses not only gave Gesell the guidelines for a correct interpretation of the articulation of economics, but at the same time it served as a source of inspiration to continue deepening and extending the economic horizon.

Gesell began by periodically noting the price fluctuations of distinct products in the national and world markets, the exchange rate changes, and the volume of transactions. He read all available newspapers and followed the congressional debates on economic topics. And as neither the ideas put forth in the press nor those expressed in congressional chambers reflected his own views, Gesell decided to formulate his own notes and ideas from three years of daily reading.

Years later, Silvio Gesell would say:

> The whole of the great complex of interrelations of a world significance, all its ties with history, politics, and economics; everything that served me for the rest of my life as the direction for my writings, gushed forward in only half an hour, with the idea of free money. So powerful was the impact that for the next three days, I was literally jumping around my bedroom. My own wife thought I was mad. I actually felt as if my head had been instantly made much heavier.
>
> (Timm 1960: 3)

Right after this event, Silvio Gesell found the necessary conviction to order his ideas and put them on paper: in this manner his first writings appeared, and the social reformer Silvio Gesell was born.

His first work *Die Reformation in Münzwesen als Brücke zum Sozialen Staat* (Currency Reform as a Bridge toward the Social State) is a notebook of forty-five pages written for the German people in Argentina and elsewhere, and therefore printed in German. We would have liked for his first work to be written in Spanish and directed towards our people as a solution to the social and economic questions, as the nature of this work was a resolution of said problems (Gesell 1988–96: I, 19).

The title of Gesell's first work refers to the name of the doctrine which he proclaims. In it, he talks of his ideas as a doctrine for the social state, or ideal social state, to emphasize its contrast with the deformed doctrine of the capitalist state. From the moment in which the organic failures of the capitalist system can be solved according to Gesell's ideas:

we shall have the social state, the ideal social state, a system in which, founded on the principle of 'suum cuique' (to each his own), allowing each person his freedom and having as a goal to guarantee to each member of society, his liberty, his right, and his property.

(Gesell 1891a: 6)

This first work carries in its title the suggestive idea of a bridge toward the social state (*Brücke zum Sozialem Staat*). Beginning in 1906, Gesell opted for the name of 'natural economic order', as the two basic principles of his doctrine, personal interest and competition, are deeply rooted in the nature of mankind, according to Karl Walker's 'Werk und Weltanschauung' (Walker 1949: 363–70). It is also the name he chose as the title of his basic work, and which would be maintained throughout all later re-editions.[2] The 'natural economic order' reminds one of the doctrine of Quesnay and the physiocratic movement. Silvio Gesell never felt bothered by this linkage; to the contrary, he missed no opportunity to harp on the ideological link with the great predecessors of economic science.

The first centre of his associates in Berlin of 1907 was called the Physiocratic Association (Physiokratische Vereinigung) and the newsletter of this group was *Der Physiokratí*. In the prologue to the second edition of *El Orden Económico Natural* (The Natural Economic Order), Paul Klüpfel energetically emphasized the nexus between the doctrine of Gesell and that of Quesnay: 'Gesell does not take into consideration the doctrine of Quesnay; this is his reference point everywhere, there can be no other' (Gesell 1916: ii).

Later, in 1924, there arose a branch of this movement under the name of the Union for the Physiocratic Struggle (Physiokratischer Kampfbund), and at times, Gesell himself designated his doctrine as a physiocratic doctrine. It is also useful to remember that even the associates of Silvio Gesell in Argentina had designated their movement as the Argentinian Physiocratic Federation. Nevertheless, there is no lack of suggestions to designate the doctrine of Gesell as 'neo-physiocratric' (Blumenthal 1924: 501–6).

In the third edition of his work, Gesell ponders that his natural economic system could also be called 'Manchesterian', a system that the true spirits always held as an ideal. Of this 'Manchesterianism', one may only speak today to people who do not put down failed experiments as an error or gloat when the failures of objectives prove to be the failure of the entire system. For the majority, what they know of this 'Manchesterianism' is sufficient to make them curse the system (Gesell 1988–96: I, 264).

Silvio Gesell, who is also the head of a movement, could not remain insensitive to the lexicographical preferences of the masses, precisely at the time when the word socialism floated through the air. At the beginning of

1919, in the hope of being able to test his doctrine, it was thrown into a whirlpool of political action by a socialist government. Silvio Gesell was very sympathetic to the possibility of guiding a political movement under the label of Socialist Liberal Union (Sozialistische Freiheitsbund), which was as opposed to capitalism as to Marxism, and other statist organizations. But the unpleasant time he had during the few days of his collaboration with the socialists of the frustrated government in Munich, led Gesell to abandon the idea of designating his doctrine as 'liberal socialism'. After 1919, the label which will enjoy his highest preference would be 'free economy' (Freiwirtschaft), a term already used by Paul Klüpfel in the prologue to the second edition of *The Natural Economic Order*, and a few months after Gesell's trial in Munich, a brochure titled 'The Free Economy before Justice' appeared. In his defence before the court of justice in Munich, Gesell labels his doctrine several times with this new name, and reminds us that among the distinct branches of his movement, there is one called the 'free economy'.

In May 1921, in the Congress of Kassel, the four branches of Gesell's movement are unified in the 'union of free economics'. On 30 November 1921, in the prologue to the fifth edition of his basic work, he designated his movement as 'the movement of the free economy'. In 1924, Gesell published an article titled, 'Was ist Freiwirtschaft?' (What is Free Economics?), in issue number 10 of *Der Entscheidungskampf*. Gesell was attracted to this movement, for his spirit of individualism grew after the disaster in Munich. It is possible that Max Stirner's book, *Der Einzige und sein Eigentum* (The Unique and its Property), could have influenced Gesell's thinking somewhat (Schmid 1954: 178).[3]

The prologue to the fourth edition of his work demonstrates his new radical individualism. For Gesell 'the transformation of the human herd of mankind's flock into a complete and independent individual, that is to say, a person who rejects the yoke by his similars' is the expression of a law of the development for human society. This law would have been realized a long time ago had it not been tripped up by the retarding failures of capitalism and Marxism. Precisely to liberate our economic system from these organic barriers was the reason for Gesell's doctrine. The natural economic order, which arises by itself, without need of legal means, nor of any tutelage, and which respects the laws of natural selection, provides to each progressive man the possibility of fully developing himself. Gesell's ideal is to liberate man from all outer domination and form a personality responsible only to himself; 'the ideal of Schiller, Stirner, Nietzsche, and Landauer' (Gesell 1920: vii). With the appearance of his writings from 1919–27, the individualism of Gesell reached frightening dimensions; individual freedom knows no practical limits!

Gesell reduced the ideas of the decalogue to one: man should do whatever seems right to him, and the absolute criterion of this behaviour is the following, as stated in *Der Aufstieg des Abendlandes* (The Ascension of

Occident): 'I do whatever seems right to me, because I act in agreement with my interests. Truth is all that increases my welfare, falsehood is all that diminishes it. Therefore, I am the absolute measure of everything' (Gesell 1923: 14).

Now that the state has been transformed by the dominant class into an instrument of individual repression, we must proceed to dismantle all the state's injurious functions:

> It will come to that it is indispensable the entire demolition of all its institutions with the exception of those that entail the traffic of money, postal service, railroads, telegraph, navy, and merchant marines. All the rest, the ministries of war, commerce, education, justice, etc., could be transferred advantageously to private hands and local organisms.
>
> (Gesell 1919: 14)

Gesell does not fear stepping into anarchist territory, he only fears a confusion of his ideals with communist anarchism, which he labels a vicious circle. The only fruitful way to anarchism is that opened by the liberal path, and Gesell, in *Der Abgebaute Staat* (The Dismantled State), claims that his doctrine of natural economic order, or free economics, constitutes the most adequate vehicle (Gesell 1927: 4). His political adversaries now began to label Gesell as an anarchist. Even collaborators of Gesell's began erroneously to label him as an anarchist, thinking this would be to his credit. Evidently, there was no other possible interpretation of Gesell's ideas in favour of liberal anarchism.

The formula of 'free economics' having been carried to its ultimate consequences by Gesell himself, it is not surprising to learn that after Gesell's death, some of his followers suggested replacing the name 'free economics' with the old tag of 'physiocrat' (Bader 1932: 112). Finally, one faction of his followers, among them Schmid and Schwarz, preferred to name the movement as 'liberal socialism', while another faction, more moderate and closer to the contemporary neo-liberalism, opted for the neutral expression 'free social order' (Freisoziale Ordnung). The fact that at the Schweinfurt meeting of the Freisoziale Union, on 23–29 July 1961, it was resolved to officially substitute the expressions 'free economy' and 'free economics' for 'free social order' and 'free social', respectively, is very significant and can be found in 'Informationen für Kultur, Wirtschaft und Politik' of September 1961, page 28.

But whatever were the turns that the doctrine of Gesell took during its long trajectory of forty years of evolution, what is certain is that its central seed expressed in the ideas of liberty, competition, and individual interest, and its guarantee by way of the abolition of income coming from other people's work, has remained unchanged.

As regards the aspects of economic theory we can enumerate the following: in the first place, Gesell certainly perceived by intuition the quantitative fundamentals of precious metals. For this, he used one of the stories of Ali Baba concerning the discovery of the Semsi mountain of gold. The effect would have been more powerful if he had resorted to the impact produced on the price level by the discovery of the gold in Potosí. For Argentinian scholars, it is difficult to believe that for a piece of writing done in Buenos Aires in 1891, neither the courses on political economics at the University of Buenos Aires, nor the works translated from French and Italian authors and published in Argentina between 1850–90 have been quoted. Then Gesell developed an idea following a vigorous criticism of the gold ownership system, showing the monetary aspects as well as those related to social policy. In the last chapters Gesell posed the problem of monetary reform through the introduction of 'Rostende Banknoten', that is free money, and the discussion with socialist doctrines about his economic and social tactics.

With this discussion it was established the starting point of the principal subjects which would continue being the object of permanent research throughout the following decades, and would culminate in 1916 in the fundamental work of Gesell, *Die Naturlich Wirtschaftsordnung durch Freiland und Freigeld* (The Natural Economic Order through Free Land and Free Money), published first in German, and later in Spanish, English, and French and later to be the object of special studies as much by disciples of Gesell as by his detractors.

Die Reformation im Münzwesen als Brücke zum Sozialen Staat was one of Gesell's works which was in highest demand, and the stock ran out before he died. An abbreviated re-edition (purged of the excess of allegories and parables which the naive author utilized, due to his pedagogical intentions), dedicated to the memory of Silvio Gesell, was prepared under the direction of Leonhard Jenni and published under the same title by the Pestalozzi-Fellenberg-Haus editorial company of Bern in 1931. In the *Obra Completa de Silvio Gesell*, volume I, the entire text is reprinted. Finally, it is noteworthy that an English translation by Phillip Pye (1951) exists, under the title of 'Currency Reform as a Bridge to the Social State' found in Palgrave's 1987 *Dictionary of Political Economy*, page 520. The only thing hampering scholars of Argentina from researching more of the works by this adopted son is the fact that most of Gesell's works were written in German, and no translations have been attempted into Spanish.

When Gesell first began publishing his works, these writings were the object of intense academic scrutiny. At first, the reviews of his works were not favourable, but in the 1920s, they became common material for lectures and debate in many universities throughout the world. Although the critiques were mostly negative, Gesell's works began to gain favourable reviews over time. This was in part due to the contributions to economics of Wicksell, Schumpeter, and Keynes in the area of monetary theory.

Beginning in 1933 and until the end of the Second World War, the attitudes of economic professionals changed notably as regards the theories of Gesell. This period was the golden age of Gesellian thought, as the problems brought on by the Great Depression were the main factor which changed opinions. The great crisis of 1929–32 gave an opportunity to the proponents of interest-free currency (Chick 1987: 520) to put their theories to the test as therapies for the ailing world economy. The best known among the various small scale experiments were those of Schwanenkirchen, Bavaria in 1931, and Wörgl, Tirol in 1932–3. The immediate success of these experiments rapidly caught the attention of national and foreign experts in politics and economics. The experiments' promoters, Hebecker in Schwanenkirchen and the mayor of Wörgl, Unterguggenberger, soon became famous. In the summer of 1933, the ex-president of the Council of Ministers of France, Eduard Daladir, resolved to study in situ the 'miracle' of Wörgl. His highly favourable impressions were the subject of a lengthy report given to the socialist congress in Nantes on 15 April 1935. The news especially attracted attention in the United States, the nation hardest hit by the effects of the Great Depression. On remembering the thousands of consultants who had come from every region of the United States, Irving Fisher felt obligated to undertake exhaustive research into interest-free currency, the conclusions of which were the object of a special work, *Stamp Script*, published in 1933. Even if he refused to accept Gesell's theory on interest, Irving Fisher conceded that in order to ward off the depression: 'the idea of free money was as useful an invention as was the laryngoscope for the master of song Manuel García' (Fisher 1933: 17).[4]

Gesell achieved celebrity status with the appearance of the *General Theory of Employment, Interest and Money* of John Maynard Keynes. Just the mere fact of having been quoted by Keynes would have been enough to draw the attention of academic economists to Gesell. Keynes, in his very reduced list of predecessors, actually placed Gesell in a very elevated position. After having recognized his debt to the mercantilist thinkers and having accused the classical authors of having 'mixed in an inextricable manner the interest rate and the marginal efficiency of capital', John Maynard Keynes proceeded to contemplate the ideas of 'the strange, unduly neglected prophet Silvio Gesell (1862–1930) whose work contains flashes of deep insight and who only failed to reach down to the essence of the matter' (Keynes 1936: 353).

At first glance, not even Keynes could find any merit in the works of Gesell. Keynes did not see the inherent brilliance of Gesell's work until he himself arrived at the same conclusions. In addition, the merit of having discovered Gesell is conceded to 'Professor Irving Fisher, alone amongst academic economists, has recognised its significance' (Keynes 1936: 355). Despite evident defects in Gesell's arguments, for Keynes, 'Gesell's main book is written in a cool, scientific language, though it is suffused throughout by a more passionate, a more emotional devotion to social justice than some think decent in a scientist' (Keynes 1936: 355). Keynes' judgement as regards the social philosophy of Gesell is also favourable:

> The purpose of the book as a whole may be described as the establishment of an anti-Marxian socialism, a reaction against laissez-faire built on theoretical foundations totally unlike those of Marx in being based on a repudiation instead of on an acceptance of the classical hypotheses, and on a fettering of competition instead of its abolition. I believe that the future will learn more from the spirit of Gesell than from that of Marx. The preface to *The Natural Economic Order* will indicate to the reader, if he will refer to it, the moral quality of Gesell. The answer to Marxism is, I think, to be found along the lines of this preface.
>
> (Keynes 1936: 355)

But beside the ideological affinity between Keynes and Gesell there was a theoretical bond. As much in the *General Theory* as in *The Natural Economic Order*, the monetary theory of the interest rate is the key to the system. Keynes takes special note of the contribution of Gesell in the construction of the new theory:

> In the first place, he distinguishes clearly between the rate of interest and the marginal efficiency of capital, and he argues that it is the rate of interest which sets a limit to the rate of growth of real capital. Next, he points out that the rate of interest is a purely monetary phenomenon and that the peculiarity of money, from which flows the importance of the money rate of interest, lies in the fact that its ownership as a means of storing wealth involves the holder in negligible carrying charges, and that forms of wealth, such as stocks of commodities which do involve carrying charges, in fact yield a return because of the standard set by money. He cites the comparative stability of the rate of interest throughout the ages as evidence that it cannot depend on purely physical characters, inasmuch as the variation of the latter from one epoch to another must have been incalculably greater than the observed change in the rate of interest.
>
> (Keynes 1936: 355–6)

If Gesell had known to incorporate in his theory of interest the notion of liquidity preference, his contribution would have been complete. Unfortunately, he only arrived half way to elaborating the theory of interest rates. According to Keynes, Gesell 'had carried his theory for far enough to lead him to a practical recommendation, which may carry with it the essence of what is needed, though it is not feasible in the form in which he proposed it' (Keynes 1936: 356–7). This reference is directed towards stamped money. Like Fisher, Keynes also thinks that 'the idea behind stamped money is sound' (Keynes 1936: 357), even when in the following lines he emphasizes:

money was not unique in having a liquidity-premium attached to it, but differed only in degree from many other articles, deriving its importance from having a greater liquidity-premium than any other article.

(Keynes 1936: 357–8)

Keynes' intervention in favour of Gesell produced a strong commotion among the followers of Gesell. It is certain that the redeeming words of Keynes, if not decisive, contributed in great measure to the recovery of the Gesellian movement from the grave crisis into which it had fallen with the death of its leader and the interdiction that was imposed upon him by the national socialist regime. Keynes' reflection that 'in the future more will be learned from Gesell than from Marx' has become the true flag of the movement. Some Gesellians, such as Wilhelm Radecke, have even taken positions against the negative criticisms of Keynes, as shown in the Epilogue Radecke wrote to Walker's *Die Überwindung des Kapitalismus*.

But an impact was produced among academic economists also, some of whom remain perplexed by it all. Schumpeter said in his criticism of the *General Theory*: 'I am not a Marxist; nevertheless, I sufficiently recognize the greatness of Marx not to offend him by considering him to be in the same category as Gesell' (Schumpeter 1936: 793). Others, on the contrary, received Gesell with glee, such as Prados Arrarte, who said:

Without having deserved the pen of a commentator, it has been the city of Buenos Aires which can be proud of being the cradle of the Keynesian revolution, since Gesell published in this city in 1891 a work which has been received by Keynes as a principal forerunner of his doctrine. Silvio Gesell is found to be, then, in the same relation of ignored inventor in opposition to the modern theories, as Cournot is in opposition to mathematical economics.

(Prados Arrarte 1950: 16)

What is certain is that after Keynes, the contributions of Gesell began to be pondered by academic economists with greater interest and above all else, with greater consideration. One decisive step in this direction was made by Dupley Dillard, the well-known American Keynesian, who chose as the topic of his doctoral thesis the doctrine of Gesell, and to which he returned on other occasions (Dillard 1940, 1942, 1952). We should keep in mind the fruitful comments on Gesell's ideas found in Lawrence R. Klein's *La Revolución Keynesiana* (Klein 1952). Deserving special mention is the French economist Maurice Allais, who, in a two-volume work on *The Economy and Interest*, affirms that he widely agrees with the Gesellian reforms 'as much as that which concerns the necessity of coincidental organization, as that in respect to the nationalization of ownership of land, the annulling of the interest rate, and the depreciation of currency' (Allais 1947: 43), even when these reforms are based on differing arguments.

Internationally, those who violently attack the ideas of Gesell are concentrated in the Marxist camps. In Latin America, the focus is on the technical aspects of Gesell's works, which the rest of the world did in the period 1920–30. Finally, a Brazilian economist, Santiago Fernandes, is undertaking a critical study of Gesell's works, pointing toward a Keynesian focus.

To be fair to Gesell, his doctrines and their technical aspects do not deserve such detailed observation as they have received. What should be studied is his theory of interest. Gesell's doctrine lives and dies by his theory of interest. Until Gesell's death, the focal point of discussion has been his analysis of real theory of interest, not his monetary theory of interest, which is his forte. This is one reason that Gesell's doctrines have met with so much resistance in the academic world. Until Keynes' monumental work, which included monetary theory, no one took Gesell's monetary theory of interest seriously.

Economic fluctuations dominate not only facts, but ideas. This is definitely true in the area of interest theory, perchance the most difficult part to understand in economics. Keynes may have brought the monetary theory of interest to the limelight, but others have since undertaken a refinement of his basically crude theory. This 'refinement' has led to the elaboration of a more comprehensive theory of interest, which day by day appears more like a synthesis of classical and Keynesian ideas. This 'general theory' provides the direction of the two previously protagonistic schools of thought, and can be viewed in the output of a very complete contemporary researcher, Friedrich A. Lutz of the University of Zurich in his work *Zinstheorie* of 1956.

Contemplating Gesell's interest theory, from the viewpoint of the new integration which dominates current economic sciences, lends an increasing degree of vulnerability to it. The paling of Keynes' brilliance is also a dampening of Gesell's ideas. Even so, Keynes' ideas and Gesell's contributions should remain equally the objects of research, and neither should fall into the abyss of the forgotten. On concluding his chapter dedicated to Gesell, Lawrence R. Klein suggests:

> As a final thought, we should point out that the academic economists are quick to ignore the 'insignificant ones', especially the reformers of currency. Johannsen, Foster and Catching, Hobson, and Gesell, all had brilliant contributions to make in their days, but they were not listened to. It is hoped that in the future, the economists lend more collective sympathy to those who possess great economic intuition.
>
> (Klein 1952: 185–6)

How should one view the contributions of Gesell, when they are surrounded by so much controversy? It is the opinion of this author that the doctrine of Gesell should be considered as an original contribution originating from the economic facts of the Argentina of his time, even when such ideas had been displayed before in the writings of other thinkers, such as Law, Proudhon, and Paltauf (Paltauf 1847). Gesell's system would lie between the modern doctrines of 'social liberalism' and 'liberal socialism'. Even if Gesell's theory of interest is not technically sound, it should be viewed as a forerunner of the monetary manipulation technique for combatting fiscal cycles. In addition, Gesell wrote on ideas such as the monetary theory of economic fluctuations, and the idea of economic growth made possible by a stable monetary system. Further proof of this author's stance in defence of Gesell can be found in the monumental work of that giant of economic thought, Keynes, and in works by other important figures already mentioned. Also worthy of mention is Gesell's doctrine on actual economic life. Support of his importance in this respect can be found in the monetary manipulation in Argentina's legislation (1899), or in the monetary reforms carried out in Bavaria (1919), or in the experiments with interest-free currency in Schwanenkirchen (1931) and Wörgl (1932), and also in the movement produced in Switzerland in 1950 by plebiscite to introduce numerical monetary indices. Finally, I would like to close by noting that to Gesell is owed the merit of having been a forerunner of today's International Monetary Fund.

17

RAÚL PREBISCH

The same age which produces great philosophers and politicians, renowned
generals and poets, usually abounds with skillful weavers and ship
carpenters. . . . The spirit of the age affects all the arts; and the minds of men,
being once roused from their lethargy and put into a fermentation . . . carry
improvements into every art and science.

(Hume 1928: 31)

During the ministerial meeting of the twenty-first conference period of the
Economic Commission of the United Nations for Latin America (or CEPAL
in Spanish), celebrated on 23–5 April 1986 in Mexico, Raúl Prebisch gave
his last speech, in which he reiterated to the developed countries his
renowned thesis that

> the politics of adjustment always fall back on the weakest elements of
> the system. In the specific case of debt, the weakest elements are the
> countries in development. . . . The debt is basically a problem of polit-
> ical character that requires future vision and understanding of the
> grave dangers which blossom upon the earth.

These ideas were developed in his posthumous *La Crisis del Desarrollo
Argentino (Prebisch 1986), particularly the matter of the political character of the
debt.*

Days later, he was back in the Chilean CEPAL centre, where he continued
to work, by then as director of *La Revista de la CEPAL*. Prebisch had his residence at the foot of the mountain range in Cajón de Maipo, near Santiago,
Chile, and it was there that death surprised him in the dawn of 29 April, at
the age of 85. The news was spread to the world by CEPAL, whose telex of
the same day had as its title: 'Latin America lost its most prominent
economist'.

There is no doubt that Raúl Prebisch was one of the Latin American
economists with the highest international prestige of the last four decades.
The news of his death jolted the scientific and political world. The press
emphasized on its front pages that 'a prominent Argentinian' (Jaime de
Pinies, Spain), 'a giant in the world of development' (Carlos Alzamora,

Perú), 'the fundamental guide in the formulation of Latin American development policies' (Sebastián Alegrett, secretary of SELA), 'a great Argentinian and a great American' (Gabriel Valdés, president of Chile's Christian Democrat party), 'the most influential Latin American economist of all times' (Celso Furtado, Brazil) had died. His fatherland, by a special decree, adhered to a period of mourning caused by the loss of one who had always responded to his country's call by liberally offering his advice, without hesitation, at crucial times. CEPAL, the organization founded and directed by Prebisch between the years 1950–63, manifested that his death 'caused great anguish for everyone at CEPAL'. In New York, the representatives of 159 member countries meeting in the General Assembly of the United Nations had a minute of silence, as a homage to the 'figure of great stature in the history of the United Nations' (Javier Pérez de Cuéllar, Secretary General of the UN); in Santiago, Chile in the hall of honour of CEPAL, where his followers, collaborators, and admirers, together with the special delegations of almost all Latin American nations rendered him homage, the requiem mass was celebrated by the ex-primate of the Chilean Catholic church, Cardinal Raúl Silva Henríquez.

With the death of Prebisch, economic science lost a man who dedicated to it his untiring will for exploration and construction for sixty-six years. His first steps, certainly of initiation in scientific labour through critical commentaries and briefs, are testified to by his publications, beginning in June 1919 in *La Revista de Ciencias Económicas* of Buenos Aires. Shortly before his death, he managed to correct and have ready to send for printing his final work, dedicated to the real analysis of Argentina's economic situation.

His formative years were also years of study and work. Prebisch was born on 17 April 1901 in Tucumán, Argentina to an Alsatian father of German origin and Linares Uriburu, his mother, who was of old inter-mixed colonial roots. In an interview granted to Agustín R. Maniglia (*La Nación*, Buenos Aires), Prebisch said:

> I completed my primary studies and went to the third year in a national secondary school run by French Lourdist fathers, who taught me to read and write in Spanish and in French, in my province of Tucumán. I am Tucumanian, of a mother from Salta, and a graduate of the National College [high school] of Jujuy, where I received my diploma at the age of seventeen. Then, I came to study economic science in the same department at the National University, where I graduated as a public accountant and from where I graduated with a PhD in 1923. And I worked as a research assistant in the same department from my second year and this is how I paid for my education.
>
> (Maniglia 1985: 3)

We should add that he worked as an assistant under the direction of Alejandro Bunge, another no less famous or great Argentinian economist, at the Institute of the Cost of Living and Acquisitive Power of Money, which Bunge had created and directed, beginning in 1919. From such timber, what a chip, we would say with pride and complacency. Prebisch was and continues to be a coveted model for all generations of Argentinian and Latin American youth who feel a vocation for the study of economic science.

The scientific production of Raúl Prebisch has been the object of various collections, but after effecting a very reduced test of just the first years of his performance in the science, I am convinced that the bibliographic inventory of his writings remains a task to be undertaken. But even so, if we only take the three most important collections that have been done recently, we come to no less than 150 works published by Prebisch whilst working as an investigator, teacher, director of institutes, magazines, and great enterprises of both national and international character.

The long list of publications cannot be analysed, or even mentioned here, as this would occupy seven or eight pages. But what should be emphasized is that this impressive list, in which figure at least some twenty works which span a great area, can only be compared to the prodigious scientific production of Prebisch's teacher Alejandro Bunge, just to give one example from the list of our great late colleagues. Also, I think that Prebisch's complete works, which were recently compiled by the Fundación Raúl Prebisch in a collection in three volumes (Prebisch 1992), will be objects of painstaking study and reflection, as much by the present generation of Latin American economists as by those to come. These complete works can be considered one of the most coveted legacies for the history of economic thought, be it at the national, Latin American, or even the world level.

The fundamental idea that shapes Prebisch's theory is the centre-periphery concept that, as students of economics know, has its beginnings in the works of Friedrich List (1848), popularized in Argentina by Vicente Fidel López, professor of political economy in 1874–6, and also in Alejandro Bunge's *Revista de Economía*, beginning in 1918. From this idea Prebisch infers all the rest of his analytical and political economic ideas: the imperative of industrialization; the tendency towards deterioration of exchange rates; structural inflation and unemployment; the imperative of a common market; and the discipline of Latin American development. Prebisch's doctrine has been the source of inspiration for various generations of Latin American economists. Therefore, he was not only the founder of a school of Latin American economics, but also a social engineer of the planning of the economic and social development of Latin America.

The best critical demonstration of Prebisch's doctrine at the time of his greatest splendour was done by Dr Roberto T. Alemann in *The Economic Thought of Prebisch – The Theory of the Peripheral Economy*, published originally in German (Alemann 1955a), later in Italian (Alemann 1955b), and in Spanish (Alemann 1956). Authors today who objectively study the present evolution of the economic thinking of Prebisch include Isidro Parra-Peña, in the prologue to the *Obras Escogidas de Raúl Prebisch* (Selected Works of Raúl Prebisch) (Consuegra 1981), and Benjamin Hopenhayn in 'Algunas Notas sobre el "Capitalismo Periférico" de Raúl Prebisch' in *Desarrollo Económico* (1982).

I must not forget to mention that Prebisch has been the object of many distinctions, of many honorary doctorates from universities in Argentina and throughout the world, and also of awards and distinctions granted by international organizations. The list would be too long to enumerate here. On the other hand, I would like to say that at the beginning of 1985, Prebisch wanted to honour his fellow Argentinian economists and thus joined the Argentinian Association of Political Economy, the only Argentinian member adhering to the International Economists Association. What is more, he actively participated in its twentieth annual congress, held in Mendoza (Argentina) in November 1985, where he gave the inaugural address on 'Latin American periphery in the global crisis of capitalism', and where he received his last honorary doctorate, this time from the National University in Mendoza.

For quite some time, in specialized volumes, in Argentinian and Latin American textbooks, and even in some of the works on the history of economic thought, both in Argentina and worldwide, the contributions of Prebisch have been the object of attentive consideration. Besides, I should like to recall some of the works of the last two decades that have been published in his honour: the work of Dr Luis Eugenio Di Marco, *International Economics and Development: Essays in Honour of Raúl Prebisch* (Di Marco 1972); of Dr José Consuegra, who in his *Antología del Pensamiento Económico y Social de América Latina* incorporates as a third volume the *Obras Escogidas de Raúl Prebisch* (Consuegra 1981); the anthology of Dr Adolfo Gurrieri, *La Obra de Prebisch en la CEPAL – Antología de Textos 1949–1982* (Gurrieri 1982); and finally, the collection of the last conferences of Raúl Prebisch given in part in Buenos Aires, published under the direction of Dr Bernardo Grinspun, *Raúl Prebisch, contra el Monetarismo* (Grinspun 1982).

As regards the essence of Prebisch's thought, the current of permanent renovation and mutation in his ideas has lately been much insisted upon. This is true, if looking at his gradual estrangement from the neo-classical school of thought, in which Prebisch received instruction from Luis Roque Gondra, another great master among masters of the post-First World War economics scene in Argentina. Prebisch stimulated this vision of confrontation with neo-classicism recently in his last books, also emphasized in his *Five Stages in My Thinking of Development* (Prebisch 1982), later translated into Spanish under the title, 'Cinco Etapas de mi Pensamiento sobre el Desarrollo' (Prebisch 1983), in *Trimestre Económico*.

Prebisch's heterodoxy, if this term can be used, is very close to another heterodoxy which also arose in Argentina, and whose author, Silvio Gesell, developed his doctrine during his stay in Argentina at the end of the last

271

century. Gesell was remembered by Keynes as one of the forerunners of Keynesian economics.

Rather than by changes and mutations, Prebisch's methodology is characterized by enlargements. To the analysis of the dynamic forces produced by the centre on the periphery, is added the study of internal dynamics of the Latin American periphery. Prebisch's viewpoint is quite similar to my course given at the University of San Marcos of Lima in 1963, entitled 'Regional development of Latin America'. My course used the language of spatial economic theory, which reinforced my feeling of confidence in Prebisch's theories, which I have also used since then in my *Introducción a la Ciencia Económica Contemporánea* (Popescu 1960, 1964c, 1968d, 1985).

Therefore, the grandeur of the writings of Prebisch, which starts with his work *Capitalismo Periférico: Crisis y Transformación* (Prebisch 1981), is the methodological widening that today is credited to Schumpeter, but really had been favoured since 1750 by David Hume. I believe that Prebisch's overall views on the Latin American system, with his feeling of incorporating not only economic variables, but also political, social, and cultural variables into the analysis, will signal the beginning of a new landmark in the history of Latin American economic thought. Of course, in his work many of the problems posed are susceptible to discussion, but this will also be fruitful.

On the other hand, it seems to me it is important to emphasize the constancy, over a period of sixty-six years of scientific labour, of the set of characteristics of his social philosophy, economic theory, and regional political economic theory, which together make up his fundamental economic doctrine. Above everything else, it is his social philosophy that has an impressive constancy, even allowing for Prebisch's occasional oscillations. One could read the articles written in the 1920s and compare them to his five-stage doctrine (presented at the Sixth Congress of the World Economists Association in 1980), which is related to the imperative need for efficient intervention by the state to guarantee the social usage of the economic surplus. Prebisch claims that:

> In substance, there are only two forms of regulatory action: that the state control the property and the force of the means of production, from which arises the surplus; or that the state use the surplus with collective rationality without concentrating property in its hands, but socially spreading it. Let it be said in passing, the great failures of the system do not arise from property itself, but in the private appropriation of the surplus and the noxious consequences of concentrating the means of production. It deals with two versions fundamentally different from socialism by their political and economic significance. Then, as the first is incompatible with the primordial concept of democracy and inherent human rights, the second makes possible the

certain compatibility of this concept in theory and in practice, just as with the vigour of development and distributive equality. . . . The transforming option that attempts to find itself on these pages represents a synthesis between socialism and liberalism. Socialism as regards collective decision, the pace of accumulation and the state regulating accumulation and distribution. Liberalism as regards the voluntary provision of capital as well as essentially consecrating economic freedom, intimately united with political freedom in its primitive philosophical version.

(Prebisch 1981: 47–9)

It must be also noted that this formulation of Prebisch, exposed in the above mentioned conference, was by no means isolated, for it was almost exactly reproduced in his book *Capitalismo Periférico: Crisis y Transformación* (Prebisch 1981).

Another constant in his analytical and political-economic apparatus is the concept of social justice, so dear to the social doctrine of the Church and which Prebisch designates with the terms 'equity' and 'social equity'. This analytical orientation should not be surprising in the admirer and translator of Adolf Wagner, attested to by Prebisch since November 1919.

Prebisch died in full brilliancy and in full activity. And he died exercising the position of director of *La Revista de la CEPAL* at the age of 85 years, a position similar to that which he held at the beginning of his career. Actually, in May 1921, the director of *La Revista de Ciencias Económicas* of the department of economic sciences at the University of Buenos Aires was none other than Raúl Prebisch – at the age of 20. What an extraordinary lesson given to all the economists of the world.

NOTES

2 INDIAN ECONOMICS

1 This book had three editions besides that of Buenos Aires: a second edition published in Paris (J. Smith's Press) in 1827 in two small volumes that can be found in the City Library of La Paz, Bolivia; and a third edition dating from 1831, published in Madrid by M. Burgos, that can be found in the library of the Colegio de Buenos Aires.

2 The anonymous translation of 'A Treatise on Political Economy in Santafé of Bogotá', published in 1810, caused a great shock at that time and remained for a long time a mystery in Colombia and thus attracted many scholars to investigate the mentioned work, causing an important discussion on the subject. Thus the interest in this anonymous author was kept alive for so long, until Professor Popescu, on the occasion of a UNDP mission to Colombia was confronted with the text, and produced a paper called 'A Treatise of Political Economy in Santafé de Bogotá in 1810: The Enigma of Father Diego Padilla' (Popescu 1968b: 360–472) in which Padilla's treatise is reproduced. The subject interests not only economists, managers, politicians and historians of Colombia: Padilla's work is of importance to all Latin American scholars. Colombian historians will find new elements to the discussion of Suarezism versus encyclopaedism, economists and administrators will be surprised by the systematic approach to these topics by Padilla, while politicians will find in his writings that he adhered to many ideas which are cherished by them today.

3 JUAN DE MATIENZO AND TOMÁS DE MERCADO

1 Juan de Matienzo published the following works of interest: *Dialogus Relatoris et Advocati Pintiani Senatus* (Valladolid 1558); *Commentaria in Librum Quintum Recollectionis Legum Hispaiae* (Madrid 1580); and *Gobierno del Perú* (Chuquisaca 1567). Matienzo was born on 22 February 1520 in Valladolid, where he studied at the university and graduated in law. After seventeen years of working for the Audience in Valladolid, he was appointed magistrate of the Audience of Charcas and remained as such from 7 September 1561 until his death on 15 August 1579. If Mercado founded a Mexican School of economics, then Matienzo should be given the credit for founding the School of Chuquisaca in Latin America.

2 The fundamental work of Fray Tomás de Mercado is, for our purposes, the *Summa de Tratos y Contratos*, published in Salamanca in 1569 and re-edited in

274

Seville in 1571 and 1587. According to the contemporary Spanish publishers, Mercado was born in Seville in 1525, while Nicolás Antonio (1684) and Wilhelm Weber (1962) both stated that he was born in Mexico. There are no doubts about his incorporation as a very young student in the convent of Santo Domingo in Mexico, or that he obtained the degree of Master in Theology in the University of Mexico as well as that he was a lecturer in the convent of that city. Once Mercado had the manuscript of his *Summa*, he went to Spain to publish it, his doctrine being elaborated upon the realities of the Indian economic life, and shared by his order in the Mexican province (Dávila Padilla 1596). In 1575, after the great success of the two editions of his work, Mercado decided to return to Mexico. During his return journey, he fell ill and died within sight of the shores of his beloved country. His body rests in the waters of San Juan de Ullúa (Veracruz). His work is one of the most important, not only at the American, but also at the universal level, as was already reported by Sayous (1928) and Weber (1962).

3 The work has also enjoyed an editorial success, which can be proved by a second edition from the office of Pedro Madrigal in Madrid, 1597, and a third edition from the printing house of Luis Sánchez in 1613 in Madrid.

4 The royal permit for the printing of the work was granted in Madrid, 28 February 1579, but it is not known if this news reached La Plata de los Charcas before the death of Matienzo, which occurred five and a half months earlier. For a more complete orientation upon the life and work of Matienzo, one should consult the excellent monograph (Lohmann Villena 1966: 35) and notes 1–8, in which is also found a bibliographical listing of the previous works on Matienzo.

5 Due to the generous subsidy by the National Council of Scientific and Technical Research of the Argentine Republic (CONICET in Spanish), I have been able to count on the assistance of two experienced Latin translators, Juan Carlos del Pino and Marino Ayerra, who were in charge of putting into Spanish part of the work by Matienzo.

6 'Your Royal Catholic Majesty: Since arriving to this city (La Plata) where I am serving in the position of Magistrate, which Your Majesty entrusted to me for the next eight years, I have written some letters giving advice as to what seemed to me to be advantageous for this land and its conservation and for the increase in the royal treasury without prejudicing anyone. . . . To compile in a better order that which I have written and many other things, I remembered to write a book which is entitled, *Gobierno del Perú* (Government of Peru) in which I deal with many subjects touching upon good government and the police, as much for the Indians . . . as for the Spaniards. . . . Likewise, in this period, I have written another book which I entitled "Stilo de Chancelleria" (Stylus of Chancellery), with the text in Romance language and the glossary in Latin, in which are examined many practical problems which arise in the chancelleries every day . . . which I also direct to Your Majesty and because they have cost me a lot of labour and I believe them to be fruitful, I wish for them to be printed, even though with my poverty and multitude of children, I do not know if I can do this at my expense. I plead of Your Majesty that you send for to see them and examine them and finding them to be all that I have mentioned, you will grant me a permit to be able to print them . . . ' (Levillier 1918: I, 236).

7 There is an edition prepared under the direction of, and with the preliminary analysis written in French by Guillermo Lohmann Villena, published under the auspices of the Ministry of Foreign Relations of France (in the collection

Travaux de l'Institut Français d'Etudes Andines, 11), in Paris and Lima, 1967. An important role has been played by the work prepared by the Department of Philosophy and Letters at the University of Buenos Aires in 1910, even though today it is known that it actually deals with a 'Relación del Libro Intitulado Gobierno del Perú, que Hizo el Licenciado Matienço, Oydor de la Ciudad de La Plata' ('Account of the Book entitled Government of Peru, written by Matienço, Magistrate of the City of La Plata'), which means that it is simply a summary or briefing on the work and not the work itself, as is indicated in Lohmann Villena (1966: 93).

8 This work of Matienzo of 1576 is unfortunately lost. 'The "Stylus of Chancellery" did not enjoy the luxury of being viewed by the public and is known only through references' (Lohmann Villena 1966: 90). But, Abecia makes the following marginal note: 'Solorzano and Francisco Gutiérrez de Escobar [of Chuchuito] have taken advantage of the Latin tract entitled "Stilum Cancellariae"' (Abecia 1939: 95).

9 One of the few authors who occupies himself with the *Commentaria* of Matienzo says: 'This work consisted of a detailed glossary of the book concerning the jurisprudential regulation of the family under Philippine law' (Lohmann Villena 1966: 91). The reflection regarding the family of this untiring researcher can be shared with my own, as long as it is understood to mean the family broadened as much in the quantitative sense as in the qualitative one, particularly in the world of the problems that are posed in Xenophon's *Oikonomikos* and Aristotle's *Oikonomika*.

10 His work, which for more than a century has occupied a special place in the universal history of economic thought (later Schumpeter chooses it as a proto-type of Hispanic scholasticism, but without knowing that Mercado was Mexican), enters into subjects which could have led to the title being changed to *Economic Policy*. The work is divided into six areas: the natural law; the treaty of the merchants; the pragmatic of wheat; exchange; usury; and restitution.

11 The Hispanic hue in Matienzo's thinking is inspired in Diego de Covarrubias y Leyva (1512–77), Domingo de Soto (1494–1560), and as indirect sources, Francisco de Vitoria (1480–1546), who is known to Matienzo thanks to Soto's work (Soto 1968).

12 Roover's opinion that the principle of social or common valuation had a distinct origin, is not founded. For reference, please see Roover (1968), where it is stated: 'The medieval glossarists added the phrase *sed communiter* (but in common) to the principle, according to which goods are valued by what they are sold for (*res tantum valet, quantum vendi potest*)' (Roover 1968: 731). This is true, but it is not all the truth. The plain truth is that the doctrine was formu-lated by Paulo and unanimously accepted by the theologians and jurisconsultants of a Christian orientation and that, for this reason, the axiom of *res tantum valet had to be changed*.

13 John Duns Scotus (1254–1308) was contemporary with Thomas Aquinas, though much younger; he was probably born in Scotland, and was considered a great philosopher and theologian, 'main ornament of the Order of Saint Francis'. He taught in Oxford, Paris and Cologne. For further reference see Gilson (1946: 183–96).

14 From his professorship at the University of Salamanca between 1526 and 1544, Francisco de Vitoria (1480–1546) gives new impulse to the scholastic school (here the expression 'Hispanic Scholastic School' is much more appropriate than the 'School of Salamanca' coined in the Anglo-Saxon world) through his writings and especially through his students. A true teacher among teachers,

his effort found a response in the brilliant fulfilment of duty by three of his students: Diego de Covarrubias y Leyva; Dr Navarro (Martín de Azpilcueta) (1493–1586); and Domingo de Soto (1495–1560), whose writings, along with those of the other teacher of Salamanca, Juan de Medina (1495–1560), are found on the reading table of de Matienzo and are consulted and quoted in an assiduous manner. It is precisely the writings of these authors, followed by another dozen of the great writers who continued in their efforts, which still today are the subject of attentive consultation and study by the historians of the economic thought of the Hispanic Scholastics. A fine image of the impulse taken in this area will be formulated through the readings of the following authors: Höffner 1941; Roover 1955: 161–190; Weber 1959, 1962; Larraz 1963.

15 In agreement with the cover of his work, 'De Contractibus Licitis atque Illicitis Tractus Conradi Summenhart de Calw', first edition, Hagenau (1500), reprinted in Venecia (1580), the author should be called Conrado Summenhart de Calw, but while the Spanish scholastics refer to him only as Conrado (from the Latin Conradus), in the modern German bibliography he figures as Konrad Summenhart. Conradus was born in the Calw in the state of Württemberg (in the southwest of Germany) between the years 1450 and 1460. He studied at Heidelberg, Tubingen, and Paris and afterwards was named professor at the University of Tubingen. He figures along with Saint Anthony (1389–1459) and Johannes Nider (1380–1438) among the three most important Thomistic theologians of the fifteenth century, in the area of scholastic economic ethics. The main subject of his lifetime studies, as was the case with Nider, was the treaties and contracts of merchants. His work culminated in 1500 with the publication of his work in Hagenau. Two years later, on 20 October 1502, he died in the monastery at Schuttern. This brief note on the life and work of Conrado is owed to Joseph Höffner, whose work has here been textually transcribed. We are also in debt to him for a detailed critical analysis of the Contracts of Conradus, 'the most minutely precise and mature work on economic ethics of the fifteenth century' (Höffner 1941: 84–96, 103).

16 Höffner identifies José Anglés (1500–87) and Domingo Bañez (1528–1604) as open defenders of the thesis of Conrado-Soto-Matienzo; and Weber (1962: 88) mentions Francisco de Vitoria and Diego de Covarrubias, as well as Luis Saravia de la Calle and Luis Lopez (1500–95) as followers of the same criterion. By this way, when the generation of Luis Molina (1535–1600), Juan de Lugo (1583–1660) and Leonard Lessius (1554–1623) came along, it can be said with total certainty that the idea had been floated for a long time in the environment and, consequently, the merit of this latter group, so celebrated by contemporary foreign critics, was actually much weakened.

17 Taking notice of the Hispanic scholastics, and especially the last generation of them, is neither a matter of the present nor of yesterday. Almost a century ago, the Belgian Catholic economist Victor Brants wrote the following in his seventh book dedicated to the history of economic thought: 'Theologians study and examine (from the fifteenth century to the eighteenth century) the new deeds, attempting to maintain the crushing moral rule: it is important to point out the economic writings of Lessius in Belgium (1583–1600), Luis de Molina, Cardinal de Lugo (1583–1660), etc., who are rarely quoted in economic histories' (Brants 1908: 239). What is more, in a work published in 1895, although obliged to limit his research to the thirteenth and fourteenth centuries, Brants does not miss the opportunity in the body of the work to refer to the

Scholastics of the sixteenth and seventeenth centuries and their more representative writers.

18 According to the study of Sierra Bravo, it is affirmed, though with certain reserve, that Mercado based the just price on the 'objective theory of value with a basis on costs' (Sierra Bravo 1973: 293). This is a false statement. A correction, or better, retraction by the author written a few lines below, ratifies the opposite thesis. But with all this, serious damage has been done to the actual edition of the work of Mercado and even greater damage to the unprepared reader or, which is even more possible, to the reader who trusts in the scientific director of the re-edited work.

19 Matienzo could have been more open-minded and could have incorporated two other sources from ancient Greco-Roman times, Xenophon (430–355 BC) and Pliny the Elder (23–79 AD), whose writings he knew, but which he ignored and which in general are ignored even today, thus disregarding important contributions to the theory of subjective value. Ignorance of the work of Xenophon was not grave, as his reflections were assimilated by Aristotle. More important was the failure arising from the ignorance of the theory of value according to Pliny. But this was overcome by Davanzatti (1529–1606), a fervent scholar of the scholastic doctrines, an Italian contemporary of Matienzo, who in 1588, by joining the theory of the mouse of Saint Augustine with that of the mouse of Pliny the Elder, managed to untangle the threads of what was later known as the 'paradox of value'.

20 'This passage attracted profound attention for centuries of scholastic thought and it can be found, quoted directly or paraphrased, in almost all the important treatments of the subject' (Dempsey 1935: 64).

21 It was impossible to locate the work by Conrado de Summenhart, but by the study performed by Höffner (1941: 87), we can deduce that what was assumed by Matienzo was correct.

22 I believe Edgar Salin is right when claiming that we are not faithful to the particular and historical sense of the Latin concept of 'complacibilitas' if we translate it – as Roover does – as 'désir ou besoin', which lacks the subjective character of value (Salin 1967: 37). This reference to Salin – despite its polemic character – is most useful for the lexicon of our science. And Salin's reference to Roover can be extended to Schumpeter who uses 'desiredness' for the concept of Saint Bernardino and Saint Augustine. Besides, it is also false when Schumpeter says that 'complacibilitas' is the equivalent of Professor Fisher's 'desiredness' (Schumpeter 1971: 137). The author who introduced this concept in the economic lexicon was Charles Gide since 1883 and called 'désirabilité' (Gide 1929). Fisher 'doing nothing but following Professor Gide's example' incorporates it in his book (Fisher 1915). And finally, Professor Griziotti Kretschmann claims that 'Saint Anthony adds to the subjective elements of utility and scarcity, which are not enough to determine value, the concept of complacibilitas, that is the merit, an objective quality of the good that also affects the price' (Griziotti Kretschmann 1951: 38).

23 'Prima conclusio: Pretia rerum non secundum ipsarum naturam aestimanda sunt, sed quatenus in usus veniunt humanos. Conclusionis huius ratio naturalis est, quod cum mundus & quae eo continentur propter hominem facta sint, tanti civili aestimatione res valent quantum hominibus inserviunt. Qua propter Arist. 5 Eticorum cap. 5 ait indigentiam causam mesuramque esse humanarum commutationum. Si enim nullus alterius re vel opera indigeret, omnis cessaret commutation rerum humanarum: ergo indigentia admetiri debemus pretia' (Soto 1556: Libri Decem, Tomo 2, Book 6, Q. 2, Art. 3).

24 With this, new light is shed on the thesis of the subjective theory of value in

Thomas Aquinas. For further reference see Hollander 1965: 616–20; Spiegel 1971: 83ff; Curia 1980: 77–150.

25 'Molina even introduces the concept of competition by stating that concurrence or rivalry among buyers will enhance prices . . . ' (Roover 1955: 169).

26 'Luis de Molina employed, without doubt for the first time as had been emphasized by Joseph Höffner since 1941, the expression concurrence among the buyers' (Willeke 1961: 10). The fact that this author remembers Höffner's discovery can be interpreted as a reference to Raymond de Roover, in the article quoted in the previous footnote, who if he knows about the work of Höffner does not mention it in relation to this subject, as he should have done.

27 It was precisely in 1528 in Madrid that King Charles and Queen Jane, in the Royal Decree related to the 'advanced purchase of bread', incorporated as a norm of economic right, that the 'public granaries of the cities . . . of these rulers . . . be favoured in the said advanced purchase of bread, to all ecclesiastical and lay persons, who concur to buy bread, which would not be purchased'. Matienzo incorporates this law into his *Commentaria* (Title 11, Law 19) and takes advantage of the opportunity to add a glossary which he entitles 'Concurren a comprar pan, que no estuviere comprado' (They go to buy bread, which would not be purchased). It is not difficult to construct the bridge between this norm of common right and the sources of the doctrine and jurisprudence which should have been accumulated in the area of 'concurrence' in a market such as that for bread (wheat, barley and derived products), in which reigned the most rigorous fixation of prices (the bread tariff).

28 The jurisconsultant Julio Paulus was one of the most productive Roman authors in the economic field. On speaking on the origin of the exchange of goods and the functions of money, he left a text which is quoted with extraordinary frequency in the Scholastic and later writings until our own day, and in which appears the word that is of such interest for our subject. The entire text is reproduced in *Palgrave's Dictionary of Political Economy*, 1894–9, reprinted in the 1963 revised edition in Vol. 3, p. 20.

29 This admiration could be due in part to the fact that Covarrubias was in the favour of the President of the Council of Castilla. It is certain that throughout the length and breadth of the bibliographical documentation to the *Commentaria*, the only author to whom the respectful title of 'Don' is given, is Covarrubias. In this sense, the reflection made in the first paragraph in the present footnote is correct. But I doubt very much that the admiration arose from such a modern source. I believe that an author, above all a man of science such as Matienzo, could not dedicate his work to Covarrubias due to cheap Phoenician reasons. It is true that when Covarrubias died in 1577, Matienzo transferred his dedication to the Bishop of La Paz, Mauriño de Pazos, but this in no way diminishes the feeling of admiration that was attested to by the disciple of Vitoria.

30 'Prices rise with the abundance of buyers, but with their scarcity they go down; while the abundance of sellers leads to the lowering of prices and their scarcity, rises prices' (Soto 1556: Book 6, Q. 2, Art. 3, fourth conclusion).

31 'We see in the market that if there is lots of clothes, they are cheap; if there are few buyers, even cheaper; and even more so if there is not much money. On the contrary, if there are just a few clothes in the market, they are expensive, more so if there are many buyers and even more if there is plenty of money' (Mercado 1977: 41). Mercado not only suggests a general formulation of Soto's idea but also seems to point to the fact that what would later be called 'the paradox of value' has no sense since it is evident that there are things which, though very

useful to life, are given for free or even wasted or burnt when there is abundance of them.

32 It is also very difficult for today's readers to understand the literal transcription of all the points of view which the author collected, and which support his own conclusions. Our modern tendency is to go more towards the other extreme, of disdaining or forgetting to mention not only those who taught us certain truths, but even the living authorities whose writings we use without making mention of them.

33 'We do not ignore', says Pliny in his *Natural History*, Book 35, last chapter, 'that prices ... change according to places and differ from year to year' (Matienzo 1580: Title 11, Law 1, Gl.2, No. 1).

34 'Also the person of the buyer, or the seller, sometimes increases and sometimes decreases the price, as when the seller is surrounded by debts or if given guarantees. . . . Then real estate is worth less when it is difficult to claim it' (Matienzo 1580: Title 11, Gl.2, No. 34).

35 'The value of the house, object of the sale, also diminishes if one has an evil and quarrelsome neighbor. . . . To the contrary, the house or the fund have higher value if there are good neighbors' (Matienzo 1580: Title 11, Gl.2, No. 35).

36 In general, Matienzo refers the reader to de Soto's work, where besides the condemnation of monopolies for the injustice of its prices, it distinguishes between the monopolies of sellers whether they be individual or collective which 'increase the price', and the monopolies of purchasers with the aim of decreasing the prices, and finally de Soto has a clear idea of bilateral monopolies, even though he does not use this name: 'When the sellers constituted their monopoly, in this case the purchasers, repelling force by force, they will be able to serve fairly the contrary agreement, for example, to pact among themselves that no one buy more expensively than an indicated price' (de Soto 1556: Book VI). Broadening de Soto's doctrine, Juan de Matienzo mentions the case of the monopolies of the artisans, who agree not to teach their trade to any others, and the royal monopoly on the selling of salt, which he condemns as unjust. In the *Gobierno del Perú*, he suggests that there should be no government monopoly in Potosí since it will all be more expensive.

37 Luis Saravia de la Calle, contemporary of Matienzo, coined a phrase in his *Instrucción a los Mercaderes*, published in 1544, that is related to auctions: 'because he who sells pleading ordinarily sells cheaper than he who pleads to sell' (Weber 1962: 89). Molina stated that the fall in prices in auctions could even come to 30 per cent.

4 SCHOLASTIC ECONOMICS

1 Bartolomé de Albornoz published his *Arte de los Conctratos* in Valencia in 1573. In the last two centuries, his name has been written as Díaz Albornoz (Canga Argüelles 1808), Bartolomé Frías de Albornoz (Iparraguirre 1954), Dr Frías (Picón Salas 1944), and Fray Bartolomé de Albornoz (Rahola 1885). This does not happen with the title of his book, which is always mentioned as *Arte de los Contratos*. He was born in Talavera, probably between 1510 and 1515, and studied law as a disciple of Diego de Covarrubias at the University of Osuna. He arrived in the Indies in 1150, and was the first professor of civil law in the recently founded University of Mexico. Due to his argumentative and aggressive spirit, his works were censored. It should be noted, however, that Nicolás Antonio, as well as Oñate and Solórzano, dared to quote him and the latter was quite flattering in his opinions about Albornoz. It is most important that in

his work, Albornoz asks questions and then supplies the answers in the best scholastic tradition. His doctrine was elaborated taking into account his American experience and probably also his experience as a teacher during his long stay at the University of Mexico. He died c. 1576.

2 Luis López (Ludovicus López) published his works, *Instructorium Conscientiae, Duabus Contentum Partibus* (Salamanca 1585) and the *Tractatus de Contractibus et Negotiationibus* (Salamanca 1589). The Dominican theologian was born in Madrid about 1530. He later came to Latin America where he worked as a missionary in the Chiapas and Guatemala provinces, and where *'plures anos Indorum saluti vigilanter incubuit'* (Antonio 1783–8). During his long stay in the New World, he became well acquainted with the policy carried out by the *encomenderos* as well as by the merchants. His two works reflect the large number of problems he had to confront in America. We do not know the exact date of his return to Spain, but we know that he returned to Madrid to induce King Philip II to do something to favour the natives. Höffner says that he became professor of theology at Salamanca (Höffner 1941). He also became provincial of the Dominican order in Spain. In Spain he supervised the publication of his two works which have had a profound influence in the scientific world due to the many editions and translations. He died in 1595.

3 Oñate published his work *De Contractibus*, distributed in four volumes with a total of 3,586 pages of two columns each, between 1646 and 1654. This work was rescued by Father Guillermo Furlong, who received the attention of the Argentinian jurist Vicente Osvaldo Cutolo (b. 1922), author of a paper entitled, 'La Primera Obra de Derecho Escrita en la Argentina del Siglo XVII' (The First Book of Law Written in Argentina in the XVII Century), which he published in 1954. Cutolo's work, which has been acknowledged by the Argentinian historian Vicente D. Sierra (1893–1982) (*Historia de la Argentina*, Buenos Aires, 1957), infers that this may be the first work in economics in the Argentina of this time. This is deduced because both parts of the third volume of *De Contractibus* were an economic treatise, probably the main writing of economic scholastics, and of outstanding dimension, which was centred around three major topics: bargain and sale; exchange; and usury. The fact that the bibliographic material used in its final part is centred around the first twenty years of the seventeenth century does support the hypothesis that the work dealing with economic topics could have been started in Oñate's days in Córdoba as 'provincial' of the Jesuit province of Paraguay (1615–24), though it is not denied that the accumulation of documents and the examination of the cases were probably done previously, in the period 1592–1614, when Oñate was teacher of novices in Lima and director of the schools of Potosí, La Paz and Chuquisaca. Shortly after the appearance of the last volumes of Oñate's work, there came another work called *Thesaurus Indicus* by Professor Diego de Avendaño (1594–1668) in six volumes (with a total of 2,500 pages in Latin, published in Antwerp, 1660–78). It is difficult to determine which of these two works is of greater significance. Still, if we limit ourselves to the grounds of our economic science, it seems to me that Diego de Avendaño could compete with Oñate, yet the former's strength does not lie in the analytical field where Oñate is outstanding but in the area of economic policy, in the wider sense of the term, including specific aspects of economic welfare in the area of social policy. We should emphasize the great effort made by Oñate to systematize and synthesize the many nuances which start to appear in the scientific production of the seventeenth century. In this sense, I think it is

correct to place Oñate on the same level with the great synthetic works of Juan de Lugo in Spain, and Giambattista de Luca in Italy.

It appears that Oñate was born in Valladolid on 7 January 1567. After graduating with a Bachelor of Arts degree from Salamanca and a degree in law from the University of Alcalá, where he also studied theology, we know that 'still as a student he was sent to Perú' under the supervision of Father Diego de Zúñiga, who obtained the authorization by royal decree on 11 July 1590, or when Oñate was 23 years old. He entered the Society of Jesus in 1586 and arrived in Lima in 1592. Oñate's professional and missionary formation was continued in Perú. From 1604–14, he was professor of philosophy of the Jesuit universities in Potosí, La Paz, and Chuquisaca. From 1615–24, he was provincial of the Jesuit province of Paraguay and Río de la Plata, and founded various schools but he also took great pains in ensuring a high educational standard at the University of Córdoba, which obtained papal recognition during his office, and whose ordinances were personally dictated by him. After this, Oñate retired to the Colegio Máximo of Lima, where he occupied important posts in the Jesuit province of Perú. He died a week before his eightieth birthday in Lima in 1646.

4 In 1791, Cyriaco Morelli's *Rudimenta Juris Naturae et Gentium* was published in Venice, in one volume of 388 pages. For more than one hundred years, the critics ignored this author with an Italian name who wrote in Latin. When, at the beginning of the present century, due to various testimonies at the end of the eighteenth century, these critics began their research, they finally discovered that the Italianized Morelli and the Hellenized Cyriaco (Kyrios in Greek, Dominicus in Latin, and Domingo in Spanish) was the pen name of Domingo Muriel. He was born at Tamanes, Salamanca in 1718 and joined the Society of Jesus in 1734, he was 'one of the most illustrious Latin American writers on a wide variety of subjects and the pride of the University of Córdoba del Tucumán', where he had been professor of philosophy (1751), moral theology (1753), and had also been elected president (1767), even though as a result of the expulsion of the Jesuits from the New World he was unable to hold this last position. Even more adverse was the destiny of his book, whose translation was not only poor, but whose editor continued to ignore Muriel's real name. He died in Faenza in 1795.

Muriel's work follows the line of late scholasticism, but to be able to evaluate it properly, we should remember that it was written in a period of upheaval brought about by the appearance of the *Encyclopaedia*, the United States Declaration of Independence, and the outbreak of the French Revolution. These events could not help but influence a book entitled *Elementos de Derecho Natural y Derecho de Gentes* (*Elements of Natural and Civil Law*). This work is rooted in the Aristotelian-Thomistic tradition and takes into consideration the works of the great Spanish and Latin American scholastics as well as those of the philosophers of the Enlightenment. In this way, Muriel established a strong link between the latter part of scholasticism (mid-sixteenth to seventeenth centuries) and neo-scholasticism (mid-nineteenth century). The doctrine of Muriel is one of the first scientific works to follow the line of the Spanish scholastics, but at the same time, it is one of the first to begin the renaissance of scholasticism in Europe, and in Hispanic America via Italy.

5 THE QUANTITY THEORY OF MONEY

1 It is not easy to determine precisely the references gathered by Matienzo of Cieza's *Chronicle of Perú*. This is due to the fact that the original of Matienzo's manuscript *The Government of Perú* up to now has not been found. Effectively, as he reported in his 'Letter to the King' of La Plata, 28 November 1567, with which he sent the original manuscript for approval and publication in Spain, this had 'marginal notes about philosophers, theologians and many other serious authors' (Levillier 1918: I, 238). Unfortunately Matienzo's original manuscript sent to the Counsel of Indies has 'disappeared into thin air' and none of the copies found up to now carry the original marginal notes made by Matienzo himself. The contemporary editor of the *Government of Perú*, Dr Guillermo Lohmann Villena, has found four or five of Matienzo's extracts of *The Chronicle of Cieza*, without specific mention in the corpus of the text. This is a sure indication that the scrupulous and learned magistrate of Chuquisaca has added his bibliographic learning to the marginal notes of the original manuscript. To elucidate this matter it is necessary to consult, in addition to the work of Guillermo Lohmann Villena, Juan de Matienzo, *Gobierno del Perú* (1567), Prologue in French by Guillermo Lohmann Villena, in the collection 'Travaux de l'Institut Français d'Etudes Andines', 11, Paris-Lima, 1967, especially all the references made on pages LXIX, 7, 89, 162, 275 and 332.

2 'I believe that the high prices we suffer come from three causes: the principal and almost the only one is the abundance of gold and silver; the second cause is due to the monopolies, the third to the penury originated by the exportations as by the ravage; the last is the entertainment of the kings and great lords, that raise the price of the things they like' in Jean Bodin, *Responses aux Paradoxes du Sire de Malestroit*, Paris 1568. The Spanish version of the text can be found in Popescu 1968d: 240.

3 In a letter to the king dated 23 December 1577, Juan de Matienzo has in mind the same image when he says that when using a new method of melting in the Potosinian mines, 'more silver could be extracted from those mines than iron extracted from Bizcaya' (Levillier 1918: 462).

6 INDO-AMERICAN DEVELOPMENT DOCTRINES

1 From the following text of the Italian humanist Pedro Martir, who was a member of the Counsel of the Indies, it is proved that there was a consciousness of the causes of the evils: 'You go to such separate worlds, so strange, so far away, by the currents of an ocean which seems to be like the rotating pattern of the heavens, distant from all authority, dragged down by the greedy blindness for gold, those from here go there as meek lambs, arriving there they become predatory wolves' (Hanke 1949: 146).

2 This fragment was discovered by the Mexican scholar, Nicolás Leon, and published in León, Mexico, in 1866.

3 In this manner More's *Utopia* had a double meaning in the history of Latin American culture: on the one hand, the work was elaborated by using the ideal state of the Golden Age of the Americas, the institutions of which are discovered with the help of the capable narrator Rafael Hitlodeo, imaginary companion of Vespucii, as a model; and on the other hand, the work serves as a model for Vasco de Quiroga, to convert it into the Magna Carta of the Hispanic Indian society. This famous work, *Libellus vere aureus nec minus salutaris quam festivus de optimo*

reipublicae statu, deque nova Insul Utopia, elaborated in 1515–1516, was published in 1516 and re-edited and translated many times.

4 This refers to the work *Luciani dialogi compluria ópuscula longe festissimo ab Erasmo Roterddamo et Thoma Moro interpretibus optimus in latinorum lingua traducta*, Paris 1506.

5 As is to be expected, there has arisen the inevitable discussion between Catholics and Marxists as regards the ideological interpretation of the Christian Republic of Quiroga. And as is also to be expected, Quiroga was influenced by the ideological nature of More's *Utopia*, since he follows this work in almost all its aspects. As is well known, the controversy as to the interpretation of More's work continues even today, with special intensity since the beatification of Thomas More by Pope Pius XI in 1935.

6 The Society of Jesus, confirmed by the pope in 1540, is reduced to an army of missionaries, upon whose flag, beside the three vows common to all the rest of the religious orders of personal poverty, chastity and unbreakable discipline, is inscribed a fourth vow: 'That when the Roman Pontifical . . . orders us as regards the saving of souls and the spreading of the faith, and to whichever territory he wishes to send us, we must carry it out exactly, without any tergiversation or excess.' The carrying out of this vow required qualifications, which in addition to virtue, obedience, and vocation, guaranteed the presence of adequate knowledge, corporal resistance, denial and humility. To be admitted into the Society of Jesus, the candidate underwent two years' trial, but in order to achieve the privilege of leaving as a missionary, these trials were extended to ten and even twenty years.

7 The bibliography on the Jesuit activities is large. (Astrain 1901–25; Pastells 1912–49; Hernández 1913; Lette 1938–50; Decorme 1941; Jouanen 1941–3; Santos 1943; Furlong 1962).

8 For a map of the distribution of the Jesuit reductions take a look at Felix Plattner's *Ein Reislaufer Gottes, des Abenteurlichen Leben der Schweizer Jesuiten Martin Schmid aus Baar (1694–1772)*.

9 Limiting myself only to the viceroyalty of the Río de La Plata, I shall recall some of the more brilliant names: Sánchez Labrador, geographer, botanist and linguist; Joaquín Camaño, encyclopaedist; Domingo Muriel, theologian, philosopher, jurist and historian; Tomás Falkner, ethnographer; Lorenzo Hervás y Panduro, philologist; Buenaventura Suárez, astronomer; Nicolás Techo, historian; we must not omit also the cultivators of economics, like Francisco Javier Iturri, to whom is attributed a 'Tratado acerca de los Males que España ha Sufrido por el Exceso de Oro proveniente de América y acerca de las Fábricas y Compañías de Comercio de España' ('Treatise concerning the Evils that Spain has Suffered due to the Excess of Gold coming from the Americas and concerning the Factories and Commercial Companies of Spain'). Further details may be found in Furlong 1946.

10 The main universities were: University of San Tomás in Santo Domingo, created in 1538 on the foundation of a Jesuit secondary school; the University of Mexico created by King Carlos V in 1551 on the foundation of the School of the Rosary of the Dominican friars, established in 1553 in the convent of Santo Domingo and transferred in 1574 to San Marcelo parish, where it remains to this day; San Francisco de Quito University, founded in 1586; and San Bartolomé University in Bogotá, Colombia, founded in 1610.

11 Colegio Máximó of Mexico founded in 1576; Colegio Máximó of Saint Peter and Saint Paul of Lima, founded in 1568; Academy of Sao Paulo, founded in 1554.

12 University of Loyola obtained such a level in 1622 above the basis of the Colegio Máximo of 1610. San Francisco Xavier University, founded in 1624 on the basis of the schools of Santiago and San Bautista of Chuquisaca, Xaverian University of Bogotá, founded in 1622.

13 'The crisis was undeniable and the true historian must not silence it . . . but, we let it be known that if the Jesuits did not found new settlements among the Guaranís, outside of that jurisdiction they founded and carried forward other towns of savage men, not any less difficult' (Furlong 1962: 631).

7 CAMERALISM

1 The work also contains a third part, 'Conservandum', which is indicated on the title page of the book, but it is not known if it was ever incorporated in the book.

2 'The Viceroyal Francisco de Toledo . . . foresaw the necessity that the tribunal had that it be understood only in this material without any dependence on another exercise . . . and thus, by the year 1607 it was resolved to erect of the Tribunal of Accountability, with all the necessary orders, instructions and form, communicating for the Royal Counsel of the Indies and the great Accountancy of Castilla, which influenced their jurisdiction and correct dispositions and their preeminences . . . they are three the Tribunals of Accountancy for all the Indies: one in New Spain and another in the New Kingdom; and another in Peru: "triad to which all the harmony of the accounts is charged"' (Escalona y Agüero 1941: 77).

8 JOSÉ CARDIEL

1 Guillermo Furlong discovered an unedited manuscript of Cardiel's, entitled 'Advertencias para las Consultas que Tratan de Haciendas, Compras y Ventas de Tierras y Pleitos Tocantes a Ellas' ('Warnings on the Consultations which Deal with Plantations, the Selling and Purchasing of Lands and Litigations which Touch upon Them'), which has Cardiel's signature and which is found in the Archivo de Loyola in Spain, and appears to be rich in economic reflections. As I have not had direct access to this manuscript, I must be content with the summary which Furlong made in this respect: 'An interesting work of an economic character to which Cardiel assigns many valuable data as to the colonial American economy. One can judge the value of this little work by the following lines: 'How is each league in Paraguay sold? My response is that I heard said that in the territory of Buenos Aires, or Río de La Plata which is the same, when I moved through those parts, each league was sold for 6,000 silver reals. . . . In the territory around the city of Santa Fé our school bought some land for grazing cattle of more than ten leagues in length and six or seven leagues in width for 13,000 pesos.' It is evident that the writing was elaborated while in exile, which is to say around 1770.

2 Thanks to the prolific bibliographic research, for which we are indebted to Guillermo Furlong, we know that José Cardiel had been working on this project since 1741. Actually, among the unedited writings of Cardiel mentioned by Furlong, we find at least three related to his project, the first of which is 'Dificultades que Suele Haber en la Conversion de los Infieles, y Medios para Vencerlas' ('Difficulties which Usually Arise in the Conversion of the Infidels, and Methods to Overcome Them'), 20 August 1741, now found

in the Biblioteca Nacional de Buenos Aires. The second book is entitled 'Dificultades que Hay en la Conversion de los Infieles de esta Provincia del Paraguay, y Medios para Vencerlas' ('Difficulties which Exist in the Conversion of the Infidels in this Province of the Paraguayan River, and Methods to Overcome Them'), which seems to be a slight variation of the first book, and is also found in the Biblioteca Nacional de Buenos Aires. Finally, in this triad is found 'Medios para Reducir a Vida Racional y Cristiana a los Indios que viven Vagabundos sin Pueblos ni Sementeras' ('Methods for Reducing to a Rational and Christian Life the Indians who live like Vagabonds without Towns or Cultivated Fields'), dated 11 January 1748 in Buenos Aires, and now found in the Archivo de la Provincia de Toledo, Madrid.

Again, we are in debt to Furlong for a summary of this valuable work: 'This writing is comprised of two parts divided into twenty-one points or numerations. The first part (numbers 1–11) is a succinct exposition of the variety of Indian races in existence in these regions, the variety of their languages, the multiplicity of their characteristics, the difficulty of forming towns or reductions and the scarcity of resources of an economic nature. This last point is of the greatest importance for Cardiel, and he does not hesitate in affirming that "the only method for the conversion for so many nations is to have a lot of money with which to be able to give them food, clothing and with which to pay many day labourers to make their houses and plots of ground" (number 12). In order to obtain this money, Cardiel proposes five methods (numbers 12–21), all of them based on mercantilism; diverse operations which should be carried out in the name of Our Lord; but whose product would come to benefit the missionaries and those to whom they preached. These methods are such, by Cardiel's judgement, that even though they may be a detriment to the Royal Exchequer they should not be allowed to not be put in motion, being so necessary for such Christian achievements; the more that they cause no damage, the sooner they should be increased'. Up to this point the quotation is Furlong's. The mention of mercantilism, which in Furlong's context has a derogatory flavour, has no substance, as the works of the Jesuits in the Indian settlements cannot be placed within the framework of the word mercantilism. Of course, all these works have been in the service of the economic and social development of our indigenous communities, and only in this sense could the works of the Jesuits and other religious orders be described as mercantilism. But even so, the fact that spiritual things were the ultimate objectives pursued by them, we should add as an attribute to this mercantilism, and name it without hesitation as Christian mercantilism, as it truly was. A second reflection on this manuscript, is that it definitely appears to be a broadening of the ideas put forth in the *Carta-Relación* of 1747.

9 COLOMBIAN ECONOMIC DEVELOPMENT

1 This chapter resulted from a speech entitled 'Economistas de la Costa' (Economists of the Coast), given upon receipt of an honorary doctoral degree from the Universidad del Atlantico, Barranquilla, Colombia, on 22 October 1971. The literature on economic development has reached unprecedented dimensions in the history of the social sciences. An orientation to this branch of economics is only possible through bibliographical works, although these are too numerous to mention here. Among the works we should mention are Arthur Hazlewood (1964) *The Economics of Development– An Annotated List of Books and Articles Published 1958–62*, Jacques Austry (1965) *Le Scandale du*

Développement and Hannah Stobbe (1965) *Methodisch-Theoretisch Schriftum zur Entwicklunswirtschaft und Schriftum zur Entwicklungs Politik.* Also in the field of development of underdeveloped countries we should keep in mind various works (UNESCO 1962; OECD 1964; Cookson and Tryon 1965; Waterston 1965; Wish 1965; BIRF 1966).

2 This current was crystallized in two great journals: *Administración y Desarrollo* (Bogotá), begun in 1962; and *Desarrollo Indoamericano,* (Barranquilla), begun in 1966.

3 Refer to *Estudios sobre las Condiciones de Desarrollo en Colombia,* published in 1958 by Centro de Economía y Humanismo, directed by Louis Joseph Lebret; *El Desarrollo Económico de Colombia,* a report produced by CEPAL in 1957 and *Bases de un Programa de Fomento para Colombia,* BIRF, mission led by Lauchlin Currie in 1950.

4 This author, one on whose ideas very little critical review has been done, has been given an excellent critique in Jaramillo Uribe 1964: 204–17.

10 THE ECONOMIC DEVELOPMENT OF ARGENTINA IN THE THINKING OF MANUEL BELGRANO

1 Son of a wealthy merchant, Domingo Belgrano y Peri, and of María González Casero, the creator of the Argentinian flag was born in 1770 in Buenos Aires. As Belgrano relates in his autobiography, in this city he learned his first letters, Latin grammar, philosophy, and a little theology. Afterwards, he left for Spain to study law in Salamanca, graduated from Valladolid, continued his studies in Madrid, and received his title as a lawyer in the Chancellery of Valladolid. Here his interest in economics was awakened. 'The ideas of political economy propagated in Spain with a fury, and I believe this to be the reason why I was placed in the secretariat of the Consulate in Buenos Aires.' While still in Spain, he translated from French the *Maxims of the Economic Government* of François Quesnay, the translation being published in Madrid in 1794. But his best known writing is another Spanish version of a physiocratic work, the *Principios de la Ciencia Económica-Política,* published in Buenos Aires in 1796. In the following years, he wrote various *Memorias,* read in the Consulate, and later, with the May Revolution, Belgrano continued on the *Correo del Comercio,* in 1810. In his memoirs and papers, the influences not only of Genovesi, Galliani, and Adam Smith are noted, but also, most powerfully, the influence of the Sociedades Económicas de Amigos del País which tended to gravitate towards what is today known as the national focus of political economy. Belgrano died in 1820. For a general review of the social-economic thinking of Belgrano, please consult Gondra 1923; Tindaro 1944; Gandia 1949: 23–88; Fernández López 1977.

2 There had also undoubtedly been a Spanish edition on the thinking of Genovesi. It deals with the work of D. Victoriano de Villara *Lecciones de Comercio, o bien de Economía Civil, del Abate Genovesi* of 1785 in Madrid, in two volumes (with a second edition published in Madrid in 1804 of three volumes), in which the translator added various critical notes to the end of each volume, based on the works of Uztariz, Ulloa, and Campomanes.

3 Nevertheless, fearful that the properties would again fall into just a few hands, Belgrano was still of the opinion that the sale of the lands should become obligatory if at least half of the land were not cultivated by the owners in a reasonable period of time; and even more should be done against those who

keep their whole lands resting fallow, and are near to rural towns, where the inhabitants are surrounded by great landowners but have none of the benefits given by the law: that, he believed, is why they do not progress, because they lack the stimuli of property.

4 'Neither Rivadavia in his decrees and messages, nor Avellaneda make the least allusion to this very wise article of Belgrano, which serves them as an antecedent, where with great wisdom and irreproachable doctrination, is planted for the first time in our country the problem of public lands, and correct solutions are given' (Gondra 1923: 268). For a comparison of the concepts of Belgrano and Rivadavia, see Lamas 1882.

5 For its content and form, this is undoubtedly the best of Belgrano's economic papers. He deals with the topic of determination of prices in a free market with unique wisdom and profound knowledge, in a strict and clear manner such as has not since been outdone.

11 THE TREATISE OF DIEGO PADILLA

1 'Motives that have obligated the New Kingdom of Granada to reassume the rights of sovereignty, to remove the authorities of the old government, and install a supreme junta under the denomination and name of our sovereign, Ferdinando VII and with independence for the Counsel of Regents and of which other representative body.'

2 Actually, it is known that Estanislao Vergara noted in an edition that is kept in the Museo 20 de Julio in Bogotá that this work was written by the venerable Father Padilla; that the secretary of the sub-presidency of Cundinamarca, Vicente de Roxas, received an official work, dated 30 January 1816 from Nicolás Ballén de Guzmán, which he alludes to explicitly as the 'Manifesto of Father Padilla'; and which the same Friar Diego in the first edition of his *Aviso al Público* of 29 September 1810 alludes to these same 'Motivos', ratifying his clear adherence to the principles maintained in them: 'Already it has been said in another paper ('Motivos') which was the origin, which were the operations of this council. But, despite the reasons that they persuade us not to recognize it, there are two castes of people . . . '

3 For outstanding critical orientation to the ideas defended in the *Aviso al Público*, consult Martinez Delgado and Ortiz 1960: 33–4; Gómez Hoyos 1962: II, 304–13.

4 Critical commentary on the essay 'Tolerancia' is found in Gómez Hoyos 1962: II, 309.

5 A sample of this addition is found in the Biblioteca Nacional, Pineda Foundation, First Wing, Vol. 99, Work 10631, Periodical Section.

6 It must be remembered that Montesquieu thinks that in order to develop the virtue of love of country, education must play a principal role in the matter.

7 The bibliography on Rousseau is much too long to mention here. Nevertheless, a good guide is *Oeuvres Complétes de Jean-Jaques Rousseau*, in four volumes, published in Paris in 1963. In this set, Volume III contains not only the two contrasted works, but also the rest of the political writings of Rousseau, each one prefaced by a valuable critical analysis by such authors as B. Gagnebin, F. Bouchard, J. Starobinski, R. Derathe, and others.

8 The first translation undertaken was of the work by Destutt de Tracy, *Treatise on Political Economy*, published in Georgetown in 1817. It was undertaken on the suggestion of Jefferson.

12 ESTEBAN ECHEVERRÍA

1 Echeverría repeats here the same idea which he defined ten years later as the law of solidarity.
2 Later in *Ojeada*, Echeverría will change his mind.
3 Still, there are diverging opinions set forward by liberal authors.
4 According to Locke's theory of work: 'Property is the sweat of one's forehead' (Echeverría 1940d: 200).
5 The name 'social democrat' seems to have been used for the first time by the main Chartist, Bronterre O'Brien, in 1839.
6 For example, the writings of Belgrano and Moreno.
7 Echeverría especially mentions economics, religion, the arts, and the sciences.
8 It is true that Echeverría thinks more of consultative measures rather than coercive ones. Besides, in this case, the idea of planning did not lose its essence.

13 A TREATISE ON POLITICAL ECONOMY IN 1823

1 The data on the demographic history of the country continues using as its starting point the census of the Archbishop-Viceroy and the estimations of Humboldt displayed in Chapter XXVI of his well known work, *Viajes a las Regiones*. For a more authentic documentation, it would be better to consider the related works of the Spanish authors, such as José Canga Argüelles, or of the Colombian authors who performed early demographic censuses, such as Pedro Fermin de Vargas, José Ignacio de Pombo, or Francisco José de Caldas.
2 In the currency system in force at that time, one silver peso was divided into eight reals.
3 Ancient right of Iberian origin of 2 per cent, later 4 per cent, and finally 5 per cent of the price paid on the sale of goods and the licensing of goods, the *Alcabala* (Arabic term), was extended to the Spanish colonies by royal decree in 1574. In 1592 in Quito and shortly thereafter in Tunja, there arose movements of rebellion against the *alcabalas*. Also, the community members of Socorro, San Gil, Vélez, Tunja, etc. sent requests that achieved a lowering of the tax to 2 per cent, but General Bolívar, based in Tunja, ordered a return to 5 per cent in 1826. Francisco Soto pushed General Santander to abolish this tax, which was accomplished in 1835.
4 It is suspected that the writing is that of Guillermo Wills, partner of the foreign company Powles, Illingworth, Wills, and Company, which explored and developed the gold mines of Supía and Marmato in Colombia.
5 From the Latin *capitatio*, it is a type of tax per person. It is a very old tax contribution system, which, according to the circumstances, was paid in services, in kind, or in money and carried many different names: money; ordinary service in Castille; morabetí in Valencia; personal in Cataluña; bobage in Aragón; tributo in the colony; and even personal service or training in Colombia.
6 A pun is made in this quotation since GPP uses the following terms in Spanish '*a Dios libertad, a Dios seguridad, a Dios subsistencia*', where *a Dios* has a double meaning: the literal one being the one used by the translator and another, trickier one if we consider that *adios* in Spanish means 'farewell'.
7 For a summary of Wagemann's ideas in Spanish, consult Popescu 1967: 102.

14 THE LÓPEZ-PELLEGRINI SCHOOL

1 Among the doctoral theses of his students written in Buenos Aires, the following are worthy of mention: Aditario Heredia (1876), 'El Sistema Proteccionista en Economía Política'; Manuel J. Heredia (1875), 'Impuesto de Aduana'; Alejo de Nevares (1874), 'Algunos Apuntes sobre las Ventajas del Sistema Protector para la República Argentina'; Servando García (1875), 'Estudio sobre el Progreso de los Principios Económicos en la República Argentina'; and last but certainly not least, that of the man who was second only to Pellegrini in importance in the movement, Dr Miguel Cané (1876), 'Protección a la Industria'. Among his contemporaries we should remember Juan María Gutiérrez (1809–78), Andrés Lamas (1817–91), Emilio de Alvear (1817–82) and Pedro Lucas Funes (1820–90). Among the members of the intermediate generation, we should remember most of Pellegrini's old mates, such as Eduardo Madero (1833–94), Ezequiel Paz (1836–1911), Juán José Montes de Oca (1840–1903), José Hernández (1834–86), Rafael Hernández (1840–1903), Dardo Rocha (1838–1921), Jerónimo Cortés Funes (1833–91) and Aristóbulo del Valle (1845–96).

2 There is now available an excellent study on the debate of 14 September 1875 (Panettieri 1960: 161–78).

3 A firm step in that direction is given by Guglialmelli (Guglialmelli 1984: 16–33).

4 Guglialmelli thinks that this is the influence of the historical school of Roscher and Schmoller.

5 Henri Richelot, *Une Revolution en Economie Politique – Exposé des Doctrines de Macleod*, 1863: 170ff. Some authors refer to this current of thought (Chiaramonte 1971; Guglialmelli 1984: 23). Chiaramonte takes a look at López' course but it is not clear whether he also looked into Richelot's book; in any case, he neither grasped completely his protectionist position nor noticed the quotation on List.

6 Schumpeter says: 'Henry Dunning Macleod (1821–1902) was an economist of several great merits, which were never recognized, nor taken seriously, due to his incapability to present his numerous good ideas in an acceptable professional form. In this book, we cannot recover his honour, except by quoting three publications in which he put the fundamentals of the modern theory of the subject [bank credit] which we discuss' (Schumpeter 1971: 1210).

15 HUMAN CAPITAL IN BOLIVIA

1 Among the best of the works performed in the early stages of the analysis of this problem, the following are worthy of quotation (Simpson and Benjamin 1958; Alexander-Frutschi 1963; Balugh 1964; Mesics 1964).

2 For a better orientation, please consult Popescu 1985: 297ff.

3 After having understood that the state of decadence prevalent in the Bolivian countryside is due to 'as much because our labourers possess no type of knowledge whatsoever, as because they lack capital' (Prudencio 1845: 12), Prudencio, convinced that 'among the positive resources that shall push agriculture toward growth is the instruction of its labourers in the rudiments of education and in the science in which they work' (ibid.: 37), proposes a new direction in primary education which would combine literacy with professional training. He suggests that the government show interest with a series of special stimulations 'the pecuniary awards, those of honour and distinction' (ibid.: 50) to push

for artisanal perfection and to attempt to 'bring from Europe the machines needed with their operators and directors' in order to improve national manufacturing. Thoroughly convinced that the destruction of Bolivian handicraft is due above all else to the competition brought on by similar foreign products, by virtue of the 'system of freedom in trade' dominant in Bolivia, Prudencio opts for an inverse restriction on the importation of goods and a fostering of immigration. 'Far from being enemies of anyone, we wish for the Europeans to come to live and stay among us, and as this is how societies have been formed to maintain traffic on the high seas, those same people should get together among themselves, and with others with the objective of establishing some industries in this country, calling upon the intelligent Europeans to direct them. In this manner, they could communicate to us their brilliance, they could inspire us by their example, the love of labour, then we could come out of our ignorance. Oh, how I wish our votes are verified and that the foreigners are invited with positive living, to come to Bolivia by the thousands, to erect industries everywhere. That would be as an immense benefit to us, as free trade is an incalculable evil' (Prudencio 1845: 70–1).

4 In this work of Dalence, an economic and demographic evaluation of Bolivia is undertaken for the first time with accompanying statistical tables. Later, Dalence proceeds to the analysis of the structure of the workforce, with the same focus. He concludes that 'the agricultural population is very numerous, but the industrial population is very scarce: which must be felt, for the manufacturing industry is that which centuplicates the value of agrarian production; and having few persons among us knowledgeable in this manner of increasing wealth, we shall be condemned to be only cultivators, always poor and miserable' (Dalence 1851: 228–9). This situation is further confirmed by Dalence's evaluation of education: 'In the republic there exists but only 100,000 people more or less out of a total of 1,373,895 inhabitants who possess the advantage of education and instruction: this is frightening and deplorable and should energetically get the attention of the government' (Dalence 1851: 240).

5 Villarroel Claure is convinced that human labour is practically 'the only source of wealth', he feels that as the first principle of Bolivian economic policy, 'all our efforts should preferably be directed toward improving the human factor' (Villarroel Claure 1929: 47–8). But 'the improvement of the human factor contains two concepts: one refers to growth in the population . . . and the other is related to its physical, intellectual, and moral progress' (Villarroel 1929: 32). Therefore, he advocates a decisive immigration policy along with an intense education policy. Of course, he rejects the encyclopaedic and abstract education policy reigning in the Bolivian educational system. For Villarroel Claure, 'speaking in terms of economics, man is so much more perfect the greater is his capacity to produce within a concrete activity' (Villarroel 1929: 53), and from here arises the need to foster a system of 'economic and technical education' (Villarroel 1929: 98–9).

6 This is a work that makes original and constructive contributions in the field of evaluation and projection of the Bolivian population. Averanga Mollinedo analyses the last two censuses, and emphasizes not only the grave sectoral imbalance in the occupations, but also the grave problem of underemployment. Actually in Bolivia, as in other underdeveloped countries, not only is a large portion of the active population seasonally employed, but there exists 'invisible or secret unemployment', which consists in the employing of many people in tasks of very low productivity, explainable by the absence of other better paying jobs' (Averanga Mollinedo 1956: 108). As regards the vocational

and commercial technical training, the author concludes that 'it has scarcely been achieved by very few persons, a fact which makes us reflect upon improving and widening these branches of public education' (Averanga Mollinedo 1956: 106).

7 *Informe de la Misión Económica de los Estados Unidos*, presided over by Merwin L. Bohan. In Part I, it is established that the progress of both agriculture and manufacturing will be for some time a function of the size of the population and per capita consumption in Bolivia. Part II is dedicated to the study of the agrarian sector, with an elaboration by Ben H. Thibodeaux. Here it is established that Bolivia's population not only is small in relation to the capacity of natural resources, but also is poorly distributed. If the cultivation in the Altiplano was carried out by tractor, 62–74 per cent less workers would be needed than are needed with a wooden plough. The excess of the population in the Altiplano could be sent to the prairies to colonize its fertile and still virginal lands. If this policy turns out to be inadequate, then foreign immigration should be encouraged. The necessity of educating the labour force is imperative, so that they may leave their current state of intraproduction and intraconsumption.

Part IV is dedicated to the mining and metallurgic sector. John Worcester presents an excellent quantitative balance of the demand and supply of labour at all levels of this sector and recommends the government to find the adequate means to overcome the noxious habit of the Indians of chewing coca, which 'continues being the main obstacle to forming an efficient working contingent', and besides this, 'to take an active position in the education of Bolivian technical personnel' (Bohan 1943: 57). The document anticipates the creation of the Corporación Boliviana de Fomento, among whose principal purposes should figure 'the development of Bolivian technical and administrative personnel' (Bohan 1943: 23).

8 In attempt to satisfy the requirement that planning must begin from the top down, this report emphasizes the need for the creation of an Institute of Labour Research, as the central organism charged with the carrying out of systematic and capable studies. The same principle should be followed in sectoral planning, since things go worse in the public sector than in the private sector and this public sector is the one responsible for the administration and elaboration of the plans for national development. By having available highly qualified functionaries, development plans can be thought out. The deficiencies in the private sector are due to alcohol and coca poisoning, the lack of instruction, scarce professional training, absenteeism, and illnesses. The mission members doubt whether the eastern sector of Bolivia can be developed by internal migration, but fear that European immigrants cannot be established there in the short run. Therefore, it is suggested that the ILO undertake a competent study on the possibilities of immigration, as much for the present as for the future. The decrease in the efficiency in mining is aggravated by the 'rigor imposed by the extreme altitude on labour' (UNO 1951: 144). In general, for the mission, 'the heterogeneous composition of the three or four million inhabitants of Bolivia constitutes what is perhaps the most difficult problem of the nation' (UNO 1951:1 5).

9 The central thesis of the diagnosis made by Zondag is that 'the Revolution of 1952 has caused a basic change in the social structure of the country . . . and upon doing this, put into motion social forces which in certain measure it cannot control; as a result of all this, the indigenous masses of Bolivia have now become a political factor, that will have to be reckoned with in the future'

(Zondag 1956: 269). This fact will have powerful repercussions on economic life. The process will be slow, but sure. If the present and the majority of the next generation still remain in the apathetic state in which they are found, it is very probable that 'future generations of Indians can gradually desire to abandon their centuries old habitat' (Zondag 1956: 108). The integration of the aborigines into the national economy is no longer an unreachable goal, as the lot of the Indian changes from that of a type of feudal serf to a low level peasant (ibid.: 109).

If in the long run there is reason for optimism, in the short run the side effects of the revolution have been felt in the economy and in the structure and efficiency in labour. The technicians, intellectuals, and middle class have been exiting Bolivia in droves. In the classes of skilled and unskilled workers, the incentives for working have dropped sharply; in the agricultural sector, the production has decreased considerably; the problem is of a social origin and stems from a lack of incentives; generally the Indian works the soil with rudimentary tools, a simple pole, the best of them using the wooden plough; 'the Indian does not work more than 60 per cent of the time, dedicating himself the rest of the time to leisure and parties of prolonged and heavy drinking' (Zondag 1956: 111); in the mining sector, productivity dropped more than 40 per cent in less than ten years, due to the lack of labour discipline, pressure by unions, the constant growth of the labour force, on one hand, and to organizational and administrative problems on the other. And in industry, the principal problem 'is naturally the lack of worker discipline in general, together with the weight of social laws lacking any common sense and the excessive control by the government' (ibid.: 172). As productivity drops, unemployment in the mining sector and underemployment in other sectors increases; which is in stark contrast with the natural wealth of Bolivia. The problem here is the scarcity of human resources. Therefore, the necessity to implement a rigorous policy of administrating the available human resources exists. Internal migration is one solution, but its effects will only be known in the long run. One solution to the agrarian problem lies in a more intensive usage of the fertile lands in the Altiplano.

10 This sociological diagnosis coincides with Zondag as regards the perspectives of a greater fluidity in social mobility, and likewise in the analysis of many of the negative aspects produced by the Revolution of 1952. It is emphasized here that to the old judgements were added new efforts to accelerate the decline in the capability and the efficiency of the Bolivian work force. In the agricultural sector, the disorientation and the lack of legal status of lands led to a decrease in production. This further led to trading on the black market, as people's inflationary expectations were fuelled by upward spiralling prices. The hardest hit sector was manufacturing, as morale on the job was broken along with old boss–worker relations. In addition, industry was beset by problems of lack of discipline, worker absenteeism, jurisprudential insecurity, administrative disorder, and the flight of human capital.

The study presents a hypothetical model of economic development, which is supported by calculations, estimations and research. Among the most important hypotheses of the model are the following: the labour force in a projected ten-year period will increase by another 26,000 people annually and must be absorbed by distinct sectors of the economy. Of these new entries every year to the workforce, only between 4,000 and 8,000 can be taken in by the farm zones near Santa Cruz and other traditional farming regions. The remaining 18–22,000 will have to be taken in by other agricultural regions, which are already underproductive. This, the study claimed, is because the other economic sectors would experience little or no increase in demand for workers.

In order to determine the structure of the economy as programmed, the study took the following steps: it projected the workforce for the entire period of the analysis, in all the possible distinct sectors. Calculations were made for all possibilities of workforce distribution and how much money was needed to finance each possibility. Next, the annual value of each sector's production and total production were calculated. Finally, the possibility of financing for the next ten years was calculated.

11 For an objective balance of the contributions of the Plan Decenal in the area of human resources, see the critical analysis of Sanford in *Informe al Gobierno* (Cohen 1964: 3).

16 SILVIO GESELL

1 The stimuli for me to write the article from which this chapter originated came from a request made in 1958 by the editor of the well-known German encyclopaedia *Handwörterbuch der Sozialwissenschaften* who wanted an article on Silvio Gesell. After conscientious research on this thinker I realized that Argentine economists must know about the life and works of this forgotten thinker who is so closely connected to our scientific heritage. This essay could not have been made without access to Carlos Idaho Gesell's private library in Villa Gesell as well as to the material found in the libraries of Ernest Fridolin Gesell, Hans Timm and Dr Hans Joachim Türke. I have also had very interesting and useful conversations with the above mentioned as well as with Mrs Laura Gesell de Gastes. I am also grateful to Karl Walker and Philip Pye who have provided not only interesting information but also certain bibliographical pieces. Parts of this essay have been read by Hans Timm and Hans Joachim Türke who, like Carlos Gesell and his wife, have made suggestions tending to guarantee a high degree of faithfulness to the reality of Gesell's life and the Gesellian movement.

2 Gesell's best-known work *Die Natürliche Wirtschaftsordnung durch Freigeld* was published in 1916 in Berlin by Physiokratischer-Verlag; fourth edition (1920) re-elaborated by the author, Rehrbrücke: Freiland-Freigeld-Verlag; seventh German edition (1931) Stirn Verlag Hans Timm; eighth German edition (1937) by F. Schwarz in *Freischafliche Zeitung – Organ des Schweizer Freiwirtschaftsbundes*, XV, 103–4; *Natural Economic Order* (1929) first English edition, edited by P. Pye, Berlin: NEO-Verlag; (1934) San Antonio, TX: H. Fack; (1958) London: P. Owen Ltd; (1936) *El Orden Natural por Libre Moneda y Libre Tierra*, first Spanish edition, Parts I and II, and (1945) Part III, Buenos Aires: E. Gesell; (1948) *L'Ordre Économique Naturel*, French edition translated by F. Swinné, Bern-Paris-Brussels.

3 Nevertheless, I was informed by Hans Timm that Stirner had no influence whatsoever on Gesell.

4 In addition more information is to be found in Schwarz 1951.

BIBLIOGRAPHY

Abecia, V. (1939) *Historia de Chuquisaca*, Sucre: Charcas.

Acevedo, C. A. (1949) 'La Enseñanza de la Ciencia de la Finanza en la Universidad de Buenos Aires desde su Fundación hasta 1830', *Revista de la Facultad de Derecho y Ciencias Sociales*, Universidad de Buenos Aires, 4, 14: 427–62.

Acosta, J. (1941) *De la Procuración de la Salvación de los Indios*, Mexico: Fondo de Cultura Económica.

—— (1962) *Historia Natural y Moral de las Indias*, Mexico: Fondo de Cultura Económica.

Agía, M. (1946) *Tratado que Contiene Tres Pareceres Graves en Derecho (1604)*, reprinted as *Servidumbre Personal de Indios*, Seville: Publicación de la Escuela de Estudios Hispanoamericanos.

Agnan, A., Demoulin, F., and Guidel, J. (1955–61) *Informe al Gobierno de Bolivia sobre Diversos Aspectos de la Formación Profesional* (two volumes), Geneva: International Labour Office.

Alberdi, J. B. (1921) *Sistema Económico y Rentístico de la Confederación Argentina según su Constitución*, Buenos Aires: Schenone Hnos & Linari Vaccaro Press.

Albornoz, B. de (1573) *Arte de los Contractos*, Valencia.

Alcedo y Herrera, A. (1786–9) *Diccionario Geográfico Histórico de las Indias Occidentales*, Madrid: Imprenta Benito Cano (English version 1812–15, James Carpenter *et al.* eds).

Alcedo y Herrera, D. (1726) 'Memorial . . . del Consulado de la Ciudad de los Reyes sobre Distintos Puntos Tocantes al Estado de la Real Hacienda', Lima: Arrchivo del Estado.

—— (1915) *Descripción Geográfica de la Real Audiencia de Quito*, Madrid: Impr. Fortanet.

Alemann, R. (1955) 'Die Theorie der Peripherischen Wirtschaft', *Weltwirtschaftliches Archiv*, 74, 1: 7–46.

—— (1955) 'La Teoría dell'Economia Periferica', *Suplemento all'Informazione SVIMEZ*, IV, 35: 947–69.

—— (1956) 'El Pensamiento Económico de Prebisch – La Teoría de la Economía Periférica', *Selección Contable*, Buenos Aires: X, 57: 195–229.

Alexander-Frutschi, M. C. (ed.) (1963) *Human Resources and Economic Growth: An International Annotated Bibliography*, Menlo Park, CA: Stanford Research Institute.

Allais, M. (1947) *Économie et Intéret*, Paris: Impr. Nationale.

Altamira y Crevea, R. (1938a) 'La Legislación Indiana como Elemento de la Historia de las Ideas Coloniales Españoles', *Revista de Historia de América*, 1: 1–24.

—— (1938b) 'El Texto de las Leyes de Burgos de 1512', *Revista de Historia de América*, 4: 5–79.

Alvear, E. de (1869) 'La Reforma Económica', *La Revista de Buenos Aires*, XXI: 248–58, 418–33, 592–606.

Antonio, N. (1783–8) *Bibliotheca Hispana Nova sive Hispanorum Scriptorum qui ab Anno MD ad MDCLXXXIV Floruere Notitia*, Matriti: Ibarra.

Anzola, N. (1936) *Conferencias sobre Economía Política*, Bogotá: Imprenta Nacional.

Aquinas, T. (1946) *La Justicia: Comentario al Libro Quinto de la Ética a Nicómaco*, Buenos Aires: Ed. Cursos de Cultura Católica.

Arboleda, S. (1951) *La República en América Española*, Bogotá: Biblioteca Popular de Cultura Colombiana.

Argentine Congress, Chamber of Deputies (1873) *Diario de Sesiones de la Cámara de Diputados*, 27 June.

—— (1875) *Diario de Sesiones de la Cámara de Diputados*, 14 September.

—— (1876) *Diario de Sesiones de la Cámara de Diputados*, 18 August.

Argentine Congress, Chamber of Senators (1895) *Carlos Pellegrini: Intervención en la Sesión Ordinaria del 28 de Setiembre de 1895 en la Cámara de Senadores*, 28 September.

Astrain, A. (1901–25) *Historia de la Compañía de Jesús en la Asistencia de España*, Madrid: Consejo Superior de Investigaciones Científicas, Instituto Santo Toribio de Mogroveyo.

Austry, J. (1965) *Le Scandale du Développement*, Paris: M. Rivière.

Auza, N. T. (1968) *La Influencia Norteamericana en el Pensamiento y la Acción de Carlos Pellegrini*, Mendoza: Impr. Universitaria.

Averanga Mollinedo, A. (1956) *Aspectos Generales de la Población Boliviana*, La Paz: Argote; reprinted (1974) La Paz: Juventud.

Baden, Margrave de (1772) 'Abrég des Principes d'Économie Politique', *Ephemerides du Citoyen*, I: 169–85.

Bader, A. (1932) 'Physiokratie oder Freiwirtschaft', *Freiwirtschaft*, 3: 112.

Baeck, L. (1988) 'Spanish Economic Thought: the School of Salamanca and the "Arbitristas"', *History of Political Economy*, III: 381ff.

Ballesteros Beretta, A. (1945) *Cristobal Colón y el Descubrimiento de América*, Barcelona-Buenos Aires: Salvat.

Balugh, M. A. (1964) *A Selected Annotated Bibliography in the Economics of Education*, London: Institute of Education, University of London.

Barcia Trelles, C. (1931) *Doctrina de Monroe y Cooperación Internacional*, Madrid: Mundo Latino.

Barreda Laos, F. (1955) 'Vida Intelectual del Virreinato del Perú', in *Historia de la Nación Argentina*, III: 95–119.

Baudin, L. (1962) *Une Theocratie Socialiste: L'Etat Jésuite du Paraguay*, Paris: Génin.

Belgrano, M. (1796) *Principios de Ciencia Económico Política Traducidos del Francés*, Buenos Aires: Imprenta del Real Consulado.

—— (1810a) 'Educación', *Correo del Comercio*, 3: 18–20.

—— (1810b) 'Economía Política', *Correo del Comercio*, 26: 197–8; 27: 200–1.

—— (1810c) 'Carta a los Editores', *Correo del Comercio*, 19: 150.

—— (1810d) 'Estadística', *Correo del Comercio*, 7: 49–51.

—— (1973a) 'Medios Generales de Fomentar la Agricultura, Animar la Industria y Proteger el Comercio en un País Agricultor. Memoria del 15 de Junio de 1796', Instituto Belgraniano *Manuel Belgrano. Documentos para su Historia*, Buenos Aires: Lito.

—— (1973b) 'Memoria del 14 de Junio de 1798', Instituto Belgraniano *Manuel Belgrano. Documentos para su Historia*, Buenos Aires: Lito.

—— (1973c) 'Discurso en la Academia de Náutica del 10 de Mayo de 1802', Instituto Belgraniano's *Manuel Belgrano. Documentos para su Historia*, Buenos Aires: Lito.

BIRF (1966) *Bibliografía Seleccionada sobre Desarrollo Económico*, Washington DC: BIRF.

Blumenthal, H. (1924) 'Die Alten Französischen Physiokraten und Wir', *Die Freiwirtschaft*, 19: 501–6.

Boccardo, G. (1872) *Tratado Teórico-Práctico de Economía Política*, translated by Federico Nin Reyes, Buenos Aires: Impresor Lit. y Fund. de Tipos de la Sociedad Anónima.

Bodin, J. (1568) *Responses aux Paradoxes du Sire de Malestroit*, Paris: Martin le Jeune.

—— (1590) *Los Seis Libros de la República*, translated from the French, Turin: Bevilogua.

Bohan, M. (1943) *Informe de la Misión Económica de los Estados Unidos*, translated into Spanish by G. Von Bilbao, La Vieja, La Paz: Secretaría Nacional de Planeación y Coordinación.

Böhm-Bawerk, E. V. (1884) *Geschichte und Kritik der Kapitalzins-Theorien*, Jena: Fischer Verlag.

—— (1908) *Las Grandes Líneas de la Economía Política*, Madrid: S. Calleja Fernández.

Bolivian-United States Labour Commission (1943) *Labor Problems in Bolivia*, Montreal: International Labour Office.

Botana, N., Di Tella, T. S., and Jaguaribe, H. (1988) *Reflexiones Socio-Políticas sobre el Pensamiento de Raúl Prebisch*, Buenos Aires: Tesis, Fundación Raúl Prebisch.

Brand, O. (1984) *Diccionario de Economía*, Colección Apesal, Bogotá: Plaza & Janés.

Brants, V. (1895) *L'Économie Politique au Moyen Age. Esquisse des Théories Économiques Profesées par les Écrivains des XIIIe et XIVe Siècles*, Louvain: Peteers.

Brocard, L. (1929–31) *Principes d'Économie Nationale et Internationale*, Paris: Sirey.

Bunge, A. E. (1927) 'Las Fuerzas Creadoras en la Economía Nacional', *Academia Nacional de Ciencias Económicas, Biblioteca*, I: 154–68.

Camacho Carreño, J. (1929) *Reflexiones Económicas*, Brussels: Impr. C. Bulens SA.

Campomanes, P. Rodríguez, Conde de (1975) *Discurso sobre la Educación Popular de los Artesanos y su Fomento (1775)*, Madrid: Instituto de Estudios Fiscales.

—— (1988) *Reflexiones sobre el Comercio Español e Indias (1762)*, Preliminary Study by V. Llombart Rosa, Madrid: Instituto de Estudios Fiscales.

Canavese, A. J. (1989) *El Pensamiento de Raúl Prebisch*, Buenos Aires: Tesis.

Capitan, L., and Lorin, H. (1948) *El Trabajo en América Antes y Después de Colón*, Buenos Aires: Argos.

Carande, R. (1977) *Carlos V y sus Banqueros*, Barcelona: Crítica-Grijalbo.

Cárcamo, M. A. (1971) *La Presidencia de Carlos Pellegrini: Política de Orden 1890–2*, Buenos Aires: Eudeba.

Cardenas Nannetti, J. (1944) *Teoría de la Economía Colombiana*, Bogotá and Medellín: Siglo XXI.

Cardiel, J. (1741) 'Dificultades que Suele Haber en la Conversión de los Infieles, y Medios para Vencerlas', Buenos Aires: Biblioteca Nacional de Buenos Aires.

—— (1748) 'Medios para Reducir a Vida Racional y Cristiana a los Indios que Viven Vagabundos sin Pueblos ni Sementeras', Buenos Aires, currently housed in the Archivo de la Provincia de Toledo.

—— (1913) 'Breve Relacion de las Misiones del Paraguay of 1770–1771', in P. González *Misiones del Paraguay. Organización Social de las Doctrinas Guaraníes de la Compañía de Jesús* Barcelona: G. Gili.

—— (1953) *Carta-Relación de las Misiones de la Provincia del Paraguay (1747)*, Prologue by G. Furlong, Buenos Aires: Librería del Plata.

—— (1980) 'Declaración de la Verdad' (1758), Buenos Aires: Imprenta de J. A. Alsina.

—— (1984) *Compendio de la Historia del Paraguay (1780)*, Prologue by J. M. Mariluz Urquijo, Buenos Aires: Fundación para la Educación, la Ciencia y la Cultura (FECyC).

Carey, M. (1814) *The Olive Branch*, Philadelphia.

Carranza, A. P. (1897) *Carlos Pellegrini, Speeches and Writings 1881–96*, Buenos Aires: Kraft.

Casas, B. de las (1542) *Brevísima Relación de la Destrucción de las Indias*, Seville: S. Trujillo; reprinted (no date) Paris-Buenos Aires: L. Michaud.

—— (1951) *Historia de las Indias* A. Millares Carlo (ed.), Buenos Aires: Fondo de Cultura Económica.

—— (1974) *Tratados*, Mexico: Fondo de Cultura Económica.

Castillo de Bovadilla, J. (1775) *Política para Corregidores*, Madrid: Impr. Real de la Gazeta.

CEPAL (1958) *El Desarrollo Económico de Bolivia*, Mexico City: United Nations.

—— (1987) *Raúl Prebisch: un Aporte a su Pensamiento*, Santiago de Chile: United Nations.

Cerviño, P. A. (1801) 'Nuevo Aspecto del Comercio del Río de la Plata' (manuscript which seems to have been lent to M. J. de Lavardén).

Céspedes del Castillo, G. (1961) 'Las Indias en el Reinado de los Reyes Católicos' in J. Vicens-Vives, *Historia de España y América*, II, Barcelona: Vicens-Vives.

Chafuén, A. A. (1986) *Christians for Freedom – Late Scholastics Economics*, San Francisco, CA: Ignatius Press; Spanish version (1991) *Económica y Ética*, Madrid: Rialp.

Chiaramonte, J. C. (1971) *Nacionalismo y Liberalismo Económico en la Argentina de 1860–1880*, Buenos Aires: Solar/Hatchette.

Chick, V. (1987) 'Silvio Gesell (1862–1930)', *New Palgrave: A Dictionary of Economics*, II, London: Macmillan, Stockton, and Maruzen Press (second edn).

Cieza de León, P. de (no date) 'Crónica del Perú', in J. Le Riverand (ed.) *Historiadores de Indias: América del sur*, Barcelona: Bruguera.

Cohen, S. (1964) *Informe al Gobierno de Bolivia sobre la Evaluación y Planificación de la Mano de Obra*, Geneva: International Labour Office.

Colombian Congress (1948) *Anales de Congreso*, Bogotá, 29 July.

Columbus, C. (1971) *Los Cuatro Viajes del Almirante y su Testamento (1492–1506)*, Prologue by I. B. Anzoátegui (ed.), Madrid: Espasa Calpe, Colección Austral (fifth edn).

Consuegra Higgins, J. (1960) *Doctrina de la Planeación Económica*, Bogotá: Fundación Universidad de América.

—— (1963) *Apuntes de Economía Política*, Bogotá: Ediciones Tercer Mundo.

—— (ed.) (1981) *Obras Escogidas de Raúl Prebisch*, Colección APESAL III, Bogotá: Plaza & Janés.

—— (1984) *El Pensamiento Económico Colombiano*, Bogotá: Plaza & Janés.

Cookson, F. E., and Tryon, J. L. (1965) *Bibliography on Project Planning*, New York: Centre for Industrial Development.

Copernicus, N. (1864) 'Monetae Cudendae Ratio', Paris: Wolowski.

Covarrubias y Leyva, D. (1552) *Variarum Resolutionum*, Salamanca; Spanish version, Selected Articles and Prologue by M. de Fraga Iribarne (1957) *Textos Jurídico Políticos*, Madrid: Instituto de Estudios Fiscales.

Cravero, J. M. J. (1993) 'La Ley Natural en la Filosofía Económica de Fray Tomás de Mercado', *Cuadernos de Ciencias Económicas y Empresariales*, 17, 24: January–June, Universidad Málaga: 75–97.

Cruz Santos, A. (1965) 'Economía y Hacienda Pública I', in *Colección Historia Extensa de Colombia*, 15, Bogotá: Ed. Lerner.

Cuccorese, H. J. (1985–6) *El Tiempo Histórico de Carlos Pellegrini*, Buenos Aires: FECyC.

Cuevas, P. M. (1921–8) *Historia de la Iglesia en Mexico* (five volumes), Mexico: Texas.

Cunninghame Graham, R. B. (1901) *A Vanished Arcadia, Being Some Account of the Jesuits in the Paraguay, 1607–1767*, London: Heinemann (revised edn New York: Lincoln McVeagh Dedeal Press Corp Inc.).

—— (1943) *Pedro de Valdivia, Conquistador de Chile. Su Biografía y Espitolario*, Buenos Aires: Interamericana.

Curia, E. L (1980) 'El Pensamiento Económico de Santo Tomás de Aquino', in E. L. Curia and C. A. Fernández Pardo *Temas de Historia del Pensamiento Económico*, Buenos Aires: Tesis.

Daire, E. (1845) 'Des Systèmes d'Économie Politique', *Annuaire d'Économie Politique*, Paris: 15–26.

Dalence, J. M. (1851) *Bosquejo Estadístico de Bolivia*, Chuquisaca (Sucre): Imprenta de Sucre.

Dávila Padilla, A. (1596) *Historia de la Fundación y Discurso de la Provincia de Santiago de Mexico por las Vidas de sus Varones Insignes y Cosas Notables de Nueva España*, Madrid: Casa Pedro Madrigal.

Decorme, G. (1941) *La Obra de los Jesuitas Mexicanos durante la Época Colonial*, Mexico: Imprenta de la Compañía.

Demaría, F. (1966) *El Pensamiento Económico de Carlos Pellegrini*, Buenos Aires: Báraga.

Dempsey, W. B. (1935) 'The Just Price in a Functional Economy', *American Economic Review*, 25: 471–86.

—— (1936) 'The Historical Emergence of Quantity Theory', *The Quarterly Journal of Economics*, 50: 174ff.

—— (1960) 'Just Price', in J. J. Spengler and W. R. Allen *Essays in Economic Thought: Aristotle to Marshall*, Chicago: Rand McNally (Spanish edn 1971).

Díaz del Castillo, B. (1943) *Historia Verdadera de la Conquista de la Nueva España*, Preliminary Study by C. de María, Barcelona: R. Sopena.

Dillard, D. (1940) 'Proudhon, Gesell and Keynes: An Investigation of Some "Anti-Marxian Socialist", Antecedents of Keynes' General Theory of Employment, Interest, and Money', Unpublished Doctoral Thesis, Berkeley, CA: University of California.

—— (1942) 'Gesell's Monetary Theory of Social Reform', *American Economic Review*, XXXII, 2: 348–52.

—— (1952) *La Teoría Económica de J. M. Keynes*, Madrid: Aguilar.

Di Marco, L. E. (1972) *International Economics and Development: Essays in Honour of Raúl Prebisch*, New York: Academic Press.

Dmochowski, J. (1925) 'Nicolas Copernic, Economiste', *Revue d'Économie Politique*, 39: 100–26.

Dumoulin, C. (1546) 'Tractatus Commerciorum et Usurarum', Köln.

Dupont de Nemours, P. S. (1768) 'De l' Origine et des Progrés d'une Science Nouvelle', in *Ephemerides du Citoyen*, Paris.

Echeverría, E. (1870–4) *Obras Completas, Cinco Tomos*, Buenos Aires: Carlos Casavalle.

—— (1940a) *Cartas*, La Plata: Palcos.

—— (1940b) *Contribución*, La Plata: Palcos.

—— (1940c) *Discurso*, La Plata: Palcos.

—— (1940d) *Dogma Socialista*, La Plata: Palcos.

—— (1940e) *Lecturas*, La Plata: Palcos.

—— (1940f) *Ojeada*, La Plata: Palcos.

—— (1940g) *Revolución*, La Plata: Palcos.

Eguino, F. and Illescas, J. M. (1962) *Analísis de la Mano de Obra, Bienio: 1963–1964*, La Paz : Junta Nacional de Planeamiento.

Escalona y Agüero, G. de (1647) *Gazophilacium Regium Perubicum*, Madrid: Imprenta Real. Abbreviated edn in L. M. Loza (1941) *Gazofilacio Real del Perú*, La Paz: Editorial de Estado de Bolivia.

Espinosa, J. M. (1935) 'Golden Years in the Paraguay', *Historical Bulletin*, Saint Louis: 33–6.

Espinosa de los Monteros, A. (1784) 'Extracto de las Primeras Juntas Celebradas por la Sociedad de Amigos del País', Mompox: Sociedad Amigos del País.

Estar Reyno, J. (1990) *La Concepción General y los Análisis sobre la Deuda de Raúl Prebisch*, Mexico: Siglo Veintiuno.

Fernández, A. (1829) 'Oración Fúnebre a la Memoria de Fray Diego Francisco Padilla', Bogotá: unpublished Augustinian files.

Fernández de Navarrete, M. (1825) *Colección de los Viajes y Descubrimientos que Hicieron los Españoles desde Fines del Siglo XV*, Madrid: Almirantazgo de Castilla.

Fernández López, M. (1976) 'Comprobaciones, Refutaciones y Problemas no Resueltos del Primer Pensamiento Económico Argentino', *11 Reunión Anual de la Asociación Argentina de Economía Política*, 1: 1–16.

—— (1980) 'La Pampa y el Análisis Espacial Algunos Predecesores de Von Thünen', *Económica*, 26, 3: 137–63.

Fisher, I. (1915) *La Naturaleza del Capital y el Ingreso*, Madrid: La España Moderna; English version (1906) *Nature of Capital and Income*, New York: Macmillan.

—— (1933a) *Stamp Scrip*, New York: Adelphi.

—— (1933b) *Booms and Depression*, London: George Allen & Unwin.

Floro Costa, A. (1902) *La Cuestión Económica en las Repúblicas del Plata*, Montevideo: Dornaleche y Reyes.

Fraga Iribarne, M. (ed.) (1957) 'Prefacio', in *Diego de Covarrubias y Leyva, Textos Jurídico Políticos*, Madrid: Instituto de Estudios Políticos.

Frondizi, A. (1987) *Carlos Pellegrini Industrialista (Su Vigencia en el Pensamiento Económico Nacional)*, Buenos Aires: Jockey Club.

Furlong, G. (1946) *Los Jesuitas y la Cultura Rioplatense*, Buenos Aires: Huarpes.

—— (1952) *Nacimiento y Desarrollo de la Filosofía en el Río de la Plata 1536–1810*, Buenos Aires: Kraft.

—— (1962) *Misiones y sus Pueblos de Guaraníes (1610–1813)* Buenos Aires: Impr. Balmes.

—— (1969) *Historia Social y Cultural del Río de la Plata 1536–1810*, Buenos Aires: TEA.

Gandía, E. de (1949) 'Las Ideas Económicas de Manuel Belgrano', *Revista Universidad*, Santa Fe, April–June: 23–88.

García Cadena, A. (1956) *Unas Ideas Elementales sobre Problemas Colombianos. Preocupaciones de un Hombre de Trabajo*, Bogotá: Imprenta del Banco de la República.

Garcilaso de la Vega, El Inca (1968) *Primera Parte de los Comentarios Reales que Tratan del Origen de los Incas*, Barcelona: Bruguera.

Gasca, P. de la (1921) 'Cartas al Consejo de Indias de 1549', in R. Levillier (ed.) *Gobernantes del Perú, Cartas y Papeles del Siglo XVI*, Collection of Historical Publications of the Library of the Argentine Congress.

Genovesi, A. (1804) *Lecciones de Comercio, o Bien de Economía Civil*, translated by V. de Villava, Madrid: Imp. J. Collado.

Gesell, S. (1891a) *Die Reformation im Münzwesen als Brücke zum Sozialen Staat*, Buenos Aires: Gesell (the author's own press); also in *Gesammelte Werke*, I: 25–68.

—— (1891b) *Nervus Rerum. Fortsetzung zur Reformation in Munzwesen*, Buenos Aires: Gesell; also in *Gesammelte Werke*, I: 69–152.

—— (1892) *Die Verstaatlichung des Geldes. Zweite Fortsetzung zur Reformation im Münzwesen*, Buenos Aires: Gesell; also in *Gesammelte Werke*, I: 153–258.

—— (1893) *El Sistema Monetario Argentino, sus Ventajas y su Perfeccionamiento*, Buenos Aires: A. Boote & Cía.

—— (1898) *La Cuestión Monetaria Argentina*, Buenos Aires: Impr. La Buenos Aires.

—— (1916) *Die Natürliche Wirtschaftsordnung durch Freigeld*, Berlin: Physiokratischer-Verlag; (1920) fourth edn, re-elaborated by the author, Rehrbrücke: Freiland-Freigeld-Verlag; (1931) seventh German edn: Stirn Verlag: Hans Timm; (1937) eighth German edn by F. Schwarz in *Freiwirtschafliche Zeitung – Organ des Schweizer Freiwirtschaftsbundes*, XV, 103–4; (1929) *Natural Economic Order*, first English edn, P. Pye (ed.), Berlin: NEO-Verlag; (1934) San Antonio, TX: H. Fack; (1958) London: P. Owen Ltd; (1936) *El Orden Natural por Libre Moneda y Libre Tierra*, first Spanish edn, Parts I and II; (1945) Part III, Buenos Aires: Gesell; (1948) *L'Ordre Économique Naturel*, French edn trans. F. Swinné, Bern-Paris-Brussels.

—— (1919) *Der Abbau des Staates nach Einfuhrung der Volksherrschaft*, Berlin: Verlag des Freiland-Freigeldes Bund.

—— (1920) *El Orden Económico Natural*, Vol. I, Berlin: Rehbrucke.

—— (1926) *Die Allgemeine Enteignung im Lichte Physiokratyscher Ziele*, Potsdam: Stirn-Verlag.

—— (1927) *Der Abgebaute Staat*, Berlin: A. Burmeister-Verlag.

—— (1988–96) *Gesammelte Werke*, 18 vols, Compiled by Stiftung für Persönl, Freiheit und Soziale Sicherheit (Foundation for Personal Liberty and Social Security) under W. Onken's 'Lektorat', Lütjenburg, Germany: Gauke Fachverlag für Sozialökonomie.

Gide, C. (1929) *Principes d'Économie Politique*, Paris: Buret.

Gilson, E. (1946) *La Filosofía en la Edad Media*, Madrid: Ed. Pegaso.

Gómez, L. (1928) *Interrogantes sobre el Progreso de Colombia*, Bogotá: Minerva.

Gómez Camacho, F. (1981) 'Introducción', in L. de Molina *La Teoría del Precio Justo*, Madrid: Ed. Nacional.

—— (1985) 'La Teoria Monetaria de los Doctores Españoles del Siglo XVI', in *Moneda y Crédito*, Madrid: 172: 55ff.

Gómez Hoyos, R. (1962) *La Revolución Granadina de 1810 – Ideario de una Generación y de una Época 1781–1821*, II, Bogotá: Temis.

Gómez Picon, A. (1967) *Las Ideas Políticas a Través de la Historia*, Bogotá: Librería Colombiana Camacho Roldán.

Gondra, L. R. (1923) *Las Ideas Económicas de Manuel Belgrano*, Buenos Aires: Facultad de Ciencias Económicas de la Universidad de Buenos Aires.

—— (1945) 'Argentina', in I. F. Normano (ed.) *El Pensamiento Económico Latinoamericano*, Mexico: Fondo de Cultura Económica.

Gonnard, R. (1852) *Historia de las Doctrinas Económicas*, Madrid: Aguilar.

Gothein, E. (1885) 'Der Christlich-Soziale Staat der Jesuiten in Paraguay', in G. Schmoller *Staats- und Sozial-Wissenschaftliche Forschungen*, Leipzig, IV, 4: 68.

GPP (1827) 'Observaciones y Argumentos sobre el Estado Político de la República de Colombia, Antecedido de un Tratado Sucinto sobre la Economía, con Notas contra Algunos de los Principios de Juan Bautista Say y Jeremías Bentham', Bogotá: Imprenta N. Lora.

Granero, P. J. M. (1930) *La Accion Misionera y los Metodos de San Ignacio de Loyola*, Burgos: Impr. Sociedad de Jesús.

Grice-Hutchinson, M. (1952) *The School of Salamanca: Readings in Spanish Monetary Theory 1544–1605*, Oxford: Clarendon Press.

—— (1978) *Early Economic Thought in Spain 1177–1740*, Madrid: Allen & Unwin.

—— (1982) *El Pensamiento Económico en España 1177–1740*, Madrid: Crítica-Grijalbo.

—— (1993) *Economic Thought in Spain. Selected Essays*, Cheltenham, Glos: Edward Elgar.

Grinspun, B. (ed.) (1982) *Raúl Prebisch, Contra el Monetarismo*, Buenos Aires: Radical.

Griziotti Kretschmann, J. (1951) *Historia de las Doctrinas Económicas*, Córdoba: Assandri.

Guaresti, J. J. (1947) 'El Curso de Economía Política que hoy se Comienza', *Revista de Ciencias Económicas*, publication of the Facultad de Ciencias Económicas, Colegio de Graduados, Buenos Aires, 35, series 2, 309: 237–41.

Guglialmelli, J. E. (1984) 'Carlos Pellegrini: Protección para la Industria Nacional', *Geopolítica. Hacia una Doctrina Nacional*, 29, 10: 16–33.

Gumplowicz, L. (1928) *Der Rassenkampf*, Innsbruck: Universitäts-Verlag Wagner.

Gurrieri, A. (1982) *La Obra de Prebisch en la CEPAL – Antología de Textos 1949–82*, Mexico City: Fondo de Cultura Económica.

Hamilton, A. (1791) 'Encouragement and Protection of Manufactures', in *Federalist*.

Hamilton, E. J. (1934) *American Treasure and the Price Revolution in Spain, 1501–1650*, Cambridge, MA: Harvard College.

Hanke, L. (1949) *The Struggle for Justice in the Spanish Conquest of America*, Spanish translation by Sudamericana, Buenos Aires: Sudamericana.

Harris, C. R. S. (1957) 'Duns Scotus, John (Doctor Subtilis)' in *Encyclopaedia of the Social Sciences*, New York/London/Toronto: Macmillan.

Hazlewood, A. (1964) *The Economics of Development – An Annotated List of Books and Articles 1958–62*, London: Oxford University Press.

Hernández, P. (1913) *Organización Social de las Doctrinas Guaraníes de la Compañía de Jesús*, Barcelona: Impr. Compañía de Jesús.

Henriquez Ureña, P. (1947) *Historia de la Cultura en la América Hispánica*, Mexico: Fondo de Cultura Económica.

—— (1949) *Las Corrientes Literarias en la América Hispánica*, Mexico: Fondo de Cultura Económica.

Höffner, J. (1941) *Wirtschaftsethik und Monopole im Fünfzehnten und Sechzehnten Jahrhundert*, Jena: Fischer Verlag.

—— (1955) 'Estática y Dinámica en la Ética Económica de la Filosofia Escolástica', in *Investigación Económica*, VXIII: 72.

Hollander, S. (1965) 'On the Interpretation of the Just Price', *Kyklos*, XVIII, 4: 615–32.

Hoover, H. (1934) *The Challenge to Liberty*, New York.

Hopenhayn, B. (1982) 'Algunas Notas sobre el "Capitalismo Periférico" de Raúl Prebisch', *Desarrollo Económico*, Buenos Aires, 22, 86: 287–94.

Humboldt, A. von (1962) *Viajes a las Regiones Equinocciales del Nuevo Continente (1818–25) – Relación Histórica*, in Colección Biblioteca Indiana, IV, Madrid: Aguilar.

Hume, D. (1928) Second essay 'Sobre el Lujo', *Ensayos Económicos*, I, Spanish translation by A. Zozaya, Madrid: Sociedad Española de Librerías.

Hurtado de Mendoza, A., Marquis of Cañete (1921) 'Carta a su Majestad del 16 de Marzo de 1556', in R. Levillier (ed.) *Gobernantes del Perú, Cartas y Papeles del Siglo XVI*, I, Madrid: Sucesores de Rivadeneyra SA.

ILO (1953) *Poblaciones Indígenas*, Geneva: International Labour Office.

—— (1958) *El Programa Andino*, Geneva: International Labour Office.

Ingenieros, J. (1946) *Sociología Argentina*, Buenos Aires: Losada.

Iparraguirre, D. (1954) 'Las Fuentes del Pensamiento Económico en España en los Siglos XIII al XVI', *Estudios de Deusto*, Biblao: II: 1–79.

Jaramillo, E. (1935) 'La Intervención del Estado en la Economía de los Pueblos', *Revista del Banco de la República*, Bogotá: VIII, 96: 268ff.

—— (1960) *Tratado de Ciencia de la Hacienda Pública*, Bogotá: Voluntad.

Jaramillo, J. (1965) 'Pensamiento Económico', *El Espectador*, Bogotá: 14 February: 2f.

Jaramillo, J. E. (1948) *Esteban Jaramillo – Su Vida, su Obra*, Medellín: Impr. Departamental de Antioquia.

Jaramillo Uribe, J. (1964) *El Pensamiento Colombiano en el Siglo XIX*, Bogotá: Temis.

Jouanen, J. (1941–3) *Historia de la Compañía de Jesús en la Antigua Provincia de Quito*, Quito: Imprenta Compañía.

Junco, A. (1940) *Sangre de Hispania*, Buenos Aires: Espasa Calpe.

Kaulla, R. (1940) *Theory of the Just Price*, London: George Allen & Unwin.

Keynes, J. M. (1936) *The General Theory of Employment, Interest and Money*, London: Macmillan (Spanish edn 1945).

Klein, L. R. (1952) *La Revolución Keynesiana*, Prologue by E. de Figueroa, translated by F. J. Osset, Madrid: Revista de Derecho Privado.

Labougle, A. (1957) *Carlos Pellegrini, un Gran Estadista: sus Ideas y su Obra*, Buenos Aires: El Ateneo.

Labra, R. de (1903) *Las Sociedades Económicas de Amigos del País – Su Historia y su Porvenir*, Madrid: La Sociedad Económica de Amigos del País.

Lafuente, M. (1858) *Historia General de España*, II, Madrid: Establecimiento Tipográfico Mellado.

Lamarca, E. (1877) *Apuntes para el Estudio de la Economía Política*, Buenos Aires: Igon Hnos.

Lamas, A. (1882) *La Legislación Agraria de Bernardino Rivadavia*, Buenos Aires.

Langenstein, H. de (no date) 'Tractatus de contractibus et Origenes Censuum', in V. Brants *Las Grandes Líneas de la Economía Política*, Madrid: S. Calleja Fernández.

Langholm, O. (1979) *Price and Value in the Aristotelian Tradition*, Bergen: Universitetsforlaget.

—— (1983) *Wealth and Money in the Aristotelian Tradition*, Bergen: Universitetsforlaget.

Larraz, J. (1963) *La Epoca del Mercantilismo en Castilla, 1500–1700*, Madrid: Aguilar; first edn (1943), Madrid: Atlas.

Lavardén, M. J. de (1955) *Nuevo Aspecto del Comercio del Río de la Plata (1799)*, reprinted with a preliminary study by Enrique Wedovoy, Buenos Aires: Raiga.

León, N. (1903) *Don Vasco de Quiroga*, Mexico: Antigua Libreria de Juan Porrúa e Hijos.

Le Riverand, J. (ed.) (no date) *Crónicas de la Conquista del Perú*, Mexico: Ed. La Nueva España.

Lestard, G. (1937) *Historia de la Evolución Económica Argentina*, Buenos Aires: La Facultad, Bernabé & Co.

Lette, S. (1938–50) *Historia da Companhia de Jesus no Brasil*, Rio de Janeiro: Civilizaçao Brasileira.

Levene, R. (1952) *Investigaciones acerca de la Historia Económica del Virreinato del Río de la Plata*, I, second edn, Buenos Aires: El Ateneo.

Levillier, R. (ed.) (1918) *La Audiencia de Charcas – Correspondencia de Presidentes y Oidores – Documentos del Archivo de Indias*, I, Madrid: Publicaciones Históricas de la Biblioteca del Congreso de la Nación Argentina.

Lhoir, A. (1962) *Informe al Gobierno de Bolivia sobre Educación Obrera*, Geneva: International Labour Office.

Lleras Restrepo, C. (1965) *Comercio Internacional*, Bogotá: Bedout.

Lohmann Villena, G. (1966) *Juan de Matienzo, Autor del 'Gobierno del Perú' (Su Personalidad y su Obra)*, Seville: Escuela de Estudios Hispano-Americanos.

Lombardo Toledano (1924) *El Problema de la Educación en Mexico*, Mexico City.

Lope de Aguirre (1972) in F. Vázquez 'Descubrimiento de Amazonas por Pedro de Orzúa (1560) . . . y el Alzamiento de Lope de Aguirre (1 enero 1561) y su Muerte en Barquisimeto, Venezuela el 7 de Octubre de 1561', in A. Macía *Historiadores de Indias: América del Sur*, Barcelona: 390–514.

López, A. (1927) *Problemas Colombianos*, Paris: América.

López, L. (1585) *Instructorium Conscientiae*, Salamanca: Haered Mathiae Gastii y Claudii Curlet.

López, V. F. (1864) 'Economía Política', Course given at the Universidad de Montevideo, Montevideo: Imprenta de la República.

—— (1896) 'Autobiografía', *La Biblioteca*, I, 1: 337–45.

López de Gómara, F. (1557) *Anales del Emperador Carlos V* (edited 1912), Madrid.

López de Jerez, F. (1534) *Verdadera Relación de la Conquista del Perú*, Seville: Imp. Bartholomé Perez; thirteenth edn, reprinted (1972) *Historiadores de Indias-América del Sur*, Barcelona: Bruguera.

Lowry, S. T. (1987) *The Archaelogy of Economic Ideas – The Classical Greek Tradition*, Durham: Duke University Press.

Lozano, J. T. (1937) 'De la Necesidad del Dinero Corriente y de la Inutilidad del Dinero Guardado', 'Plan de una Compañía Patriotica de Comercio', and 'Sobre lo Útil que sería en este Reino el Establecimiento de una Sociedad de Amigos del País', *Periodistas en los Albores de la República*, Bogotá, 62: 1–43.

Lutz, F. A. (1956) *Zinstheorie*, Zurich-Tübingen: J. C. B. Mohr.

Macía, A. (ed.) (1972) *Historiadores de Indias-América del Sur*, Barcelona: Bruguera.

Madiedo, M. M. (1863) *La Ciencia Social o el Socialismo Filosófico, derivado de las Grandes Armonías Morales del Cristianismo*, Bogotá: N. Pontón.

Maniglia, A. R. (1985) 'Interview with Raúl Prebisch', *La Nación*, Buenos Aires: 29 September.

Mariátegui, J. C. (1957) *Siete Ensayos de Interpretación de la Realidad Peruana*, Lima: Biblioteca Amauta.

Mariluz Urquijo, J. M. (1952) 'Antecedentes sobre la Política Económica de las Provincias Unidas (1810–16)', *Revista del Instituto de Historia del Derecho*, 4.

—— (1963) 'Protección y Librecambio durante el Período 1820–35', *Boletín de la Academia Nacional de la Historia*, 34.

—— (1965) 'Aspectos de la Política Proteccionista durante la Década 1810–20', *Boletín de la Academia Nacional de la Historia*, 37.

Martínez Delgado, L. and Ortiz, S. E. (1960) *El Periodismo en la Nueva Granada 1810–11*, Bogatá: Kelly.

Mason, W. (1959) *Informe al Gobierno de Bolivia sobre la Organización del Empleo y el Desarrollo de un Programa de Información sobre el Mercado del Empleo*, Geneva: International Labour Office.

Matienzo, J. de (1580) *Commentaria Ioannis Matienzo Regii Senatoris in Cancellaria Argentina Regni Peru in Librum Quintum Recollectionis Legum Hipaniae*, Madrid: F. Sánchez.

—— (1623) *Dialogus Relatoris et Advocati Pinciani Senatus MDLVIII (1558)*, third edn, Francoforte del Meno: J. Berner.

—— (1967) *Gobierno del Perú (1567)*, Prologue in French by G. Lohmann Villena, in the Collection 'Travaux de l'Institut Français d' Études Andines', 11, Paris-Lima: Institut Français d' Études Andines.

Meinvielle, J. (1973) *El Poder Destructivo de la Dialéctica Comunista*, Buenos Aires: Cruz y Fierro.

Mendoza, D. (1912) 'Cartas Inéditas de José Ignacio de Pombo a Don José Celestino Mutis', in *Lecturas Populares*, Literary Suplement of *El Tiempo*, Bogatá: V: 56–7.

Mercado, T. de ([1569] 1969) *Tratos y Contratos de Mercaderes*, Salamanca: Mathias Guast.

—— (1977) *Summa de Tratos y Contratos (1571)*, Preliminary Study by N. Sánchez Albornoz, Madrid: Instituto de Estudios Fiscales.

Mesics, E. A. (1964) *Training and Education for Manpower Development – An Annotated Bibliography*, Ithaca, NY: Cornell University, State School of Industry and Labor Relations.

Monroe, A. E. (1923) *Monetary Theory before Adam Smith*, Cambridge, MA: Harvard University Press.

Montesquieu, C. de Secondat, Baron of (1951) 'El Espíritu de las Leyes', in *Obras*, Book XX, Chapter 9, Buenos Aires: El Ateneo.

Moreno, J. J. (1939) *Don Vasco de Quiroga, Primer Obispo de Michoacán*, Mexico: Colegio de México.

Morrison, S. E. (1974) *European Discovery of America*, New York: Oxford University Press.

Muro, D. de (1910) *Carlos Pellegrini 1881–96*, Buenos Aires: M. García.

Nariño, A. (1946) 'Ensayo sobre un Nuevo Plan de Administración en el Nuevo Reino de Granada Presentado al Excelentísimo Señor Virrey para que lo Dirija a su Majestad, en 16 de Noviembre de 1797', in J. M. Vergara y Vergara *Vida y Escritos del General Antonio Nariño*, Bogotá: Imprenta Nacional.

Narváez y la Torre, A. (1965) 'Provincia de Santa Marta y Río Hacha del Virreinato de Santa Fé – mayo de 1778', *Escritos de dos Economistas Coloniales: Don Antonio de Narváez y la Torre y Don José Ignacio de Pombo*, Bogotá: Banco de la República.

Nevares, A. de (1874) 'Algunos Apuntes sobre las Ventajas del Sistema Protector para la República Argentina', in reply to Estanislao Zeballos' doctoral thesis, Buenos Aires: Facultad de Derecho y Ciencias Sociales.

New Palgrave: A Dictionary of Economics, (1987) J. Eatwell, M. Milgate and P. Newman (eds), (4 vols), London, Macmillan Press.

Newton, J. (1965) *Carlos Pellegrini: El Estadista sin Miedo*, Buenos Aires: Editorial Claridad.

Nogueira de Paula, L. (1942) *Sintese da Evaluçao do Pensamento Economico no Brasil*, published in Spanish in I. F. Normano (ed.) (1945) *El Pensamiento Económico Latinoamericano: Argentina, Bolivia, Brasil, Cuba, Chile, Haití, Paraguay, Perú*, Mexico: Fondo de Cultura Económica: 70–103.

Normano, I. F. (ed.) (1945) *El Pensamiento Económico Latinoamericano: Argentina, Bolivia, Brasil, Cuba, Chile, Haití, Paraguay, Perú*, Mexico: Fondo de Cultura Económica.

Oca Balda, J. A. (1942) *El Último Libertador. Obra Escrita en Homenaje a Carlos Pellegrini* (The Last Liberator: Work in Homage to Carlos Pellegrini), Buenos Aires: B. Chiesino.

OECD (1964) *Economic Planning – Special Annotated Bibliographies*, Paris: OECD.
—— (1966) *Organisation Gouvernamentale et Développement Économique*, Paris: OECD.
Oñate, P. de (1646–54) *De Contractibus*, Rome: Ex Tipographia Francisci Caballi.
Pabón, J.M. (1922) *Fundamentos de la Ciencia Económica*, Bogotá: Editorial Cromos.
Padilla, D. F. (1960) 'Sobre la Libertad', excerpt from his weekly publication *Aviso al Público*, in *Periodistas en los Albores de la República 1810–11*, Selección Samper Ortega de Literatura Colombiana, Section Seven, Journalism, 62: 47–268.
Palgrave, P. J. (1963) *Dictionary of Political Economy*, H. Higgs (ed.) (3 vols), New York: Augustus M. Kelly.
Paltauf, C. (1847) *Die Kunst, aus Nichts Geld zu Machen*, Tirnau.
Panettieri, J. (1960) 'Un Debate Histórico', *Humanidades*, Revista de la Facultad de Humanidades y Ciencias de la Educación de la Universidad Nacional de La Plata, 35: 161–78.
Parra Peña, I. (1984) *El Pensamiento Económico Latinoamericano*, Bogotá: Plaza & Janés.
Pastells, P. (1912–49) *Historia de la Compañía de Jesús en la Provincia de Paraguay*, Madrid: Consejo Superior de Investigaciones Científicas, Instituto Santo Toribio de Mogroveyo.
Pereyra, C. (1930) *La Obra de España en América*, Madrid: Aguilar.
—— (1938) *Breve Historia de América*, Santiago.
Perez Gómez, J. (1924) *Apuntes Históricos de las Misiones Agustinianas en Colombia*, Bogotá: La Cruzada.
Pombo, J. I. de (1965) 'Informe del Real Consulado de Cartagena de Indias', *Escritos de dos Economistas Colombianas: Don Antonio de Narváez y la Torre y Don José Ignacio de Pombo*, Bogatá: Banco de la República.
Popescu, O. (1952) 'Etienne Echeverría, Penseur Argentin des Doctrines Solidaristes', *Révue d'Histoire Économique et Social*, 4.
—— (1954) *El Pensamiento Social Económico de Esteban Echeverría*, Buenos Aires: Editorial Americana.
—— (1959) 'Tendencias Actuales del Pensamiento Económico', *Revista de la Universidad*, La Plata: 8: 61–78, 9: 65–84.
—— (1960) *Introducción a la Ciencia Económica Contemporánea*, first edn, La Plata: Instituto de Economía y Finanzas.
—— (1964a) 'En Colombia hay Tradición en Cuestiones Económicas', *El Tiempo*, Bogotá: 1 July: 19.
—— (1964b) 'El Pensamiento Económico Colombiano', *Revista de la Universidad*, Bogotá: 17: 43–4.
—— (1964c) *Introducción a la Ciencia Económica Contemporánea*, second edn, Barcelona: Ariel.
—— (1965) 'L'histoire de la Pensée Économique et sa Division en Periodes', in *Revue International Sciences Sociales*, XVII: 4.
—— (1966) 'Lehrgeschichtliche Anfänge der Sozialoekonomischen Entwicklungsbestrebungen Lateinamerikas', *Weltwirtschaftliches Archiv*, Kiel: Sondernummer für Latein Amerika): 64–96.
—— (1967) *El Sistema Económico en las Misiones Jesuíticas – Un Vasto Experimento de Desarrollo Indoamericano*, Barcelona: Ariel (second edn); first edn (1952) *El Sistema Económico en las Misiones Jesuíticas*, Bahía Blanca: Pampa-Mar.
—— (1968a) *Desarrollo y Planeamiento en el Pensamiento Económico Colombiano*, Bogotá: Imprenta E. Salazar.
—— (1968b) *Un Tratado de Economía Política en Santafé de Bogotá*, Bogotá: Imprenta E. Salazar.
—— (1968c) *Dinero y Crédito*, Bogotá: ESAP.

—— (1968d) *Introducción a la Ciencia Económica Contemporánea*, third edn, Barcelona: Ariel.

—— (1984) *Origenes Hispanoamericanos de la Teoría Cuantitativa*, Buenos Aires: Programa BIBLEH-UCA-CONICET.

—— (1985) *Introducción a la Ciencia Económica Contemporánea*, fourth edn, Bogotá: Plaza & Janés.

—— (1987) 'Price Theory in Amer. Scholastics', ILSE, 14, 3/4/5.

—— (1988) *Económica Indiana*, Buenos Aires: Academia Nacional de Ciencias Económicas.

—— (1994) *Contribuciones de Teoría Monetaria a la Económica Indiana*, Buenos Aires: Academia Nacional de Ciencias Económicas.

Popescu, O., Gomez Camacho, F. and Grice Hutchinson, M. (1986) *Aportaciones del Pensamiento Económica Iberoamericano, Siglos XVI–XX*, Madrid: Instituto de Cooperación Iberoamericana.

Posada, E. (1925) *Bibliografía Bogotana*, Bogotá: Imprenta Nacional.

Prados Arrarte, J. (1950) *Problemas Básicos de la Doctrina Económica*, Buenos Aires: Sudamericana.

Prebisch, R. (1920) 'La cuestión social', *Revista de Ciencias Económicas*, Buenos Aires, January–April: 399–401.

—— (1981) *Capitalismo Periférico: Crisis y Transformación*, Mexico: Fondo de Cultura Económica.

—— (1982) *Five Stages in My Thinking of Development*, Washington, DC: IBRD/The World Bank.

—— (1983) 'Cinco Etapas de mi Pensamiento sobre el Desarrollo', *Trimestre Económico*, Mexico: 50, 198: 1077–96.

—— (1986) *La Crisis del Desarrollo Argentino*, Buenos Aires: El Ateneo.

—— (1992) *Obras Completas 1919–48*, Buenos Aires: Fundación Raúl Prebisch.

Prudencio, Julián (1845) *Principios de Economía Política Aplicados al Estado Actual y Circunstancias de Bolivia*, Sucre: Beeche y Compañía.

Quintana, M. J. (1914) *Vidas de los Españoles Célebres*, two volumes, Madrid.

Radecke, W. (1954) 'Nachwort', in K. Walker *Die Uberwindung des Kapitalismus*, Nuremberg: Lauf Press.

Ramírez de Quiñones, P., López de Haro, J. and Matienzo, J. de (1918) 'Carta a Su Majestad del 22 de octubre de 1561', in *La Audiencia de Charcas – Correspondencia de Presidentes y Oidores – Documentos del Archivo de Indias*, I (1561–79), Madrid: Publicaciones Históricas de la Biblioteca del Congreso Argentino.

Reinaga, C. A. (1969) *Esbozo de una Historia del Pensamiento Económico del Perú*, Cuzco: Garcilaso.

Repetto, N. (1961) 'Relaciones Humanas en el Trabajo. El Pensamiento de Carlos Pellegrini', *Anales de la Academia de Ciencias Económicas*: 238–53.

Reyes, A. (1942) *Ultima Tule*, Mexico: University Press.

Richelot, H. (1863) *Une Revolution en Économie Politique – Exposé des Doctrines de Macleod*, Paris: Capelle.

—— (1876) *Una Revolución en Economía Política – Exposición de las Doctrinas de Macleod*, translated by M. Ugarte and A. Navarro Viola, Buenos Aires: Imprenta La América del Sur.

Rivero Astengo, A. (ed.) (1941) *Obras Completas de Carlos Pellegrini*, Buenos Aires: CONI.

Rodríguez Garavito, A. (1964) *José Camacho Carreño, Hijo de Prometeo*, Bogotá.

—— (1967) '¿Qué Sabemos de la Planificación?', *Administración y Desarrollo – Revista de la Escuela Superior de Administración Pública*, IX: 169.

307

Romero, E. (1945) 'Perú', in I. F. Normano (ed.) *El Pensamiento Económico Latinoamericano: Argentina, Bolivia, Brasil, Cuba, Chile, Haití, Paraguay, Perú*, Mexico: Fondo de Cultura Económica.

Romero, M. G. (1960) 'Fray Diego Francisco Padilla', in *Próceres 1810*, Bogotá: Banco de la República.

Roover, R. de (1953) *L'Évolution de la Lettre de Change*, Paris: Colin.

—— (1955) 'Scholastic Economics Survival and Lasting Influence from the Sixteenth Century to Adam Smith', *The Quarterly Journal of Economics*, LXIX: 2.

—— (1968) 'Economic Thought I: Ancient and Medieval Thought', *International Encyclopedia of the Social Sciences*, Vol. 4, New York: Crowell Collier and Macmillan.

Rossi, P. (1865) *Cours d'Économie Politique*, Paris: Librairie Guillalmine.

Rousseau, J. J. (1963) *Oeuvres Complétes*, Paris: Gallimard (Bibliothéque de la Pléiade).

Saint Agustine (1948) *La Ciudad de Dios*, Madrid: Biblioteca de Autores Cristianos.

Salin, E. (1967) *Politische Oekonomie – Geschichte der Wirtschaftspolitischen Ideen von Platon bis zur Gegenwart*, Zurich: Polygraphischer Verlag.

Samaranch, F. de (1967) *Obras de Aristóteles*, Madrid: Aguilar.

Samper, J. M. (1861) *Ensayo sobre las Revoluciones Políticas y la Condición Social de las Repúblicas Colombianas (Hispano-Americanas)* Bogotá: Centro.

Sánchez Albornoz, C. (1959) 'Un Testigo del Comercio Indiano: Tomás de Mercado y Nueva España', *Revista de Historia de América*, La Plata, 47: 95ff.

Sánchez Albornoz, C. (1977) 'Tomás de Mercado: entre la Tradición Escolástica y la Práctica del Siglo de Oro', in T. de Mercado *Summa de Tratos y Contratos*, Madrid: Instituto de Estudios Fiscales del Ministerio de Hacienda.

Santillán, F. de (1950) 'Relación del Origen, Descendencia, Política y Gobierno de los Incas', in M. Jimenez de la Espada (ed.) *Tres Relaciones de Antigüedades Peruanas*, Asunción: Guaranía; (1879) Madrid: Ministerio de Fomento de España.

Santos, A. (1943) *Jesuitas en el Polo Norte. La Misión de Alaska*, Madrid: Ultra.

Sanz, C. (ed.) (1962) *Diario de Colón: Libro de la Primera Navegación y Descubrimiento de las Indias*, Madrid: Biblioteca Americana Vetustísima; English version in S. E. Morrison (1963) *Journals and other Documents on the Life and Voyages of Christopher Columbus*, New York.

Sayous, A. E. (1928) 'Observations d'Écrivains du XVIème Siècle sur les Changes et Notamment sur l'Influence de la Disparité du Pouvoir d'Achat des Monnaies, *Revue Économique Internationale*, 20: 289ff.

Scarpetta, L., and Vergara, S. (1879) 'Padilla, Diego Francisco', in *Diccionario Biográfico de los Campeones de la Libertad de Nueva Granada, Venezuela, Ecuador, y Perú*, Bogotá.

Schmid, W. (1954) *Silvio Gesell*, Bern-Zurich: Genossenschaft Verlag Freiwirtschaftlicher Schriften.

Schumpeter, J. (1936) 'Criticism of Keynes' General Theory', *Journal of the American Statistical Association*, New Series, 31, 196: 793.

—— (1971) *Historia del Análisis Económico*, Spanish edn, Barcelona: Ariel; (1954) *History of Economic Analysis*, New York: Oxford University Press; (1996) London: Routledge.

Schwarz, F. (1951) *Das Experiment von Wörgl*, Bern-Zurich: Genossenschaft Verlag Freiwirtschaftlicher Schriften.

Scotus, J. D. (1490) 'Quaestiones in Quattuor Libros Sententiarum', Venetiis.

Segovia, F. S. (1989) *El Pensamiento Económico y Político de Carlos Pellegrini*, Mendoza: Fundación Carlos Pellegrini.

Sempere y Guarinos, J. (1797) 'Ensayos de una Biblioteca Española, Discurso Preliminar', in *Biblioteca Española Económica-Política*, Madrid.

Sicaro y Perez, A. (1883) 'Fr. Diego Francisco Padilla', in *Papel Periódico Ilustrado*, Bogotá: 52, III: 15.

Sierra, V. D. (1942) *El Sentido Misional de la Conquista de América*, Buenos Aires: Ediciones de Orientación Española.

Sierra Bravo, R. (1973) 'La Suma de Tratos y Contratos de Tomás de Mercado', *Revista de Economía Política*, Madrid: 64: 273ff.

Silva Herzog, J. (1947) *El Pensamiento Económico en México*, Mexico: Fondo de Cultura Económica.

Simpson, K., and Benjamin, H. C. (1958) *Manpower Problems in Economic Development: A Select Bibliography*, Princeton, NJ: Princeton Industrial Relations Section.

Smith, R. S. (1957) 'The Wealth of Nations in Spain and Hispanic America 1780–1850', *Journal of Political Economy*, 65, 2: 104–25.

Solórzano, J. (1930) *Política Indiana*, Madrid-Buenos Aires: Compañía Iberoamericana de Publicaciones.

Soto, D. de (1556) *De Justitia et Jure*, Madrid: Facsimile edn of the 1556 work.

—— (1968) *De la Justicia y el Derecho*, translated from Latin into Spanish by M. González Ordoñez, Madrid: Instituto de Estudios Políticos.

Spengler, J. J. and Allen, W. R. (1960) (Spanish edn 1971) *Essays in Economic Thought: Aristotle to Marshall*, Chicago: Rand McNally.

Spiegel, H. (1971) *The Growth of Economic Thought*, Englewood Cliffs, NJ: Prentice-Hall.

Stirner, M. (J. K. Schimdt) (1845) *Der Einzige und sein Eigentum*, Leipzig; English version (1907), translation by S. T. Byinton, New York; Spanish version *El Único y su Propiedad*, Madrid: La España Moderna.

Stobbe, H. (1965) *Methodisch-Theoretisches Schriftum zur Entwicklungslaender und Schriftum zur Entwicklunspolitik*, Kiel: Institut für Weltwirtschaft.

Subercaseaux, G. (1924) *Historia de las Doctrinas Económicas en América y en Especial en Chile*, Santiago de Chile: Impr. Universo.

Symposium Organized in tribute to Raúl Prebisch (1989) *Raúl Prebisch: Thinker and Builder*, New York: United Nations Conference on Trade and Development.

Thorp, W. L., and Taylor, G. R. (1957) *Price Theory: Encyclopaedia of Social Science*, 12: 375ff.

Tichauer, E. R. (1960) *Informe al Gobierno de Bolivia sobre una Misión de Productividad*, Geneva: International Labour Office.

Timm, H. (1960) 'Gerburt einer Idee und einer Bewegung', *Informationen fur Kultur, Wirtschaft, und Politik*, Hamburg, 13: 4.

Tindaro, C. (1944) *El Pensamiento de Manuel Belgrano*, Buenos Aires: Lautaro.

Torres Contreras, A. (1967) 'La Planeación en Colombia', *Administración Científica*, Bogotá: II: 2.

Torres García, G. (1942) *Nociones de Economía Política*, Bogotá: Ed. de Cromos.

Tozzi, G. (1968) *Economistas Griegos y Romanos*, Mexico: Fondo de Cultura Económica; Italian version (1961) *Economisti Greci e Romani*, Milan: G. Feltrinelli.

Tuddo, A. de (1952) *Informe de los Estudios y Observaciones sobre Higiene Industrial en los Centros Mineros Visitados por la Comisión 'De Tuddo'*, La Paz: Ministerio de Trabajo.

Ullastres Calvo, A. (1941–2) 'Martín de Azpilcueta y su Comentario Resolutorio de Cambios', *Anales de Economía*, Madrid, I: 375ff, II: 50ff.

Ulloa, B. de (1992) *Restablecimiento de las Fábricas y Gobierno Español (1740)*, Introduction by G. Anes, Madrid: Sociedad Quinto Centenario, IEF, Bosch.

UNESCO (1962) *Cooperation Internationale et Programmes de Développment Économique et Social. Bibliographie Commentée*, Paris: UNESCO.

309

Unión Internacional de Estudios Sociales (1953) *Código Social. Esbozo de la Doctrina Social Católica*, Buenos Aires: Ed. del Atlántico.

UNO (1951) *Report of the United Nations of Technical Assistance to Bolivia*, New York: United Nations.

Urdanoz, T. (1956) 'Introducción a la Cuestion 78 – El Pecado de Usura', in Thomas Aquinas *Suma Teológica, Segunda Parte, Seccion Segunda, Tratado de Justicia*, Madrid: Biblioteca de Autores Cristianos.

Uriarte y Herrera, M. de (1757) *Representación sobre los Adelantamientos de Quito y la Opulencia de España*, Quito: Imprenta Nacional.

Uribe Echeverri, C. (1936) *Nuestro Problema: Producir*, Madrid: Aguilar.

Uztáriz, G. (1968) *Theorica y Práctica de Comercio y de Marina (1724)*, Introduction by G. Franco, Madrid: Aguilar.

Valdivia, P. de (1865) 'Relación hecha por Pedro de Valdivia al Emperador', in *Colección de Documentos Inéditos Relativos al Descubrimiento, Conquista y Población de Chile Sacados de los Archivos del Reino y del de Indias*, Madrid: Ponton.

Valle, J. C. del (1958) *El Pensamiento Económico de José Cecilio del Valle*, Tegucigalpa: Publicaciones del Banco Central de Honduras.

Vallejo, J. (1959) 'Planeación Económica', *Ciencias Económicas*, Medellín: 15.

Valsecchi, F. (1941) 'La Nueva Orientación de la Economía según las Encíclicas Rerum Novarum y Quadragesimo Anno', *Revista de Ciencias Económicas*, XXIX, 238: 563–84.

Vargas, P. F. de (1944) *Pensamientos Políticos y Memorias sobre la Poblacion del Nuevo Reino de Granada*, Bogotá: Banco de la República.

Vázquez de Espinosa, A. (1948) *Compendio y Descripción de las Indias Occidentales*, Washington, DC: Smithsonian Institution.

Vázquez Varini, F. S. (1961) *Acción y Pensamiento Económicos de América Latina*, Montevideo: Palacio del Libro, A. Monteverde y Cía SA.

Vergara y Vergara, J. M. (1946) 'Vida y Escritos del General Antonio Nariño', *Biblioteca Colombiana*, 95, Bogotá: Imprenta Nacional.

Victoria, F. de (1927) *Recueil des Cours de Droit International*, III, The Hague: École Moderne de Droit International.

Villarroel Claure, N. (1929) *Educación Económica de Bolivia*, Iquique: Impr. Villarroel.

Wagemann, E. (1948) *Menschenzahl und Völkerschicksal*, Hamburg: W. Krüger-Verlag.

Walter, K. (1949) 'Werk und Weltanschauung', *Die Gefährten*, 28: 363–70.

Waterston, A. (1965) *National Plans*, Baltimore, MD: Johns Hopkins Press.

Weber, W. (1959) *Wirtschaftsetihk am Vorabend des Liberalismus*, Münster: Aschendorffsche Verlag.

—— (1962) *Geld und Zins in der Spanischen Spaetscholastik*, Münster: Aschendorffsche Verlag.

Willeke, F. U. (1961) *Entwicklung der Markttheorie von der Scholastik bis zur Klassik*, Tubingen: Mohr.

Wills, G. (1831) *Observaciones sobre el Comercio de la Nueva Granada*, Bogotá: Wills.

Wish, J. R. (1965) *Economic Development in Latin America – An Annotated Bibliography*, New York: Praeger.

Zavala, S. A. (1937) *La 'Utopia' de Tomás Moro en la Nueva España y otros Estudios*, Mexico: J. Porrúa.

—— (1947) *Filosofía de la Conquista*, Mexico: Fondo de Cultura Económica.

Zondag, C. (1956) *Problemas en el Desarrollo Económico de Bolivia*, La Paz: US Department of State.

INDEX

311